Global Issues 13/14

Twenty-Ninth Edition

EDITOR

Robert M. Jackson
California State University, Chico

Robert M. Jackson is a professor emeritus of political science and past dean of the School of Graduate, International and Sponsored Programs at California State University, Chico. In addition to teaching courses on third-world politics and globalization, he has published articles on the international political economy, international relations simulations, and political behavior. Dr. Jackson has been responsible for numerous international training programs for professionals from around the world. International educational exchanges and study-abroad programs also have been an area of special interest. His research and professional travels include China, Japan, Hong Kong, Taiwan, Singapore, Malaysia, Spain, Portugal, Morocco, Belgium, Germany, the Czech Republic, the Netherlands, Italy, Russia, Mexico, Guatemala, Honduras, Costa Rica, El Salvador, Brazil, Chile, and Argentina.

Mc Graw Hill

Connect Learn Succeed™

ANNUAL EDITIONS: GLOBAL ISSUES, TWENTY-NINTH EDITION

Published by McGraw-Hill, a business unit of The McGraw-Hill Companies, Inc., 1221 Avenue
of the Americas, New York, NY 10020. Copyright © 2014 by The McGraw-Hill Companies, Inc.
All rights reserved. Printed in the United States of America. Previous edition(s) © 2013, 2012,
2011, 2010, and 2009. No part of this publication may be reproduced or distributed in any form or
by any means, or stored in a database or retrieval system, without the prior written consent of The
McGraw-Hill Companies, Inc., including, but not limited to, in any network or other electronic
storage or transmission, or broadcast for distance learning.

Some ancillaries, including electronic and print components, may not be available to customers
outside the United States.

This book is printed on acid-free paper.

Annual Editions® is a registered trademark of The McGraw-Hill Companies, Inc.

Annual Editions is published by the **Contemporary Learning Series** group within the
McGraw-Hill Higher Education division.

1 2 3 4 5 6 7 8 9 0 QDB/QDB 1 0 9 8 7 6 5 4 3

ISBN: 978-0-07-813598-9
MHID: 0-07-813598-2
ISSN: 1093-278X (print)
ISSN: 2158-4060 (online)

Acquisitions Editor: *Joan L. McNamara*
Marketing Director: *Adam Kloza*
Marketing Manager: *Nathan Edwards*
Developmental Editor: *Dave Welsh*
Senior Project Manager: *Joyce Watters*
Buyer: *Nichole Birkenholz*
Cover Designer: *Studio Montage, St. Louis, MO*
Senior Content Licensing Specialist: *Shirley Lanners*
Media Project Manager: *Sridevi Palani*

Compositor: Laserwords Private Limited
Cover Image Credits: Pixtal/age fotostock (inset); Ingram Publishing (background)

Editors/Academic Advisory Board

Members of the Academic Advisory Board are instrumental in the final selection of articles for each edition of ANNUAL EDITIONS. Their review of articles for content, level, and appropriateness provides critical direction to the editors and staff. We think that you will find their careful consideration well reflected in this volume.

ANNUAL EDITIONS: Global Issues 13/14
29th Edition

EDITOR

Robert M. Jackson
California State University, Chico

ACADEMIC ADVISORY BOARD MEMBERS

Preface

During the three decades I have edited this book of readings, there has been change as well as continuity in the topics meriting consideration. The most significant change has been the collapse of the Soviet Union and the end of the Cold War. Today countries like China, India, and Brazil have assumed a more significant role in the global political hierarchy. In terms of economic issues, it no longer makes sense to organize articles into categories such as developed and developing countries. Two decades of rapid globalization required new organizing themes. In the years following the 2008 financial crisis, fresh perspectives on the global political economy had to be identified. In contrast to these changes, there are issues that have had an enduring priority. Beginning with the first edition, global energy resources have been a central theme. Environmental issues, it is important to note, are even more significant than they were thirty years ago, and each year there is never a shortage of new conflicts and threats to regional and global peace. The challenge is to sort through all of these and identify those disputes which provide the greatest insights into the causes and consequences of violent conflict. At the same time, there has emerged a counterbalancing pattern of increased cooperation between governments, non-profit organizations, and the corporate sector. This collaboration has resulted in considerable success in addressing some of the world's most pressing problems, including reducing extreme poverty and containing or eliminating the spread of contagious diseases such as AIDS, polio, and malaria.

While the mass media may focus on the latest international crisis for a few weeks or months, the broad forces that shape the world are seldom given an in-depth analysis by the popular media. In contrast, scholarly research about these change factors can be found in a variety of academic publications, but these are not readily accessible to students beginning the study of global issues. Furthermore, the terminology and abstract concepts that characterize much of this literature are not aimed at the student audience. In selecting and organizing the articles and learning tools for this book, my first priority is to address the needs and interests of students new to this field.

Each unit begins with an introductory article(s) providing a broad overview of the issue area. The articles that follow offer specific case studies as well as describing the efforts being made to address specific problems. There are daily reminders that people everywhere face serious challenges, the magnitude of which can discourage even the most stouthearted individual. While identifying problems is easier than solving them, it is important not to forget that many are being successfully addressed.

Perhaps the most striking feature of the study of contemporary global issues is the absence of any single, widely-held theory which adequately explains what is taking place. As a result, a conscious effort has been made to offer a variety of points of view. An important consideration, therefore, is to present global issues from an international perspective, rather than from a purely American or Western point of view. By encompassing materials originally published in different countries and written by men and women of various nationalities, the anthology represents the great diversity of opinions that people hold. Two writers examining the same phenomenon may reach very different conclusions. It is not just a question of who is right or wrong, but rather understanding that people from different vantage points can have different points of view on an issue.

Another major consideration when organizing these materials is to explore the complex interrelationship of factors that produce social problems such as poverty. Too often, debates about these issues are reduced to arguments about the fallacies of not following the correct economic policy or not having the correct form of government. As a result, many people overlook the interplay of historic, cultural, geographic, economic, and political factors that form complex webs that bring about many different problems. Every effort has been made to select materials that illustrate this complex interaction of factors, stimulating the beginning student to consider realistic rather than overly simplistic approaches to the pressing problems that threaten the existence of civilization.

To assist the reader, a number of learning tools are included in this book. In addition to an annotated *Table of Contents* and a *Topic Guide,* there are *Internet References* which can be used to further explore topics addressed in the articles.

Learning Outcomes for each unit are organized around two principles. The first: all of the articles have a central point of view (usually identified in the opening paragraphs), which is supported by specific reasons and illustrated with examples. The articles typically conclude by reconsidering the point of view in terms of counter arguments, policy implications, and/or forecasts of the future. Basic comprehension of each article requires an understanding of the author's point of view and supporting reasons. In a number of cases, articles are paired to illustrate contending points of view so that the reader is aware of on-going policy debates. The process of comparing and contrasting, therefore, requires a higher level of understanding beyond the comprehension of each article's content in and of itself.

The second principle is the interconnectedness of the units of the book. As identified in the introduction to Unit 1, the Allegory of the Balloon portrays the interconnectedness of the book's four organizing themes. An ability to identify and articulate these connections is the second focus of the *Learning Outcomes.*

At the conclusion of each article, there is a *Critical Thinking* section. This is comprised of a series of questions linked to the *Learning Outcomes* of each unit.

It is my continuing goal to work with the editors and staff at McGraw-Hill Contemporary Learning Series to provide materials that encourage the readers of this book to develop a life-long appreciation of the complex and rapidly changing world in which we live. This collection of articles is an invitation to further explore the global issues of the twenty-first century and become personally involved in the great issues of our time.

Finally, materials in this book were selected for both their intellectual insights and readability. Timely and well-written materials should stimulate good classroom lectures and discussions. I hope that students and teachers will enjoy using this book. Readers can have input into the next edition by completing and returning the postage-paid article rating form in the back of the book.

Robert M. Jackson
Editor

The Annual Editions Series

VOLUMES AVAILABLE

Adolescent Psychology

Aging

American Foreign Policy

American Government

Anthropology

Archaeology

Assessment and Evaluation

Business Ethics

Child Growth and Development

Comparative Politics

Criminal Justice

Developing World

Drugs, Society, and Behavior

Dying, Death, and Bereavement

Early Childhood Education

Economics

Educating Children with Exceptionalities

Education

Educational Psychology

Entrepreneurship

Environment

The Family

Gender

Geography

Global Issues

Health

Homeland Security

Human Development

Human Resources

Human Sexualities

International Business

Management

Marketing

Mass Media

Microbiology

Multicultural Education

Nursing

Nutrition

Physical Anthropology

Psychology

Race and Ethnic Relations

Social Problems

Sociology

State and Local Government

Sustainability

Technologies, Social Media, and Society

United States History, Volume 1

United States History, Volume 2

Urban Society

Violence and Terrorism

Western Civilization, Volume 1

World History, Volume 1

World History, Volume 2

World Politics

Contents

UNIT 1
Global Issues in the Twenty-First Century: An Overview

UNIT 2
Population and Food Production

The concepts in bold italics are developed in the article. For further expansion, please refer to the Topic Guide.

UNIT 3
The Global Environment and Natural Resources Utilization

The concepts in bold italics are developed in the article. For further expansion, please refer to the Topic Guide.

UNIT 4
Political Economy

The concepts in bold italics are developed in the article. For further expansion, please refer to the Topic Guide.

UNIT 5
Conflict

Unit Overview — 126

The concepts in bold italics are developed in the article. For further expansion, please refer to the Topic Guide.

UNIT 6
Cooperation

The concepts in bold italics are developed in the article. For further expansion, please refer to the Topic Guide.

UNIT 7
Values and Visions

The concepts in bold italics are developed in the article. For further expansion, please refer to the Topic Guide.

Correlation Guide

The *Annual Editions* series provides students with convenient, inexpensive access to current, carefully selected articles from the public press. **Annual Editions: Global Issues 13/14** is an easy-to-use reader that presents articles on important topics such as *population, environment, political economy,* and many more. For more information on *Annual Editions* and other *McGraw-Hill Contemporary Learning Series* titles, visit www.mhhe.com/cls.

This convenient guide matches the units in **Annual Editions: Global Issues 13/14** with the corresponding chapters in two of our best-selling McGraw-Hill Political Science textbooks by Rourke/Boyer and Boyer/Hudson/Butler.

Annual Editions: Global Issues 13/14	International Politics on the World Stage, Brief, 8/e by Rourke/Boyer	Global Politics by Boyer/Hudson/Butler
Unit 1: Global Issues in the Twenty-First Century: An Overview	**Chapter 1:** Thinking and Caring about World Politics **Chapter 2:** The Evolution of World Politics **Chapter 5:** Globalization: The Alternative Orientation	**Chapter 1:** Thinking about Global Politics **Chapter 2:** Interpreting Power: A Levels-of-Analysis Approach **Chapter 3:** Nations, States, and Identity **Chapter 4:** Globalization: Politics from Above and Below
Unit 2: Population and Food Production	**Chapter 8:** International Law and Human Rights	**Chapter 8:** International Law and Transitional Justice
Unit 3: The Global Environment and Natural Resources Utilization	**Chapter 12:** Preserving and Enhancing the Biosphere	**Chapter 12:** Global Political Ecology
Unit 4: Political Economy	**Chapter 6:** Power, Statecraft, and the National State: The Traditional Structure **Chapter 7:** Intergovernmental Organizations: Alternative Governance **Chapter 10:** National Economic Competition: The Traditional Road **Chapter 11:** International Economics: The Alternative Road	**Chapter 9:** Global Political Economy—Protecting Wealth in the Dominant System **Chapter 10:** Global Political Economy—Searching for Equity in the Dependent System
Unit 5: Conflict	**Chapter 6:** Power, Statecraft, and the National States: The Traditional Structure **Chapter 9:** Pursuing Security	**Chapter 3:** Nations, States, and Identity **Chapter 6:** Pursuing Security **Chapter 7:** Conflict and Conflict Management
Unit 6: Cooperation	**Chapter 8:** International Law and Human Rights **Chapter 11:** International Economics: The Alternative Road	**Chapter 8:** International Law and Transitional Justice **Chapter 11:** Human Rights: A Tool for Preserving and Enhancing Human Dignity
Unit 7: Values and Visions	**Chapter 3:** Levels of Analysis and Foreign Policy **Chapter 8:** International Law and Human Rights	**Chapter 3:** Nations, States, and Identity **Chapter 11:** Human Rights: A Tool for Preserving and Enhancing Human Dignity

Topic Guide

This topic guide suggests how the selections in this book relate to the subjects covered in your course. You may want to use the topics listed on these pages to search the Web more easily.

On the following pages a number of websites have been gathered specifically for this book. They are arranged to reflect the units of this Annual Editions reader. You can link to these sites by going to www.mhhe.com/cls.

All the articles that relate to each topic are listed below the bold-faced term.

Agriculture
1. Global Trends 2025: A Transformed World: Executive Summary
2. The New Geopolitics of Food
10. The Blue Food Revolution

Communication
17. Why the World Isn't Flat
36. War in the Fifth Domain
41. Gene Sharp: A Dictator's Worst Nightmare
42. Power of the iMob

Conservation
2. The New Geopolitics of Food
3. The End of Easy Everything
10. The Blue Food Revolution
13. The Melting North
14. Asian Carp, Other Invasive Species Make a Splash
23. Tech's Tragic Secret
28. King Coal's Comeback

Cultural customs and values
6. The New Population Bomb: The Four Megatrends That Will Change the World
7. Population and Sustainability
17. Why the World Isn't Flat
18. Globalization and Its Contents
19. The Future of History: Can Liberal Democracy Survive the Decline of the Middle Class?
25. Women and Work: Here's to the Next Half-Century
32. Unfinished Mideast Revolts
38. Geneva Conventions
41. Gene Sharp: A Dictator's Worst Nightmare
42. Power of the iMob
43. UN Women's Head Michelle Bachelet: A New Superhero?
44. The End of Men
45. Humanity's Common Values: Seeking a Positive Future

Demographics
1. Global Trends 2025: A Transformed World: Executive Summary
6. The New Population Bomb: The Four Megatrends That Will Change the World
7. Population and Sustainability
8. The Best Story in Development
9. Virus Hunter

Dependencies, international
3. The End of Easy Everything
17. Why the World Isn't Flat
18. Globalization and Its Contents
22. Bolivia and Its Lithium
23. Tech's Tragic Secret
24. Africa's Hopeful Economies: The Sun Shines Bright
26. It's Still the One
28. King Coal's Comeback

Development, economic
1. Global Trends 2025: A Transformed World: Executive Summary
2. The New Geopolitics of Food

3. The End of Easy Everything
4. China's Search for a Grand Strategy
5. Why the World Needs America
8. African Child Mortality: The Best Story in Development
9. Virus Hunter
10. The Blue Food Revolution
15. Go Glocal
16. Innovation's Long March
17. Why the World Isn't Flat
18. Globalization and Its Contents
19. The Future of History: Can Liberal Democracy Survive the Decline of the Middle Class?
22. Bolivia and Its Lithium
23. Tech's Tragic Secret
24. Africa's Hopeful Economies: The Sun Shines Bright
32. Unfinished Mideast Revolts
39. Africa: MCC and Coca-Cola's Shared Commitment to Water

Development, social
8. The Best Story in Development
9. Virus Hunter
19. The Future of History: Can Liberal Democracy Survive the Decline of the Middle Class?
21. Mafia States
24. Africa's Hopeful Economies: The Sun Shines Bright
25. Women and Work: Here's to the Next Half-Century
32. Unfinished Mideast Revolts
37. The Healing Fields
38. Geneva Conventions
39. Africa: MCC and Coca-Cola's Shared Commitment to Water
41. Gene Sharp: A Dictator's Worst Nightmare
43. UN Women's Head Michelle Bachelet: A New Superhero
44. End of Men
45. Humanity's Common Values: Seeking a Positive Future

Ecology
2. The New Geopolitics of Food
3. The End of Easy Everything
7. Population and Sustainability
10. The Blue Food Revolution
11. Climate Change
12. The Other Climate Changers
13. The Melting North
14. Asian Carp, Other Invasive Species Make a Splash
23. Tech's Tragic Secret
28. King Coal's Comeback

Economics
1. Global Trends 2025: A Transformed World: Executive Summary
2. The New Geopolitics of Food
3. The End of Easy Everything
5. Why the World Needs America
8. The Best Story in Development
10. The Blue Food Revolution
13. The Melting North
15. Go Glocal
16. Innovation's Long March
17. Why the World Isn't Flat
18. Globalization and Its Contents
19. The Future of History: Can Liberal Democracy Survive the Decline of the Middle Class?

Internet References

The following Internet sites have been selected to support the articles found in this reader. These sites were available at the time of publication. However, because websites often change their structure and content, the information listed may no longer be available. We invite you to visit www.mhhe.com/cls for easy access to these sites.

Annual Editions: Global Issues 13/14

General Sources

U.S. Information Agency (USIA)
www.america.gov

USIA's home page provides definitions, related documentation, and discussions of topics of concern to students of global issues. The site addresses today's Hot Topics as well as ongoing issues that form the foundation of the field.

World Wide Web Virtual Library: International Affairs Resources
www.etown.edu/vl

Surf this site and its extensive links to learn about specific countries and regions, to research various think tanks and international organizations, and to study such vital topics as international law, development, the international economy, human rights, and peacekeeping.

UNIT 1: Global Issues in the Twenty-First Century: An Overview

The Henry L. Stimson Center
www.stimson.org

The Stimson Center, a nonpartisan organization, focuses on issues where policy, technology, and politics intersect. Use this site to find varying assessments of U.S. foreign policy in the post–Cold War world and to research other topics.

The Heritage Foundation
www.heritage.org

This page offers discussion about and links to many sites having to do with foreign policy and foreign affairs, including news and commentary, policy review, events, and a resource bank.

The North-South Institute
www.nsi-ins.ca/ensi/index.htm

Searching this site of the North-South Institute, which works to strengthen international development cooperation and enhance gender and social equity, will help you find information and debates on a variety of global issues.

UNIT 2: Population and Food Production

The Hunger Project
www.thp.org

Browse through this nonprofit organization's site, whose goal is the sustainable end to global hunger through leadership at all levels of society. The Hunger Project contends that the persistence of hunger is at the heart of the major security issues threatening our planet.

Penn Library: Resources by Subject
www.library.upenn.edu/cgi-bin/res/sr.cgi

This vast site is rich in links to information about subjects of interest to students of global issues. Its extensive population

and demography resources address such concerns as migration, family planning, and health and nutrition in various world regions.

World Health Organization
www.who.int

This home page of the World Health Organization will provide you with links to a wealth of statistical and analytical information about health and the environment in the developing world.

WWW Virtual Library: Demography & Population Studies
http://demography.anu.edu.au/VirtualLibrary

A definitive guide to demography and population studies can be found at this site. It contains a multitude of important links to information about global poverty and hunger.

UNIT 3: The Global Environment and Natural Resources Utilization

National Geographic Society
www.nationalgeographic.com

This site provides links to material related to the atmosphere, the oceans, and other environmental topics.

National Oceanic and Atmospheric Administration (NOAA)
www.noaa.gov

Through this home page of NOAA, part of the U.S. Department of Commerce, you can find information about coastal issues, fisheries, climate, and more. The site provides many links to research materials and to other Web resources.

SocioSite: Sociological Subject Areas
www.pscw.uva.nl/sociosite/TOPICS

This huge site provides many references of interest to those interested in global issues, such as links to information on ecology and the impact of consumerism.

United Nations Environment Programme (UNEP)
www.unep.ch

Consult this home page of UNEP for links to critical topics of concern to students of global issues, including desertification, migratory species, and the impact of trade on the environment.

UNIT 4: Political Economy

Belfer Center for Science and International Affairs (BCSIA)
http://belfercenter.ksg.harvard.edu

BCSIA is the hub of Harvard University's John F. Kennedy School of Government's research, teaching, and training in international affairs related to security, environment, and technology.

U.S. Agency for International Development
www.usaid.gov

Broad and overlapping issues such as democracy, population and health, economic growth, and development are covered on this website. It provides specific information about different regions and countries.

Internet References

The World Bank Group

www.worldbank.org

News, press releases, summaries of new projects, speeches, publications, and coverage of numerous topics regarding development, countries, and regions are provided at this World Bank site. It also contains links to other important global financial organizations.

UNIT 5: Conflict

DefenseLINK

www.defenselink.mil

Learn about security news and research-related publications at this U.S. Department of Defense site. Links to related sites of interest are provided. The information systems BosniaLINK and GulfLINK can also be found here. Use the search function to investigate such issues as land mines.

Federation of American Scientists (FAS)

www.fas.org

FAS, a nonprofit policy organization, maintains this site to provide coverage of and links to such topics as global security, peace, and governance in the post–Cold War world. It notes a variety of resources of value to students of global issues.

ISN International Relations and Security Network

www.isn.ethz.ch

This site, maintained by the Center for Security Studies and Conflict Research, is a clearinghouse for information on international relations and security policy. Topics are listed by category (Traditional Dimensions of Security, New Dimensions of Security, and Related Fields) and by major world region.

The NATO Integrated Data Service (NIDS)

www.nato.int/structur/nids/nids.htm

NIDS was created to bring information on security-related matters to within easy reach of the widest possible audience. Check out this website to review North Atlantic Treaty Organization documentation of all kinds, to read *NATO Review*, and to explore key issues in the field of European security and transatlantic cooperation.

UNIT 6: Cooperation

Carnegie Endowment for International Peace

www.ceip.org

An important goal of this organization is to stimulate discussion and learning among both experts and the public at large on a wide range of international issues. The site provides links to *Foreign Policy*, to the Moscow Center, to descriptions of various programs, and much more.

OECD/FDI Statistics

www.oecd.org/statistics

Explore world trade and investment trends and statistics on this site from the Organization for Economic Cooperation and Development. It provides links to many related topics and addresses the issues on a country-by-country basis.

U.S. Institute of Peace

www.usip.org

USIP, which was created by the U.S. Congress to promote peaceful resolution of international conflicts, seeks to educate people and to disseminate information on how to achieve peace. Click on Highlights, Publications, Events, Research Areas, and Library and Links.

UNIT 7: Values and Visions

Human Rights Web

www.hrweb.org

The history of the human rights movement, text on seminal figures, landmark legal and political documents, and ideas on how individuals can get involved in helping to protect human rights around the world can be found at this valuable site.

InterAction

www.interaction.org

InterAction encourages grassroots action and engages government policymakers on advocacy issues. The organization's Advocacy Committee provides this site to inform people on its initiatives to expand international humanitarian relief, refugee, and development-assistance programs.

World Map

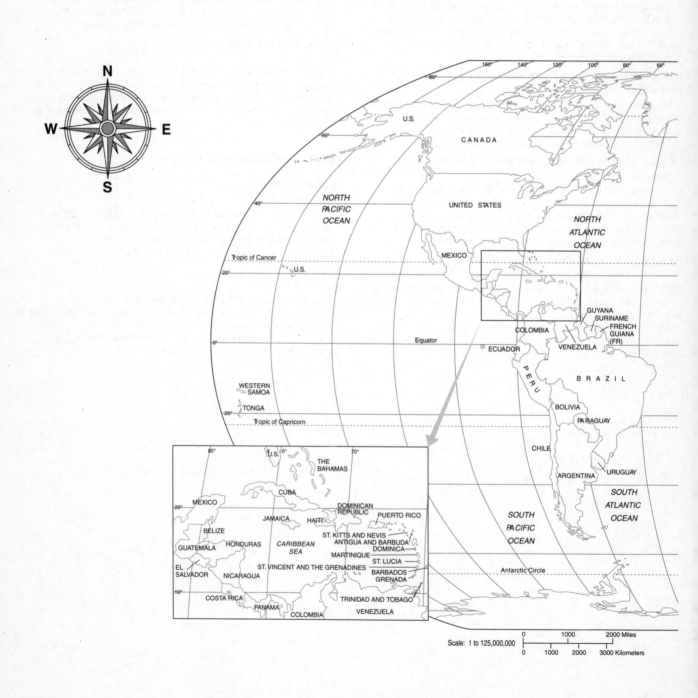

N
W E
S

160° 140° 120° 100° 80° 60°
80°

U.S.

CANADA

60°

NORTH
PACIFIC
OCEAN

UNITED STATES

40°

NORTH
ATLANTIC
OCEAN

Tropic of Cancer

MEXICO

20°

U.S.

GUYANA
SURINAME
FRENCH
GUIANA
(FR)

COLOMBIA

Equator

0°

ECUADOR

VENEZUELA

P E R U

B R A Z I L

WESTERN
SAMOA

BOLIVIA

TONGA

PARAGUAY

20°

Tropic of Capricorn

CHILE

SOUTH
ATLANTIC
OCEAN

ARGENTINA

URUGUAY

SOUTH
PACIFIC
OCEAN

Antarctic Circle

Inset map

90° 0°
U.S.
70°

THE
BAHAMAS

CUBA

MEXICO
20°

DOMINICAN
REPUBLIC

PUERTO RICO

JAMAICA
HAITI

BELIZE

ST. KITTS AND NEVIS
ANTIGUA AND BARBUDA
DOMINICA

GUATEMALA
HONDURAS

CARIBBEAN
SEA

MARTINIQUE
ST. LUCIA

EL
SALVADOR
NICARAGUA

ST. VINCENT AND THE GRENADINES

BARBADOS
GRENADA

10°

COSTA RICA

PANAMA

TRINIDAD AND TOBAGO

COLOMBIA

VENEZUELA

Scale: 1 to 125,000,000

0   1000   2000 Miles

0   1000   2000   3000 Kilometers

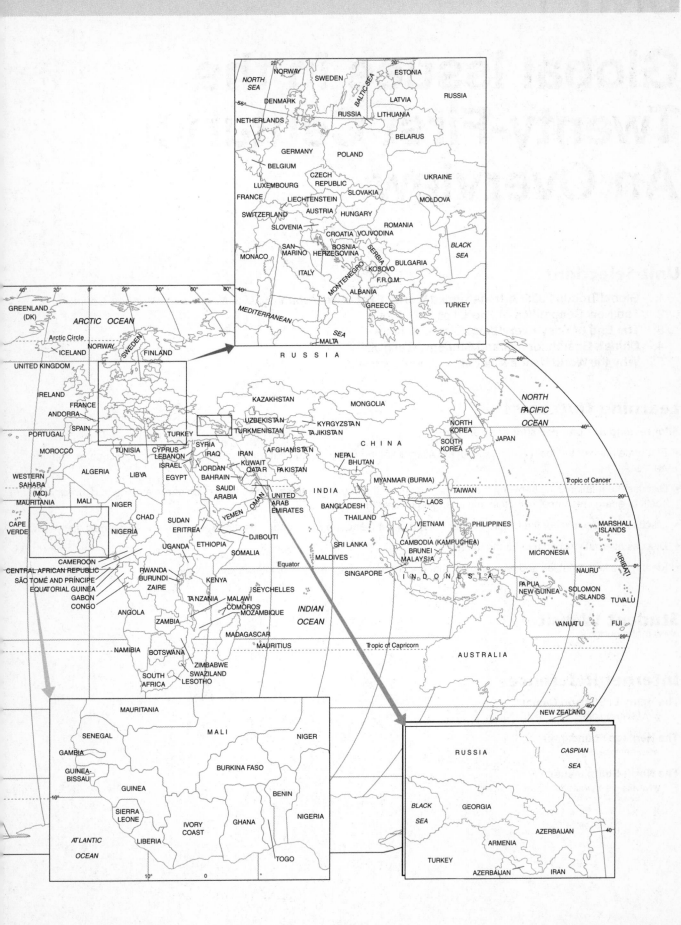

UNIT 1

Global Issues in the Twenty-First Century: An Overview

Unit Selections

1. **Global Trends 2025: A Transformed World: Executive Summary,** *U.S. National Intelligence Council*
2. **The New Geopolitics of Food,** Lester R. Brown
3. **The End of Easy Everything,** Michael T. Klare
4. **China's Search for a Grand Strategy,** Wang Jisi
5. **Why the World Needs America,** Robert Kagan

Learning Outcomes

After reading this unit you should be able to:

- Elaborate each of the four components of the Allegory of the Balloon (e.g., natural resources) with specific examples from the articles.

- Discuss the relationships between the four categories of the allegory with examples from each of the articles (e.g., the increasing costs of energy resource extraction and changing social structures).

- Discuss how the roles of the United States, Europe, Japan, and the BRIC countries are likely to change in the next fifty years

- Discuss alternative scenarios of the future.

- Identify the key variables and relationships that are central to your "theory" of international relations.

Student Website

www.mhhe.com/cls

Internet References

The Henry L. Stimson Center
www.stimson.org

The Heritage Foundation
www.heritage.org

The North-South Institute
www.nsi-ins.ca/ensi/index.htm

Imagine yellow paint being brushed onto an inflated, clear balloon. The yellow color, for purposes of this allegory, represents "people." In many ways the study of global issues is first and foremost the study of people. Today, there are more human beings occupying Earth than ever before. In addition, we are in the midst of a period of unprecedented population growth. Not only are there many countries where the majority of people are under age 16, but also due to improved health care, there are a greater number of older people alive today than ever before. The effect of a growing global population, however, goes beyond sheer numbers, for this trend has unprecedented impacts on natural resources and social services. An examination of population trends and the related topic of food production is a good place to begin an in-depth study of global issues.

Imagine that our fictional artist next dips the brush into a container of blue paint to represent "nature." The natural world plays an important role in setting the international agenda. Shortages of raw materials, climate change, regional droughts, and pollution of waterways are just a few examples of how natural resources can have global implications.

Adding blue paint to the balloon reveals one of the most important underlying concepts found in this book. Although the balloon originally was covered by both yellow and blue paint (people and nature as separate conceptual entities), the two combined produce an entirely different color: green. Talking about nature as a separate entity or people as though they were somehow removed from the forces of the natural world is a serious intellectual error. The people–nature relationship is one of the keys to understanding many of today's most important global issues.

The third color to be added to the balloon is red. This color represents "social structures." Factors falling into this category include whether a society is urban or rural, industrial or agrarian, and consumer-oriented or dedicated to the needs of the state. The relationship between this component and the others is extremely important. The impact of political decisions on the environment, for example, is one of the most significant features of the contemporary world. Will the whales or bald eagles survive? Historically, the forces of nature determined which species survived or perished. Today, survival depends on political decision or indecision. Understanding the complex relationship between social structure and nature is central to the study of global issues.

Added to the three primary colors is the fourth and final color of white. It represents the "meta" component (i.e., those qualities that make human beings different from other life forms). These include new ideas and inventions, culture and values, religion and spirituality, and art and literature. The addition of the white paint immediately changes the intensity and shade of the mixture of colors, again emphasizing the relationship among all four factors.

If the painter continues to ply the paintbrush over the miniature globe, a marbling effect becomes evident. From one area to the next, the shading varies because one element is more dominant than another. Further, the miniature system

© U.S. Fish & Wildlife Service/Robert Pos

appears dynamic. Nothing is static; relationships are continually changing. This leads to a number of important insights: (1) There are no such things as separate elements, only connections or relationships; (2) changes in one area (such as the climate) will result in changes in all other areas; and (3) complex and dynamic relationships make it difficult to predict events accurately, so observers and policymakers are often surprised by unexpected events.

This book is organized along the basic lines of the balloon allegory. The first unit provides a broad overview of a variety of perspectives on the major forces that are shaping the world of the twenty-first century. From this "big picture" perspective more in-depth analyses follow. Unit 2, for example, focuses on population and food production. Unit 3 examines the environment and related natural resource issues. The next three units look at different aspects of the world's social structures. They explore issues of economics, national security, conflict, and international cooperation. In the final unit, a number of "meta" factors are presented.

The reader should keep in mind that, just as it was impossible to keep the individual colors from blending into new colors on the balloon, it is also impossible to separate global issues into discrete units in a book. Any discussion of agriculture, for example, must take into account the impact of a growing population on soil and water resources, as well as new scientific breakthroughs in food production. Therefore, the organization of this book focuses attention on issue areas; it does not mean to imply that these factors are somehow separate.

With the collapse of the Soviet empire and the end of the Cold War, a new global system has begun to emerge. Rather than being based on the ideology and interests of two superpowers, new political, economic, environmental, cultural, and security issues are interacting in an unprecedented fashion. Rapid population growth, environmental decline, uneven economic progress, and global terrorist networks are all parts of a complex state of affairs for which there is no historic parallel.

In the second decade of the twenty-first century, signs abound that we are entering a new era. In the words of Abraham Lincoln, "As our case is new, so we must think anew." Compounding this situation, however, is a whole series of old problems such as intensifying ethnic and religious rivalries.

The authors in this first unit provide a variety of perspectives on the trends which they believe are the most important to understanding the historic changes at work. This discussion is then pursued in greater detail in the following units.

Global Trends 2025: A Transformed World

Executive Summary

U.S. National Intelligence Council

The **international system**—as constructed following the Second World War—will be almost unrecognizable by 2025 owing to the rise of emerging powers, a globalizing economy, a historic transfer of relative wealth and economic power from West to East, and the growing influence of nonstate actors. By 2025, the international system will be a **global multipolar one** with gaps in national power[1] continuing to narrow between developed and developing countries. Concurrent with the shift in power among nation-states, the relative power of various nonstate actors—including businesses, tribes, religious organizations, and criminal networks—is increasing. The players are changing, but so too are the scope and breadth of transnational issues important for continued global prosperity. Aging populations in the developed world; growing energy, food, and water constraints; and worries about climate change will limit and diminish what will still be an historically unprecedented age of prosperity.

Historically, emerging multipolar systems have been more unstable than bipolar or unipolar ones. Despite the recent financial volatility—which could end up accelerating many ongoing trends—we do not believe that we are headed toward a complete breakdown of the international system, as occurred in 1914–1918 when an earlier phase of globalization came to a halt. However, the next 20 years of transition to a new system are fraught with risks. Strategic rivalries are most likely to revolve around trade, investments, and technological innovation and acquisition, but we cannot rule out a 19th century-like scenario of arms races, territorial expansion, and military rivalries.

This is a story with **no clear outcome,** as illustrated by a series of vignettes we use to map out divergent futures. Although the United States is likely to remain the single most powerful actor, the United States' relative strength—even in the military realm—will decline and U.S. leverage will become more constrained. At the same time, the extent to which other actors—both state and nonstate—will be willing or able to shoulder increased burdens is unclear. Policymakers and publics will have to cope with a growing demand for multilateral cooperation when the international system will be stressed by the incomplete transition from the old to a still-forming new order.

Economic Growth Fueling Rise of Emerging Players

In terms of size, speed, and directional flow, the transfer of **global wealth and economic power** now under way—roughly from West to East—is without precedent in modern history. This shift derives from two sources. First, increases in oil and commodity prices have generated windfall profits for the Gulf states and Russia. Second, lower costs combined with government policies have shifted the locus of manufacturing and some service industries to Asia.

Growth projections for Brazil, Russia, India, and China (the BRICs) indicate they will collectively match the original G-7's share of global GDP by 2040–2050. **China** is poised to have more impact on the world over the next 20 years than any other country. If current trends persist, by 2025 China will have the world's second largest economy and will be a leading military power. It also could be the largest importer of natural resources and the biggest polluter. **India** probably will continue to enjoy relatively rapid economic growth and will strive for a multipolar world in which New Delhi is one of the poles. China and India must decide the extent to which they are willing and capable of playing increasing global roles and how each will relate to the other. **Russia** has the potential to be richer, more powerful, and more self-assured in 2025 if it invests in human capital, expands and diversifies its economy, and integrates with global markets. On the other hand, Russia could experience a significant decline if it fails to take these steps and oil and gas prices remain in the $50–70 per barrel range. No other countries are projected to rise to the level of China, India, or Russia, and none is likely to match their individual global clout. We expect, however, to see the political and economic power of other countries—such as Indonesia, Iran, and Turkey—increase.

For the most part, China, India, and Russia are not following the Western liberal model for self-development but instead are using a different model, **"state capitalism."** State capitalism is a loose term used to describe a system of economic management that gives a prominent role to the state. Other rising powers—South Korea, Taiwan, and Singapore—also used state capitalism to develop their economies. However, the impact of Russia, and particularly China, following this path is potentially much greater owing to their size and approach to "democratization." We remain optimistic about the *long-term* prospects for **greater democratization,** even though advances are likely to be slow and globalization is subjecting many recently democratized countries to increasing social and economic pressures with the potential to undermine liberal institutions.

Many other countries will fall further behind economically. **Sub-Saharan Africa** will remain the region most vulnerable to economic disruption, population stresses, civil conflict, and political instability. Despite increased global demand for commodities for which Sub-Saharan Africa will be a major supplier, local populations are unlikely to experience significant economic gain. Windfall profits arising from sustained increases in commodity prices might further entrench corrupt or otherwise ill-equipped governments in several regions, diminishing the prospects for democratic and market-based reforms. Although many of **Latin America's** major countries will have become middle income powers by 2025, others, particularly those such as Venezuela and Bolivia that have embraced populist policies for a protracted period, will lag behind—and some, such as Haiti, will have become even poorer and less governable. Overall, Latin America will continue to lag behind Asia and other fast-growing areas in terms of economic competitiveness.

Asia, Africa, and Latin America will account for virtually all **population growth** over the next 20 years; less than 3 percent of the growth will occur in the West. Europe and Japan will continue to far outdistance the emerging powers of China and India in per capita wealth, but they will struggle to maintain robust growth rates because the size of their working-age populations will decrease. The US will be a partial exception to the aging of populations in the developed world because it will experience higher birth rates and more immigration. The number of migrants seeking to move from disadvantaged to relatively privileged countries is likely to increase.

The number of countries with youthful age structures in the current "arc of instability" is projected to decline by as much as 40 percent. Three of every four youth-bulge countries that remain will be located in Sub-Saharan Africa; nearly all of the remainder will be located in the core of the Middle East, scattered through southern and central Asia, and in the Pacific Islands.

New Transnational Agenda

Resource issues will gain prominence on the international agenda. Unprecedented global economic growth—positive in so many other regards—will continue to put pressure on a number of **highly strategic resources,** including energy, food, and water, and demand is projected to outstrip easily available supplies over the next decade or so. For example, non-OPEC liquid hydrocarbon production—crude oil, natural gas liquids, and unconventionals such as tar sands—will not grow commensurate with demand. Oil and gas production of many traditional energy producers already is declining. Elsewhere—in China, India, and Mexico—production has flattened. Countries capable of significantly expanding production will dwindle; oil and gas production will be concentrated in unstable areas. As a result of this and other factors, the world will be in the midst of a fundamental energy transition away from oil toward natural gas, coal and other alternatives.

The World Bank estimates that **demand for food** will rise by 50 percent by 2030, as a result of growing world population, rising affluence, and the shift to Western dietary preferences by a larger middle class. Lack of access to stable supplies of water is reaching critical proportions, particularly for agricultural purposes, and the problem will worsen because of rapid urbanization worldwide and the roughly 1.2 billion persons to be added over the next 20 years. Today, experts consider 21 countries, with a combined population of about 600 million, to be either cropland or freshwater scarce. Owing to continuing population growth, 36 countries, with about 1.4 billion people, are projected to fall into this category by 2025.

Climate change is expected to exacerbate resource scarcities. Although the impact of climate change will vary by region, a number of regions will begin to suffer harmful effects, particularly water scarcity and loss of agricultural production. Regional differences in agricultural production are likely to become more pronounced over time with declines disproportionately concentrated in developing countries, particularly those in Sub-Saharan Africa. Agricultural losses

are expected to mount with substantial impacts forecast by most economists by late this century. For many developing countries, decreased agricultural output will be devastating because agriculture accounts for a large share of their economies and many of their citizens live close to subsistence levels.

New technologies could again provide solutions, such as viable alternatives to fossil fuels or means to overcome food and water constraints. However, all current technologies are inadequate for replacing the traditional energy architecture on the scale needed, and new energy technologies probably will not be commercially viable and widespread by 2025. The pace of technological innovation will be key. Even with a favorable policy and funding environment for biofuels, clean coal, or hydrogen, the transition to new fuels will be slow. Major technologies historically have had an "adoption lag." In the energy sector, a recent study found that it takes an average of 25 years for a new production technology to become widely adopted.

Despite what are seen as long odds now, we cannot rule out the possibility of an **energy transition** by 2025 that would avoid the costs of an energy infrastructure overhaul. The greatest possibility for a relatively quick and inexpensive transition during the period comes from better renewable generation sources (photovoltaic and wind) and improvements in battery technology. With many of these technologies, the infrastructure cost hurdle for individual projects would be lower, enabling many small economic actors to develop their own energy transformation projects that directly serve their interests—e.g., stationary fuel cells powering homes and offices, recharging plug-in hybrid autos, and selling energy back to the grid. Also, energy conversion schemes—such as plans to generate hydrogen for automotive fuel cells from electricity in the homeowner's garage—could avoid the need to develop complex hydrogen transportation infrastructure.

Prospects for Terrorism, Conflict, and Proliferation

Terrorism, proliferation, and conflict will remain key concerns even as resource issues move up on the international agenda. Terrorism is unlikely to disappear by 2025, but its appeal could diminish if economic growth continues and youth unemployment is mitigated in the Middle East. Economic opportunities for youth and greater political pluralism probably would dissuade some from joining terrorists' ranks, but others—motivated by a variety of factors, such as a desire for revenge or to become "martyrs"—will continue to turn to violence to pursue their objectives.

In the absence of employment opportunities and legal means for political expression, conditions will be ripe for disaffection, growing radicalism, and possible recruitment of youths into **terrorist groups.** Terrorist groups in 2025 will likely be a combination of descendants of long-established groups—that inherit organizational structures, command and control processes, and training procedures necessary to conduct sophisticated attacks—and newly emergent collections of the angry and disenfranchised that become self-radicalized. For those terrorist groups that are active in 2025, the diffusion of technologies and scientific knowledge will place some of the world's most dangerous capabilities within their reach. One of our greatest concerns continues to be that terrorist or other malevolent groups might acquire and employ biological agents, or less likely, a nuclear device, to create mass casualties.

Although **Iran's** acquisition of nuclear weapons is not inevitable, other countries' worries about a nuclear-armed Iran could lead states in the region to develop new security arrangements with external powers, acquire additional weapons, and consider pursuing their own nuclear ambitions. It is not clear that the type of stable deterrent relationship that existed between the great powers for most of the Cold War would emerge naturally in the Middle East with a nuclear-weapons capable Iran. Episodes of low-intensity conflict taking place under a nuclear umbrella could lead to an unintended escalation and broader conflict if clear red lines between those states involved are not well established.

We believe **ideological conflicts** akin to the Cold War are unlikely to take root in a world in which most states will be preoccupied with the pragmatic challenges of globalization and shifting global power alignments. The force of ideology is likely to be strongest in the Muslim world—particularly the Arab core. In those countries that are likely to struggle with youth bulges and weak economic underpinnings—such as Pakistan, Afghanistan, Nigeria, and Yemen—the radical Salafi trend of Islam is likely to gain traction.

Types of **conflict** we have not seen for awhile—such as over resources—could reemerge. Perceptions of energy scarcity will drive countries to take actions to assure their future access to energy supplies. In the worst case, this could result in interstate conflicts if government leaders deem assured access to energy resources, for example, to be essential for maintaining domestic stability and the survival of their regimes. However, even actions short of war will have important geopolitical consequences. Maritime security concerns are providing a rationale for naval buildups and modernization efforts, such as China's and India's development of blue-water naval capabilities. The buildup of regional naval capabilities could lead to increased tensions, rivalries, and counterbalancing moves but it also will create opportunities for multinational cooperation in protecting critical sea lanes. With water becoming more scarce in Asia and the Middle East, cooperation to manage changing water resources is likely to become more difficult within and between states.

The risk of **nuclear weapon use** over the next 20 years, although remaining very low, is likely to be greater than it is today as a result of several converging trends. The spread of nuclear technologies and expertise is generating concerns about the potential emergence of new nuclear weapon states and the acquisition of nuclear materials by terrorist groups. Ongoing low-intensity clashes between India and Pakistan continue to raise the specter that such events could escalate to a broader conflict between those nuclear powers. The possibility of a future disruptive regime change or collapse occurring in a nuclear weapon state such as North Korea also continues to raise questions regarding the ability of weak states to control and secure their nuclear arsenals.

If nuclear weapons are used in the next 15–20 years, the international system will be shocked as it experiences immediate humanitarian, economic, and political-military repercussions. A future use of nuclear weapons probably would bring about significant geopolitical changes as some states would seek to establish or reinforce security alliances with existing nuclear powers and others would push for global nuclear disarmament.

A More Complex International System

The trend toward greater diffusion of authority and power that has been occurring for a couple decades is likely to accelerate because of the emergence of new global players, the worsening institutional deficit, potential expansion of regional blocs, and enhanced strength of nonstate actors and networks. The **multiplicity of actors** on the international scene could add strength—in terms of filling gaps left by aging post-World War II institutions—or further fragment the international system and incapacitate international cooperation. The diversity in type of actor raises

the likelihood of fragmentation occurring over the next two decades, particularly given the wide array of transnational challenges facing the international community.

The rising BRIC powers are unlikely to challenge the international system as did Germany and Japan in the 19th and 20th centuries, but because of their growing geopolitical and economic clout, they will have a high degree of freedom to customize their political and economic policies rather than fully adopting Western norms. They also are likely to want to preserve their policy freedom to maneuver, allowing others to carry the primary burden for dealing with such issues as terrorism, climate change, proliferation, and energy security.

Existing multilateral institutions—which are large and cumbersome and were designed for a different geopolitical order—will have difficulty adapting quickly to undertake new missions, accommodate changing memberships, and augment their resources.

Nongovernmental organizations (NGOs)—concentrating on specific issues—increasingly will be a part of the landscape, but NGO networks are likely to be limited in their ability to effect change in the absence of concerted efforts by multilateral institutions or governments. Efforts at greater inclusiveness—to reflect the emergence of the newer powers—may make it harder for international organizations to tackle transnational challenges. Respect for the dissenting views of member nations will continue to shape the agenda of organizations and limit the kinds of solutions that can be attempted.

Greater **Asian regionalism**—possible by 2025—would have global implications, sparking or reinforcing a trend toward three trade and financial clusters that could become quasi-blocs: North America, Europe, and East Asia. Establishment of such quasi-blocs would have implications for the ability to achieve future global World Trade Organization (WTO) agreements. Regional clusters could compete in setting trans-regional product standards for information technology, biotechnology, nanotechnology, intellectual property rights, and other aspects of the "new economy." On the other hand, an absence of regional cooperation in Asia could help spur competition among China, India, and Japan over resources such as energy.

Intrinsic to the growing complexity of the overlapping roles of states, institutions, and nonstate actors is the **proliferation of political identities,** which is leading to establishment of new networks and rediscovered communities. No one political identity is likely to be dominant in most societies by 2025. Religion-based networks may be quintessential issue networks and overall may play a more powerful role on many transnational issues such as the environment and inequalities than secular groupings.

The United States: Less Dominant Power

By 2025 the US will find itself as one of a number of important actors on the world stage, albeit still the most powerful one. Even in the military realm, where the US will continue to possess considerable advantages in 2025, advances by others in science and technology, expanded adoption of irregular warfare tactics by both state and nonstate actors, proliferation of long-range precision weapons, and growing use of cyber warfare attacks increasingly will constrict US freedom of action. A more constrained US role has implications for others and the likelihood of new agenda issues being tackled effectively. Despite the recent rise in anti-Americanism, the US probably will continue to be seen as a much-needed regional balancer in the Middle East and Asia. The US will continue to be expected to play a significant role in using its military power to counter global terrorism. On newer security issues like climate change, US leadership will be widely perceived as critical to leveraging competing and divisive views to find solutions. At the same time, the multiplicity of influential actors and distrust of vast power means less room for the US to call the shots without the support of strong partnerships. Developments in the rest of the world, including internal developments in a number of key states—particularly China and Russia—are also likely to be crucial determinants of US policy.

2025—What Kind of Future?

The above trends suggest major **discontinuities**, shocks, and surprises, which we highlight throughout the text. Examples include nuclear weapons use or a pandemic. In some cases, the surprise element is only a matter of **timing**: an energy transition, for example, is inevitable; the only questions are when and how abruptly or smoothly such a transition occurs. An energy transition from one type of fuel (fossil fuels) to another (alternative) is an event that historically has only happened once a century at most with momentous consequences. The transition from wood to coal helped trigger industrialization. In this case, a transition—particularly an abrupt one—out of fossil fuels would have major repercussions for energy producers in the Middle East and Eurasia, potentially causing permanent decline of some states as global and regional powers.

Other discontinuities are less predictable. They are likely to result from an interaction of several trends and depend on the quality of leadership. We put uncertainties such as whether China or Russia becomes a democracy in this category. China's growing middle class increases the chances but does not make such a development inevitable. Political pluralism seems less likely in Russia in the absence of economic diversification. Pressure from below may force the issue, or a leader might begin or enhance the democratization process to sustain the economy or spur economic growth. A sustained plunge in the price of oil and gas would alter the outlook and increase prospects for greater political and economic liberalization in Russia. If either country were to democratize, it would represent another wave of democratization with wide significance for many other developing states.

Also **uncertain** are the outcomes of demographic challenges facing Europe, Japan, and even Russia. In none of these cases does demography have to spell destiny with less regional and global power an inevitable outcome. Technology, the role of immigration, public health improvements, and laws encouraging greater female participation in the economy are some of the measures that could change the trajectory of current trends pointing toward less economic growth, increased social tensions, and possible decline.

Whether global institutions adapt and revive—another key uncertainty—also is a function of leadership. Current trends suggest a dispersion of power and authority will create a global governance deficit. Reversing those trend lines would require strong leadership in the international community by a number of powers, including the emerging ones.

Some uncertainties would have greater consequences—should they occur—than would others. In this work, we emphasize the overall potential for greater conflict—some forms of which could threaten globalization. We put WMD terrorism and a Middle East nuclear arms race in this category. In the four fictionalized scenarios, we have highlighted new challenges that could emerge as a result of the ongoing global transformation. They present new situations, dilemmas, or predicaments that represent departures from recent developments. As a set, they do not cover all possible futures. *None of these is inevitable or even necessarily likely;* but, as with many other uncertainties, the scenarios are potential game-changers.

- In *A World Without the West,* the new powers supplant the West as the leaders on the world stage.
- *October Surprise* illustrates the impact of inattention to global climate change; unexpected major impacts narrow the world's range of options.
- In *BRICs' Bust-Up,* disputes over vital resources emerge as a source of conflict between major powers—in this case two emerging heavyweights—India and China.
- In *Politics Is Not Always Local,* nonstate networks emerge to set the international agenda on the environment, eclipsing governments.

Note

1. National power scores, computed by the International Futures computer model, are the product of an index combining the weighted factors of GDP, defense spending, population, and technology.

Critical Thinking

1. What is the authors' point of view, which is the basis of this article?
2. What reasons are given to support this point of view?
3. Who are the so-called BRIC countries?
4. What is meant by state capitalism?
5. What is the new transnational agenda?
6. In addition to nation-states (i.e., countries), who are some of the new international actors?
7. Are there plausible scenarios of the future that have been left out?
8. In the "note" at the end of the article, the variables are identified that comprise the National Power Score. Assess the centrality of these variables to predicting the future and identify other variables that may have been omitted. Note: this assessment reveals a general outline of your international relations theory. Is it similar or different from the theory underlying the analysis presented in this article?

U.S. National Intelligence Council. From *Atlantic Council*, November 2008, pp. vi–xiii.

The New Geopolitics of Food

From the Middle East to Madagascar, high prices are spawning land grabs and ousting dictators. Welcome to the 21st-century food wars.

LESTER R. BROWN

In the United States, when world wheat prices rise by 75 percent, as they have over the last year, it means the difference between a $2 loaf of bread and a loaf costing maybe $2.10. If, however, you live in New Delhi, those sky-rocketing costs really matter: A doubling in the world price of wheat actually means that the wheat you carry home from the market to hand-grind into flour for chapatis costs twice as much. And the same is true with rice. If the world price of rice doubles, so does the price of rice in your neighborhood market in Jakarta. And so does the cost of the bowl of boiled rice on an Indonesian family's dinner table.

Welcome to the new food economics of 2011: Prices are climbing, but the impact is not at all being felt equally. For Americans, who spend less than one-tenth of their income in the supermarket, the soaring food prices we've seen so far this year are an annoyance, not a calamity. But for the planet's poorest 2 billion people, who spend 50 to 70 percent of their income on food, these soaring prices may mean going from two meals a day to one. Those who are barely hanging on to the lower rungs of the global economic ladder risk losing their grip entirely. This can contribute—and it has—to revolutions and upheaval.

Already in 2011, the U.N. Food Price Index has eclipsed its previous all-time global high; as of March it had climbed for eight consecutive months. With this year's harvest predicted to fall short, with governments in the Middle East and Africa tee-tering as a result of the price spikes, and with anxious markets sustaining one shock after another, food has quickly become the hidden driver of world politics. And crises like these are going to become increasingly common. The new geopolitics of food looks a whole lot more volatile—and a whole lot more contentious—than it used to. Scarcity is the new norm.

Until recently, sudden price surges just didn't matter as much, as they were quickly followed by a return to the rela-tively low food prices that helped shape the political stability of the late 20th century across much of the globe. But now both the causes and consequences are ominously different.

In many ways, this is a resumption of the 2007–2008 food crisis, which subsided not because the world somehow came together to solve its grain crunch once and for all, but because the Great Recession tempered growth in demand even as favorable weather helped farmers produce the larg-est grain harvest on record. Historically, price spikes tended to be almost exclusively driven by unusual weather—a mon-soon failure in India, a drought in the former Soviet Union, a heat wave in the U.S. Midwest. Such events were always disruptive, but thankfully infrequent. Unfortunately, today's price hikes are driven by trends that are both elevating demand and making it more difficult to increase production: among them, a rapidly expanding population, crop-withering temperature increases, and irrigation wells running dry. Each night, there are 219,000 additional people to feed at the global dinner table.

More alarming still, the world is losing its ability to soften the effect of shortages. In response to previous price surges, the United States, the world's largest grain producer, was effectively able to steer the world away from poten-tial catastrophe. From the mid-20th century until 1995, the United States had either grain surpluses or idle cropland that could be planted to rescue countries in trouble. When the Indian monsoon failed in 1965, for example, President Lyndon Johnson's administration shipped one-fifth of the U.S. wheat crop to India, successfully staving off famine. We can't do that anymore; the safety cushion is gone.

That's why the food crisis of 2011 is for real, and why it may bring with it yet more bread riots cum political revo-lutions. What if the upheavals that greeted dictators Zine el-Abidine Ben Ali in Tunisia, Hosni Mubarak in Egypt, and Muammar al-Qaddafi in Libya (a country that imports 90 percent of its grain) are not the end of the story, but the beginning of it? Get ready, farmers and foreign ministers alike, for a new era in which world food scarcity increas-ingly shapes global politics.

The doubling of world grain prices since early 2007 has been driven primarily by two factors: accelerat-ing growth in demand and the increasing difficulty of rapidly expanding production. The result is a world that looks strikingly different from the bountiful global grain economy of the last century. What will the geopolitics of food look like in a new era dominated by scarcity? Even at this early stage, we can see at least the broad outlines of the emerging food economy.

On the demand side, farmers now face clear sources of increasing pressure. The first is population growth. Each year the world's farmers must feed 80 million additional people, nearly all of them in developing countries. The world's population has nearly doubled since 1970 and is headed toward 9 billion by midcentury. Some 3 billion people, meanwhile, are also trying to move up the food chain, consuming more meat, milk, and eggs. As more families in China and elsewhere enter the middle class, they expect to eat better. But as global consumption of grain-intensive livestock products climbs, so does the demand for the extra corn and soybeans needed to feed all that livestock. (Grain consumption per person in the United States, for example, is four times that in India, where little grain is converted into animal protein. For now.)

At the same time, the United States, which once was able to act as a global buffer of sorts against poor harvests elsewhere, is now converting massive quantities of grain into fuel for cars, even as world grain consumption, which is already up to roughly 2.2 billion metric tons per year, is growing at an accelerating rate. A decade ago, the growth in consumption was 20 million tons per year. More recently it has risen by 40 million tons every year. But the rate at which the United States is converting grain into ethanol has grown even faster. In 2010, the United States harvested nearly 400 million tons of grain, of which 126 million tons went to ethanol fuel distilleries (up from 16 million tons in 2000). This massive capacity to convert grain into fuel means that the price of grain is now tied to the price of oil. So if oil goes to $150 per barrel or more, the price of grain will follow it upward as it becomes ever more profitable to convert grain into oil substitutes. And it's not just a U.S. phenomenon: Brazil, which distills ethanol from sugar cane, ranks second in production after the United States, while the European Union's goal of getting 10 percent of its transport energy from renewables, mostly biofuels, by 2020 is also diverting land from food crops.

This is not merely a story about the booming demand for food. Everything from falling water tables to eroding soils and the consequences of global warming means that the world's food supply is unlikely to keep up with our collectively growing appetites. Take climate change: The rule of thumb among crop ecologists is that for every 1 degree Celsius rise in temperature above the growing season optimum, farmers can expect a 10 percent decline in grain yields. This relationship was borne out all too dramatically during the 2010 heat wave in Russia, which reduced the country's grain harvest by nearly 40 percent.

While temperatures are rising, water tables are falling as farmers overpump for irrigation. This artificially inflates food production in the short run, creating a food bubble that bursts when aquifers are depleted and pumping is necessarily reduced to the rate of recharge. In arid Saudi Arabia, irrigation had surprisingly enabled the country to be self-sufficient in wheat for more than 20 years; now, wheat production is collapsing because the non-replenishable aquifer the country uses for irrigation is largely depleted. The Saudis soon will be importing all their grain.

Saudi Arabia is only one of some 18 countries with water-based food bubbles. All together, more than half the world's people live in countries where water tables are falling. The politically troubled Arab Middle East is the first geographic region where grain production has peaked and begun to decline because of water shortages, even as populations continue to grow. Grain production is already going down in Syria and Iraq and may soon decline in Yemen. But the largest food bubbles are in India and China. In India, where farmers have drilled some 20 million irrigation wells, water tables are falling and the wells are starting to go dry. The World Bank reports that 175 million Indians are being fed with grain produced by overpumping. In China, overpumping is concentrated in the North China Plain, which produces half of China's wheat and a third of its corn. An estimated 130 million Chinese are currently fed by overpumping. How will these countries make up for the inevitable shortfalls when the aquifers are depleted?

Even as we are running our wells dry, we are also mismanaging our soils, creating new deserts. Soil erosion as a result of overplowing and land mismanagement is undermining the productivity of one-third of the world's cropland. How severe is it? Look at satellite images showing two huge new dust bowls: one stretching across northern and western China and western Mongolia; the other across central Africa. Wang Tao, a leading Chinese desert scholar, reports that each year some 1,400 square miles of land in northern China turn to desert. In Mongolia and Lesotho, grain harvests have shrunk by half or more over the last few decades. North Korea and Haiti are also suffering from heavy soil losses; both countries face famine if they lose international food aid. Civilization can survive the loss of its oil reserves, but it cannot survive the loss of its soil reserves.

Beyond the changes in the environment that make it ever harder to meet human demand, there's an important intangible factor to consider: Over the last half-century or so, we have come to take agricultural progress for granted. Decade after decade, advancing technology underpinned steady gains in raising land productivity. Indeed, world grain yield per acre has tripled since 1950. But now that era is coming to an end in some of the more agriculturally advanced countries, where farmers are already using all available technologies to raise yields. In effect, the farmers have caught up with the scientists. After climbing for a century, rice yield per acre in Japan has not risen at all for 16 years. In China, yields may level off soon. Just those two countries alone account for one-third of the world's rice harvest. Meanwhile, wheat yields have plateaued in Britain, France, and Germany—Western Europe's three largest wheat producers.

In this era of tightening world food supplies, the ability to grow food is fast becoming a new form of geopolitical leverage, and countries are scrambling to secure their own parochial interests at the expense of the common good.

The first signs of trouble came in 2007, when farmers began having difficulty keeping up with the growth in global demand for grain. Grain and soybean prices started to climb, tripling by mid-2008. In response, many exporting countries tried to control the rise of domestic food prices by restricting exports. Among them were Russia and Argentina, two leading wheat exporters. Vietnam, the No. 2 rice exporter, banned exports entirely for several months in early 2008. So did several other smaller exporters of grain.

With exporting countries restricting exports in 2007 and 2008, importing countries panicked. No longer able to rely on the market to supply the grain they needed, several countries took the novel step of trying to negotiate long-term grain-supply agreements with exporting countries. The Philippines, for instance, negotiated a three-year agreement with Vietnam for 1.5 million tons of rice per year. A delegation of Yemenis traveled to Australia with a similar goal in mind, but had no luck. In a seller's market, exporters were reluctant to make long-term commitments.

Fearing they might not be able to buy needed grain from the market, some of the more affluent countries, led by Saudi Arabia, South Korea, and China, took the unusual step in 2008 of buying or leasing land in other countries on which to grow grain for themselves. Most of these land acquisitions are in Africa, where some governments lease cropland for less than $1 per acre per year. Among the principal destinations were Ethiopia and Sudan, countries where millions of people are being sustained with food from the U.N. World Food Program. That the governments of these two countries are willing to sell land to foreign interests when their own people are hungry is a sad commentary on their leadership.

By the end of 2009, hundreds of land acquisition deals had been negotiated, some of them exceeding a million acres. A 2010 World Bank analysis of these "land grabs" reported that a total of nearly 140 million acres were involved—an area that exceeds the cropland devoted to corn and wheat combined in the United States. Such acquisitions also typically involve water rights, meaning that land grabs potentially affect all downstream countries as well. Any water extracted from the upper Nile River basin to irrigate crops in Ethiopia or Sudan, for instance, will now not reach Egypt, upending the delicate water politics of the Nile by adding new countries with which Egypt must negotiate.

The potential for conflict—and not just over water—is high. Many of the land deals have been made in secret, and in most cases, the land involved was already in use by villagers when it was sold or leased. Often those already farming the land were neither consulted about nor even informed of the new arrangements. And because there typically are no formal land titles in many developing-country villages, the farmers who lost their land have had little backing to bring their cases to court. Reporter John Vidal, writing in Britain's *Observer,* quotes Nyikaw Ochalla from Ethiopia's Gambella region: "The foreign companies are arriving in large numbers, depriving people of land they have used for centuries. There is no consultation with the indigenous population. The deals are done secretly. The only thing the local people see is people coming with lots of tractors to invade their lands."

Local hostility toward such land grabs is the rule, not the exception. In 2007, as food prices were starting to rise, China signed an agreement with the Philippines to lease 2.5 million acres of land slated for food crops that would be shipped home. Once word leaked, the public outcry—much of it from Filipino farmers—forced Manila to suspend the agreement. A similar uproar rocked Madagascar, where a South Korean firm, Daewoo Logistics, had pursued rights to more than 3 million acres of land. Word of the deal helped stoke a political furor that toppled the government and forced cancellation of the agreement. Indeed, few things are more likely to fuel insurgencies than taking land from people. Agricultural equipment is easily sabotaged. If ripe fields of grain are torched, they burn quickly.

Not only are these deals risky, but foreign investors producing food in a country full of hungry people face another political question of how to get the grain out. Will villagers permit trucks laden with grain headed for port cities to proceed when they themselves may be on the verge of starvation? The potential for political instability in countries where villagers have lost their land and their livelihoods is high. Conflicts could easily develop between investor and host countries.

These acquisitions represent a potential investment in agriculture in developing countries of an estimated $50 billion. But it could take many years to realize any substantial production gains. The public infrastructure for modern market-oriented agriculture does not yet exist in most of Africa. In some countries it will take years just to build the roads and ports needed to bring in agricultural inputs such as fertilizer and to export farm products. Beyond that, modern agriculture requires its own infrastructure: machine sheds, grain-drying equipment, silos, fertilizer storage sheds, fuel storage facilities, equipment repair and maintenance services, well-drilling equipment, irrigation pumps, and energy to power the pumps. Overall, development of the land acquired to date appears to be moving very slowly.

So how much will all this expand world food output? We don't know, but the World Bank analysis indicates that only 37 percent of the projects will be devoted to food crops. Most of the land bought up so far will be used to produce biofuels and other industrial crops.

Even if some of these projects do eventually boost land productivity, who will benefit? If virtually all the inputs—the farm equipment, the fertilizer, the pesticides, the seeds—are brought in from abroad and if all the output is shipped out of the country, it will contribute little to the host country's economy. At best, locals may find work as farm laborers, but in highly mechanized operations, the jobs will be few. At worst, impoverished countries like Mozambique and Sudan will be left with less land and water with which to feed their already hungry populations. Thus far the land grabs have contributed more to stirring unrest than to expanding food production.

And this rich country-poor country divide could grow even more pronounced—and soon. This January, a new stage in the scramble among importing countries to secure food began to unfold when South Korea, which imports 70 percent of its grain, announced that it was creating a new public-private entity that will be responsible for acquiring part of this grain. With an initial office in Chicago, the plan is to bypass the large international trading firms by buying grain directly from U.S. farmers. As the Koreans acquire their own grain elevators, they may well sign multiyear delivery contracts with farmers, agreeing to buy specified quantities of wheat, corn, or soybeans at a fixed price.

Other importers will not stand idly by as South Korea tries to tie up a portion of the U.S. grain harvest even before it gets to market. The enterprising Koreans may soon be joined by China, Japan, Saudi Arabia, and other leading importers. Although South Korea's initial focus is the United States, far and away the world's largest grain exporter, it may later consider brokering deals with Canada, Australia, Argentina, and other major exporters. This is happening just as China may be on the verge of entering the U.S. market as a potentially massive importer of grain. With China's 1.4 billion increasingly affluent consumers starting to compete with U.S. consumers for the U.S. grain harvest, cheap food, seen by many as an American birthright, may be coming to an end.

No one knows where this intensifying competition for food supplies will go, but the world seems to be moving away from the international cooperation that evolved over several decades following World War II to an every-country-for-itself philosophy. Food nationalism may help secure food supplies for individual affluent countries, but it does little to enhance world food security. Indeed, the low-income countries that host land grabs or import grain will likely see their food situation deteriorate.

After the carnage of two world wars and the economic missteps that led to the Great Depression, countries joined together in 1945 to create the United Nations, finally realizing that in the modern world we cannot live in isolation, tempting though that might be. The International Monetary Fund was created to help manage the monetary system and promote economic stability and progress. Within the U.N. system, specialized agencies from the World Health Organization to the Food and Agriculture Organization (FAO) play major roles in the world today. All this has fostered international cooperation.

But while the FAO collects and analyzes global agricultural data and provides technical assistance, there is no organized effort to ensure the adequacy of world food supplies. Indeed, most international negotiations on agricultural trade until recently focused on access to markets, with the United States, Canada, Australia, and Argentina persistently pressing Europe and Japan to open their highly protected agricultural markets. But in the first decade of this century, access to supplies has emerged as the overriding issue as the world transitions from an era of food surpluses to a new politics of food scarcity. At the same time, the U.S. food aid program that once worked to fend off famine wherever it threatened has largely been replaced by the U.N. World Food Program (WFP), where the United States is the leading donor. The WFP now has food-assistance operations in some 70 countries and an annual budget of $4 billion. There is little international coordination otherwise. French President Nicolas Sarkozy—the reigning president of the G-20—is proposing to deal with rising food prices by curbing speculation in commodity markets. Useful though this may be, it treats the symptoms of growing food insecurity, not the causes, such as population growth and climate change. The world now needs to focus not only on agricultural policy, but on a structure that integrates it with energy, population, and water policies, each of which directly affects food security.

But that is not happening. Instead, as land and water become scarcer, as the Earth's temperature rises, and as world food security deteriorates, a dangerous geopolitics of food scarcity is emerging. Land grabbing, water grabbing, and buying grain directly from farmers in exporting countries are now integral parts of a global power struggle for food security.

With grain stocks low and climate volatility increasing, the risks are also increasing. We are now so close to the edge that a breakdown in the food system could come at any time. Consider, for example, what would have happened if the 2010 heat wave that was centered in Moscow had instead been centered in Chicago. In round numbers, the 40 percent drop in Russia's hoped-for harvest of roughly 100 million tons cost the world 40 million tons of grain, but a 40 percent drop in the far larger U.S. grain harvest of 400 million tons would have cost 160 million tons. The world's carryover stocks of grain (the amount in the bin when the new harvest begins) would have dropped to just 52 days of consumption. This level would have been not only the lowest on record, but also well below the 62-day carryover that set the stage for the 2007–2008 tripling of world grain prices.

Then what? There would have been chaos in world grain markets. Grain prices would have climbed off the charts. Some grain-exporting countries, trying to hold down domestic food prices, would have restricted or even banned exports, as they did in 2007 and 2008. The TV news would have been dominated not by the hundreds of fires in the Russian countryside, but by footage of food riots in low-income grain-importing countries and reports of governments falling as hunger spread out of control. Oil-exporting countries that import grain would have been trying to barter oil for grain, and low-income grain importers would have lost out. With governments toppling and confidence in the world grain market shattered, the global economy could have started to unravel.

We may not always be so lucky. At issue now is whether the world can go beyond focusing on the symptoms of the deteriorating food situation and instead attack the underlying causes. If we cannot produce higher crop yields with less water and conserve fertile soils, many agricultural areas will cease to be viable. And this goes far beyond farmers. If we cannot move at wartime speed to stabilize the climate, we may not be able to avoid runaway food prices. If we cannot accelerate the shift to smaller families and stabilize the world population sooner rather than later, the ranks of the hungry will almost certainly continue to expand. The time to act is now—before the food crisis of 2011 becomes the new normal.

Critical Thinking

1. Identify Lester Brown's point of view, which is the basis for this article.
2. What are the primary reasons he offers to support his point of view?
3. What are the reasons for grain prices doubling since 2007?
4. What impact on food prices does the demand for crop-based fuels have?
5. What three environmental trends are making it more difficult to expand grain supply?
6. How does this article illustrate the relationship between natural resources and social structures?
7. How is the concept of sustainability illustrated in this article?
8. What alternatives to current practices does Brown propose?
9. Do the authors of Article 1 give the same priority to threats to the food supply that Brown does?

LESTER R. BROWN, president of the Earth Policy Institute, is author of *World on the Edge: How to Prevent Environmental and Economic Collapse.*

Brown, Lester R. Reprinted in entirety by McGraw-Hill with permission from *Foreign Policy,* May/June 2011, pp. 56–58, 61–62. www.foreignpolicy.com. © 2011 Washingtonpost. Newsweek Interactive, LLC.

The End of Easy Everything

The transition from an easy to a tough resource era will come at a high price.

MICHAEL T. KLARE

According to some experts, many of the world's key energy and mineral supplies are being rapidly depleted and will soon be exhausted. Other experts say that new technology is opening up vast reserves of hitherto inaccessible supplies. Oil, coal, uranium, and natural gas will soon be scarce commodities or will be more plentiful than ever, depending on whom you ask. The same holds true for copper, cobalt, lithium, and other critical minerals.

Those unfamiliar with the distinctive characteristics of the extractive industries can find it difficult to make sense of all this. But in truth, the contending positions on resource availability largely obscure an essential reality: Instead of moving from plenty to scarcity or from plenty to even greater abundance, we are moving from "easy" sources of supply to "tough" ones. This distinction carries immense implications for international politics, the world economy, and the health of the global environment.

Toughest for Last

Extraction of resources, whatever the material, follows a predictable pattern. Whenever a natural resource is first found to possess desirable characteristics (whether as a trade commodity, source of energy, manufacturing input, or luxury product), producers seek out and exploit the most desirable deposits of that material—those easiest to extract, purest, closest to markets, and so on. In time, however, these deposits are systematically depleted, and so producers must seek out and develop less attractive deposits—those harder to extract, of poorer quality, further from markets, and posing hazards of various sorts.

Very often technology is brought to bear to exploit these tougher deposits. Mining and drilling go deeper underground and extend into harsher climate zones. In the case of oil and gas, drilling moves from land to coastal waters, and then from shallow to deeper waters. Technological innovations allow increasingly unappealing sources of supply to be exploited—but they also pose evergrowing risks of accidents, environmental contamination, and political strife.

The Deepwater Horizon disaster that began on April 20, 2010, is a perfect expression of this phenomenon. Until relatively recently, offshore oil and gas drilling had been confined to relatively shallow waters, at depths of less than 1,000 feet. Over the past few decades, however, the major oil firms have developed incredibly sophisticated offshore drilling rigs that can operate in waters over one mile deep. One such rig, called Mars, was deployed in deep Gulf of Mexico waters six months before NASA's celebrated 1996 launch of its Pathfinder probe to the planet Mars. At a total cost of $1 billion, Shell's Mars platform was more than three times as expensive as Pathfinder, and its remote-sensing technologies and engineering systems are arguably more sophisticated.

The use of such costly and advanced technology has allowed BP, Shell, and other well-heeled companies to extract ever-increasing volumes of oil from the Gulf's deep waters, helping to compensate for production declines at America's onshore and shallow coastal deposits. But operating in the Gulf's deep waters is far more difficult and hazardous than doing so in shallow waters, and the deep underground pressures encountered by these rigs are proportionally more difficult to manage. Intricate safety devices have been developed to reduce the risk of accident, but, as shown by the fate of the Deepwater Horizon, these cannot always be relied on to prevent catastrophe.

Despite this reality, oil companies will continue to drill in the Gulf's deep waters—and other challenging environments—because they see no other choice. Most of the "easy" oil and gas deposits on land and in shallow coastal waters in the United States and in friendly countries around the world have now been discovered and exploited, leaving only "tough" deposits in deep waters, the Arctic, areas with problematic geological formations, and dangerous or inhospitable countries like Iran, Iraq, and Russia. However daunting a task, the giant firms must find ways to operate in such areas if they intend to survive as major energy providers in the years to come.

And there is no question but that a vast abundance of "tough" oil and natural gas remains to be exploited. Resources in this category, which are often grouped together as "unconventional" fuels, include Canadian tar sands, Venezuelan heavy oil, shale oil and oil shale (two different things), shale gas, ultra-deepwater oil and gas, and Arctic hydrocarbons. The Orinoco Belt of Venezuela, for example, is said by the US Geological Survey (USGS) to contain as many as 1.7 trillion barrels of oil equivalent—easily exceeding the world's 1.3 trillion barrels in "proven" reserves of conventional (liquid) petroleum. The Arctic region, claims the USGS, harbors an estimated 1,700 billion cubic feet of natural gas, or the equivalent of 320 billion barrels of oil.

The Deepwater Horizon disaster may be the first ominous sign of what we can expect as we rely more heavily on unconventional fuels.

Even more astonishing is the amount of kerogen (an immature form of oil) contained in the oil shales of western Colorado and eastern Utah: as many as 2.8 trillion barrels of oil equivalent, or twice the tally of proven conventional reserves. Mature oil and gas deposits encased in hard shale formations, such as the Bakken oil formation of North Dakota, Montana, and Saskatchewan and the Marcellus gas formation of Pennsylvania, New York, and West Virginia are thought to be of a comparable scale.

Peak and Plateau

Such assessments of potential resource availability, coupled with recent advances in extractive technology, have led many energy experts to proclaim a new golden age of fossil fuel production—contradicting those in the field who speak of an imminent peak (and subsequent decline) in the output of oil, natural gas, and coal. Adherents of the "peak oil" theory see a significant contraction in petroleum supplies just around the corner, while the new-energy optimists believe that with sufficient investment, new technologies, and the relaxation of environmental regulations, all of humankind's future energy needs can be met.

Among the most vocal and prominent critics of production pessimism is Daniel Yergin, the author of a classic history of the oil industry, *The Prize: The Epic Quest for Oil, Money, and Power* and a just published study of energy's future, *The Quest: Energy, Security, and the Remaking of the Modern World.* "The peak oil theory," Yergin writes in his new volume, "embodies an 'end of technology/end of opportunity' perspective, that there will be no more significant innovation in oil production, nor significant new resources that can be developed. . . . But there is another, more appropriate way to visualize the course of supply: as a plateau. The world has decades of further production growth before flattening out into a plateau—perhaps some time around midcentury—at which time a more gradual decline will begin."

To buttress this contention, Yergin highlights the promising outlook for deep offshore drilling, shale oil, and Canadian tar sands. He also speaks with great enthusiasm about the "natural gas revolution"—the potential for recovering vast quantities of gas from shale rock through the use of horizontal drilling and hydraulic fracturing ("hydro-fracking," or simply "fracking"). When combined, these techniques allow for the extraction of gas

from the shale deposits of the giant Marcellus formation, as well as others in the United States and around the world. "As a result of the shale revolution," he asserts, "North America's natural gas base, now estimated at 3,000 trillion cubic feet, could provide for current levels of consumption for over a hundred years—plus."

Yergin's writings, in turn, have spawned an outpouring of Pollyannaish commentary about the unlimited future for unconventional oil and gas production in the United States and elsewhere. Writing in *The New York Times,* columnist David Brooks has described shale gas as a "wondrous gift" and a "blessing."

That production of unconventional oil and gas is rising, and that these fuels will constitute an increasing share of America's energy supply, are unquestionable—as long as we rely on fossil fuels for the lion's share of our energy supply. But to view such options as blessings, wondrous gifts, or even as easily obtainable resources is misleading. Even putting aside the fact that continued dependence on fossil fuels will lead to increased emissions of greenhouse gases and an acceleration in climate change, the extraction of these materials will involve ever greater cost, danger, and environmental risk as energy firms operate deeper underground, further offshore, further north, and in more problematic rock formations. Indeed, the Deepwater Horizon disaster may be the first ominous sign of what we can expect as we rely more heavily on unconventional fuels.

The Turning Point

Perhaps the first person to grasp the significance of this shift toward tough energy was David O'Reilly, the former chairman and chief executive officer of Chevron. In February 2005, O'Reilly startled participants at an annual oil-industry conference in Houston by declaring that their business was at an epochal turning point. After more than a hundred years during which the global availability of petroleum had always kept pace with rising world demand, he said, "oil is no longer in plentiful supply. The time when we could count on cheap oil and even cheaper natural gas is clearly ending." In an open letter published in many newspapers, O'Reilly then put the matter in even starker terms: "The era of easy oil is over. . . . New discoveries are mainly occurring in places where resources are difficult to extract, physically, economically, and even politically."

Nations will fight for access to new supply sources as easy reserves are depleted.

A closer look at O'Reilly's speech and accompanying advertisements shows that he was less interested in defining a momentous historic transition than in lobbying for more favorable government policies and reduced environmental regulation. Nevertheless, his description of the global situation has been widely embraced as an explanation for prevailing energy trends. *The Wall Street Journal,* for example, recently summed up a story about the rise of unconventional petroleum in Saudi Arabia with the headline "Facing up to End of 'Easy Oil.'"

As the paper explained, "As demand for energy grows and fields of 'easy oil' around the world start to dry up, the Saudis are turning to a much tougher source: the billions of barrels of heavy oil trapped beneath the desert."

The impact of the changeover from "easy oil" to tougher alternatives is partly financial and technical. Extracting light crude in Saudi Arabia once was accomplished for a few dollars per barrel, whereas making a barrel of usable liquid from sulfurous heavy oil requires sophisticated technology and can cost as much as $60 or $70 per barrel. But the pursuit of new petroleum sources to replace the exhausted "easy" deposits also has other costs, such as a growing reliance on oil acquired from countries in conflict or controlled by corrupt dictators.

Nigeria, for example, has become America's fourth-leading supplier of oil—yet Nigerian production is constantly imperiled by sabotage and the kidnapping of oil workers by militants opposed to the inequitable allocation of the country's petroleum revenues. Russia is another large source of oil and gas, yet Prime Minister Vladimir Putin's relentless drive to impose state control over the extraction of natural resources has resulted in the de facto seizure of foreign assets by government-owned firms. Iraq, with the world's second largest petroleum reserves, is theoretically capable of producing three or four times as much as it does now, but any such increase would require a significant increase in domestic security as well as a predictable legal regime—neither of which appears in the offing any time soon.

The Arctic is another promising source of tough oil and gas. According to the USGS, the land above the Arctic Circle, representing about 6 percent of the world's total surface area, contains approximately 30 percent of the world's undiscovered hydrocarbon reserves. As the planet warms and new technologies are perfected, it will become increasingly possible to extract this untapped energy. But operations in the Arctic are exceedingly difficult and hazardous. Winter temperatures can drop to well below minus 40 degrees Fahrenheit, and severe storms are common. Thick ice covers the Arctic Ocean throughout the winter, and drifting ice threatens ships and oil platforms in the summer. Many endangered species inhabit the area, and any oil spill is likely to prove devastating—especially since the oil companies' capacity to conduct cleanup operations in the Arctic (such as those performed in the Gulf of Mexico following the Deepwater Horizon spill) is severely limited.

Of all unconventional sources of oil and gas, none perhaps is more controversial than shale gas, when extracted by the hydro-fracking method. To obtain gas in this manner, a powerful drill is used to reach a gas-bearing shale formation, often thousands of feet underground, and then turned sidewise to penetrate the shale layer in several directions. After concrete is applied to the outer walls of the resulting channels, explosives are set off to penetrate the rock; then millions of gallons of water—usually laced with lubricants and toxic chemicals—are poured into the openings to fracture the stone and release the gas. The "frack" water is then pumped back up and stored on site or sent for disposal elsewhere, after which the gas is sucked out of the ground.

The big problem here is the risk of water contamination. Water extracted from the wells (or "flowback") contains toxic chemicals and radioactive materials released from underground rock and cannot be returned to local streams and rivers; any seepage, either from the well itself (due to cracks in the well bore) or from on-site storage ponds could contaminate local drinking supplies—a major worry in New York and Pennsylvania, where the Marcellus formation overlaps with the watershed for major metropolitan areas, including New York City. Cavities created by the fracturing process could also connect to other underground fissures and allow methane to escape into underground aquifers, with the same risk of water contamination. Dangers like these have led some states and municipalities to place a moratorium on hydro-fracking, or ban its use near major watershed areas.

Advocates of shale gas and hydro-fracking say that the technique can be performed safely and to great benefit—if only regulators and environmentalists will stand aside and let the companies get on it with it. "There have been over a million wells hydraulically fractured in the history of the industry, and there is not one, not one, reported case of a freshwater aquifer having ever been contaminated from hydraulic fracturing," said Rex W. Tillerson, the chief executive of ExxonMobil, in testimony before Congress. But investigation by reporters for *The New York Times* has uncovered numerous examples of contamination, including cases in which flowback that contained unsafe levels of radioactive materials has been dumped into rivers that supply drinking water to major communities.

Coal, too, is becoming increasingly difficult and dangerous to extract. In the American West, many once-prolific coal deposits have been exhausted, forcing miners to dig ever deeper into the earth—increasing the risk of cave-ins and seismic jolts known as "bounces," since less stone is left after the mining process to support the weight of the mountains above. The end of easy coal is also evident in a growing reliance on "mountain-top removal," a technique used to uncover buried coal seams in Appalachia by blasting off the peaks of mountains and dumping the rubble in the valleys below. While considered a practical method for reaching otherwise inaccessible coal deposits, the technique has devastating environmental consequences, such as the destruction of woodland habitats and the contamination of valley streams with toxic chemicals.

Never Had It So Hard

What is true of oil, gas, and coal is also true of many other natural resources necessary for modern industry, including iron, copper, cobalt, and nickel. "With easy nickel fading fast, miners go after the tough stuff," read one characteristic headline in *The Wall Street Journal,* describing ongoing mining difficulties in the South Pacific islands of New Caledonia. At one time, New Caledonia's ore had been so rich—as much as 15 percent nickel—that miners could simply dig it out with pickaxes and haul it away on donkeys.

Those reserves are long gone, however, and the mine's current owner, the Brazilian mining giant Vale, has been left trying to extract the valuable metal from ores that contain less than 2 percent nickel. This requires treating the rough ore with acid under intense heat and pressure, an inherently costly and risky process. Massive acid spills have occurred on several occasions, delaying the opening of Vale's $4 billion nickel refinery in New

Caledonia. Adding to the company's problems, indigenous groups have repeatedly stormed the site, demanding that Vale halt its operations and restore the original forested landscape.

Copper, another critical mineral, likewise is seeing the end of easy supplies. With many existing mines in decline, the major mining firms are searching for new sources of supply in the Arctic and in countries recovering from conflict. Freeport-McMoRan Copper and Gold, for example, has acquired a majority stake in the Tenke Fungurume copper/cobalt mine in the southern Katanga region of the Democratic Republic of the Congo, one of the most war-ravaged countries on the planet. Said to contain ore that is up to 10 times as rich as copper found in older mines elsewhere, Tenke Fungurume was originally developed by other companies, but was abandoned in the 1990s when fighting among various militias and rebel factions made it unsafe to operate in the area. Freeport has now rebuilt much of the damaged infrastructure at the site and hired a small army of private guards to protect the installation and its staff from continuing outbursts of violence. But security conditions remain a concern.

As easy-to-access deposits of all these natural resources disappear, the price of many basic commodities will rise, requiring lifestyle changes from people in wealthy countries—and extreme hardship for the poor, especially when it comes to food prices. The cost of corn, rice, wheat, and other key staples doubled or tripled in 2008, provoking riots around the world and leading to the collapse of Haiti's government; then, after a brief retreat, food prices rose again in 2010 and 2011, reaching record highs and sparking a fresh round of protests.

Analysts have given many reasons for this alarming trend, including soaring global demand, scarcity of cropland, and prolonged drought in many parts of the world (widely attributed to climate change). But according to a World Bank analysis, the catastrophic 2008 spike in food prices, at least, was largely driven by rising energy costs. With oil prices expected to remain high in the years ahead, food will remain costly, producing not just hardship for the poor but also a continuing risk of social instability.

Ferocious Competition

Skyrocketing commodity prices are among the most visible effects of the end of "easy" resources, and they will be felt by virtually everyone on the planet. But the transition away from an easy resource world will not only affect individuals. It will also set the stage for ferocious competition among major corporations and for perilous wrangling among nation-states.

As existing reserves of vital materials are exhausted, the major energy and minerals firms will have to acquire new sources of supply in distant and uninviting areas—an undertaking that will prove increasingly costly and dangerous, exposing many smaller and less nimble companies to a risk of seizure by larger and more powerful firms. It has been reported, for example, that Shell and ExxonMobil both considered an unfriendly takeover of BP following the Deepwater Horizon disaster, when that company's stock fell to record lows. Many mining firms have also been targets of corporate attack as existing deposits

of key minerals have been exhausted and industry giants compete for control over the few promising alternative reserves.

Nations, too, will fight among themselves for access to new supply sources as easy reserves are depleted and everyone must rely on the same assortment of tough deposits. This is evident, for example, in the Arctic, where formerly neglected boundary disputes have acquired fresh urgency with the growing appeal of the region's oil, gas, and mineral reserves. Canada and Russia have been particularly assertive in their claims to Arctic territory, saying not only that they will not back down in disputes over the location of contested offshore boundaries but that they will employ force if necessary to protect their Arctic space.

A similar pugnaciousness is evident in the East and South China Seas, where China has claimed ownership over a constellation of undersea oil and gas deposits but faces challenges from neighboring states that also assert ownership over the subsea reserves. In the East China Sea, China is squared off against Japan for control of the Chunxiao natural gas field (called Shirakaba by the Japanese), located in an offshore area claimed by both countries. Periodically, Chinese and Japanese ships and planes deployed in the area have engaged in menacing maneuvers toward one another, though no shots have yet been fired.

The situation in the South China Sea is even more complex and volatile. China and Taiwan claim the entire region, while parts are claimed by Brunei, Malaysia, Vietnam, the Philippines, and Indonesia—and here, shots have been fired on several occasions, when Chinese warships have sought to drive off oil-exploration vessels sanctioned by Vietnam and the Philippines.

The end of easy everything will not result in scarcity, as predicted by some—at least not in the short term. Instead, the use of advanced technologies to extract resources from hitherto inaccessible reserves will result in a continued supply of vital energy and mineral supplies. But the transition from an easy to a tough resource era will come at a high price, both in economic costs and in terms of environmental damage, social upheaval, and political strife. Only by reducing consumption of traditional fuels and metals and accelerating the development of renewable alternatives will it be possible to avert these perils.

Critical Thinking

1. What is the predictable pattern in resources extraction?

2. What is the "shale revolution"?

3. How does Klare assess this so-called revolution?

4. What is meant by the end of easy oil?

5. Compare the prospects of energy resources to mineral resources.

6. Do the authors of Article 1 give the same priority to the changing circumstances of natural resource extraction that Klare gives?

MICHAEL T. KLARE, a *Current History* contributing editor, is a professor at Hampshire College and author of the forthcoming *The Race for What's Left* (Metropolitan Books, 2012), from which this article is drawn.

China's Search for a Grand Strategy

Wang Jisi

A Rising Great Power Finds Its Way

Any country's grand strategy must answer at least three questions: What are the nation's core interests? What external forces threaten them? And what can the national leadership do to safeguard them? Whether China has any such strategy today is open to debate. On the one hand, over the last three decades or so, its foreign and defense policies have been remarkably consistent and reasonably well coordinated with the country's domestic priorities. On the other hand, the Chinese government has yet to disclose any document that comprehensively expounds the country's strategic goals and the ways to achieve them. For both policy analysts in China and China watchers abroad, China's grand strategy is a field still to be plowed.

In recent years, China's power and influence relative to those of other great states have outgrown the expectations of even its own leaders. Based on the country's enhanced position, China's international behavior has become increasingly assertive, as was shown by its strong reactions to a chain of events in 2010: for example, Washington's decision to sell arms to Taiwan, U.S.–South Korean military exercises in the Yellow Sea, and Japan's detention of a Chinese sailor found in disputed waters. It has become imperative for the international community to understand China's strategic thinking and try to forecast how it might evolve according to China's interests and its leaders' vision.

The Enemy within and without

A unique feature of Chinese leaders' understanding of their country's history is their persistent sensitivity to domestic disorder caused by foreign threats. From ancient times, the ruling regime of the day has often been brought down by a combination of internal uprising and external invasion. The Ming dynasty collapsed in 1644 after rebelling peasants took the capital city of Beijing and the Manchu, with the collusion of Ming generals, invaded from the north. Some three centuries later, the Manchu's own Qing dynasty collapsed after a series of internal revolts coincided with invasions by Western and Japanese forces. The end of the Kuomintang's rule and the founding of the People's Republic in 1949 was caused by an indigenous revolution inspired and then bolstered by the Soviet Union and the international communist movement.

Since then, apprehensions about internal turbulences have lingered. Under Mao Zedong's leadership, from 1949 to 1976, the Chinese government never formally applied the concept of "national interest" to delineate its strategic aims, but its international strategies were clearly dominated by political and military security interests—themselves often framed by ideological principles such as "proletarian internationalism." Strategic thinking at the time followed the Leninist tradition of dividing the world into political camps: archenemies, secondary enemies, potential allies, revolutionary forces. Mao's "three worlds theory" pointed to the Soviet Union and the United States as China's main external threats, with corresponding internal threats coming from pro-Soviet "revisionists" and pro-American "class enemies." China's political life in those years was characterized by recurrent struggles against international and domestic schemes to topple the Chinese Communist Party (CCP) leadership or change its political coloring. Still, since Mao's foreign policy supposedly represented the interests of the "international proletariat" rather than China's own, and since China was economically and socially isolated from much of the world, Beijing had no comprehensive grand strategy to speak of.

Then came the 1980s and Deng Xiaoping. As China embarked on reform and opened up, the CCP made economic development its top priority. Deng's foreign policy thinking departed appreciably from that of Mao. A major war with either the Soviet Union or the United States was no longer deemed inevitable. China made great efforts to develop friendly and cooperative relations with countries all over the world, regardless of their political or ideological orientation; it reasoned that a nonconfrontational posture would attract foreign investment to China and boost trade. A peaceful international environment, an enhanced position for China in the global arena, and China's steady integration into the existing economic order would also help consolidate the CCP's power at home.

But even as economic interests became a major driver of China's behavior on the international scene, traditional security concerns and the need to guard against Western political interference remained important. Most saliently, the Tiananmen Square incident of 1989 and, in its wake, the West's sanctions against Beijing served as an alarming reminder to China's leaders that internal and external troubles could easily intertwine. Over the next decade, Beijing responded to Western censure by contending that the state's sovereign rights trumped human rights. It resolutely refused to consider adopting Western-type democratic institutions. And it insisted that it would never give up the option of using force if Taiwan tried to secede.

Despite those concerns, however, by the beginning of the twenty-first century, China's strategic thinkers were depicting a generally favorable international situation. In his 2002 report to the CCP National Congress, General Secretary Jiang Zemin foresaw a "20 years' period of strategic opportunity," during which China could continue to concentrate on domestic tasks. Unrest has erupted at times—such as the violent riots in Tibet in March 2008 and in Xinjiang in July 2009, which the central government blamed on "foreign hostile forces" and responded

16

to with harsh reprisals. And Beijing claims that the awarding of the 2010 Nobel Peace Prize to Liu Xiaobo, a political activist it deems to be a "criminal trying to sabotage the socialist system," has proved once again Westerners' "ill intentions." Still, the Chinese government has been perturbed by such episodes only occasionally, which has allowed it to focus on redressing domestic imbalances and the unsustainability of its development.

Under President Hu Jintao, Beijing has in recent years formulated a new development and social policy geared toward continuing to promote fast economic growth while emphasizing good governance, improving the social safety net, protecting the environment, encouraging independent innovation, lessening social tensions, perfecting the financial system, and stimulating domestic consumption. As Chinese exports have suffered from the global economic crisis since 2008, the need for such economic and social transformations has become more urgent.

With that in mind, the Chinese leadership has redefined the purpose of China's foreign policy. As Hu announced in July 2009, China's diplomacy must "safeguard the interests of sovereignty, security, and development." Dai Bingguo, the state councilor for external relations, further defined those core interests in an article last December: first, China's political stability, namely, the stability of the CCP leadership and of the socialist system; second, sovereign security, territorial integrity, and national unification; and third, China's sustainable economic and social development.

Apart from the issue of Taiwan, which Beijing considers to be an integral part of China's territory, the Chinese government has never officially identified any single foreign policy issue as one of the country's core interests. Last year, some Chinese commentators reportedly referred to the South China Sea and North Korea as such, but these reckless statements, made with no official authorization, created a great deal of confusion. In fact, for the central government, sovereignty, security, and development all continue to be China's main goals. As long as no grave danger—for example, Taiwan's formal secession—threatens the CCP leadership or China's unity, Beijing will remain preoccupied with the country's economic and social development, including its foreign policy.

The Principle's Principle

The need to identify an organizing principle to guide Chinese foreign policy is widely recognized today in China's policy circles and scholarly community, as well as among international analysts. However, defining China's core interests according to the three prongs of sovereignty, security, and development, which sometimes are in tension, means that it is almost impossible to devise a straightforward organizing principle. And the variety of views among Chinese political elites complicates efforts to devise any such grand strategy based on political consensus.

One popular proposal has been to focus on the United States as a major threat to China. Proponents of this view cite the ancient Chinese philosopher Mencius, who said, "A state without an enemy or external peril is absolutely doomed." Or they reverse the political scientist Samuel Huntington's argument that "the ideal enemy for America would be ideologically hostile, racially and culturally different, and militarily strong enough to pose a credible threat to American security" and cast the United States as an ideal enemy for China. This notion is based on the long-held conviction that the United States, along with other Western powers and Japan, is hostile to China's political values and wants to contain its rise by supporting Taiwan's separation from the mainland. Its proponents also point to U.S. politicians' sympathy for

the Dalai Lama and Uighur separatists, continued U.S. arms sales to Taiwan, U.S. military alliances and arrangements supposedly designed to encircle the Chinese mainland, the currency and trade wars waged by U.S. businesses and the U.S. Congress, and the West's argument that China should slow down its economic growth in order to help stem climate change.

This view is reflected in many newspapers and on many Web sites in China (particularly those about military affairs and political security). Its proponents argue that China's current approach to foreign relations is far too soft; Mao's tit-for-tat manner is touted as a better model. As a corollary, it is said that China should try to find strategic allies among countries that seem defiant toward the West, such as Iran, North Korea, and Russia. Some also recommend that Beijing use its holdings of U.S. Treasury bonds as a policy instrument, standing ready to sell them if U.S. government actions undermine China's interests.

This proposal is essentially misguided, for even though the United States does pose some strategic and security challenges to China, it would be impractical and risky to construct a grand strategy based on the view that the United States is China's main adversary. Few countries, if any, would want to join China in an anti-U.S. alliance. And it would seriously hold back China's economic development to antagonize the country's largest trading partner and the world's strongest economic and military power. Fortunately, the Chinese leadership is not about to carry out such a strategy. Premier Wen Jiabao was not just being diplomatic last year when he said of China and the United States that "our common interests far outweigh our differences."

Well aware of this, an alternative school of thought favors Deng's teaching of tao guang yang hui, or keeping a low profile in international affairs. Members of this group, including prominent political figures, such as Tang Jiaxuan, former foreign minister, and General Xiong Guangkai, former deputy chief of staff of the People's Liberation Army, argue that since China remains a developing country, it should concentrate on economic development. Without necessarily rebuffing the notion that the West, particularly the United States, is a long-term threat to China, they contend that China is not capable of challenging Western primacy for the time being—and some even caution against hastily concluding that the West is in decline. Meanwhile, they argue, keeping a low profile in the coming decades will allow China to concentrate on domestic priorities.

Although this view appears to be better received internationally than the other, it, too, elicits some concerns. Its adherents have had to take great pains to explain that tao guang yang hui, which is sometimes mistranslated as "hiding one's capabilities and biding one's time," is not a calculated call for temporary moderation until China has enough material power and confidence to promote its hidden agenda. Domestically, the low-profile approach is vulnerable to the charge that it is too soft, especially when security issues become acute. As nationalist feelings surge in China, some Chinese are pressing for a more can-do foreign policy. Opponents also contend that this notion, which Deng put forward more than 20 years ago, may no longer be appropriate now that China is far more powerful.

Some thoughtful strategists appreciate that even if keeping a low profile could serve China's political and security relations with the United States well, it might not apply to China's relations with many other countries or to economic issues and those nontraditional security issues that have become essential in recent years, such as climate change, public health, and energy security. (Beijing can hardly keep a low profile when it actively participates in mechanisms such as BRIC, the informal group formed by Brazil, Russia, India, China, and the new member South Africa.) A foreign policy that insists merely on keeping China's profile low cannot cope effectively with the multi-faceted challenges facing the country today.

Home Is Where the Heart Is

A more sophisticated grand strategy is needed to serve China's domestic priorities. The government has issued no official written statement outlining such a vision, but some direction can be gleaned from the concepts of a "scientific outlook on development" and "building a harmonious society," which have been enunciated by Hu and have been recorded in all important CCP documents since 2003. In 2006, the Central Committee of the CCP announced that China's foreign policy "must maintain economic construction as its centerpiece, be closely integrated into domestic work, and be advanced by coordinating domestic and international situations." Moreover, four ongoing changes in China's strategic thinking may suggest the foundations for a new grand strategy.

The first transformation is the Chinese government's adoption of a comprehensive understanding of security, which incorporates economic and nontraditional concerns with traditional military and political interests. Chinese military planners have begun to take into consideration transnational problems such as terrorism and piracy, as well as cooperative activities such as participation in UN peacekeeping operations. Similarly, it is now clear that China must join other countries in stabilizing the global financial market in order to protect its own economic security. All this means that it is virtually impossible to distinguish China's friends from its foes. The United States might pose political and military threats, and Japan, a staunch U.S. ally, could be a geopolitical competitor of China's, but these two countries also happen to be two of China's greatest economic partners. Even though political difficulties appear to be on the rise with the European Union, it remains China's top economic partner. Russia, which some Chinese see as a potential security ally, is far less important economically and socially to China than is South Korea, another U.S. military ally. It will take painstaking efforts on Beijing's part to limit tensions between China's traditional political–military perspectives and its broadening socioeconomic interests—efforts that effectively amount to reconciling the diverging legacies of Mao and Deng. The best Beijing can do is to strengthen its economic ties with great powers while minimizing the likelihood of a military and political confrontation with them.

A second transformation is unfolding in Chinese diplomacy: it is becoming less country-oriented and more multilateral and issue-oriented. This shift toward functional focuses—counterterrorism, nuclear nonproliferation, environmental protection, energy security, food safety, post-disaster reconstruction—has complicated China's bilateral relationships, regardless of how friendly other states are toward it. For example, diverging geostrategic interests and territorial disputes have long come between China and India, but the two countries' common interest in fending off the West's pressure to reduce carbon emissions has drawn them closer. And now that Iran has become a key supplier of oil to China, its problems with the West over its nuclear program are testing China's stated commitment to the nuclear nonproliferation regime.

Changes in the mode of China's economic development account for a third transformation in the country's strategic thinking. Beijing's preoccupation with GDP growth is slowly giving way to concerns about economic efficiency, product quality, environmental protection, the creation of a social safety net, and technological innovation. Beijing's understanding of the core interest of development is expanding to include social dimensions. Correspondingly, China's leaders have decided to try to sustain the country's high growth rate by propping up domestic consumption and reducing over the long term the country's dependence on exports and foreign investment. They are now more concerned with global economic imbalances and financial fluctuations, even as international economic frictions are becoming more intense because of the global financial crisis. China's long-term interests will require some incremental appreciation of the yuan, but its desire to increase its exports in the short term will prevent its decision-makers from taking the quick measures urged by the United States and many other countries. Only the enhancement of China's domestic consumption and a steady opening of its capital markets will help it shake off these international pressures.

The fourth transformation has to do with China's values. So far, China's officials have said that although China has a distinctive political system and ideology, it can cooperate with other countries based on shared interests—although not, the suggestion seems to be, on shared values. But now that they strongly wish to enhance what they call the "cultural soft power of the nation" and improve China's international image, it appears necessary to also seek common values in the global arena, such as good governance and transparency. Continuing trials and tribulations at home, such as pervasive corruption and ethnic and social unrest in some regions, could also reinforce a shift in values among China's political elite by demonstrating that their hold on power and the country's continued resurgence depend on greater transparency and accountability, as well as on a firmer commitment to the rule of law, democracy, and human rights, all values that are widely shared throughout the world today.

All four of these developments are unfolding haltingly and are by no means irreversible. Nonetheless, they do reveal fundamental trends that will likely shape China's grand strategy in the foreseeable future. When Hu and other leaders call for "coordinating domestic and international situations," they mean that efforts to meet international challenges must not undermine domestic reforms. And with external challenges now coming not only from foreign powers—especially the United States and Japan—but also, and increasingly, from functional issues, coping with them effectively will require engaging foreign countries cooperatively and emphasizing compatible values.

Thus, it would be imprudent of Beijing to identify any one country as a major threat and invoke the need to keep it at bay as an organizing principle of Chinese foreign policy—unless the United States, or another great power, truly did regard China as its main adversary and so forced China to respond in kind. On the other hand, if keeping a low profile is a necessary component of Beijing's foreign policy, it is also insufficient. A grand strategy needs to consider other long-term objectives as well. One that appeals to some Chinese is the notion of building China into the most powerful state in the world: Liu Mingfu, a senior colonel who teaches at the People's Liberation Army's National Defense University, has declared that replacing the United States as the world's top military power should be China's goal. Another idea is to cast China as an alternative model of development (the "Beijing consensus") that can challenge Western systems, values, and leadership. But the Chinese leadership does not dream of turning China into a hegemon or a standard-bearer. Faced with mounting pressures on both the domestic and the international fronts, it is sober in its objectives, be they short- or long-term ones. Its main concern is how best to protect China's core interests—sovereignty, security, and development—against the messy cluster of threats that the country faces today. If an organizing principle must be established to guide China's grand strategy, it should be the improvement of the Chinese people's living standards, welfare, and happiness through social justice.

The Birth of a Great Nation

Having identified China's core interests and the external pressures that threaten them, the remaining question is, how can China's leadership safeguard the country's interests against those threats? China's continued success in modernizing its economy and lifting its people's standards of living depends heavily on global stability. Thus, it is in China's interest to contribute to a peaceful international environment. China should seek peaceful solutions to residual sovereignty and security issues, including the thorny territorial disputes between it and its neighbors. With the current leadership in Taiwan refraining from seeking formal independence from the mainland, Beijing is more confident that peace can be maintained across the Taiwan Strait. But it has yet to reach a political agreement with Taipei that would prevent renewed tensions in the future. The Chinese government also needs to find effective means to pacify Tibet and Xinjiang, as more unrest in those regions would likely elicit reactions from other countries.

Although the vast majority of people in China support a stronger Chinese military to defend the country's major interests, they should also recognize the dilemma that poses. As China builds its defense capabilities, especially its navy, it will have to convince others, including the United States and China's neighbors in Asia, that it is taking their concerns into consideration. It will have to make the plans of the People's Liberation Army more transparent and show a willingness to join efforts to establish security structures in the Asia-Pacific region and safeguard existing global security regimes, especially the nuclear nonproliferation regime. It must also continue to work with other states to prevent Iran and North Korea from obtaining nuclear weapons. China's national security will be well served if it makes more contributions to other countries' efforts to strengthen security in cyberspace and outer space. Of course, none of this excludes the possibility that China might have to use force to protect its sovereignty or its security in some special circumstances, such as in the event of a terrorist attack.

China has been committed to almost all existing global economic regimes. But it will have to do much more before it is recognized as a full-fledged market economy. It has already gained an increasingly larger say in global economic mechanisms, such as the G-20, the World Bank, and the International Monetary Fund. Now, it needs to make specific policy proposals and adjustments to help rebalance the global economy and facilitate its plans to change its development pattern at home. Setting a good example by building a low-carbon economy is one major step that would benefit both China and the world.

A grand strategy requires defining a geostrategic focus, and China's geostrategic focus is Asia. When communication lines in Central Asia and South Asia were poor, China's development strategy and economic interests tilted toward its east coast and the Pacific Ocean. Today, East Asia is still of vital importance, but China should and will begin to pay more strategic attention to the west. The central government has been conducting the Grand Western Development Program in many western provinces and regions, notably Tibet and Xinjiang, for more than a decade. It is now more actively initiating and participating in new development projects in Afghanistan, India, Pakistan, Central Asia, and throughout the Caspian Sea region, all the way to Europe. This new western outlook may reshape China's geostrategic vision as well as the Eurasian landscape.

Still, relationships with great powers remain crucial to defending China's core interests. Notwithstanding the unprecedented economic interdependence of China, Japan, and the United States, strategic trust is still lacking between China and the United States and China and Japan. It is imperative that the Chinese–Japanese–U.S. trilateral interaction be stable and constructive, and a trilateral strategic dialogue is desirable. More generally, too, China will have to invest tremendous resources to promote a more benign image on the world stage. A China with good governance will be a likeable China. Even more important, it will have to learn that soft power cannot be artificially created: such influence originates more from a society than from a state.

Two daunting tasks lie ahead before a better-designed Chinese grand strategy can take shape and be implemented. The first is to improve policy coordination among Chinese government agencies. Almost all institutions in the central leadership and local governments are involved in foreign relations to varying degrees, and it is virtually impossible for them to see China's national interest the same way or to speak with one voice. These differences confuse outsiders as well as the Chinese people.

The second challenge will be to manage the diversity of views among China's political elite and the general public, at a time when the value system in China is changing rapidly. Mobilizing public support for government policies is expected to strengthen Beijing's diplomatic bargaining power while also helping consolidate its domestic popularity. But excessive nationalism could breed more public frustration and create more pressure on the government if its policies fail to deliver immediately, which could hurt China's political order, as well as its foreign relations. Even as it allows different voices to be heard on foreign affairs, the central leadership should more vigorously inform the population of its own view, which is consistently more moderate and prudent than the inflammatory remarks found in the media and on Web sites.

No major power's interests can conform exactly to those of the international community; China is no exception. And with one-fifth of the world's population, it is more like a continent than a country. Yet despite the complexity of developing a grand strategy for China, the effort is at once consistent with China's internal priorities and generally positive for the international community. China will serve its interests better if it can provide more common goods to the international community and share more values with other states.

How other countries respond to the emergence of China as a global power will also have a great impact on China's internal development and external behavior. If the international community appears not to understand China's aspirations, its anxieties, and its difficulties in feeding itself and modernizing, the Chinese people may ask themselves why China should be bound by rules that were essentially established by the Western powers. China can rightfully be expected to take on more international responsibilities. But then the international community should take on the responsibility of helping the world's largest member support itself.

Critical Thinking

1. What is Wang Jisi's point of view?

2. What are the main reasons he offers to support his point of view?

3. How do domestic concerns such as economic and social development influence China's foreign policy?

4. Why is an anti-United States strategy unlikely to be adopted?

5. What are two challenges that China must overcome before a grand strategy takes shape?

6. Do the authors of Article 1 view China in a similar or different perspective than Wang Jisi?

WANG JISI is Dean of the School of International Studies at Peking University, in Beijing.

Why the World Needs America

Foreign-policy pundits increasingly argue that democracy and free markets could thrive without U.S. predominance. If this sounds too good to be true, writes Robert Kagan, that's because it is.

ROBERT KAGAN

lasting only for a short time.

History shows that world orders, including our own, are transient. They rise and fall, and the institutions they erect, the beliefs and "norms" that guide them, the economic systems they support—they rise and fall, too. The downfall of the Roman Empire brought an end not just to Roman rule but to Roman government and law and to an entire economic system stretching from Northern Europe to North Africa. Culture, the arts, even progress in science and technology, were set back for centuries.

Modern history has followed a similar pattern. After the Napoleonic Wars of the early 19th century, British control of the seas and the balance of great powers on the European continent provided relative security and stability. Prosperity grew, personal freedoms expanded, and the world was knit more closely together by revolutions in commerce and communication.

With the outbreak of World War I, the age of settled peace and advancing liberalism—of European civilization approaching its pinnacle—collapsed into an age of hyper-nationalism, despotism and economic calamity. The once-promising spread of democracy and liberalism halted and then reversed course, leaving a handful of outnumbered and besieged democracies living nervously in the shadow of fascist and totalitarian neighbors. The collapse of the British and European orders in the 20th century did not produce a new dark age—though if Nazi Germany and imperial Japan had prevailed, it might have—but the horrific conflict that it produced was, in its own way, just as devastating.

Would the end of the present American-dominated order have less dire consequences? A surprising number of American intellectuals, politicians and policy makers greet the prospect with equanimity. There is a general sense that the end of the era of American pre-eminence, if and when it comes, need not mean the end of the present international order, with its widespread freedom, unprecedented global prosperity (even amid the current economic crisis) and absence of war among the great powers.

American power may diminish, the political scientist G. John Ikenberry argues, but "the underlying foundations of the liberal international order will survive and thrive." The commentator Fareed Zakaria believes that even as the balance shifts against the U.S., rising powers like China "will continue to live within the framework of the current international system." And there are elements across the political spectrum—Republicans who call for retrenchment, Democrats who put their faith in international law and institutions—who don't imagine that a "post-American world" would look very different from the American world.

If all of this sounds too good to be true, it is. The present world order was largely shaped by American power and reflects American interests and preferences. If the balance of power shifts in the direction of other nations, the world order will change to suit their interests and preferences. Nor can we assume that all the great powers in a post-American world would agree on the benefits of preserving the present order, or have the capacity to preserve it, even if they wanted to.

Take the issue of democracy. For several decades, the balance of power in the world has favored democratic governments. In a genuinely post-American world, the balance would shift toward the great-power autocracies. Both Beijing and Moscow already protect dictators like Syria's Bashar al-Assad. If they gain greater relative influence in the future, we will see fewer democratic transitions and more autocrats hanging on to power. The balance in a new, multipolar world might be more favorable to democracy if some of the rising democracies—Brazil, India, Turkey, South Africa—picked up the slack from a declining U.S. Yet not all of them have the desire or the capacity to do it.

What about the economic order of free markets and free trade? People assume that China and other rising powers that have benefited so much from the present system would have a stake in preserving it. They wouldn't kill the goose that lays the golden eggs.

Unfortunately, they might not be able to help themselves. The creation and survival of a liberal economic order has depended, historically, on great powers that are both willing and able to support open trade and free markets, often with naval power. If a declining America is unable to maintain its long-standing hegemony on the high seas, would other nations take on the burdens and the expense of sustaining navies to fill in the gaps?

Even if they did, would this produce an open global commons—or rising tension? China and India are building bigger navies, but the result so far has been greater competition, not greater security. As Mohan Malik has noted in this newspaper, their "maritime rivalry could spill into the open in a decade or two," when India deploys an aircraft carrier in the Pacific Ocean and China deploys one in the Indian Ocean. The move from American-dominated oceans to collective policing by several great powers could be a recipe for competition and conflict rather than for a liberal economic order.

And do the Chinese really value an open economic system? The Chinese economy soon may become the largest in the world, but it will be far from the richest. Its size is a product of the country's enormous population, but in per capita terms, China remains relatively poor. The U.S., Germany and Japan have a per capita GDP of over $40,000. China's is a little over $4,000, putting it at the same level as Angola, Algeria and Belize. Even if optimistic forecasts are correct, China's per capita GDP by 2030 would still only be half that of the U.S., putting it roughly where Slovenia and Greece are today.

As Arvind Subramanian and other economists have pointed out, this will make for a historically unique situation. In the past, the largest and most dominant economies in the world have also been the richest. Nations whose peoples are such obvious winners in a relatively unfettered economic system have less temptation to pursue protectionist measures and have more of an incentive to keep the system open.

China's leaders, presiding over a poorer and still developing country, may prove less willing to open their economy. They have already begun closing some sectors to foreign competition and are likely to close others in the future. Even optimists like Mr. Subramanian believe that the liberal economic order will require "some insurance" against a scenario in which "China exercises its dominance by either reversing its previous policies or failing to open areas of the economy that are now highly protected." American economic dominance has been welcomed by much of the world because, like the mobster Hyman Roth in "The Godfather," the U.S. has always made money for its partners. Chinese economic dominance may get a different reception.

Another problem is that China's form of capitalism is heavily dominated by the state, with the ultimate goal of preserving the rule of the Communist Party. Unlike the eras of British and American pre-eminence, when the leading economic powers were dominated largely by private individuals or companies, China's system is more like the mercantilist arrangements of previous centuries. The government amasses wealth in order to secure its continued rule and to pay for armies and navies to compete with other great powers.

Although the Chinese have been beneficiaries of an open international economic order, they could end up undermining it simply because, as an autocratic society, their priority is to preserve the state's control of wealth and the power that it brings. They might kill the goose that lays the golden eggs because they can't figure out how to keep both it and themselves alive.

Finally, what about the long peace that has held among the great powers for the better part of six decades? Would it survive in a post-American world?

Most commentators who welcome this scenario imagine that American predominance would be replaced by some kind of multipolar harmony. But multipolar systems have historically been neither particularly stable nor particularly peaceful. Rough parity among powerful nations is a source of uncertainty that leads to miscalculation. Conflicts erupt as a result of fluctuations in the delicate power equation.

War among the great powers was a common, if not constant, occurrence in the long periods of multipolarity from the 16th to the 18th centuries, culminating in the series of enormously destructive Europe-wide wars that followed the French Revolution and ended with Napoleon's defeat in 1815.

The 19th century was notable for two stretches of great-power peace of roughly four decades each, punctuated by major conflicts. The Crimean War (1853–1856) was a mini-world war involving well over a million Russian, French, British and Turkish troops, as well as forces from nine other nations; it produced almost a half-million dead combatants and many more wounded. In the Franco-Prussian War (1870–1871), the two nations together fielded close to two million troops, of whom nearly a half-million were killed or wounded.

The peace that followed these conflicts was characterized by increasing tension and competition, numerous war scares and massive increases in armaments on both land and sea. Its climax was World War I, the most destructive and deadly conflict that mankind had known up to that point. As the political scientist Robert W. Tucker has observed, "Such stability and moderation as the balance brought rested ultimately on the threat or use of force. War remained the essential means for maintaining the balance of power."

There is little reason to believe that a return to multipolarity in the 21st century would bring greater peace and stability than it has in the past. The era of American predominance has shown that there is no better recipe for great-power peace than certainty about who holds the upper hand.

President Bill Clinton left office believing that the key task for America was to "create the world we would like to live in when we are no longer the world's only superpower," to prepare for "a time when we would have to share the stage." It is an eminently sensible-sounding proposal. But can it be done? For particularly in matters of security, the rules and institutions of international order rarely survive the decline of the nations that erected them. They are like scaffolding around a building: They don't hold the building up; the building holds them up.

Many foreign-policy experts see the present international order as the inevitable result of human progress, a combination of advancing science and technology, an increasingly global economy, strengthening international institutions, evolving "norms" of international behavior and the gradual but inevitable triumph of liberal democracy over other forms of government—forces of change that transcend the actions of men and nations.

Americans certainly like to believe that our preferred order survives because it is right and just—not only for us but for everyone. We assume that the triumph of democracy is the triumph of a better idea, and the victory of market capitalism is the victory of a better system, and that both are irreversible. That is why Francis Fukuyama's thesis about "the end of history" was so attractive at the end of the Cold War and retains its appeal even now, after it has been discredited by events. The idea of inevitable evolution means that there is no requirement to impose a decent order. It will merely happen.

But international order is not an evolution; it is an imposition. It is the domination of one vision over others—in America's case, the domination of free-market and democratic principles, together with an international system that supports them. The present order will last only as long as those who favor it and benefit from it retain the will and capacity to defend it.

There was nothing inevitable about the world that was created after World War II. No divine providence or unfolding Hegelian dialectic required the triumph of democracy and capitalism, and there is no guarantee that their success will outlast the powerful nations that have fought for them. Democratic progress and liberal economics have been and can be reversed and undone. The ancient democracies of Greece and the republics of Rome and Venice all fell to more powerful forces or through their own failings. The evolving liberal economic order of Europe collapsed in the 1920s and 1930s. The better idea doesn't have to win just because it is a better idea. It requires great powers to champion it.

If and when American power declines, the institutions and norms that American power has supported will decline, too. Or more likely, if history is a guide, they may collapse altogether as we make a transition to another kind of world order, or to disorder. We may discover then that the U.S. was essential to keeping the present world order together and that the alternative to American power was not peace and harmony but chaos and catastrophe—which is what the world looked like right before the American order came into being.

Critical Thinking

1. Describe the debate about the future international order and the role of the US.

2. What is Kagan's point of view on this debate?

3. How does he contrast his point of view from alternative perspectives?

4. What is meant by the term "multipolarity"?

5. How does this article complement or contradict the analysis offered in Article 1?

MR. KAGAN is a senior fellow in foreign policy at the Brookings Institution. Adapted from "The World America Made," published by Alfred A. Knopf. Copyright © 2012 by Robert Kagan.

UNIT 2

Population and Food Production

Unit Selections

Learning Outcomes

After reading this unit you should be able to:

• Describe major demographic trends and the variations in these trends between regions of the world.

• Describe the concerns about diseases migrating from primates to humans.

• Describe the Blue Food movement in comparison to traditional livestock production.

• Offer examples of how demographic changes impact natural resources and social structures.

• Assess your initial effort at identifying your theory of international relations and how this unit changes/complements it.

Student Website

www.mhhe.com/cls

Internet References

The Hunger Project
www.thp.org

Penn Library: Resources by Subject
www.library.upenn.edu/cgi-bin/res/sr.cgi

World Health Organization
www.who.int

WWW Virtual Library: Demography & Population Studies
http://demography.anu.edu.au/VirtualLibrary

After World War II, the world's population reached an estimated 2 billion people. It had taken 250 years to triple to that level. In the six decades following World War II, the population tripled again to 6 billion. When the typical reader of this book reaches the age of 50, demographers estimate that the global population will have reached 8.5 billion! By 2050, or about 100 years after World War II, some experts forecast that 10 to 12 billion people may populate the world. A person born in 1946 (a so-called baby boomer) who lives to be 100 could see a six-fold increase in population.

Nothing like this has ever occurred before. To state this in a different way: In the next 50 years there will have to be twice as much food grown, twice as many schools and hospitals available, and twice as much of everything else just to maintain the current and rather uneven standard of living. We live in an unprecedented time in human history.

One of the most interesting aspects of this population growth is that there is little agreement about whether this situation is good or bad. The government of China, for example, has a policy that encourages couples to have only one child. In contrast, there are a few governments that use various financial incentives to promote large families.

In the second decade of the new millennium, there are many population issues that transcend simple numeric or economic considerations. The disappearance of indigenous cultures is a good example of the pressures of population growth on people who live on the margins of modern society. Finally, while demographers develop various scenarios forecasting population growth, it is important to remember that there are circumstances that could lead not to growth but to a significant decline in global population. The spread of AIDS and other infectious diseases reveals that confidence in modern medicine's ability to control these scourges may be premature. Nature has its own checks and balances to the population dynamic. This factor is often overlooked in an age of technological optimism.

The lead article in this section provides an overview of general demographic trends, with a special focus on issues related to aging. In the second article, the often-overlooked issue of reversing the increase in human population as a strategy for achieving long-term balance with the environment is described.

There are, of course, no greater checks on population growth than the availability of an adequate food supply and control of the spread of infectious diseases. Some experts question whether current agricultural technologies are sustainable over the long run. How much food are we going to need, and how are farmers and fishermen going to provide it? Will markets deliver food to those in greatest need?

© Ingram Publishing

Making predictions about the future of the world's population is a complicated task, for there are a variety of forces at work and considerable variation from region to region. The danger of oversimplification must be overcome if governments and international organizations are going to respond with meaningful policies. Perhaps one could say that there is not a global population problem but rather many population challenges that vary from country to country and region to region.

The New Population Bomb: The Four Megatrends That Will Change the World

Jack A. Goldstone

Forty-two years ago, the biologist Paul Ehrlich warned in The Population Bomb that mass starvation would strike in the 1970s and 1980s, with the world's population growth outpacing the production of food and other critical resources. Thanks to innovations and efforts such as the "green revolution" in farming and the widespread adoption of family planning, Ehrlich's worst fears did not come to pass. In fact, since the 1970s, global economic output has increased and fertility has fallen dramatically, especially in developing countries.

The United Nations Population Division now projects that global population growth will nearly halt by 2050. By that date, the world's population will have stabilized at 9.15 billion people, according to the "medium growth" variant of the UN's authoritative population database World Population Prospects: The 2008 Revision. (Today's global population is 6.83 billion.) Barring a cataclysmic climate crisis or a complete failure to recover from the current economic malaise, global economic output is expected to increase by two to three percent per year, meaning that global income will increase far more than population over the next four decades.

But twenty-first-century international security will depend less on how many people inhabit the world than on how the global population is composed and distributed: where populations are declining and where they are growing, which countries are relatively older and which are more youthful, and how demographics will influence population movements across regions.

These elements are not well recognized or widely understood. A recent article in *The Economist,* for example, cheered the decline in global fertility without noting other vital demographic developments. Indeed, the same UN data cited by *The Economist* reveal four historic shifts that will fundamentally alter the world's population over the next four decades: the relative demographic weight of the world's developed countries will drop by nearly 25 percent, shifting economic power to the developing nations; the developed countries' labor forces will substantially age and decline, constraining economic growth in the developed world and raising the demand for immigrant workers; most of the world's expected population growth will increasingly be concentrated in today's poorest, youngest, and most heavily Muslim countries, which have a dangerous lack of quality education, capital, and employment opportunities; and, for the first time in history, most of the world's population will become urbanized, with the largest urban centers being in the world's poorest countries, where policing, sanitation, and health care are often scarce. Taken together, these trends will pose challenges every bit as alarming as those noted by Ehrlich. Coping with them will require nothing less than a major reconsideration of the world's basic global governance structures.

Europe's Reversal of Fortunes

At the beginning of the eighteenth century, approximately 20 percent of the world's inhabitants lived in Europe (including Russia). Then, with the Industrial Revolution, Europe's population boomed, and streams of European emigrants set off for the Americas. By the eve of World War I, Europe's population had more than quadrupled. In 1913, Europe had more people than China, and the proportion of the world's population living in Europe and the former European colonies of North America had risen to over 33 percent. But this trend reversed after World War I, as basic health care and sanitation began to spread to poorer countries. In Asia, Africa, and Latin America, people began to live longer, and birthrates remained high or fell only slowly. By 2003, the combined populations of Europe, the United States, and Canada accounted for just 17 percent of the global population. In 2050, this figure is expected to be just 12 percent—far less than it was in 1700. (These projections, moreover, might even understate the reality because they reflect the "medium growth" projection of the UN forecasts, which assumes that the fertility rates of developing countries will decline while those of developed countries will increase. In fact, many developed countries show no evidence of increasing fertility rates.) The West's relative decline is even more dramatic if one also considers changes in income. The Industrial Revolution made Europeans not only more numerous than they had been but also considerably richer per capita than others worldwide. According to the economic historian Angus Maddison, Europe, the United States, and Canada together produced about 32 percent of the world's GDP at the beginning of the nineteenth century. By 1950, that proportion had increased to a remarkable 68 percent of the world's total output (adjusted to reflect purchasing power parity).

This trend, too, is headed for a sharp reversal. The proportion of global GDP produced by Europe, the United States, and Canada fell from 68 percent in 1950 to 47 percent in 2003 and will decline even more steeply in the future. If the growth rate of per capita income (again, adjusted for purchasing power parity) between 2003 and 2050 remains as it was between 1973 and 2003—averaging 1.68 percent annually in Europe, the United States, and Canada and 2.47 percent annually in the rest of the world—then the combined GDP of Europe, the United States, and Canada will roughly double by 2050, whereas the GDP of the rest of the world will grow by a factor of five. The portion of global GDP produced by Europe, the United States, and Canada in 2050 will then be less than 30 percent—smaller than it was in 1820.

These figures also imply that an overwhelming proportion of the world's GDP growth between 2003 and 2050—nearly 80 percent—will occur outside of Europe, the United States, and Canada. By the middle of this century, the global middle class—those capable of purchasing durable consumer products, such as cars, appliances, and electronics—will increasingly be found in what is now considered the developing world. The World Bank has predicted that by 2030 the number of middle-class people in the developing world will be 1.2 billion—a rise of 200 percent since 2005. This means that the developing world's middle class alone will be larger than the total populations of Europe, Japan, and the United States combined. From now on, therefore, the main driver of global economic expansion will be the economic growth of newly industrialized countries, such as Brazil, China, India, Indonesia, Mexico, and Turkey.

Aging Pains

Part of the reason developed countries will be less economically dynamic in the coming decades is that their populations will become substantially older. The European countries, Canada, the United States, Japan, South Korea, and even China are aging at unprecedented rates. Today, the proportion of people aged 60 or older in China and South Korea is 12–15 percent. It is 15–22 percent in the European Union, Canada, and the United States and 30 percent in Japan. With baby boomers aging and life expectancy increasing, these numbers will increase dramatically. In 2050, approximately 30 percent of Americans, Canadians, Chinese, and Europeans will be over 60, as will more than 40 percent of Japanese and South Koreans.

Over the next decades, therefore, these countries will have increasingly large proportions of retirees and increasingly small proportions of workers. As workers born during the baby boom of 1945–65 are retiring, they are not being replaced by a new cohort of citizens of prime working age (15–59 years old).

Industrialized countries are experiencing a drop in their working-age populations that is even more severe than the overall slowdown in their population growth. South Korea represents the most extreme example. Even as its total population is projected to decline by almost 9 percent by 2050 (from 48.3 million to 44.1 million), the population of working-age South Koreans is expected to drop by 36 percent (from 32.9 million to 21.1 million), and the number of South Koreans aged 60 and older will increase by almost 150 percent (from 7.3 million to 18 million). By 2050, in other words, the entire working-age population will barely exceed the 60-and-older population. Although South Korea's case is extreme, it represents an increasingly common fate for developed countries. Europe is expected to lose 24 percent of its prime working-age population (about 120 million workers) by 2050, and its 60-and-older population is expected to increase by 47 percent. In the United States, where higher fertility and more immigration are expected than in Europe, the working-age population will grow by 15 percent over the next four decades—a steep decline from its growth of 62 percent between 1950 and 2010. And by 2050, the United States' 60-and-older population is expected to double.

All this will have a dramatic impact on economic growth, health care, and military strength in the developed world. The forces that fueled economic growth in industrialized countries during the second half of the twentieth century—increased productivity due to better education, the movement of women into the labor force, and innovations in technology—will all likely weaken in the coming decades. College enrollment boomed after World War II, a trend that is not likely to recur in the twenty-first century; the extensive movement of women into the labor force also was a one-time social change; and the technological change of the time resulted from innovators who created new products and leading-edge consumers who were willing to try them out—two groups that are thinning out as the industrialized world's population ages.

Overall economic growth will also be hampered by a decline in the number of new consumers and new households. When developed countries' labor forces were growing by 0.5–1.0 percent per year, as they did until 2005, even annual increases in real output per worker of just 1.7 percent meant that annual economic growth totaled 2.2–2.7 percent per year. But with the labor forces of many developed countries (such as Germany, Hungary, Japan, Russia, and the Baltic states) now shrinking by 0.2 percent per year and those of other countries (including Austria, the Czech Republic, Denmark, Greece, and Italy) growing by less than 0.2 percent per year, the same 1.7 percent increase in real output per worker yields only 1.5–1.9 percent annual overall growth. Moreover, developed countries will be lucky to keep productivity growth at even that level; in many developed countries, productivity is more likely to decline as the population ages.

A further strain on industrialized economies will be rising medical costs: as populations age, they will demand more health care for longer periods of time. Public pension schemes for aging populations are already being reformed in various industrialized countries—often prompting heated debate. In theory, at least, pensions might be kept solvent by increasing the retirement age, raising taxes modestly, and phasing out benefits for the wealthy. Regardless, the number of 80- and 90-year-olds—who are unlikely to work and highly likely to require nursing-home and other expensive care—will rise dramatically. And even if 60- and 70-year-olds remain active and employed, they will require procedures and medications—hip replacements, kidney transplants, blood-pressure treatments—to sustain their health in old age.

All this means that just as aging developed countries will have proportionally fewer workers, innovators, and consumerist young households, a large portion of those countries' remaining economic growth will have to be diverted to pay for the medical bills and pensions of their growing elderly populations. Basic services, meanwhile, will be increasingly costly because fewer young workers will be available for strenuous and labor-intensive jobs. Unfortunately, policymakers seldom reckon with these potentially disruptive effects of otherwise welcome developments, such as higher life expectancy.

Youth and Islam in the Developing World

Even as the industrialized countries of Europe, North America, and Northeast Asia will experience unprecedented aging this century, fast-growing countries in Africa, Latin America, the Middle East, and Southeast Asia will have exceptionally youthful populations. Today, roughly nine out of ten children under the age of 15 live in developing countries. And these are the countries that will continue to have the world's highest birthrates. Indeed, over 70 percent of the world's population growth between now and 2050 will occur in 24 countries, all of which are classified by the World Bank as low income or lower-middle income, with an average per capita income of under $3,855 in 2008.

Many developing countries have few ways of providing employment to their young, fast-growing populations. Would-be laborers, therefore, will be increasingly attracted to the labor markets of the aging developed countries of Europe, North America, and Northeast Asia. Youthful immigrants from nearby regions with high unemployment—Central America, North Africa, and Southeast Asia, for example—will be drawn to those vital entry-level and manual-labor jobs that sustain advanced economies: janitors, nursing-home aides, bus drivers, plumbers, security guards, farm workers, and the like. Current levels of immigration from developing to developed countries are paltry compared to those that the forces of supply and demand might soon create across the world.

These forces will act strongly on the Muslim world, where many economically weak countries will continue to experience dramatic population growth in the decades ahead. In 1950, Bangladesh, Egypt, Indonesia, Nigeria, Pakistan, and Turkey had a combined population of 242 million. By 2009, those six countries were the world's most populous Muslim-majority countries and had a combined population of 886 million. Their populations are continuing to grow and indeed are expected to increase by 475 million between now and 2050—during which time, by comparison, the six most populous developed countries are projected to gain only 44 million inhabitants. Worldwide, of the 48 fastest-growing countries today—those with annual population growth of two percent or more—28 are majority Muslim or have Muslim minorities of 33 percent or more.

It is therefore imperative to improve relations between Muslim and Western societies. This will be difficult given that many Muslims live in poor communities vulnerable to radical appeals and many see the West as antagonistic and militaristic. In the 2009 Pew Global Attitudes Project survey, for example, whereas 69 percent of those Indonesians and Nigerians surveyed reported viewing the United States favorably, just 18 percent of those polled in Egypt, Jordan, Pakistan, and Turkey (all U.S. allies) did. And in 2006, when the Pew survey last asked detailed questions about Muslim-Western relations, more than half of the respondents in Muslim countries characterized those relations as bad and blamed the West for this state of affairs.

But improving relations is all the more important because of the growing demographic weight of poor Muslim countries and the attendant increase in Muslim immigration, especially to Europe from North Africa and the Middle East. (To be sure, forecasts that Muslims will soon dominate Europe are outlandish: Muslims compose just three to ten percent of the population in the major European countries today, and this proportion will at most double by midcentury.) Strategists worldwide must consider that the world's young are becoming concentrated in those countries least prepared to educate and employ them, including some Muslim states. Any resulting poverty, social tension, or ideological radicalization could have disruptive effects in many corners of the world. But this need not be the case; the healthy immigration of workers to the developed world and the movement of capital to the developing world, among other things, could lead to better results.

Urban Sprawl

Exacerbating twenty-first-century risks will be the fact that the world is urbanizing to an unprecedented degree. The year 2010 will likely be the first time in history that a majority of the world's people live in cities rather than in the countryside. Whereas less than 30 percent of the world's population was urban in 1950, according to UN projections, more than 70 percent will be by 2050.

Lower-income countries in Asia and Africa are urbanizing especially rapidly, as agriculture becomes less labor intensive and as employment opportunities shift to the industrial and service sectors. Already, most of the world's urban agglomerations—Mumbai (population 20.1 million), Mexico City (19.5 million), New Delhi (17 million), Shanghai (15.8 million), Calcutta (15.6 million), Karachi (13.1 million), Cairo (12.5 million), Manila (11.7 million), Lagos (10.6 million), Jakarta (9.7 million)—are found in low-income countries. Many of these countries have multiple cities with over one million residents each: Pakistan has eight, Mexico 12, and China more than 100. The UN projects that the urbanized proportion of sub-Saharan Africa will nearly double between 2005 and 2050, from 35 percent (300 million people) to over 67 percent (1 billion). China, which is roughly 40 percent urbanized today, is expected to be 73 percent urbanized by 2050; India, which is less than 30 percent urbanized today, is expected to be 55 percent urbanized by 2050. Overall, the world's urban population is expected to grow by 3 billion people by 2050.

This urbanization may prove destabilizing. Developing countries that urbanize in the twenty-first century will have far lower per capita incomes than did many industrial countries when they first urbanized. The United States, for example, did not reach 65 percent urbanization until 1950, when per capita income was nearly $13,000 (in 2005 dollars). By contrast, Nigeria, Pakistan, and the Philippines, which are approaching similar levels of urbanization, currently have per capita incomes of just $1,800–$4,000 (in 2005 dollars).

According to the research of Richard Cincotta and other political demographers, countries with younger populations are especially prone to civil unrest and are less able to create or sustain democratic institutions. And the more heavily urbanized, the more such countries are likely to experience Dickensian poverty and anarchic violence. In good times, a thriving economy might keep urban residents employed and governments flush with sufficient resources to meet their needs. More often, however, sprawling and impoverished cities are vulnerable to crime lords, gangs, and petty rebellions. Thus, the rapid urbanization of the developing world in the decades ahead might bring, in exaggerated form, problems similar to those that urbanization brought to nineteenth-century Europe. Back then, cyclical employment, inadequate policing, and limited sanitation and education often spawned widespread labor strife, periodic violence, and sometimes—as in the 1820s, the 1830s, and 1848—even revolutions.

International terrorism might also originate in fast-urbanizing developing countries (even more than it already does). With their neighborhood networks, access to the Internet and digital communications technology, and concentration of valuable targets, sprawling cities offer excellent opportunities for recruiting, maintaining, and hiding terrorist networks.

Defusing the Bomb

Averting this century's potential dangers will require sweeping measures. Three major global efforts defused the population bomb of Ehrlich's day: a commitment by governments and nongovernmental organizations to control reproduction rates; agricultural advances, such as the green revolution and the spread of new technology; and a vast increase in international trade, which globalized markets and thus allowed developing countries to export foodstuffs in exchange for seeds, fertilizers, and machinery, which in turn helped them boost production. But today's population bomb is the product less of absolute growth in the world's population than of changes in its age and distribution. Policymakers must therefore adapt today's global governance institutions to the new realities of the aging of the industrialized world, the concentration of the world's economic and population growth in developing countries, and the increase in international immigration.

During the Cold War, Western strategists divided the world into a "First World," of democratic industrialized countries; a "Second World," of communist industrialized countries; and a "Third World," of developing countries. These strategists focused chiefly on deterring or managing conflict between the First and the Second Worlds and on launching proxy wars and diplomatic initiatives to attract Third World countries into the First World's camp. Since the end of the Cold War, strategists have largely abandoned this three-group division and have tended to believe either that the United States, as the sole superpower, would maintain a Pax Americana or that the world would become multipolar, with the United States, Europe, and China playing major roles.

Unfortunately, because they ignore current global demographic trends, these views will be obsolete within a few decades. A better approach would be to consider a different three-world order, with a new First World of the aging industrialized nations of North America, Europe, and Asia's Pacific Rim (including Japan, Singapore, South Korea, and Taiwan, as well as China after 2030, by which point the one-child policy will have produced significant aging); a Second World comprising fast-growing and economically dynamic countries with a healthy mix of young and old inhabitants (such as Brazil, Iran, Mexico, Thailand, Turkey, and Vietnam, as well as China until 2030); and a Third World of fast-growing, very young, and increasingly urbanized countries with poorer economies and often weak governments. To cope with the instability that will likely arise from the new Third World's urbanization, economic strife, lawlessness, and potential terrorist activity, the aging industrialized nations of the new First World must build effective alliances with the growing powers of the new Second World and together reach out to Third World nations. Second World powers will be pivotal in the twenty-first century not just because they will drive economic growth and consume technologies and other products engineered in the First World; they will also be central to international security and cooperation. The realities of religion, culture, and geographic proximity mean that any peaceful and productive engagement by the First World of Third World countries will have to include the open cooperation of Second World countries.

Strategists, therefore, must fundamentally reconsider the structure of various current global institutions. The G-8, for example, will likely become obsolete as a body for making global economic policy. The G-20 is already becoming increasingly important, and this is less a short-term consequence of the ongoing global financial crisis than the beginning of the necessary recognition that Brazil, China, India, Indonesia, Mexico, Turkey, and others are becoming global economic powers. International institutions will not retain their legitimacy if they exclude the world's fastest-growing and most economically dynamic countries. It is essential, therefore, despite European concerns about the potential effects on immigration, to take steps such as admitting Turkey into the European Union. This would add youth and economic dynamism to the EU—and would prove that Muslims are welcome to join Europeans as equals in shaping a free and prosperous future. On the other hand, excluding Turkey from the EU could lead to hostility not only on the part of Turkish citizens, who are expected to number 100 million by 2050, but also on the part of Muslim populations worldwide.

NATO must also adapt. The alliance today is composed almost entirely of countries with aging, shrinking populations and relatively slow-growing economies. It is oriented toward the Northern Hemisphere and holds on to a Cold War structure that cannot adequately respond to contemporary threats. The young and increasingly populous countries of Africa, the Middle East, Central Asia, and South Asia could mobilize insurgents much more easily than NATO could mobilize the troops it would need if it were called on to stabilize those countries. Long-standing NATO members should, therefore—although it would require atypical creativity and flexibility—consider the logistical and demographic advantages of inviting into the alliance countries such as Brazil and Morocco, rather than countries such as Albania. That this seems far-fetched does not minimize the imperative that First World countries begin including large and strategic Second and Third World powers in formal international alliances.

The case of Afghanistan—a country whose population is growing fast and where NATO is currently engaged—illustrates the importance of building effective global institutions. Today, there are 28 million Afghans; by 2025, there will be 45 million; and by 2050, there will be close to 75 million. As nearly 20 million additional Afghans are born over the next 15 years, NATO will have an opportunity to help Afghanistan become reasonably stable, self-governing, and prosperous. If NATO's efforts fail and the Afghans judge that NATO intervention harmed their interests, tens of millions of young Afghans will become more hostile to the West. But if they come to think that NATO's involvement benefited their society, the West will have tens of millions of new friends. The example might then motivate the approximately one billion other young Muslims growing up in low-income countries over the next four decades to look more kindly on relations between their countries and the countries of the industrialized West.

Creative Reforms at Home

The aging industrialized countries can also take various steps at home to promote stability in light of the coming demographic trends. First, they should encourage families to have more children. France and Sweden have had success providing child care, generous leave time, and financial allowances to families with young children. Yet there is no consensus among policymakers—and certainly not among demographers—about what policies best encourage fertility.

More important than unproven tactics for increasing family size is immigration. Correctly managed, population movement can benefit developed and developing countries alike. Given the dangers of young, underemployed, and unstable populations in developing countries, immigration to developed countries can provide economic opportunities for the ambitious and serve as a safety valve for all. Countries that embrace immigrants, such as the United States, gain economically by having willing laborers and greater entrepreneurial spirit. And countries with high levels of emigration (but not so much that they experience so-called brain drains) also

benefit because emigrants often send remittances home or return to their native countries with valuable education and work experience.

One somewhat daring approach to immigration would be to encourage a reverse flow of older immigrants from developed to developing countries. If older residents of developed countries took their retirements along the southern coast of the Mediterranean or in Latin America or Africa, it would greatly reduce the strain on their home countries' public entitlement systems. The developing countries involved, meanwhile, would benefit because caring for the elderly and providing retirement and leisure services is highly labor intensive. Relocating a portion of these activities to developing countries would provide employment and valuable training to the young, growing populations of the Second and Third Worlds.

This would require developing residential and medical facilities of First World quality in Second and Third World countries. Yet even this difficult task would be preferable to the status quo, by which low wages and poor facilities lead to a steady drain of medical and nursing talent from developing to developed countries. Many residents of developed countries who desire cheaper medical procedures already practice medical tourism today, with India, Singapore, and Thailand being the most common destinations. (For example, the international consulting firm Deloitte estimated that 750,000 Americans traveled abroad for care in 2008.)

Never since 1800 has a majority of the world's economic growth occurred outside of Europe, the United States, and Canada. Never have so many people in those regions been over 60 years old. And never have low-income countries' populations been so young and so urbanized. But such will be the world's demography in the twenty-first century. The strategic and economic policies of the twentieth century are obsolete, and it is time to find new ones.

Reference

Goldstone, Jack A. "The new population bomb: the four megatrends that will change the world." *Foreign Affairs* 89.1 (2010): 31. *General OneFile*. Web. 23 Jan. 2010. http://0-find.galegroup .com.www.consuls.org/gps/start.do?proId=IPS& userGroupName=a30wc.

Critical Thinking

1. Identify the four demographic trends.
2. How does the author argue that international politics is changing due to these trends?
3. Summarize the Afghanistan case study.
4. How does this discussion of demographic trends relate to the Allegory of the Balloon?

Population and Sustainability

Reversing the rise in human numbers is the most overlooked and essential strategy for achieving long-term balance with the environment. Contrary to widespread opinion, it does not require "population control."

ROBERT ENGELMAN

In an era of changing climate and sinking economies, Malthusian limits to growth are back—and squeezing us painfully. Whereas *more people* once meant more ingenuity, more talent, and more innovation, today it just seems to mean *less for each*. Less water for every cattle herder in the Horn of Africa. (The United Nations projects there will be more than four billion people living in nations defined as water-scarce or water-stressed by 2050, up from half a billion in 1995.) Less land for every farmer already tilling slopes so steep they risk killing themselves by falling off their fields. (At a bit less than six tenths of an acre, global per capita cropland today is little more than half of what it was in 1961, and more than 900 million people are hungry.) Less capacity in the atmosphere to accept the heat-trapping gases that could fry the planet for centuries to come. Scarcer and higher-priced energy and food. And if the world's economy does not bounce back to its glory days, less credit and fewer jobs.

It's not surprising that this kind of predicament brings back an old sore topic: human population and whether to do anything about it. Let's concede up front that nothing short of a catastrophic population crash (think of the film *Children of Men*, set in a world without children) would make much difference to climate change, water scarcity or land shortages over the next decade or so. There are 6.8 billion of us today, and more are on the way. To make a dent in these problems in the short term without throwing anyone overboard, we will need to radically reduce individuals' footprint on the environment through improvements in technology and possibly wrenching changes in lifestyle.

But until the world's population stops growing, there will be no end to the need to squeeze individuals' consumption of fossil fuels and other natural resources. A close look at this problem is sobering: short of catastrophic leaps in the death rate or unwanted crashes in fertility, the world's population is all but certain to grow by at least one billion to two billion people. The low-consuming billions of the developing world would love to consume as Americans do, with similar disregard for the environment—and they have as much of a right to do so. These facts suggest that the coming ecological impact will be of a scale that we will simply have to manage and adapt to as best we can.

Population growth constantly pushes the consequences of any level of individual consumption to a higher plateau, and reductions in individual consumption can always be overwhelmed by increases in population. The simple reality is that acting on both, consistently and simultaneously, is the key to long-term environmental sustainability. The sustainability benefits of level or falling human numbers are too powerful to ignore for long.

In the U.S., this discussion remains muted all the same. Population concerns may lurk within the public anger over illegal immigration or over the unwed California mother of octuplets earlier this year. But to the extent that the news media address domestic population growth at all, it is through euphemisms such as "sprawl" (the theoretical culprit in pollution of the Chesapeake Bay, for example) or the economy (the theoretical driver of increased greenhouse gas emissions). You are more likely to read about population growth in a letter to the editor than in a news story or editorial.

When President-elect Barack Obama pledged in late 2008 to bring U.S. carbon dioxide emissions to their 1990 levels by 2020, environmentalists struggled to swallow their dismay. The European Union, after all, had committed itself to 20 percent *reductions* from 1990 levels. But on a per capita basis, President Obama's pledge was somewhat *more* ambitious than the E.U.'s was. Because of much more rapid population growth than in the E.U., Americans would be cutting their individual emissions by 26 percent under his plan and Europeans by 25 percent under theirs. Any pledges to lower emissions by a uniform percentage among industrial countries will be much harder for the U.S. to achieve, simply because it is gaining people so fast through immigration and a birthrate that is higher than average for a developed nation.

The bitterness of the immigration debate has helped keep U.S. population growth off-limits in the national conversation. In industrial countries outside of North America, however, population is creeping back into public and even political consciousness. In the U.K., an all-party parliamentary panel issued a report called "Return of the Population Growth Factor" and called for stronger efforts to slow that growth. And the concern in the U.K.

is not just about the people "over there" in developing countries. In early 2009 Jonathon Porritt, chair of the government's Sustainable Development Commission, whacked a hornet's nest by calling parents of more than two children "irresponsible" and blasting mainstream environmental groups for "betraying" their members by fearing to call for small families. "It is the ghost at the table," Porritt said of population in an interview with the *Daily Telegraph,* a London broadsheet. Blog comments on his remarks, most of them supportive, soared into the thousands.

Meanwhile, in Australia, as summer temperatures hovered near 117 degrees Fahrenheit (47 degrees Celsius) and murderous flames converted forests into carbon dioxide, a new book entitled *Overloading Australia: How Governments and Media Dither and Deny on Population* issued an unusual ecological battle cry: ignore all admonitions to conserve the country's increasingly scarce water supplies until the government eliminates "baby bonuses" in the tax code and clamps down on immigration. A former premier of New South Wales spoke at the book's launch.

With comments such as these gaining attention—and in some circles, approval—are environmentalists and eventually policy makers likely to renew the decades-old call for "population control"? Would they be wise to do so?

A Number of Us

Two big questions present themselves as population reemerges from the shadows: Can any feasible downshift in population growth actually put the environment on a more sustainable path? And if so, are there measures that the public and policy makers would support that could actually bring about such a change?

Nature, of course, couldn't care less how many of us there are. What matters to the environment are the sums of human pulls and pushes, the extractions of resources and the injections of wastes. When these exceed key tipping points, nature and its systems can change quickly and dramatically. But the magnitudes of environmental impacts stem not just from our numbers but also from behaviors we learn from our parents and cultures. Broadly speaking, if population is the number of us, then consumption is the way each of us behaves. In this unequal world, the behavior of a dozen people in one place sometimes has more environmental impact than does that of a few hundred somewhere else.

Consider how these principles relate to global warming. The greenhouse gases already released into the atmosphere are likely to bring us quite close to the 3.6 degree F (two degree C) increase from the preindustrial global temperature average that many scientists see as the best-guess threshold of potential climate catastrophe. Already the earth is experiencing harsher droughts, fiercer storms and higher sea levels. If the scientists are right, these impacts will worsen for decades or centuries. Indeed, even if we ended all emissions tomorrow, additional warming is on the way thanks to the momentum built into the earth's intricate climate system. (The oceans, for example, have yet to come into equilibrium with the extra heat-trapping capacity of the atmosphere. As the oceans continue to warm, so will the land around them.)

Our species' demographic growth since its birth in Africa 200,000 years ago clearly contributed to this crisis. If world population had stayed stable at roughly 300 million people—a number that demographers believe characterized humanity from the birth of Christ to A.D. 1000 and that equals the population of just the U.S. today—there would not be enough of us to have the effect of relocating the coastlines even if we all drove Hummers. But instead we kept growing our numbers, which are projected to reach 9.1 billion by midcentury.

Humanity's consumption behaviors consequently did and do matter, and in this arena, all people have not been created equal. Greenhouse gas release has been linked overwhelmingly, at least up until recently, to the high-consumption habits of the industrial nations. As a result, in an ethical outrage as big as all outdoors, the coming shifts in climate and sea level will most harm the world's poor, who are least responsible for the atmosphere's composition, and will least harm the wealthy, who bear the biggest responsibility.

All-Consuming Passions

What part can the size of the human race play in finding a happy ending to this morality play? Population scenarios cannot directly address the inequity in emissions patterns—but they are far from unimportant.

Countries with the highest emissions per capita tend to have smaller families on average, whereas those with low emissions per capita tend to have larger ones. Americans, for example, consumed 8.6 tons of oil or its commercial energy equivalent per capita in 2007, according to data kept by British Petroleum; Indians consumed just 0.4 ton per capita. (These figures somewhat distort the gap because they exclude biomass and other noncommercial forms of energy, for which data are unreliable.)

So while India gained 17 million people in that year and the U.S. gained three million, by this simplified math the U.S. growth in population counted for the equivalent of an additional 25.6 million tons of oil consumed, whereas India's much greater growth counted for only 6.6 million additional tons. With such large disparities, the climate would be better served if the Americans emulated Indian consumption than if India emulated U.S. population.

End of story? For a variety of reasons, not quite. Population is not a contrasting force to consumption but something very close to its parent. Alone, each of us has no significant impact on the planet, even when our collective behavior overwhelms its natural processes. Historically, population has grown fastest when per capita consumption is modest. Later, consumption tends to explode on the base of a population that is large, but it is by then growing more slowly. Throughout the 19th century, the U.S. population grew at rates typical of Africa today. That century of rapid growth helped to make 21st-century America (with 307 million people now) a consumption behemoth.

The same one-two punch of population growth followed by consumption growth is now occurring in China (1.34 billion people) and India (1.2 billion). Per capita commercial energy use has been growing so rapidly in both countries (or at least it

Human Population Growth.

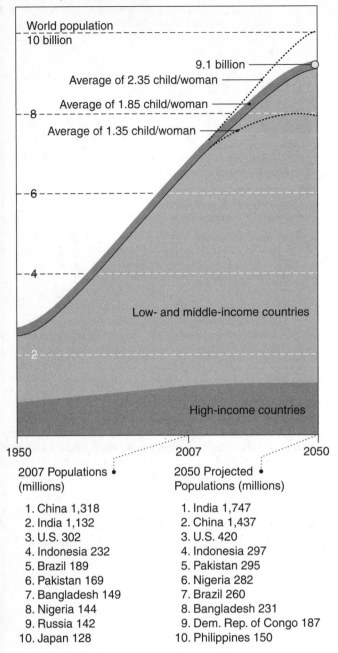

World population
10 billion

9.1 billion

Average of 2.35 child/woman

Average of 1.85 child/woman

Average of 1.35 child/woman

—8—

—6—

—4—

—2—

Low- and middle-income countries

High-income countries

1950   2007   2050

2007 Populations •
(millions)

1. China 1,318
2. India 1,132
3. U.S. 302
4. Indonesia 232
5. Brazil 189
6. Pakistan 169
7. Bangladesh 149
8. Nigeria 144
9. Russia 142
10. Japan 128

2050 Projected •
Populations (millions)

1. India 1,747
2. China 1,437
3. U.S. 420
4. Indonesia 297
5. Pakistan 295
6. Nigeria 282
7. Brazil 260
8. Bangladesh 231
9. Dem. Rep. of Congo 187
10. Philippines 150

The challenge to sustainability. For most of its history, the human race has numbered no more than several million and has expanded only slowly. As late as A.D. 1000, our species was smaller than the current population of the U.S. Only in the past few centuries have our numbers exploded, especially (during recent decades) in low- and middle-income nations, with increases in consumption habits following suit. Projections suggest that by 2050 or so, the population will probably stabilize around 9.1 billion. But very small changes in fertility could shift that figure up or down by about a billion—with a powerful impact on innumerable sustainability issues.

was through 2007 on the eve of the economic meltdown) that if the trends continue unabated the typical Chinese will out-consume the typical American before 2040, with Indians sur-

passing Americans by 2080. Population and consumption thus feed on each other's growth to expand humans' environmental footprint exponentially over time.

Moreover, because every human being consumes and disposes of multiple natural resources, a birth that does not occur averts consumption impacts in every direction. A person reducing her carbon footprint, conversely, does not automatically use less water. A wind turbine displaces coal-fired electricity but hardly prevents the depletion of forests (now disappearing in the tropics at the rate of one Kentucky-size swath a year) or fisheries (at current depletion rates facing exhaustion by the middle of the century). But unlike wind turbines, humans reproduce themselves. So every smaller generation means that the multipliers of consumption linked to population also shrink on into the future.

Because most environmental challenges emerge on scales of decades and centuries, population growth packs a long-term wallop. With respect to saving the planet, over a few short years it is hard for smaller families to beat sharp reductions in per capita consumption. Since the early 1990s, however, published calculations have demonstrated that slower population growth over decades yields significant reductions of greenhouse gas emissions even in countries where per capita fossil-fuel consumption is modest.

Slower population growth that leads to eight billion people in 2050 rather than to the currently projected 9.1 billion would save one billion to two billion tons of carbon annually by 2050, according to estimates by climate scientist Brian O'Neill of the National Center for Atmospheric Research and his colleagues. The subsequent savings in emissions would grow year by year ever afterward—while the billion-plus fewer people would need less land, forest products, water, fish and other foodstuffs.

Those improvements still would not be enough on their own to avert significant climate change. Other similar billion-ton savings in emissions (what Princeton University professors Stephen Pacala and Robert Socolow have dubbed "stabilization wedges") are desperately needed and can come only from reduction in fossil-fuel consumption through energy efficiency, low-carbon technologies and changes in way of life. If two billion automobiles getting 30 miles per gallon traveled only 5,000 miles a year instead of 10,000, that change would save another billion tons of carbon emissions. So would replacing coal-fired power plants that produce 1.4 trillion watts of electricity with equivalent plants burning natural gas. But without a population that stops growing, comparable technology improvements or lifestyle downshifts will be needed indefinitely to keep greenhouse gas emissions sustainable.

The complications that population growth poses to every environmental problem are not to be dismissed. In fact, they are accepted and understood best by the governments of poorer countries, where the impacts of dense and rapidly growing populations are most obvious. During the past few years, most of the reports that developing countries have filed with the U.N. on how they plan to adapt to climate change mention population growth as a complicating factor.

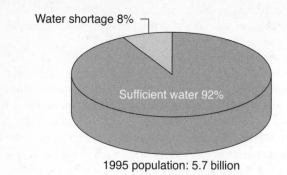

Water shortage 8%

Sufficient water 92%

1995 population: 5.7 billion

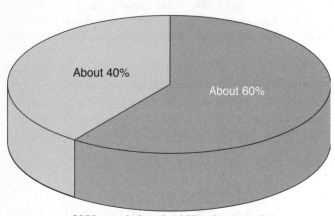

About 40%

About 60%

2050 population: 9.1 billion (projected)

More of the population will suffer water shortages.

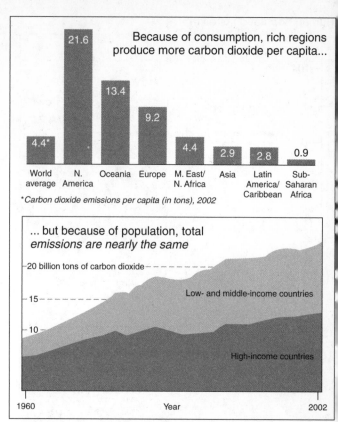

Because of consumption, rich regions produce more carbon dioxide per capita...

21.6 — N. America
13.4 — Oceania
9.2 — Europe
4.4* — World average
4.4 — M. East/ N. Africa
2.9 — Asia
2.8 — Latin America/ Caribbean
0.9 — Sub-Saharan Africa

Carbon dioxide emissions per capita (in tons), 2002

... but because of population, total *emissions are nearly the same*

20 billion tons of carbon dioxide

Low- and middle-income countries

15

10

High-income countries

1960   Year   2002

Consumption and the greenhouse gap. Citizens of industrial nations produce far more climate-warming carbon dioxide per capita than their peers in poorer countries. Because of population size, however, the developing world now produces slightly more of the gas. Thus, population exerts a powerful multiplier effect on the toll of consumption on the earth.

Instruments of Policy

A commonsense strategy for dealing with rising environmental risk would be to probe every reasonable opportunity for shifting to sustainability as quickly, easily and inexpensively as possible. No single energy strategy—whether nuclear, efficiency, wind, solar or geothermal—shows much promise on its own for eliminating the release of carbon dioxide into the air. Obstacles such as high up-front costs hamper most of those energy strategies even as part of a collective fix for the climate problem. No single change in land use will turn soils and plants into net absorbers of heat-trapping gases. Without technological breakthroughs in energy or land use, only higher prices for fossil fuels show much potential for edging down per capita emissions—a "solution" that policy makers have yet to grapple with effectively.

Given the long-term contribution that a turnaround in population growth could make in easing our most recalcitrant challenges, why doesn't the idea get more respect and attention? Politicians' apathy toward long-term solutions is part of the answer. But the more obvious reason is the discomfort most of us feel in grappling with the topics of sex, contraception, abortion, immigration and family sizes that differ by ethnicity and income. What in the population mix is *not* a hot button? Especially when the word "control" is added, and when the world's biggest religions have fruitful multiplication embedded in their philosophical DNA. And so critics from left, right and the intellectual center gang up on the handful of environmentalists and other activists who try to get population into national and global discussions.

Population and consumption feed on each other's growth to expand humans' environmental footprint exponentially.

Yet newly released population data from the U.N. show that developed countries, from the U.S. to Spain, have been experiencing (at least up through the beginnings of the economic crisis in 2008), if not baby booms, at least reproductive "rat-a-tat-tats." For the first time since the 1970s, the average number of children born to U.S. women has topped 2.1—the number at which parents replace themselves in the populations of developed and many developing countries. Even if net immigration ended tomorrow, continuation of that fertility rate would guarantee further growth in U.S. population for decades to come.

Those who do consider population to be a key to the problem typically say little about which policies would spare the planet many more billions of people. Should we restructure tax rates to favor small families? Propagandize the benefits of small families for the planet? Reward family-planning workers for clients they have sterilized? Each of those steps alone or in combination might help bend birthrates downward for a time, but none has proved to affect demographic trends over the long term or, critically, to gain and keep public support. When the

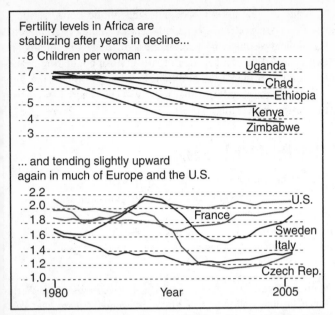

Fertility levels in Africa are stabilizing after years in decline...

... and tending slightly upward again in much of Europe and the U.S.

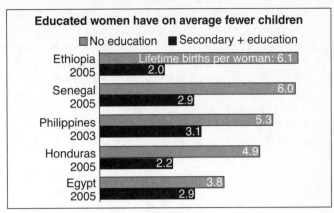

Educated women have on average fewer children

Education and fertility. Data from around the world testify to a robust trend: birthrates fall where women have more access to education. Improving women's access to schooling (and the opportunities it opens) may be one of the most powerful ways to reduce population growth.

Reason for concern. Declines in fertility rates cannot be taken for granted. In parts of Africa, the rates seem to be flattening out well above the replacement rate. Surprisingly, the U.S. and parts of Europe seem to be experiencing a small but significant increase in fertility, compounding the population increases from immigration.

government of India rewarded health workers for meeting sterilization quotas in 1976, the zeal of some of them for wielding scalpels regardless of their patients' wishes contributed to the downfall of Indira Gandhi's government in 1977.

And how can we reduce consumption? Ideas such as cap-and-trade plans for limiting greenhouse gas emissions and allowing companies to trade emission rights are based on the same principle: raise the price of what harms the environment to reduce consumption of it. Beyond the consumption cuts, however, such schemes don't have much to recommend them. Governments can also eliminate subsidies of polluting behavior, an approach that is more palatable—except to the often powerful interests that benefit from the subsidies. Or governments can subsidize low consumption through tax deductions and credits, but the funds to do so on the needed scale will likely be increasingly scarce.

The Zen of Population

Mostly ignored in the environmental debates about population and consumption is that nearly all the world's nations agreed to an altogether different approach to the problem of growth 15 years ago, one that bases positive demographic outcomes on decisions individuals make in their own self-interest. (If only something comparable could be imagined to shrink consumption.) The strategy that 179 nations signed onto at a U.N. conference in Cairo in 1994 was: forget population control and instead help every woman bear a child in good health when she wants one.

That approach, which powerfully supports reproductive liberty, might sound counterintuitive for shrinking population growth, like handing a teenager the keys to the family car without so much as a lecture. But the evidence suggests that what women want—and have always wanted—is not so much to have *more*

children as to have *more for* a smaller number of children they can reliably raise to healthy adulthood. Women left to their own devices, contraceptive or otherwise, would collectively "control" population while acting on their own intentions.

More than 200 million women in developing countries are sexually active without effective modern contraception even though they do not want to be pregnant anytime soon, according to the Guttmacher Institute, a reproductive health research group. By the best estimates, some 80 million pregnancies around the world are unintended. Although the numbers aren't strictly comparable—many unplanned pregnancies end in abortion—the unintended pregnancies exceed the 78 million by which world population grows every year.

In the U.S., which is well informed and spends nearly 20 cents per dollar of economic activity on health care, nearly one out of every two pregnancies is unintended. That proportion has not changed much for decades. In every nation, rich and poor, in which a choice of contraceptives is available and is backed up by reasonably accessible safe abortion for when contraception fails, women have two or fewer children. Furthermore, educating girls reduces birthrates. Worldwide, according to a calculation provided for this article by demographers at the International Institute for Applied Systems Analysis in Austria, women with no schooling have an average of 4.5 children, whereas those with a few years of primary school have just three. Women who complete one or two years of secondary school have an average of 1.9 children apiece—a figure that over time leads to a decreasing population. With one or two years of college, the average childbearing rate falls even further, to 1.7. And when women enter the workforce, start businesses, inherit assets and otherwise interact with men on an equal footing, their desire for more than a couple of children fades even more dramatically.

Forget population control and instead help every woman bear a child in good health when she wants one.

True, old-style population control seems to have helped slow population growth in China. The country's leaders brag that their one-child policy has spared the world's climate 300 million greenhouse gas emitters, the population equivalent of a U.S. that never happened. But most of the drop in Chinese fertility occurred before that coercive policy went into effect in 1979, as the government brought women by the millions into farm and industry collectives and provided them with the family planning they needed to stay on the job. Many developing countries—from Thailand and Colombia to Iran—have experienced comparable declines in family size by getting better family-planning services and educational opportunities to more women and girls in more places.

With President Obama in the White House and Democrats dominant in Congress, the signs are good that the U.S. will support the kind of development abroad and reproductive health at home most likely to encourage slower population growth. Like almost all politicians, however, Obama never mentions population or the way it bridges problems from health and education all the way to food, energy security and climate change.

Bringing population back into the public conversation is risky, but the world has come a long way in understanding that the subject is only one part of most of today's problems and that "population control" can't really control population. Handing control of their lives and their bodies to women—the right thing to do for countless other reasons—can. There is no reason to fear the discussion.

Critical Thinking

1. Identify Robert Engelman's point of view.
2. What are some of the proposed policies to reduce the number of new babies?
3. Summarize his argument that a "downshift" in population will put the environment on a more sustainable path.

ROBERT ENGELMAN is vice president for programs at the Worldwatch Institute and author of *More: Population, Nature, and What Women Want* (Island Press).

African Child Mortality

The Best Story in Development

Africa is experiencing some of the biggest falls in child mortality ever seen, anywhere.

THE ECONOMIST

It is, says Gabriel Demombynes, of the World Bank's Nairobi office, "a tremendous success story that has only barely been recognised". Michael Clemens of the Centre for Global Development calls it simply "the biggest, best story in development". It is the huge decline in child mortality now gathering pace across Africa.

According to Mr. Demombynes and Karina Trommlerova, also of the World Bank, 16 of the 20 African countries which have had detailed surveys of living conditions since 2005 reported falls in their child-mortality rates (this rate is the number of deaths of children under five per 1,000 live births). Twelve had falls of over 4.4% a year, which is the rate of decline that is needed to meet the millennium development goal (MDG) of cutting by two-thirds the child-mortality rate between 1990 and 2015 (see chart). Three countries—Senegal, Rwanda and Kenya—have seen falls of more than 8% a year, almost twice the MDG rate and enough to halve child mortality in about a decade. These three now have the same level of child mortality as India, one of the most successful economies in the world during the past decade.

The decline in African child mortality is speeding up. In most countries it's now falling about twice as fast as during the early 2000s and 1990s. More striking, the average fall is faster than it was in China in the early 1980s, when child mortality was declining around 3% a year, admittedly from a lower base.

The only recent fall comparable to the largest of those in Africa occurred in Vietnam between 1985–90 and 1990–95, when child mortality fell by 37%—and even that was slower than in Senegal and Rwanda. Rwanda's child-mortality rate more than halved between 2005–06 and 2010–11. Senegal cut its rate from 121 to 72 in five years (2005–10). It took India a quarter of centaury to make that reduction. The top rates of decline in African child mortality are the fastest seen in the world for at least 30 years.

The striking thing about the falls is how widespread they have been. They have happened in countries large and small, Muslim and Christian, and in every corner of the continent. The three biggest successes are in east, west and central Africa. The success stories come from Africa's two most populous countries, Nigeria and Ethiopia, and from tiddlers such as Benin (population: 9m).

You might expect that countries which reduced their birth rates the most would also have cut child mortality comparably. This is because such countries have moved furthest along the demographic transition from poor, high-fertility status to richer, low-fertility status. But it turns out that is only partly true. Senegal, Ethiopia and Ghana all reduced fertility and child mortality a lot. But Kenya and Uganda also did well on child deaths, though their fertility declines have stalled recently. So it cannot all be just about lower birth rates. Liberia, where fertility remains high, did badly on child mortality—but so did low-fertility places such as Namibia and Lesotho. The link between mortality and broader demographic change seems weak.

What makes a bigger difference, Mr. Demombynes argues, is some combination of broad economic growth and specific public-health policies, notably the increase in the use of insecticide-treated bednets (ITNs) which discourage mosquitoes, which cause malaria.

Ethiopia, Ghana, Rwanda and Uganda have been among Africa's star economic performers recently, with annual GDP growth averaging over 6.5% in 2005–10.

Less is more
Under-five mortality rate per 1,000 live births*
Annual % change†

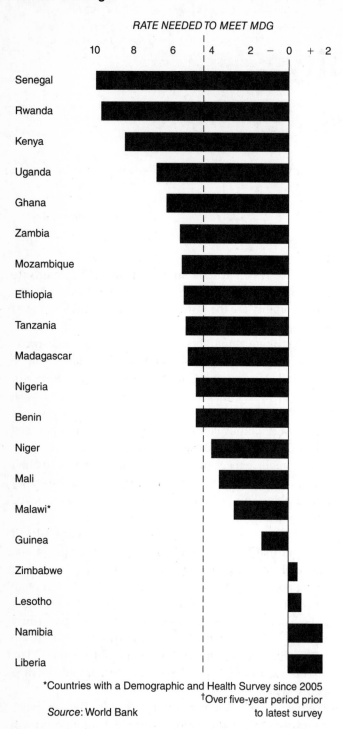

RATE NEEDED TO MEET MDG

*Countries with a Demographic and Health Survey since 2005
†Over five-year period prior
Source: World Bank   to latest survey

and better nutrition but also because growth can be a proxy for other good things: more sensible economic policies; more democratic, accountable governments; and a greater commitment to improving people's living standards.

But growth offers no guarantees. High-mortality Liberia actually saw impressive GDP increases whereas Senegal, whose record in child mortality is second to none, had a rather anaemic growth rate by recent African standards (3.8% a year, half that of Rwanda). That what Mr. Demombynes calls "the miracle of low mortality" has taken place in different circumstances suggests there can be no single cause. To look for other explanations, therefore, he studied Kenya in more detail*.

And Good Riddance

Kenya is a test case. It has cut the rate of infant mortality (deaths of children under one year old) by more than any other country. It has had healthy economic growth (4.8% a year in 2005–10) and a functioning democracy, albeit after horrendous post-election violence in 2008. But Mr. Demombynes noticed something else: it increased the use of treated bednets from 8% of all households in 2003 to 60% in 2008. Using figures on the geographical variation of malaria, he calculated that half the overall drop in Kenya's infant mortality can be explained by the huge rise in the use of ITNs in areas where malaria is endemic.

Bednets are often taken as classic examples of the benefits of aid, since in the past they were pioneered by foreign charities. Consistent with the view that aid is vital, Jeffrey Sachs, an American economist, recently claimed that a big drop in child mortality in his Millennium Villages project (a group of African villages that his Earth Institute of Columbia University, New York, is helping) is the result of large increases in aid to villagers. In fact, argues Mr. Demombynes, the mortality decline in these villages was no better than in the countries as a whole.

The broad moral of the story is different: aid does not seem to have been the decisive factor in cutting child mortality. No single thing was. But better policies, better government, new technology and other benefits are starting to bear fruit. "This will be startling news for anyone who still thinks Africa is mired in unending poverty and

At the other end of the scale, Zimbabwe saw its GDP fall and mortality rise. This seems intuitively right. An increase in national income should reduce mortality not just because it is usually associated with lower poverty

*What has driven the decline in infant mortality in Kenya? Policy Research Working Paper 6057. World Bank

death," says Mr. Clemens. But "that Africa is slipping quickly away."

Correction: The original version of this article identified Michael Clemens as coming from the Kennedy School of Government at Harvard. He is actually a senior fellow at the Centre for Global Development. This was corrected on May 17th 2012.

Critical Thinking

1. What is the point of view of this case study?
2. What reasons are offered to support this point of view?
3. What conclusion is offered regarding the roles of international aid and new technology in this demographic shift?
4. Does this article support the main point of view presented in Article 6?

Virus Hunter

Nathan Wolfe has a mission: to prevent new pathogens from making the jump from animals to humans—and stop the next deadly pandemic before it starts.

Bryan Walsh

Junior creeps through the tropical forest, searching for his prey. The hardwood trees in southern Cameroon are some of the most valuable in Central Africa, their branches towering above 50 ft. (15 m), but Junior's eyes are on the jungle floor. He's a hunter, and his target is bush meat: wild forest animals like porcupines, the cat-size antelopes called dik-diks, perhaps even monkeys. One would be enough to feed his family for a couple of days, or he could sell it to truckers passing along the new, Chinese-made logging roads that cut through this once untouched part of the forest. When Junior arrives at one of his traps after hours of walking, though, he kneels to find that the wire snare has snapped but is empty. Something living has already come and gone.

Nathan Wolfe leans over Junior and examines the spent trap. A 41-year-old with close-cropped black hair and sleepy Buddha eyes, Wolfe is a hunter in this forest as well, though one of a different sort. He stalks viruses—new ones—and the Cameroonian forest is one of the best places to find them. As the founder and head of Global Viral Forecasting (GVF), Wolfe has set up projects in Africa, Southeast Asia and southern China—all hot spots where humans and wild animals intermingle and new viruses can leap from one species to another.

Wolfe's big idea is as simple as it is ambitious. Pandemics and outbreaks of new infectious diseases usually begin when a novel microbe in an animal mutates and passes to a human being who lacks immunity to it. HIV, SARS, swine flu—they all began in animals. But instead of waiting for viruses to appear in humans, Wolfe is going on the offensive, using hunters like Junior to gather blood from animals that Wolfe and his colleagues can screen for unknown pathogens. "This is the sort of place where people can have contact with animals and their viruses and spark a real pandemic," he says. "It all comes together here."

This is a revolution in epidemiology—working to predict and prevent rather than simply respond to pandemics. The world is more vulnerable to infectious new pathogens than ever. For one thing, there are simply more of us—7 billion, to be exact—often packed into dense cities, where an aggressive disease could spread fast. We're also more connected; thanks to air travel, there's barely a spot on this planet, including the deep forests of Cameroon, that isn't within 24 hours of a major city. A new disease that might have burned out in a rural village years ago now

stands a better chance of finding fresh victims. Meanwhile, as we clear-cut forests and expand into what was once wilderness, we expose ourselves to new animals and microbes.

The panic, chaos and death in the recent film *Contagion*—for which Wolfe served as a technical adviser—aren't exaggerations. "We are at greater risk because of our greater interconnectedness," says Dr. Donald Burke, dean of the graduate school of public health at the University of Pittsburgh and one of Wolfe's mentors. "That's why we need to get better at figuring out where these things start." If we fail, Hollywood's take on the problem could turn out to be a portent of what we'll all experience.

Wolfe is not alone in trying to prevent that from happening. The experience of SARS—which in 2003 moved from bats to civets before infecting humans—and the threat of avian flu sent jolts though the public-health field. The World Health Organization and the U.S. Centers for Disease Control and Prevention (CDC) have upped surveillance for new diseases, while the U.S. Agency for International Development, which disburses foreign assistance, has launched an innovative program to help beef up infectious-disease surveillance. And groups like Wolfe's GVF are bringing the concepts of intelligence gathering to epidemiology, sifting through viral chatter to detect what new biothreat might be brewing. "Virus hunters like Nathan are our first line of protection," says Dr. Larry Brilliant, the president of the Skoll Global Threats Fund and an infectious-disease veteran. "He can make a huge difference."

Where Pandemics Are Born

You think you know the story of HIV. AIDS first appeared in the U.S. in 1981, and HIV, the virus that causes AIDS, was identified in 1983. In just a few decades, HIV has become a global killer, on par with smallpox and bubonic plague, with millions infected each year. Though antiviral drugs have reduced the toll, there is no vaccine.

Wolfe tells a different tale: HIV was active among people in Central Africa for decades before it spread to the rest of the world, aided by air travel, changing sexual mores and the mass distribution of cheap syringes. The best guess is that the virus jumped from primates to humans more than a century ago, when some unlucky hunter killed and butchered a chimp infected with simian immunodeficiency virus (SIV), the primate version of HIV.

But it goes back even further. SIV has long been common in many African monkeys, in which it appears to do little harm. When viruses remain in one population for a long time, they can attenuate and lose their virulence—but viruses that jump to a new species are often extremely deadly because the new host's immune system has no means of defense. Wolfe imagines a possible Patient Zero chimpanzee millions of years ago that might have acquired different SIV strains while hunting monkeys in Central Africa. "If you look at the chimp virus that led to HIV, it's a mix of two monkey viruses," says Wolfe.

There are a few lessons here for Wolfe's work. One is that while human beings love to think our species is special, to microbes there's not much difference between a *Pan troglodytes,* or common chimp, and a *Homo sapiens*. To viruses, we all look the same—which is one reason nearly 20% of all major infectious diseases in humans began in primates, even though primates make up just 0.5% of all vertebrate species. Another point is that viruses make that leap between species when bodily fluids are shared—as tends to happen when one animal hunts, kills and eats another. Hunting and butchering, writes Wolfe in his new book, *The Viral Storm,* "provide superhighways connecting a hunting species directly with the microbes in every tissue of their prey."

In the most basic and ambitious sense, Wolfe's goal is to prevent the next HIV. In 1998, Wolfe, who has a Ph.D. in immunology from Harvard University, published a paper that raised the possible links between the hunting of wild animals and the spread of emerging infectious diseases. At the time, few researchers were exploring that idea, but Burke was one of them. Burke, then at Johns Hopkins, had spent time in Cameroon working on HIV, and he wanted to start a project that could detect when novel viruses were jumping from animals to humans. Wolfe seemed like the perfect person for the job, in part because of his personality. "Nathan has the ability to be very persuasive," says Burke. More important was Wolfe's scientific experience; he'd done research tracking pathogens in primate populations in Malaysia.

Wolfe set up shop in Cameroon in 2000 with barely a word of French—the country is largely francophone—to start what eventually became GVF. He immediately put his persuasiveness to work: Lucky Gunasekara, who runs GVF's digital-epidemiology program and met Wolfe at Stanford, where the virus hunter teaches, told me Wolfe almost instantly talked him into putting medical school on hold and working for him instead. The objective in Cameroon was simple enough: collect blood samples from bush-meat hunters and their prey and find out what microbes were out there. Hunters are what Wolfe calls

a sentinel population. "It's amazing the amount of information you can get from a single drop of blood," he says.

The real challenge is getting that blood in the first place, especially in a desperately poor country where the roads range from rough to impassable. GVF distributes filter paper to villages throughout the country; when hunters make a kill, they squeeze a few drops of blood from the animal onto the paper, noting what they butchered, when and where. "We're looking for unknown things," Wolfe says. "If you want to be able to forecast, you need to know what's out there." Every few months, GVF staffers collect the papers, which can preserve blood samples for months. After a decade of work, Wolfe has over 20,000 blood samples.

It didn't take long for the project to pay off. In 2004, Wolfe and his colleagues found evidence that simian foamy virus (SFV) had spread to Cameroonian hunters. SFV—so called because of the way it makes infected cells appear under a microscope—hasn't been connected to any known symptoms, but it was nevertheless worrying that a novel primate retrovirus from the same genetic tree that produced HIV had made the jump to humans. More important, the discovery served as tangible proof that the concept driving GVF was sound. "That was a pivotal moment for this project," says Wolfe. "We knew that this method worked, and if we look for more, we'll find more."

That's what happened. Screening those blood samples, Wolfe and his colleagues soon discovered new variants of a virus called HTLV. Millions of people around the world are infected with the HTLV-1 strain, which can sometimes lead to adult T-cell leukemia, or HTLV-2, which may cause neurological diseases. But the hunters' blood contained two variants the researchers called HTLV-3 and HTLV-4. Though it's not clear yet whether the new HTLV variants cause disease, they're retroviruses like HIV—and they've been spreading silently among humans. "If we're going to find the kind of new viruses that might trigger pandemics, we need to do the kind of work Nathan is doing," says Charles Chiu, a microbiologist at the University of California, San Francisco, who collaborates with Wolfe.

There's never been a better time to be a virus hunter like Wolfe, thanks in part to inexpensive genetic sequencing and other techniques that allow scientists to rapidly isolate pathogens. Wolfe is a preternaturally calm guy—you have to be if you're going to work in the field, where the occasional flooded bridge keeps you from your appointed rounds—but get him talking about the microscopic world and he lights up. "We're just at the dawn of a new age of microbial discovery," he says. "You could spend your career as a scientist trying to find one new primate, but we find new viruses every year."

But pandemic prevention isn't just about cataloging new pathogens; it's also about trying to contain them. And that goes back to the bush-meat hunters, the people coming into direct contact with wild animals and their blood. Stop the bush-meat hunt and you might rob viruses of the chance to leap the species barrier. You'd also benefit conservation. One of the leading threats to endangered animals, especially primates in Central Africa, is the bush-meat trade.

'**We're looking for unknown things." If you want to be able to forecast, you need to know what's out there.'**

—Nathan Wolfe, Founder, Global Viral Forecasting

It's not so simple just to shut the ad hoc business down, though. Villagers in Cameroon and elsewhere in Central Africa aren't scouring the forest for prey because they want to, as anyone who's shadowed a hunter on an hours-long trek knows. Bush meat is virtually the only source of protein available in the countryside, and as African cities have swelled, there's additional demand at the market from urbanites who crave a taste of dik-dik or monkey. (It's common to see Cameroonians selling freshly killed bush meat along the roadsides.) "If we could snap our fingers and eliminate all contact with wild game, that would be great, but it's an impossibility," says Wolfe. "This is an issue of rural poverty." That puts Wolfe and his colleagues in a tough spot. They know that bush-meat hunting is a danger to the entire planet. But desperately poor people need to eat.

Preventing pandemics, then, also means addressing basic issues of development. That's a tall order, and Wolfe would like to see more aid focused on alternative sources of protein, like domestic animals, rarely seen in rural Cameroon. In the meantime, GVF promotes what you might call safe hunting.

At a hamlet in southern Cameroon, Joseph Diffo, a local GVF staffer, gathers villagers for his healthy-hunters talk. Using graphic pictures of sick and dead animals, Diffo explains the danger of infection that the blood of a primate might pose to a hunter and his family. "You can't always tell the difference between a sick animal and a healthy one," Diffo tells his audience in French. "Even if you think hunting is safe, there's a problem of viruses out there." He urges them to be mindful of cuts and scrapes on their hands as they butcher prey and to wrap the carcass in plastic or leaves if possible—all to prevent blood-to-blood virus transmission.

Central Africans already know plenty about the risk of disease. Ebola, which is transmitted by sick primates, is a real threat, not just the stuff of Hollywood outbreak thrillers. But safety doesn't always win out over hunger, and most hunters seem more concerned about stampeding elephants than novel viruses. After Diffo's talk, we walk to a nearby hut to watch a woman and her son butcher a recently killed porcupine. First they skin the animal; then they boil the carcass to strip off the quills. With the animal's flesh pink and raw, the woman tears into its belly with a machete and pulls out the yellow, glistening internal organs. Blood begins to flow as she chops the quivering carcass into quarters, kneading the meat with her hands. This is an encounter with the blood and attendant microbes of another species that, as Brilliant puts it, is "more intimate than

sex." Multiply that interaction—each of which could seed a devastating new infection—a thousandfold every day throughout Central Africa and other viral hot spots, and you can see why Wolfe is worried. "It's as if there is a lottery going on and the odds are getting better and better for the microbe," he says. "And the stakes are getting higher and higher all the time."

The New Age of Epidemiology

While our growing global connectedness makes us more vulnerable to new diseases, it also gives us powerful weapons. With the Internet and mobile phones, epidemiologists can quickly track new outbreaks as they happen—even in the most remote corners of the world. Groups like GVF and the New York City—based EcoHealth Alliance have set up lasting partnerships on the ground with local governments, building scientific and organizational capacities to respond to new viral threats. Even the Department of Defense is playing a vital role, thanks to a network of high-tech microbiology labs in vulnerable countries like Egypt, Kenya and Indonesia. (The armed forces have been deeply involved in infectious-disease research for decades, in part to ensure the health of troops deployed overseas.)

"We can maintain active surveillance on new pathogens in these countries," says Captain Kevin Russell, director of the military's Global Emerging Infections Surveillance and Response System. "Maybe preventing a pandemic is beyond our means now, but we can get ahead of the curve."

Wolfe sees it as a competition: Can our technological connectedness trump the risks of our biological and geographic connectedness? That's one reason he's pushed GVF to pioneer what he calls digital epidemiology, which uses the resources of the Internet to make predictive sense of the viral chatter picked up in the field. When he at last became a medical student, Gunasekara, now GVF's chief innovation officer, helped develop a system called Medic Mobile, which allows health workers in remote areas of developing countries to connect to hospitals. Now he and his team are setting up a bioinformatics strategy that could mine data from Internet searches and social media to pinpoint new outbreaks as they dawn—and potentially predict which newly discovered viruses might pose real threats to humanity. That work is culminating in a project called Epidemic IQ that will, Wolfe hopes, provide the ability to predict new pandemics the way the CIA might predict a terrorist attack.

Table 1   Fever Chart. New diseases often emerge in animals and then spread to humans

	ORIGIN	HOW IT SPREAD
HIV	The virus began in monkeys in **Africa** and was acquired by chimps that ate monkey meat	A century ago, humans first likely contracted HIV by **butchering infected chimps.** Now the virus has killed millions
SARS	The virus emerged in **China,** first among bats and then in civet cats sold in markets	SARS jumped from civet cats to human beings. Thanks to **air travel,** the virus spread to more than 25 countries
H1N1	H1N1, a mix of human-, bird- and swine-flu viruses, first emerged in pigs in **Mexico**	After jumping to human beings, H1N1 triggered the first **flu pandemic** in more than 40 years, infecting billions

GVF isn't the only place practicing digital epidemiology. At Harvard, bioinformatics expert John Brownstein has developed HealthMap, an app that scours the Web for information on emerging diseases and displays it geographically. Dr. Kamran Khan at the University of Toronto has helped create Bio.Diaspora, a project that integrates real-time information on infectious diseases with data on global travel patterns. But it's San Francisco–based GVF, with its Silicon Valley connections, that seems best poised to push the field forward. "Forecasting has been the missing piece of the puzzle," says Gunasekara. "We can mine data from the field and the Internet and try to come up with algorithms that forecast where these things are going next."

Wolfe's larger goal is to yank epidemiology into the digital age, to stop chasing pandemics as opposed to predicting and preventing them. "On infectious disease, we're where cardiology was in the 1950s," he says. "We're finally beginning to understand why pandemics happen instead of just reacting to them." What's needed is a global effort to scale up that kind of proactive work to ensure that every hot spot has surveillance running for new pathogens in animals and in human beings and that it has its own GVF-type group to do the work. Viruses don't respect borders—whether between nations or between species—and in a world where airlines act like bloodlines, global health is only as strong as its weakest link. We got lucky with the relatively weak swine-flu pandemic in 2009, but history tells us our luck won't last. "We sit here dodging bullets left and right, assuming we have an invisible shield," says Wolfe. "But you can't dodge bullets forever."

Critical Thinking

1. What is the relationship between animals and human infectious diseases?

2. Describe the work of the organization Global Viral Forecasting in preventing a pandemic?

3. What roles do non-governmental organizations and technology play in the field of epidemiology?

4. Do the authors of Articles 1 and 6 give adequate consideration of the possibility of a pandemic?

The Blue Food Revolution

New fish farms out at sea, and cleaner operations along the shore, could provide the world with a rich supply of much needed protein.

SARAH SIMPSON

Neil Sims tends his rowdy stock like any devoted farmer. But rather than saddling a horse like the Australian sheep drovers he grew up with, Sims dons a snorkel and mask to wrangle his herd: 480,000 silver fish corralled half a mile off the Kona coast of Hawaii's Big Island.

Tucked discretely below the waves, Sims's farm is one of 20 operations worldwide that are trying to take advantage of the earth's last great agricultural frontier: the ocean. Their offshore locations offer a distinct advantage over the thousands of conventional fish farms—flotillas of pens that hug the coastline. Too often old-style coastal farms, scorned as eyesores and ocean polluters, exude enough fish excrement and food scraps to cloud the calm, shallow waters, triggering harmful algal blooms or snuffing out sea life underneath the pens. At offshore sites such as Kona Blue Water Farms, pollution is not an issue, Sims explains. The seven submerged paddocks, each one as big as a high school gymnasium, are anchored within rapid currents that sweep away the waste, which is quickly diluted to harmless levels in the open waters.

Rather than taking Sims's word for it, I put swim fins on my feet and a snorkel around my neck, high-step to the edge of his small service boat, and take the plunge. From the water, the double-cone-shape cage is aglow like a colossal Chinese lantern, with shimmering streams of sunlight and glinting forms of darting fish. To the touch, the material that stretches taut around the outside of the cage's frame feels more like a fence than a net. The solid, Kevlar-esque material would repel hungry sharks as effectively as it contains teeming masses of Seriola rivoliana, a local species of yellowtail that Kona Blue has domesticated as an alternative to wild tuna.

Why yellowtail? Many wild tuna fisheries are collapsing, and sushi-grade yellowtail fetches a high price. Sims and fellow marine biologist Dale Sarver founded Kona Blue in 2001 to raise popular fish sustainably. But the company's methods could just as well be applied to run-of-the-mill fish—and we may need them. The global population of 6.9 billion people is estimated to rise to 9.3 billion by 2050, and people with higher living standards also tend to eat more meat and seafood. Yet the global catch from wild fisheries has been stagnant or declining for a decade. Raising cows, pigs, chickens and other animals consumes vast amounts of land, freshwater, fossil fuels that pollute the air and fertilizers that run off and choke rivers and oceans.

Where will all the needed protein for people come from? The answer could well be new offshore farms, if they can function efficiently, and coastal farms, if they can be cleaned up.

Cleaner Is Better

To some scientists, feeding the world calls for transferring the production of our animal protein to the seas. If a blue food revolution is to fill such an exalted plate at the dinner table, however, it must operate in environmentally sound ways—and make its benefits better known both to a jaded public and to policy makers with the power to help or retard its spread.

In the past, condemnation might have been apt. When modern coastal fish farming began about 30 years ago, virtually no one was doing things right, either for the environment or for the industry's long-term sustainability. Fish sewage was just one of the issues. Shrimp farmers in Southeast Asia and Mexico clearcut coastal mangrove forests to make ponds to grow their shrimp. In the salmon farms of Europe and the Americas, animals were often too densely packed, helping disease and parasites sweep through the populations. Fish that escaped farms sometimes spread their diseases to native species. Making matters worse, the aquaculture industry represented (and still does) a net drain on fish mass; wild forage fish—small, cheap species that humans do not prefer but that bigger, wild fish eat—are captured in large quantities and ground into feed for the bigger, tastier, more expensive farmed fish folks favor.

Clearly, such ills were not good for business, and the industry has devised innovative solutions. Kona Blue's strategy of situating the farm within rapid offshore currents is one example. Other farmers are beginning to raise seaweed and filter-feeding animals such as mollusks near the fish pens to gobble up waste. Throughout the industry, including freshwater pens, improvements in animal husbandry and feed formulations are reducing disease and helping fish grow faster, with less forage fish in their diets. It may still be a long time before environmental groups remove farmed fish from "don't buy" lists, however.

Some cutting-edge thinkers are experimenting with an even bolder move. Nations exercise sole rights to manage waters out to 200 nautical miles from their shores—a vast frontier untapped for domesticated food production. Around the U.S., that frontier measures 3.4 million square nautical miles. Submerged fish pens, steered by large propellers, could ride in stable ocean currents, returning months later to their starting points or a distant destination to deliver fresh fish for market.

Ocean engineer Clifford Goudey tested the world's first self-propelled, submersible fish pen off the coast of Puerto Rico in late 2008. A geodesic sphere 62 feet in diameter, the cage proved surprisingly maneuverable when outfitted with a pair of eight-foot propellers, says Goudey, former director of M.I.T. Sea Grant's Offshore Aquaculture Engineering Center. Goudey imagines launching dozens of mobile farms in a steady progression within a predictable current that traverses the Caribbean Sea every nine months.

Feeding Frenzy

The aspect of marine (saltwater) aquaculture that has been hardest to fix is the need to use small, wild fish as food for the large, farmed varieties. (The small fish are not farmed, because a mature industry already exists that catches and grinds them into fish meal and oil.) The feed issue comes into pungent focus for me when Sims and I climb aboard an old U.S. Navy transport ship cleverly transformed into a feeding barge. The sea swell pitches me sideways as I make my way to the bow, calling to mind a bumpy pickup truck ride I took long ago, across a semi-frozen Missouri pasture to deliver hay to my cousin's Herefords. The memory of sweet-smelling dried grass vanishes when I grab a handful of oily brown feed from a 2,000-pound sack propped open on the deck. The pellets look like kibble for a small terrier but reek of an empty anchovy tin.

The odor is no surprise; 30 percent of Kona Blue's feed is ground up Peruvian anchovy. Yellowtail could survive on a vegetarian diet, but they wouldn't taste as good, Sims explains. Nor would their flesh include all the fatty acids and amino acids that make them healthy to eat. Those ingredients come from fish meal and fish oil, and that is the issue. "We are often pilloried because we're killing fish to grow fish," Sims says. Salmon farming, done in coastal pens, draws the same ire.

Detractors worry that rising demand from fish farms will wipe out wild anchovies, sardines and other forage fish. Before modern fish farming began, most fish meal was fed to pigs and chickens, but today aquaculture consumes 68 percent of the fish meal. Consumption has lessened under advanced feed formulas, however. When Kona Blue started raising yellowtail in 2005, its feed pellets were 80 percent anchovy. By early 2008 the company had reduced the share to 30 percent—without sacrificing taste or health benefit, Sims says—by increasing the concentration of soybean meal and adding chicken oil, a byproduct of poultry processing. The compound feed pellets are a big improvement over the egregious practice of dumping whole sardines into the fish cages. Unfortunately, this wasteful habit remains the norm among less responsible farmers.

A goal for the more enlightened proprietors is a break-even ratio, in which the amount of fish in feed equals the weight of fish produced for market. Farmers of freshwater tilapia and catfish have attained this magic ratio, but marine farmers have not. Because 70 percent of Kona Blue's feed is agricultural protein and oil, it now needs only 1.6 to 2.0 pounds of anchovies to produce one pound of yellowtail. The average for the farmed salmon industry is around 3.0. To achieve no net loss of marine protein, the industry would have to reduce that ratio. Still, farmed fish take a far smaller bite than their wild equivalents do: over its lifetime, a wild tuna may consume as much as 100 pounds of food per pound of its own weight, all of it fish.

The pressure to reduce sardine and anchovy catches will increase as the number of fish farms grows. Aquaculture is the fastest-growing food production sector in the world, expanding at 7.5 percent a year since 1994. At that pace, fish meal and fish oil resources could be exhausted by 2040. An overarching goal, therefore, is to eliminate wild fish products from feed altogether, within a decade or so, asserts marine ecologist Carlos M. Duarte, who directs the International Laboratory for Global Change at the Spanish Council for Scientific Research in Majorca.

One breakthrough that could help is coaxing the coveted omega-3 fatty acid DHA out of microscopic algae, which could replace some of the forage fish content in feed. Advanced Bio-Nutrition in Columbia, Md., is testing feed that contains the same algae-derived DHA that enhances infant formula, milk and juice now sold in stores. Recently researchers at Australia's Commonwealth Scientific and Industrial Research Organization coaxed DHA out of land plants for the first time. Duarte suggests that fierce competition for agricultural land and freshwater means that fish farmers should eventually eliminate soy, chicken oil and other terrestrial products as well, instead feeding their flocks on zooplankton and seaweed, which is easy to grow. (Seaweed already accounts for nearly one quarter of all marine aquaculture value.)

Despite improvements in marine fish farming, prominent environmentalists and academics still shoot it down. Marine ecologist Jeremy Jackson of the Scripps Institution of Oceanography says he is "violently opposed" to aquaculture of predatory fish and shrimp—basically, any fish people like to eat sashimi-style. He calls the practice "environmentally catastrophic" in the pressure it puts on wild fish supplies and insists it should be "illegal."

Smarter than Beef

Jackson's point, echoed by other critics, is that the risk of collapsing forage fisheries, which are already overexploited, is too great to justify serving up a luxury food most of the world will never taste. Far better would be to eat the herbivorous sardines and anchovies directly instead of farmed, top-end predators.

Sims agrees that we should fish lower on the food web but says that does not mean we need to eat lower. "Let's get real. I eat anchovies on my pizza, but I can't get anyone else in my family to do it," he says. "If you can get a pound of farmed sushi for every pound of anchovy, why not give people the thing they want to eat?"

Certain people scoff at fish consumption—whether wild-caught or farm-raised—on the premise that the planet and its human inhabitants would be healthier if people ate more plants. But society is not rushing to become vegetarian. More people are eating more meat, particularly as populations in the developing world become wealthier, more urban and more Western. The World Health Organization predicts a 25 percent increase in per capita meat consumption by 2050. Even if consumption held steady, crop and grazing areas would have to increase by 50 to 70 percent, at current yields, to produce the food required in 2050.

That reality begs for a comparison rarely made: fish farming versus terrestrial farming. Done right, fish farming could provide much needed protein for the world while minimizing the expansion of land-based farming and the attendant environmental costs.

Land-based farmers have already transformed 40 percent of the earth's terrestrial surface. And after 10,000 years to work out the kinks, major problems still abound. Cattle eat tremendous amounts of heavily fertilized crops, and pig and chicken farms are notorious polluters. The dead zones underneath coastal fish farms pale in comparison to the huge dead zones that fertilizer run-off triggers in the Gulf of Mexico, Black Sea and elsewhere and to the harmful algal blooms that pig farm effluent has caused in Chesapeake Bay.

A growing number of scientists are beginning to compare the environmental impacts of all the various protein production systems, so that society can "focus its energies on efficiently solving the most demanding problems," writes Kenneth M. Brooks, an independent aquatic environmental consultant in Port Townsend, Wash. Brooks estimates that raising Angus beef requires 4,400 times more high-quality pasture land than sea-floor needed for the equivalent weight of farmed Atlantic salmon filets. What is more, the ecosystem below a salmon farm can recover in less than a decade, instead of the centuries it would take for a cattle pasture to revert to mature forest.

An even more compelling reason to raise protein in the sea may be to reduce humanity's drain on freshwater. As Duarte points out, animal meat products represent only 3.5 percent of food production but consume 45 percent of the water used in agriculture. By shifting most protein production to the ocean, he says, "land agriculture could grow considerably without exceeding current levels of water use."

Of course, collecting and transporting soybean meal and chicken oil and feeding fish flocks all consume energy and create emissions, too. Fuel consumption and emissions are greater for farms that are farther from shore, but both types of farming rate better than most fishing fleets. The only way offshore farmers can be profitable right now is to raise high-priced fish, but costs can come down: a few experimental farms are already raising cost-competitive mussels in the ocean.

Environmental Distinctions

If providing more fish to consumers is an answer to meeting global demands for protein, why not just catch more fish directly? Many wild fisheries are maxed out, right at a time when global

population, as well as per capita demand for fish, is booming. North Americans, for example, are heeding health experts' advice to eat fish to help reduce the risk of heart attacks and improve brain function.

What is more, fishing fleets consume vast amounts of fuel and emit volumes of greenhouse gases and pollutants. Widely used, indiscriminate fishing methods, such as trawling and dredging, kill millions of animals; studies indicate that at least half the sea life fishers haul in this way is discarded as too small, overquota or the wrong species. All too often this so-called by-catch is dead by the time it is tossed overboard. Aquaculture eliminates this waste altogether: "Farmers only harvest the fish in their pens," Sims notes.

Goudey points out another often overlooked reality: you can grow fish more efficiently than you can catch them. Farmed fish convert food into flesh much more effectively than their wild brethren, which expend enormous amounts of energy as they hunt for food and evade predators, seek a mate and reproduce. Farmed fish have it easy by comparison, so most of their diet goes into growth.

Kona Blue's yellowtail and most farmed salmon are between one and three years old at harvest, one-third the age of the large, wild tuna targeted for sushi. The younger age also means farmed fish have less opportunity to accumulate mercury and other persistent pollutants that can make mature tuna and swordfish a potential health threat.

Indeed, fish farming already accounts for 47 percent of the seafood people consume worldwide, up from only 9 percent in 1980. Experts predict the share could rise to 62 percent of the total protein supply by 2050. "Clearly, aquaculture is big, and it is here to stay. People who are against it really aren't getting it," says Jose Villalon, aquaculture director at the World Wildlife Fund. Looking only at the ills of aquaculture is misleading if they are not compared with the ills of other forms of food production. Aquaculture affects the earth, and no number of improvements will eliminate all problems. But every food production system taxes the environment, and wild fish, beef, pork and poultry producers impose some of the greatest burdens.

To encourage good practices and help distinguish clean fish farms from the worst offenders, the World Wildlife Fund has co-founded the Aquaculture Stewardship Council to set global standards for responsible practices and to use independent auditors to certify compliant farms. The council's first set of standards is expected early this year. The council believes certification could have the greatest effect by motivating the world's 100 to 200 big seafood retailers to buy fish from certified farms, rather than trying to crack down directly on thousands of producers.

The Ocean Conservancy's aquaculture director George Leonard agrees that this kind of farm-to-plate certification program is an important way to encourage fish farmers to pursue better sustainability practices. As in any global industry, he says, cheap, unscrupulous providers will always exist. Setting a regulatory "floor" could require U.S. farmers to behave responsibly "without making it impossible for them to compete."

That point is key. Only five of the world's 20 offshore installations are in U.S. waters. Goudey thinks more aquaculture entrepreneurs would dive in if the U.S. put a licensing system into place for federal waters, from three nautical miles offshore to the 200-mile boundary. "No investor is going to back a U.S. operation when there are no statutes granting rights of tenancy to an operation," Goudey asserts. All U.S. farms exist inside the three-mile-wide strip of water that states control, and only a few states, such as Hawaii, allow them. California has yet to grant permits, despite government estimates that a sustainable offshore fish-farming industry in less than 1 percent of the state's waters could bring in up to $1 billion a year.

Protein Policy

To grow, and do so sustainably, the fish-farming industry will need appropriate policies and a fairer playing field. At the moment, robust government fuel subsidies keep trawling and dredging fleets alive, despite their well-known destruction of the sea-floor and the terrible volume of dead by-catch. Farm subsidies help to keep beef, pork and poultry production profitable. And powerful farm lobbies continue to block attempts to curtail the flow of nitrogen-rich fertilizer down the Mississippi River. "Almost none of these more traditional ways of producing food have received the scrutiny that aquaculture has," Brooks says. The public has accepted domestication of the land but maintains that the ocean is a wild frontier to be left alone, even though this imbalance may not be the most sustainable plan for feeding the world.

Policy shifts at the federal and regional levels may soon open up U.S. federal waters. In January 2009 the Gulf of Mexico Fishery Management Council voted in favor of an unprecedented plan for permitting offshore aquaculture within its jurisdiction, pending approval from higher levels within the U.S. National Oceanic and Atmospheric Administration. NOAA will evaluate the plan only after it finalizes its new national aquaculture policy, which addresses all forms of the industry and will probably include guidance for the development of a consistent, nationwide framework for regulating commercial activities. "We don't want the blue revolution to repeat the mistakes of the green revolution," says NOAA director Jane Lubchenco. "It's too important to get it wrong, and there are so many ways to get it wrong."

Given relentlessly rising demand, society has to make hard choices about where greater protein production should occur.

"One of my goals has been to get us to a position where, when people say food security, they don't just mean grains and livestock but also fisheries and aquaculture," Lubchenco says. Duarte suggests we take some pressure off the land and turn to the seas, where we have the opportunity to do aquaculture right, rather than looking back 40 years from now wishing we had done so.

As for Neil Sims's part of the blue food revolution, he is courting technology companies for upgrades. Tools such as robotic net cleaners, automated feeders and satellite-controlled video cameras to monitor fish health and cage damage would help Kona Blue's crew manage its offshore farms remotely. "Not just so we can grow more fish in the ocean," Sims says. "So we can grow more fish better."

In Brief

Meat consumption is rising worldwide, but production involves vast amounts of energy, water and emissions. At the same time, wild fisheries are declining. Aquaculture could become the most sustainable source of protein for humans.

Fish farming already accounts for half of global seafood production. Most of it is done along coastlines, which creates substantial water pollution.

Large, offshore pens that are anchored to the seafloor are often cleaner. Those farms, other new forms of aquaculture. and practices that clean up coastal operations could expand aquaculture significantly.

Questions remain about how sustainable and cost-effective the approaches can be.

Critical Thinking

1. What is the Blue Food Revolution?
2. What are some of the environmental challenges facing large-scale fish farming?
3. Can fish farming be more sustainable than raising livestock?
4. How does this article complement or contradict Article 2?

Sarah Simpson is a freelance writer and contributing editor for *Scientific American*. She lives in Riverside, Calif.

Simpson, Sarah. From *Scientific American*, February 2011, pp. 54–61. Copyright © 2011 by Scientific American, a division of Nature America, Inc. All rights reserved. Reprinted by permission.

UNIT 3

The Global Environment and Natural Resources Utilization

Unit Selections

11. **Climate Change,** Bill McKibben
12. **The Other Climate Changers,** Jessica Seddon Wallack and Veerabhadran Ramanathan
13. **The Melting North,** *The Economist*
14. **Asian Carp, Other Invasive Species Make a Splash,** David Harrison

Learning Outcomes

After reading this unit you should be able to:

- Discuss the basic pro and con arguments regarding the causes of climate change.

- Describe the impact of human activities on glaciers, oceans, tropical forests, and other ecological systems.

- Identify some of the policy debates related to mitigating climate change impacts.

- Assess your on-going effort at identifying your theory of international relations and how this unit changes/complements it.

- Describe a case study of an invasive species.

Student Website
www.mhhe.com/cls

Internet References

National Geographic Society
www.nationalgeographic.com

National Oceanic and Atmospheric Administration (NOAA)
www.noaa.gov

SocioSite: Sociological Subject Areas
www.pscw.uva.nl/sociosite/TOPICS

United Nations Environment Programme (UNEP)
www.unep.ch

In the eighteenth century, the modern nation-state emerged, and, over many generations, it evolved to the point where it is difficult to imagine a world without national governments. These legal entities have been viewed as separate, self-contained units that independently pursue their "national interests." Scholars often described the world as a political community of sovereign units that interact with each other (a concept described as a billiard ball model).

This perspective of the international community as comprised of self-contained and self-directed units has undergone major rethinking in the past 45 years. One of the reasons for this is the international consequences of the growing demands being placed on natural resources. The Middle East, for example, contains a majority of the world's known oil reserves. The United States, Western Europe, China, India, and Japan are dependent on this vital source of energy. The unbalanced oil supply and demand equation has created an unprecedented lack of self-sufficiency for the world's major economic powers.

The increased interdependence of countries is further illustrated by the fact that air and water pollution do not respect political boundaries. One country's smoke is often another country's acid rain. The concept that independent political units control their own destiny makes less sense than it might have a century ago. In order to more fully understand why this is so, one must first look at how natural resources are being utilized and how this is effecting the climate.

The first two articles examine the debate surrounding global climate change and the challenges facing policymakers. Climate change directly or indirectly impacts everyone, and if these changes are to be mitigated, international collaboration will be required. The consequences of basic human activities such as growing, processing, and cooking food are profound when multiplied billions of times every day. A single country or even a few countries working together cannot have a significant impact on redressing these problems. Solutions will have to be conceived that are truly global in scope. Just as there are shortages of natural resources, there are also shortages of new ideas for solving many of these problems.

© Lucidio Studio Inc./Corbis

Unit 3 continues by offering a number of case studies. Implicit in these is the challenge of moving from the perspective of the environment as primarily an economic resource to be consumed to a perspective that has been defined as "sustainable development." This change is easily called for, but in fact it goes to the core of social values and basic economic activities. Developing sustainable practices, therefore, is a challenge of unprecedented magnitude.

Nature is not some object "out there" to be visited at a national park. It is the food we eat and the energy we consume. Human beings are joined in the most intimate of relationships with the natural world in order to survive from one day to the next. It is ironic how little time is spent thinking about this relationship. This lack of attention, however, is not likely to continue, for rapidly growing numbers of people and the increased use of energy consuming technologies are placing unprecedented pressures on Earth's carrying capacity.

Climate Change

BILL MCKIBBEN

"Scientists Are Divided"

No, they're not. In the early years of the global warming debate, there was great controversy over whether the planet was warming, whether humans were the cause, and whether it would be a significant problem. That debate is long since over. Although the details of future forecasts remain unclear, there's no serious question about the general shape of what's to come.

Every national academy of science, long lists of Nobel laureates, and in recent years even the science advisors of President George W. Bush have agreed that we are heating the planet. Indeed, there is a more thorough scientific process here than on almost any other issue: Two decades ago, the United Nations formed the Intergovernmental Panel on Climate Change (IPCC) and charged its scientists with synthesizing the peer-reviewed science and developing broad-based conclusions. The reports have found since 1995 that warming is dangerous and caused by humans. The panel's most recent report, in November 2007, found it is "very likely" (defined as more than 90 percent certain, or about as certain as science gets) that heat-trapping emissions from human activities have caused "most of the observed increase in global average temperatures since the mid-20th century."

If anything, many scientists now think that the IPCC has been too conservative—both because member countries must sign off on the conclusions and because there's a time lag. Its last report synthesized data from the early part of the decade, not the latest scary results, such as what we're now seeing in the Arctic.

In the summer of 2007, ice in the Arctic Ocean melted. It melts a little every summer, of course, but this time was different—by late September, there was 25 percent less ice than ever measured before. And it wasn't a one-time accident. By the end of the summer season in 2008, so much ice had melted that both the Northwest and Northeast passages were open. In other words, you could circumnavigate the Arctic on open water. The computer models, which are just a few years old, said this shouldn't have happened until sometime late in the 21st century. Even skeptics can't dispute such alarming events.

"We Have Time"

Wrong. Time might be the toughest part of the equation. That melting Arctic ice is unsettling not only because it proves the planet is warming rapidly, but also because it will help speed up the warming. That old white ice reflected 80 percent of incoming solar radiation back to space; the new blue water left behind absorbs 80 percent of that sunshine. The process amps up. And there are many other such feedback loops. Another occurs as northern permafrost thaws. Huge amounts of methane long trapped below the ice begin to escape into the atmosphere; methane is an even more potent greenhouse gas than carbon dioxide.

Such examples are the biggest reason why many experts are now fast-forwarding their estimates of how quickly we must shift away from fossil fuel. Indian economist Rajendra Pachauri, who accepted the 2007 Nobel Peace Prize alongside Al Gore on behalf of the IPCC, said recently that we must begin to make fundamental reforms by 2012 or watch the climate system spin out of control; NASA scientist James Hansen, who was the first to blow the whistle on climate change in the late 1980s, has said that we must stop burning coal by 2030. Period.

All of which makes the Copenhagen climate change talks that are set to take place in December 2009 more urgent than they appeared a few years ago. At issue is a seemingly small number: the level of carbon dioxide in the air. Hansen argues that 350 parts per million is the highest level we can maintain "if humanity wishes to preserve a planet similar to that on which civilization developed and to which life on Earth is adapted." But because we're already past that mark—the air outside is currently about 387 parts per million and growing by about 2 parts annually—global warming suddenly feels less like a huge problem, and more like an Oh-My-God Emergency.

"Climate Change Will Help as Many Places as It Hurts"

Wishful thinking. For a long time, the winners-and-losers calculus was pretty standard: Though climate change will cause some parts of the planet to flood or shrivel up, other frigid, rainy regions would at least get some warmer days every year. Or so the thinking went. But more recently, models have begun to show that after a certain point almost everyone on the planet will suffer. Crops might be easier to grow in some places for a few decades as the danger of frost recedes, but over time the threat of heat stress and drought will almost certainly be stronger.

A 2003 report commissioned by the Pentagon forecasts the possibility of violent storms across Europe, megadroughts across the Southwest United States and Mexico, and unpredictable monsoons causing food shortages in China. "Envision Pakistan, India, and China—all armed with nuclear weapons—skirmishing at their borders over refugees, access to shared rivers, and arable land," the report warned. Or Spain and Portugal "fighting over fishing rights—leading to conflicts at sea."

Of course, there are a few places we used to think of as possible winners—mostly the far north, where Canada and Russia could theoretically produce more grain with longer growing seasons, or perhaps explore for oil beneath the newly melted Arctic ice cap. But even those places will have to deal with expensive consequences—a real military race across the high Arctic, for instance.

Want more bad news? Here's how that Pentagon report's scenario played out: As the planet's carrying capacity shrinks, an ancient pattern of desperate, all-out wars over food, water, and energy supplies would reemerge. The report refers to the work of Harvard archaeologist Steven LeBlanc, who notes that wars over resources were the norm until about three centuries ago. When such conflicts broke out, 25 percent of a population's adult males usually died. As abrupt climate change hits home, warfare may again come to define human life. Set against that bleak backdrop, the potential upside of a few longer growing seasons in Vladivostok doesn't seem like an even trade.

"It's China's Fault"

Not so much. China is an easy target to blame for the climate crisis. In the midst of its industrial revolution, China has overtaken the United States as the world's biggest carbon dioxide producer. And everyone has read about the one-a-week pace of power plant construction there. But those numbers are misleading, and not just because a lot of that carbon dioxide was emitted to build products for the West to consume. Rather, it's because China has four times the population of the United States, and per capita is really the only way to think about these emissions. And by that standard, each Chinese person now emits just over a quarter of the carbon dioxide that each American does. Not only that, but carbon dioxide lives in the atmosphere for more than a century. China has been at it in a big way less than 20 years, so it will be many, many years before the Chinese are as responsible for global warming as Americans.

What's more, unlike many of their counterparts in the United States, Chinese officials have begun a concerted effort to reduce emissions in the midst of their country's staggering growth. China now leads the world in the deployment of renewable energy, and there's barely a car made in the United States that can meet China's much tougher fuel-economy standards.

For its part, the United States must develop a plan to cut emissions—something that has eluded Americans for the entire two-decade history of the problem. Although the U.S. Senate voted down the last such attempt, Barack Obama has promised that it will be a priority in his administration. He favors some variation of a "cap and trade" plan that would limit the total amount of carbon dioxide the United States could release, thus putting a price on what has until now been free.

Despite the rapid industrialization of countries such as China and India, and the careless neglect of rich ones such as the United States, climate change is neither any one country's fault, nor any one country's responsibility. It will require sacrifice from everyone. Just as the Chinese might have to use somewhat more expensive power to protect the global environment, Americans will have to pay some of the difference in price, even if just in technology. Call it a Marshall Plan for the environment. Such a plan makes eminent moral and practical sense and could probably be structured so as to bolster emerging green energy industries in the West. But asking Americans to pay to put up windmills in China will be a hard political sell in a country that already thinks China is prospering at its expense. It could be the biggest test of the country's political maturity in many years.

"Climate Change Is an Environmental Problem"

Not really. Environmentalists were the first to sound the alarm. But carbon dioxide is not like traditional pollution. There's no Clean Air Act that can solve it. We must make a fundamental transformation in the most important part of our economies, shifting away from fossil fuels and on to something else. That means, for the United States, it's at least as much a problem for the Commerce and Treasury departments as it is for the Environmental Protection Agency.

And because every country on Earth will have to coordinate, it's far and away the biggest foreign-policy issue we face. (You were thinking terrorism? It's hard to figure out a scenario in which Osama bin Laden destroys Western civilization. It's easy to figure out how it happens with a rising sea level and a wrecked hydrological cycle.)

Expecting the environmental movement to lead this fight is like asking the USDA to wage the war in Iraq. It's not equipped for this kind of battle. It may be ready to save Alaska's Arctic National Wildlife Refuge, which is a noble undertaking but on a far smaller scale. Unless climate change is quickly deghettoized, the chances of making a real difference are small.

"Solving It Will Be Painful"

It depends. What's your definition of painful? On the one hand, you're talking about transforming the backbone of the world's industrial and consumer system. That's certainly expensive. On the other hand, say you manage to convert a lot of it to solar or wind power—think of the money you'd save on fuel.

And then there's the growing realization that we don't have many other possible sources for the economic growth we'll need to pull ourselves out of our current economic crisis. Luckily, green energy should be bigger than IT and biotech combined.

Almost from the moment scientists began studying the problem of climate change, people have been trying to estimate the costs of solving it. The real answer, though, is that it's such a huge transformation that no one really knows for sure. The bottom line is, the growth rate in energy use worldwide could be cut in half during the next 15 years and the steps would, net, save more money than they cost. The IPCC included a cost estimate in its latest five-year update on climate change and looked a little further into the future. It found that an attempt to keep carbon levels below about 500 parts per million would shave a little bit off the world's economic growth—but only a little. As in, the world would have to wait until Thanksgiving 2030 to be as rich as it would have been on January 1 of that year. And in return, it would have a much-transformed energy system.

Unfortunately though, those estimates are probably too optimistic. For one thing, in the years since they were published, the science has grown darker. Deeper and quicker cuts now seem mandatory.

But so far we've just been counting the costs of fixing the system. What about the cost of doing nothing? Nicholas Stern, a renowned economist commissioned by the British government to study the question, concluded that the costs of climate change could eventually reach the combined costs of both world wars and the Great Depression. In 2003, Swiss Re, the world's biggest reinsurance company, and Harvard Medical School explained why global warming would be so expensive. It's not just the infrastructure, such as sea walls against rising oceans, for example. It's also that the increased costs of natural disasters begin to compound. The diminishing time between monster storms in places such as the U.S. Gulf Coast could eventually mean that parts of "developed countries would experience developing nation conditions for prolonged periods." Quite simply, we've already done too much damage and waited too long to have any easy options left.

"We Can Reverse Climate Change"

If only. Solving this crisis is no longer an option. Human beings have already raised the temperature of the planet about a degree Fahrenheit. When people first began to focus on global warming (which is, remember, only 20 years ago), the general consensus was that at this point we'd just be standing on the threshold of realizing its consequences—that the big changes would be a degree or two and hence several decades down the road. But scientists seem to have systematically underestimated just how delicate the balance of the planet's physical systems really is.

The warming is happening faster than we expected, and the results are more widespread and more disturbing. Even that rise of 1 degree has seriously perturbed hydrological cycles: Because warm air holds more water vapor than cold air does, both droughts and floods are increasing dramatically. Just look at the record levels of insurance payouts, for instance. Mosquitoes, able to survive in new places, are spreading more malaria and dengue. Coral reefs are dying, and so are vast stretches of forest.

None of that is going to stop, even if we do everything right from here on out. Given the time lag between when we emit carbon and when the air heats up, we're already guaranteed at least another degree of warming.

The only question now is whether we're going to hold off catastrophe. It won't be easy, because the scientific consensus calls for roughly 5 degrees more warming this century unless we do just about everything right. And if our behavior up until now is any indication, we won't.

Critical Thinking

1. What is Bill McKibben's point of view?
2. What reasons does McKibben offer to support his point of view?
3. Identify some of the challenges to reversing climate change.

McKibben, Bill. Reprinted in entirety by McGraw-Hill with permission from *Foreign Policy,* January/February 2009, pp. 32–38. www.foreignpolicy.com. © 2009 Washingtonpost. Newsweek Interactive, LLC.

The Other Climate Changers

JESSICA SEDDON WALLACK AND VEERABHADRAN RAMANATHAN

Why Black Carbon and Ozone Also Matter

At last, world leaders have recognized that climate change is a threat. And to slow or reverse it, they are launching initiatives to reduce greenhouse gases, especially carbon dioxide, the gas responsible for about half of global warming to date. Significantly reducing emissions of carbon dioxide is essential, as they will likely become an even greater cause of global warming by the end of this century. But it is a daunting task: carbon dioxide remains in the atmosphere for centuries, and it is difficult to get governments to agree on reducing emissions because whereas the benefits of doing so are shared globally, the costs are borne by individual countries. As a result, no government is moving fast enough to offset the impact of past and present emissions. Even if current emissions were cut in half by 2050—one of the targets discussed at the 2008 UN Climate Change Conference— by then, humans' total contribution to the level of carbon dioxide in the atmosphere would still have increased by a third since the beginning of this century.

Meanwhile, little attention has been given to a low-risk, cost-effective, and high-reward option: reducing emissions of light-absorbing carbon particles (known as "black carbon") and of the gases that form ozone. Together, these pollutants' warming effect is around 40–70 percent of that of carbon dioxide. Limiting their presence in the atmosphere is an easier, cheaper, and more politically feasible proposition than the most popular proposals for slowing climate change—and it would have a more immediate effect.

Time is running out. Humans have already warmed the planet by more than 0.5 degrees Celsius since the nineteenth century and produced enough greenhouse gases to make it a total of 2.4 degrees Celsius warmer by the end of this century. If the levels of carbon dioxide and nitrous oxide in the atmosphere continue to increase at current rates and if the climate proves more sensitive to greenhouse gases than predicted, the earth's temperature could rise by as much as five degrees before the century ends.

A temperature change of two to five degrees would have profound environmental and geopolitical effects. It would almost—certainly melt all the Arctic summer sea ice. As a result, the Arctic Ocean would absorb more sunlight, which, in turn, would further amplify the warming. Such a rise could eliminate the Himalayan and Tibetan glaciers, which feed the major water systems of some of the poorest regions of the world. It would also accelerate the melting of the Greenland and Antarctic ice sheets, raising the sea level worldwide and provoking large-scale emigration from low-lying coastal regions. Cycles of droughts and floods triggered by global warming would spell disaster for agriculture-dependent economies.

Some of global warming's environmental effects would be irreversible; some of its societal impacts, unmanageable. Given these consequences, policymakers worldwide seeking to slow climate change must weigh options beyond just reducing carbon dioxide, especially those that would produce rapid results. Cutting black carbon and ozone is one such strategy.

Powerful Pollutants

The warming effect of carbon dioxide has been known since at least the 1900s, and that of ozone since the 1970s, but the importance of black carbon was discovered only recently. During the past decade, scientists have used sophisticated instruments on drones, aircraft, ships, and satellites to track black carbon and ozone from their sources to remote locations thousands of miles away and measure and model how much atmospheric heating they cause. Black carbon, a widespread form of particulate air pollution, is what makes sooty smoke look blackish or brownish. It is a byproduct of incomplete, inefficient combustion—a sign of energy waste as much as energy use. Vehicles and ships fueled by diesel and cars with poorly maintained engines release it. So do forest fires and households and factories that use wood, dung, crop waste, or coal for cooking, heating, or other energy needs.

Black carbon alters the environment in two ways. In the sky, the suspended particles absorb sunlight, warming up the atmosphere and in turn the earth itself. On the earth's surface, deposits of black carbon on snowpacks and ice absorb sunlight, thereby heating the earth and melting glaciers. The Arctic sea ice and the Himalayan and Tibetan glaciers, for example, are melting as much as a result of black carbon as they are as a result of the global warming caused by carbon dioxide. The warming effect of black carbon is equal to about 20–50 percent of the effect of carbon dioxide, making it the second- or third-largest contributor to global warming. No one knows exactly how much warming it causes, but even the most conservative estimates indicate a nontrivial impact. And its large contribution to the melting of glaciers and sea ice, one of the most alarming near-term manifestations of climate change, is well documented.

The ozone in the lower level of the atmosphere is another major contributor to global warming that deserves attention. (This is different from the ozone in the stratosphere, which shields life on earth from the sun's ultraviolet rays.) A potent greenhouse gas, its warming effect is equal to about 20 percent of that of carbon dioxide. Unlike black carbon, which exists as particles, ozone is a gas. Ozone in the atmosphere is not emitted directly but formed from other gases, "ozone precursors," such as carbon monoxide (from the burning of fossil fuels or biomass), nitrogen oxides (from lightning, soil, and the burning of fossil fuels), methane (from agriculture, cattle, gas leaks, and the burning of wood), and other hydrocarbons (from the burning of organic materials and fossil fuels, among other sources).

Most important, black carbon and ozone stay in the atmosphere for a much shorter time than does carbon dioxide. Carbon dioxide remains in the atmosphere for centuries—maybe even millennia—before it is absorbed by oceans, plants, and algae. Even if all carbon dioxide emissions were miraculously halted today, it would take several centuries for the amount of carbon dioxide in the atmosphere to approach its preindustrial-era level. In contrast, black carbon stays in the atmosphere for only days to weeks before it is washed away by rain, and ozone (as well as some of its precursors) only stays for weeks to months before being broken down. Nonetheless, because both are widespread and continuously emitted, their atmospheric concentrations build up and cause serious damage to the environment.

Although reducing the emissions of other greenhouse gases, such as methane and halocarbons, could also produce immediate results, black carbon and ozone are the shortest-lived climate-altering pollutants, and they are relatively under-recognized in efforts to stem climate change. Reducing the emissions of these pollutants on earth would quickly lower their concentrations in the atmosphere and, in turn, reduce their impact on global warming.

An Easier Extra Step

Another promising feature of black carbon and ozone precursor emissions is that they can be significantly limited at relatively low cost with technologies that already exist. Although the sources of black carbon and ozone precursors vary worldwide, most emissions can be reduced without necessarily limiting the underlying activity that generated them. This is because, unlike carbon dioxide, black carbon and ozone precursors are not essential byproducts of energy use.

The use of fossil fuels, particularly diesel, is responsible for about 35 percent of black carbon emissions worldwide. Technologies that filter out black carbon have already been invented: diesel particulate filters on cars and trucks, for example, can reduce black carbon emissions by 90 percent or more with a negligible reduction in fuel economy. A recent study by the Clean Air Task Force, a U.S. nonprofit environmental research organization, estimated that retrofitting one million semitrailer trucks with these filters would yield the same benefits for the climate over 20 years as permanently removing over 165,000 trucks or 5.7 million cars from the road.

The remaining 65 percent of black carbon emissions are associated with the burning of biomass—through naturally occurring forest fires, man-made fires for clearing cropland, and the use of organic fuels for cooking, heating, and small-scale industry. Cleaner options for the man-made activities exist. The greenest options for households are stoves powered by the sun or by gas from organic waste, but updated designs for biomass-fueled stoves can also substantially cut the amount of black carbon and other pollutants emitted. Crop waste, dung, wood, coal, and charcoal are the cheapest, but also the least efficient and dirtiest, fuels, and so households tend to shift away from them as soon as other options become reliably available. Thus, the challenge in lowering black carbon emissions is not convincing people to sacrifice their lifestyles, as it is with convincing people to reduce their carbon dioxide emissions. The challenge is to make other options available.

Man-made ozone precursors are mostly emitted through industrial processes and fossil-fuel use, particularly in the transportation sector. These emissions can be reduced by making the combustion process more efficient (for example, through the use of fuel additives) or by removing these gases after combustion (for example, through the use of catalytic converters). Technologies that both minimize the formation of ozone precursors and filter or break down emissions are already widely used and are reducing ozone precursors in the developed world. The stricter enforcement of laws that forbid adulterating gasoline and diesel with cheaper, but dirtier, substitutes would also help.

Fully applying existing emissions-control technologies could cut black carbon emissions by about 50 percent. And that would be enough to offset the warming effects of one to two decades' worth of carbon dioxide emissions. Reducing the human-caused ozone in the lower atmosphere by about 50 percent, which could be possible through existing technologies, would offset about another decade's worth. Within weeks, the heating effect of black carbon would lessen; within months, so, too, would the greenhouse effect of ozone. Within ten years, the earth's overall warming trend would slow down, as would the retreat of sea ice and glaciers. The scientific argument for reducing emissions of black carbon and ozone precursors is clear.

A Political Possibility

Reducing emissions of black carbon and ozone precursors is also a politically promising project. It would yield significant benefits apart from slowing climate change, giving governments economic and developmental incentives to reduce them. Reducing ozone precursors, for its part, would have recognizable agricultural benefits. Ozone lowers crop yields by damaging plant cells and interfering with the production of chlorophyll, the pigment that enables plants to derive energy from sunlight. One recent study estimated that the associated economic loss (at 2000 world prices) ranged from $14 billion to $26 billion, three to five times as large as that attributed to global warming. For policymakers concerned about agricultural productivity and food security, these effects should resonate deeply.

In countries where a large portion of the population still depends on biomass fuels, reducing black carbon emissions from households would improve public health and economic productivity. Nearly 50 percent of the world's population, and up to 95 percent of the rural population in poor countries, relies on solid fuels, including biomass fuels and coal. The resulting indoor air pollution is linked to about a third of the fatal acute respiratory infections among children under five, or about seven percent of child deaths worldwide. Respiratory illnesses associated with the emissions from solid fuels are the fourth most important cause of excess mortality in developing countries (after malnutrition, unsafe sex, and waterborne diseases).

These health problems perpetuate poverty. Exposure to pollutants early in life harms children's lung development, and children who suffer from respiratory illnesses are less likely to attend school. Air pollution leaves the poor, who often earn a living from manual labor, especially worse off. Collectively, workers in India lose an estimated 1.6–2.0 billion days of work every year to the effects of indoor air pollution. Reducing black carbon emissions from households would thus promote economic growth and, particularly for rural women and children, improve public health.

Furthermore, both black carbon and ozone precursor emissions tend to have localized consequences, and governments are more likely to agree to emissions-reduction strategies that can deliver local benefits. With carbon dioxide and other long-lasting, far-spreading greenhouse gases, emissions anywhere contribute to global warming everywhere. But the effects of black carbon and ozone are more confined. When it first enters the atmosphere, black carbon spreads locally and then, within a week, dissipates more regionally before disappearing from the atmosphere entirely in the form of precipitation. Ozone precursors, too, are more regionally confined than carbon dioxide, although background levels of ozone are increasing around the globe.

Because the effects of black carbon and ozone are mostly regional, the benefits from reducing them would accrue in large part to the areas where reductions were achieved. The melting of the Himalayan and Tibetan glaciers is almost reason enough for countries in South and East Asia to take rapid action to eliminate black carbon emissions. So is the retreat of the Arctic sea ice for countries bordering the Arctic Ocean. Regional groupings are also more likely than larger collections of countries to have dense networks of the economic, cultural, and diplomatic ties that sustain difficult negotiations. Moreover, both black carbon and ozone can be contained through geographically targeted strategies because many of the sources of black carbon and ozone are largely fixed. And so even if one country in a region seeks to regulate emissions, that country's polluting activities are unlikely to move to another country with less stringent policies—a common concern with agreements to reduce carbon dioxide emissions.

Cleaning Up

So what can be done to curb black carbon and ozone precursor emissions? A logical first step is for governments, international development agencies, and philanthropists to increase financial support for reduction efforts. Although some money for this is currently available, neither pollutant has emerged as a mainstream target for public or private funding. Simply recognizing black carbon and ozone as environmental problems on par with carbon dioxide would make policymakers more inclined to spend development funds and the "green" portions of stimulus packages on initiatives to tackle them. Developed countries could put their contributions toward customizing emissions-reduction technologies for the developing world and promoting their deployment—an important gesture of goodwill that would kick-start change.

Regardless of the source of the funding, aid should support the deployment of clean-energy options for households and small industries in the developing world and of emissions-reduction technologies for transportation around the world. This could mean distributing solar lanterns and stoves that use local fuel sources more efficiently or paying for small enterprises to shift to cleaner technologies. The specific fixes for small-scale industry will vary by economic activity—making brick kilns cleaner is different from making tea and spice driers more efficient—but the number of possible customers for the new technologies offers some economies of scale. When it comes to transportation, policy options include subsidizing engine and filter upgrades, shifting to cleaner fuels, and removing the incentives, created by government subsidies that favor some fuels over others, for adulterating fuel and for using diesel.

Deploying technologies to reduce emissions from so many culturally embedded activities, from cooking to driving, will not be easy. Enforcing emissions controls on many small, mobile polluters is harder than regulating larger sources, such as power plants. And in customizing technologies, close attention will need to be paid to the varied needs of households and industry. But creating and enforcing regulations and subsidizing and disseminating energy-efficient technologies are challenges that have been met before. The "green revolution"—the remarkable growth in agricultural productivity that occurred in the second half of the twentieth century—introduced radical changes to small-scale farming. Other development initiatives have influenced fertility, gender equality, schooling, and other household decisions more sensitive than those about cooking and driving.

Moreover, the infrastructure for international financial and technological transfers already exists in the form of the World Bank, regional development banks, and UN programs that have supported development around the world for decades. The Global Environment Facility, a development and environmental fund that started as a World Bank program and is now the world's largest funder of environmental projects, is well suited to finance cleaner technologies.

Governments and international agencies should also finance technology that tracks air quality, which is generally under-monitored. In the major cities of most developing countries, the number of sensors has not kept up with the growth in population or economic activity. In rural areas, air pollution is not tracked at all. Improving the monitoring of air quality and disseminating the data would inform policymakers and environmental activists. And tracking individuals' emissions—through indoor air-pollution monitors or devices attached to cars' tailpipes—could help motivate people to curb their emissions. Experimental initiatives to measure individuals' carbon footprints and energy use have been shown to change people's behavior in some settings.

Aid alone will not be enough, however. International organizations must also help governments identify and act on opportunities that mitigate climate change and promote development. International development institutions, such as the UN Environment Program and the multilateral and regional development banks, could sponsor research, set up interministerial working groups, and establish standards for monitoring and reporting public expenditures. These initiatives would make it easier to identify possible areas of coordination among public health, agricultural, environmental, and anti-poverty programs. In most countries, domestic institutions are not designed to encourage cooperation among different authorities. Pitching the reduction of black carbon and ozone precursor emissions as public health and agricultural policies could help such efforts compete for scarce funds; enabling the clearer calculation of the environmental benefits of development policies would make policymaking more informed. Much in the same way that international development organizations currently support good governance to improve infrastructure and services, they should also promote better environmental governance.

Responding Regionally

The current piecemeal approach to climate science—in particular, the tendency to treat air pollution and climate change as separate issues—has at times led to bad policy. The decision of many countries to promote diesel as a means to encourage fuel efficiency, for example, may have had the inadvertent effect of increasing black carbon emissions. And air-pollution laws designed to reduce the use of sulfate aerosols, which cause acid rain, have ironically led to more warming because sulfates also have a cooling effect. Had policymakers instead integrated efforts to reduce air pollution with those to slow global warming, they could have ensured that the reduction of sulfates was accompanied by an equivalent reduction in greenhouse gases.

A single global framework would be the ideal way to integrate various strategies for mitigating climate change. Bilateral or multilateral agreements are more feasible for getting started on reducing black carbon and ozone precursor emissions. These can strengthen governments' incentives to act by discouraging free-riding and by motivating governments to take into account the larger-scale impacts of their own emissions. Because the sources of black carbon and ozone vary from region to region, agreements to reduce them need to be tailored to suit regional conditions. In the Northern Hemisphere, for example, ozone precursors mostly come from industrial processes and transportation, whereas in the Southern Hemisphere, especially tropical regions, they mostly come from natural emissions (soils, plants, and forest fires). The sources of black carbon vary by region, too: in Europe and North America, transportation and industrial activity play a larger role than the burning of biomass, whereas the reverse is true in developing regions.

The impact of emissions on the climate is scientifically complex, and it depends on a number of factors that have not yet been adequately taken into account when devising climate models. The challenge, then, is to quickly create agreements that consider the complex links between human activities, emissions, and climate change and that can adjust over time as the scientific understanding of the problem evolves. Regional air-pollution agreements are easier to update than global agreements with many signatories. The UN Convention on Long-Range Transboundary Air Pollution (most of whose signatories are European or Central Asian states) and its subsequent pollutant-specific protocols provide a ready model for regional agreements on short-lived climate-changing pollutants. The specific provisions of these agreements are based on the costs of reductions, scientists' knowledge of the sources and distribution of air pollution, and the ability to measure reductions—considerations that should also inform the regulation of black carbon and ozone precursor emissions. Moreover, these agreements commit countries to particular actions, not just specific outcomes. This is wise, given that emissions are difficult to monitor and quantify precisely.

Black carbon and ozone can also be built into existing bilateral discussions. The High-Level India-EU Dialogue, a working group of scientists and policymakers from Europe and India, is one such existing forum. In February 2009, it was already urging governments from Europe and India to work together to recognize and reduce the threat from black carbon. Participants proposed an interdisciplinary research project that would determine the effects of biomass-based cooking and heating on health and the climate and assess the obstacles to a large-scale deployment of cleaner stoves. Black carbon and ozone are also natural candidates for U.S.-Chinese cooperation on energy and climate change: China would reap public health and agricultural benefits from reducing emissions, and the United States would earn goodwill for helping China do so.

By building on existing air-pollution agreements, the risk of distracting climate-change negotiations from the substantial task of promoting the reduction of carbon dioxide emissions could be avoided. Putting black carbon and ozone on the table in high-level climate talks could backfire if developing nations thought that they would be tacitly admitting responsibility for global warming by committing to reducing emissions of black carbon and ozone precursors or believed that the issue was an effort by developed countries to divert attention from the need for them to reduce their carbon dioxide emissions. Therefore, efforts to reduce emissions of black carbon and ozone precursors should be presented not as substitutes for commitments to reducing carbon dioxide emissions but as ways to quickly achieve local environmental and economic benefits.

The Low-Hanging Fruit

Historically, initiatives to slow global warming have focused on reducing the emissions of carbon dioxide and other greenhouse gases and largely ignored the role played by air pollution. This strategy makes sense for the long run, since carbon dioxide emissions are, and will continue to be, the most important factor in climate change. But in the short run, it alone will not be enough. Some scientists have proposed geoengineering—manipulating the climate through the use of technology—as a potential option of last resort, but the reduction of black carbon and ozone precursor emissions offers a less risky opportunity for achieving the same end.

Such an approach would quickly lower the level of black carbon and ozone in the atmosphere, offsetting the impact of decades of greenhouse gas emissions, decelerating the rush toward a dangerously warm planet, and giving efforts to reduce carbon dioxide emissions time to get off the ground. These pollutants are also tractable policy targets: they can be reduced through the use of existing technologies, institutions, and strategies, and doing so would lead to local improvements in air quality, agricultural output, and public health. In short, reducing black carbon and ozone precursor emissions is a low-risk, high-potential addition to the current arsenal of strategies to mitigate climate change.

At the current rate of global warming, the earth's temperature stands to career out of control. Now is the time to look carefully at all the possible brakes that can be applied to slow climate change, hedge against near-term climate disasters, and buy time for technological innovations. Of the available strategies, focusing on reducing emissions of black carbon and ozone precursors is the low-hanging fruit: the costs are relatively low, the implementation is feasible, and the benefits would be numerous and immediate.

Critical Thinking

1. What other contributors to climate change are there in addition to greenhouse gases?

2. How does black carbon alter the environment?

3. Why is it less expensive to combat black carbon and ozone precursor emissions than greenhouse gases?

4. What can be done by governments and international organizations to curb these pollutants?

JESSICA SEDDON WALLACK is Director of the Center for Development Finance at the Institute for Financial Management and Research, in Chennai, India. **VEERABHADRAN RAMANATHAN** is Distinguished Professor of Climate and Atmospheric Sciences at the Scripps Institute of Oceanography at the University of California, San Diego; Distinguished Visiting Fellow at the Energy and Resources Institute, in New Delhi; and a recipient of the 2009 Tyler Prize for Environmental Achievement.

The Melting North

The Arctic is warming twice as fast as the rest of the planet, says James Astill. The retreating ice offers access to precious minerals and new sea lanes—but also carries grave dangers.

THE ECONOMIST (US)

Standing on the Greenland ice cap, it is obvious why restless modern man so reveres wild places. Everywhere you look, ice draws the eye, squeezed and chiselled by a unique coincidence of forces. Ghormenghastian ice ridges, silver and lapis blue, ice mounds and other frozen contortions are minutely observable in the clear Arctic air. The great glaciers impose order on the icy sprawl, flowing down to a semi-frozen sea.

The ice cap is still, frozen in perturbation. There is not a breath of wind, no engine's sound, no bird's cry, no hubbub at all. Instead of noise, there is its absence. You feel it as a pressure behind the temples and, if you listen hard, as a phantom roar. For generations of frosty-whiskered European explorers, and still today, the ice sheet is synonymous with the power of nature.

The Arctic is one of the world's least explored and last wild places. Even the names of its seas and rivers are unfamiliar, though many are vast. Siberia's Yenisey and Lena each carries more water to the sea than the Mississippi or the Nile. Greenland, the world's biggest island, is six times the size of Germany. Yet it has a population of just 57,000, mostly Inuit scattered in tiny coastal settlements. In the whole of the Arctic—roughly defined as the Arctic Circle and a narrow margin to the south—there are barely 4m people, around half of whom live in a few cheerless post-Soviet cities such as Murmansk and Magadan. In most of the rest, including much of Siberia, northern Alaska, northern Canada, Greenland and northern Scandinavia, there is hardly anyone. Yet the region is anything but inviolate.

Fast Forward

A heat map of the world, colour-coded for temperature change, shows the Arctic in sizzling maroon. Since 1951 it has warmed roughly twice as much as the global average.

In that period the temperature in Greenland has gone up by 1.5°C, compared with around 0.7°C globally. This disparity is expected to continue. A 2°C increase in global temperatures—which appears inevitable as greenhouse-gas emissions soar—would mean Arctic warming of 3–6°C.

Almost all Arctic glaciers have receded. The area of Arctic land covered by snow in early summer has shrunk by almost a fifth since 1966. But it is the Arctic Ocean that is most changed. In the 1970s, 80s and 90s the minimum extent of polar pack ice fell by around 8% per decade. Then, in 2007, the sea ice crashed, melting to a summer minimum of 4.3m sq km (1.7m square miles), close to half the average for the 1960s and 24% below the previous minimum, set in 2005. This left the north-west passage, a sea lane through Canada's 36,000-island Arctic Archipelago, ice-free for the first time in memory.

Scientists, scrambling to explain this, found that in 2007 every natural variation, including warm weather, clear skies and warm currents, had lined up to reinforce the seasonal melt. But last year there was no such remarkable coincidence: it was as normal as the Arctic gets these days. And the sea ice still shrank to almost the same extent.

There is no serious doubt about the basic cause of the warming. It is, in the Arctic as everywhere, the result of an increase in heat-trapping atmospheric gases, mainly carbon dioxide released when fossil fuels are burned. Because the atmosphere is shedding less solar heat, it is warming—a physical effect predicted back in 1896 by Svante Arrhenius, a Swedish scientist. But why is the Arctic warming faster than other places?

Consider, first, how very sensitive to temperature change the Arctic is because of where it is. In both hemispheres the climate system shifts heat from the steamy equator to the frozen pole. But in the north the exchange is much more efficient. This is partly because of the ofty mountain ranges of Europe, Asia and America that help mix warm and cold fronts, much as boulders churn water in a stream. Antarctica, surrounded by the vast southern seas, is subject to much less atmospheric mixing.

The land masses that encircle the Arctic also prevent the polar oceans revolving around it as they do around Antarctica. Instead they surge, north-south, between the Arctic land masses in a gigantic exchange of cold and warm water: the Pacific pours through the Bering Strait, between Siberia and Alaska, and the Atlantic through the Fram Strait, between Greenland and Norway's Svalbard archipelago.

That keeps the average annual temperature for the high Arctic (the northernmost fringes of land and the sea beyond) at a relatively sultry −15°C; much of the rest is close to melting-point for much of the year. Even modest warming can therefore have a dramatic effect on the region's ecosystems. The Antarctic is also warming, but with an average annual temperature of −57°C it will take more than a few hot summers for this to become obvious.

The Albedo Effect

The efficient north-south mixing of air may also play a part in the Arctic's amplified warming. The winds that rush northwards carry pollutants, including soot from European and Asian smokestacks, which has a powerful warming effect over snow. In recent decades there has also been a rise in levels of mercury, a by-product of burning coal, in the tissues of beluga whales, walruses and polar bears, all of which the Inuit eat. This is another reason why the Arctic is not virgin.

But the main reason for Arctic amplification is the warming effect of replacing light-coloured snow and ice with darker-coloured land or water. Because dark surfaces absorb more heat than light ones, this causes local warming, which melts more snow and ice, revealing more dark land or water, and so on. Known as the albedo effect, this turns out to be a more powerful positive feedback than most researchers had expected. Most climate models predicted that the Arctic Ocean could be ice-free in summer by the end of this century; an analysis published in 2009 in *Geophysical Research Letters* suggested it might happen as early as 2037. Some now think it will be sooner.

It is hard to exaggerate how dramatic this is. Perhaps not since the felling of America's vast forests in the 19th century, or possibly since the razing of China's and western Europe's great forests a thousand years before that, has the world seen such a spectacular environmental change. The consequences for Arctic ecosystems will be staggering.

As their ancient ice buffers vanish, Arctic coastlines are eroding; parts of Alaska are receding at 14 metres (45 feet) a year. Niche habitats, such as meltwater pools on multiyear ice, are dwindling. Some highly specialised Arctic species will probably become extinct as their habitats shrink and southern interlopers rush in. Others will thrive. The early signs of this biological reshuffle are already evident. High-Arctic species, including the polar bear, are struggling. Species new to the region, such as mackerel and Atlantic cod, are coming up in Arctic trawler nets. Yet the shock waves of Arctic change will be felt much more widely.

Melting sea ice will not affect global sea levels, because floating ice displaces its own mass in seawater. But melting glaciers will, and the Arctic's are shedding ice at a great rate. Greenland's ice cap is losing an estimated 200 gigatonnes of ice a year, enough to supply a billion people with water. The Arctic's smaller ice caps and glaciers together are losing a similar amount. Before this became clear, the Intergovernmental Panel on Climate Change (IPCC) had predicted a sea-level rise of up to 59cm during this century. Given what is happening up north, many now think this too modest.

A wilder fear is that a deluge of Arctic meltwater could disrupt the mighty "overturning circulation" of the global oceans, the exchange of warm tropical and cold polar water. It has happened before, at least seven times in the past 60,000 years, and needs watching. But recent evidence suggests that such a calamity is not imminent. Another concern, that thawing Arctic permafrost could release vast quantities of carbon dioxide and methane, looms larger. That, too, has happened before, around 55m years ago, leading to a global temperature increase of 5°C in a few thousand years.

Such risks are hard to pin down, and possibly small. Many elements of the change in the Arctic, including the rates of snow melt and glacier retreat, are still within the range of historical variations. Yet the fact that the change is man-made is unprecedented, which introduces huge uncertainty about how far and fast it will proceed. For those minded to ignore the risks, it is worth noting that even the more extreme predictions of Arctic warming have been outpaced by what has happened in reality.

Riches of the North

In the long run the unfrozen north could cause devastation. But, paradoxically, in the meantime no Arctic species will profit from it as much as the one causing it: humans.

Disappearing sea ice may spell the end of the last Eskimo cultures, but hardly anyone lives in an igloo these days anyway. And the great melt is going to make a lot of people rich.

As the frozen tundra retreats northwards, large areas of the Arctic will become suitable for agriculture. An increasingly early Arctic spring could increase plant growth by up to 25%. That would allow Greenlanders to grow more than the paltry 100 tonnes of potatoes they manage now. And much more valuable materials will become increasingly accessible. The Arctic is already a big source of minerals, including zinc in Alaska, gold in Canada, iron in Sweden and nickel in Russia, and there is plenty more to mine.

Melting sea ice will not affect global sea levels, because floating ice displaces its own mass in seawater. But melting glaciers will.

The Arctic also has oil and gas, probably lots. Exploration licences are now being issued across the region, in the United States, Canada, Greenland, Norway and Russia. On April 18th ExxonMobil finalised the terms of a deal with Russia's Rosneft to invest up to $500 billion in developing offshore reserves, including in Russia's Arctic Kara sea. Oil companies do not like to talk about it, but this points to another positive feedback from the melt. Climate change caused by burning fossil fuels will allow more Arctic hydrocarbons to be extracted and burned.

These new Arctic industries will not emerge overnight. There is still plenty of sea ice to make the north exceptionally tough and expensive to work in; 24-hour-a-day winter darkness and Arctic cyclones make it tougher still. Most of the current exploration is unlikely to lead to hydrocarbon production for a decade at least. But in time it will happen. The prize is huge, and oil companies and Arctic governments are determined to claim it. Shortly before the ExxonMobil-Rosneft deal was announced, Vladimir Putin, Russia's president, announced plans to make it much more attractive for foreigners to invest in Russian offshore energy production. "Offshore fields, especially in the Arctic, are without any exaggeration our strategic reserve for the 21st century," he said.

For half the 20th century the Arctic, as the shortest route between Russia and America, was the likeliest theatre for a nuclear war, and some see potential for fresh conflict in its opening. Russia and Canada, the two biggest Arctic countries by area, have encouraged this fear:

the Arctic stirs fierce nationalist sentiment in both. With a new regard to their northern areas, some of the eight Arctic countries are, in a modest way, remilitarising them. Norway shifted its military command centre to the Arctic town of Reitan in 2009. Russia is replacing and upgrading its six nuclear icebreakers, a piece of civilian infrastructure with implications for security too. Yet this special report will suggest that warnings about Arctic conflict are, like the climate, overcooked.

The Arctic is no *terra nullius*. Unlike Antarctica, which is governed by an international treaty, most of it is demarcated. Of half a dozen territorial disputes in the region, the biggest is probably between the United States and Canada, over the status of the north-west passage. Those two countries will not go to war. And the majority of Arctic countries are members of NATO.

Yet the melting Arctic will have geostrategic consequences beyond helping a bunch of resource-fattened countries to get fatter. An obvious one is the potentially disruptive effect of new trade routes. Sailing along the coast of Siberia by the north-east passage, or Northern Sea Route (NSR), as Russians and mariners call it, cuts the distance between western Europe and east Asia by roughly a third. The passage is now open for four or five months a year and is getting more traffic. In 2010 only four ships used the NSR; last year 34 did, in both directions, including tankers, refrigerated vessels carrying fish and even a cruise liner.

Asia's big exporters, China, Japan and South Korea, are already investing in ice-capable vessels, or planning to do so. For Russia, which has big plans to develop the sea lane with trans-shipment hubs and other infrastructure, this is a double boon. It will help it get Arctic resources to market faster and also, as the NSR becomes increasingly viable, diversify its hydrocarbon-addicted economy.

There are risks in this, of dispute if not war, which will require management. What is good for Russia may be bad for Egypt, which last year earned over $5 billion in revenues from the Suez Canal, an alternative east-west shipping route. So it is good that the regional club, the Arctic Council, is showing promise. Under Scandinavian direction for the past half-decade, it has elicited an impressive amount of Arctic co-operation, including on scientific research, mapping and resource development.

Yet how to reconcile the environmental risks of the melting Arctic with the economic opportunities it will present? The shrinkage of the sea ice is no less a result of human hands than the ploughing of the prairies. It might even turn out as lucrative. But the costs will also be huge. Unique ecosystems, and perhaps many species, will be lost in a tide of environmental change. The cause is global pollution, and the risks it carries are likewise global. The Arctic, no longer distant or inviolable, has emerged, almost overnight, as a powerful symbol of the age of man.

Critical Thinking

1. What is the central point of view of this article?

2. What reasons are offered to support this point of view?

3. How does this article relate to articles 1, 3, and 11?

Asian Carp, Other Invasive Species Make a Splash

DAVID HARRISON

Last month, a commercial angler netted a 19-pound Asian carp on Chicago's Lake Calumet, part of the waterway system that connects the Mississippi River to Lake Michigan. The fisherman's haul was ominous, suggesting that the carp, a prehistoric-looking behemoth, had somehow gotten past an underwater electric fence designed to keep the species from entering the Great Lakes.

Since then, officials from the Great Lakes states have been fretting about the invasive fish, which has been working its way up the Mississippi River since it was first introduced in the Southeast almost 20 years ago, crowding out native species along the way. Asian carp are just the latest alien species to threaten the lakes, following other creatures such as the zebra and quagga mussel and the sea lamprey, all of which have found homes in the lakes' waters.

But the carp have attained a degree of notoriety that has eluded the other species, owing to their size and their distressing habit of thrashing out of the water at the sound of passing motorboats. Politicians have cast the fish as a voracious invader that would annihilate the lakes' ecosystems and cause the collapse of the $7 billion fishing and tourism industry.

Scientists have disputed that claim, noting that other invasive species already have depleted food sources in the Great Lakes so much that carp could find the waters to be inhospitable. The uproar nevertheless has brought renewed attention to the problem of invasive species, which have been washing into U.S. waters for years thanks to international shipping.

Michigan Attorney General Mike Cox has been particularly vocal, calling on Illinois to close locks and gates on the Chicago River that connect the Mississippi River with the lakes. But behind his rhetoric lies the disconcerting fact that states are powerless to combat most invasive species. Fish and mollusks don't respect state sovereignty, which makes it impossible for one state to completely seal off its waters from another. The best way to effectively control the spread of invasive species, advocates say, is for the federal government to step in.

In an attempt to force Washington's hand, Michigan, Minnesota, Ohio, Pennsylvania and Wisconsin filed a lawsuit against the federal government last week to force the U.S. Army Corps of Engineers to speed up its efforts to protect the lakes from the fish. "President Obama and the Army Corps of Engineers have failed to fight Asian carp aggressively," Cox said in a statement. "Asian carp will kill jobs and ruin our way of life."

This is not the first time Cox has used the courts to combat Asian carp. Late last year, Michigan sued Illinois in the U.S. Supreme Court to try to force Illinois to close the Chicago-area locks, which are crucial to shipping. Right now, carp are massed behind an electric fence and officials fear that all it would take is a power outage for them to flood into the lakes. The court declined to take the case.

The Illinois Chamber of Commerce has criticized the latest lawsuit, calling it politically motivated — Cox is running for governor in Michigan. The state of Illinois did not join the suit. Instead Illinois Governor Pat Quinn has suggested harvesting the fish and sending them to China, where they are considered a delicacy.

Big Eaters

Despite all the attention they've gotten recently, Asian carp are not the most dangerous invasive species to threaten the Great Lakes. Their impact pales in comparison to that of the quagga mussel which first showed up in the lakes in the late 1990s and has become ensconced there. The mussels reproduce rapidly and devour plankton, disrupting the lower levels of a food chain that native species rely upon.

"We're probably looking at one of the biggest invasions in the Great Lakes right now with the quagga mussels," says Gary Fahnenstiel, a senior ecologist at the National Oceanic and Atmospheric Administration.

Notwithstanding the dire warnings from politicians, Fahnenstiel says, should Asian carp make it to Lake Michigan they probably would have a difficult time competing with the quagga mussels for food. "They beat them to the buffet table, you might say," Fahnenstiel says.

Also, while state officials argue about sealing the lakes from the Mississippi, the biggest threat is likely to come from the north, where the Saint Lawrence Seaway connects the Great Lakes to the Atlantic Ocean. Many of the 185 invasive species in the lakes hitched rides in the cargo holds of ships sailing through the seaway.

Transatlantic cargo vessels often unload their cargo in New York or New Jersey, then take on ocean water to settle themselves. They travel through the seaway to the Great Lakes where they unload the ballast water and pick up cargo before embarking on their return trips. Over time, the mud and residual water that settles in the ships' holds becomes an ideal place for invasive species to settle before they get flushed out into the Great Lakes. That's how quagga and zebra mussels from Eastern Europe arrived on the shores of Michigan, Wisconsin and other Great Lakes states.

Heading West

Unfortunately, it now seems that the mussels' journey didn't end there. About three years ago, a recreational boater drove a mussel-encrusted boat from the Great Lakes to Lake Mead in Nevada. That introduced the species to the inland West, where it is continuing to spread as boaters move their craft from one waterway to the next. Quagga and zebra mussels have been found in Colorado, Nebraska and Utah.

They haven't come to Wyoming or Idaho yet, and those two states want to keep it that way. Recently, officials there started inspecting boats and requiring boaters to buy stickers certifying that their boats are mussel-free.

Yet officials in these states are afraid the mussels will inevitably evade their efforts. Like their Great Lakes counterparts, Western states are blaming what is widely believed to be an inadequate federal response.

"We're doing everything we can to protect our waterways here and the federal government is doing nothing," says Idaho state Representative Eric Anderson, who lives on a lake at the northern tip of the state. "To me it's an absolute crime."

One possible solution would be for the federal government to enforce strict rules on treating the ballast water of international cargo ships. Environmentalists have called on the U.S. Environmental Protection Agency, the Coast Guard or Congress to address the issue without success so far. Some also have suggested closing the Saint Lawrence Seaway to ocean ships, forcing them to transfer their cargo to lake vessels.

States have put in place a patchwork of their own ballast-water rules, which have been upheld in court challenges. But that system encourages shipping companies to find the state with the weakest regulations, putting all the other Great Lakes states at risk, says Nick Schroeck, executive director of the Great Lakes Environmental Law Center.

"Why can't we just get a national standard and be done with it?" Schroeck says. "That's what makes the most sense."

In 2008, the U.S. House of Representatives passed a bill that would have regulated treatment of ballast water, but the measure died in the Senate.

"I don't know that there's much of an appetite right now to take that up again," says Schroek. "You'd think that with the Asian carp situation there would be, but I guess they've got a lot on their plate."

Critical Thinking

1. What is an invasive species?
2. What challenges to governmental agencies does the Asian carp present?
3. What are some other examples of invasive species?

Harrison, David. From *Stateline.org*, July 30, 2010. Copyright © 2010 by Stateline.org. Reprinted by permission. Stateline.org is a nonpartisan, nonprofit news service of the Pew Center on the States that reports and analyzes trends in state policy.

UNIT 4

Political Economy

Unit Selections

Learning Outcomes

After reading this unit you should be able to:

• Describe the basic structure of the contemporary global political economy.

• Describe the changes in the globalized economy since 2008 and the perspectives on different types of capitalism, including the challenges facing US and European businesses.

• Compare and contrast the insights into the global political economy that the various case studies offer.

• Describe the central role of fossil fuels in the global political economy.

• Identify the challenges in managing the energy transition to alternative, sustainable sources.

• Assess your on-going effort at identifying your theory of international relations and how this unit changes/complements it.

Student Website

www.mhhe.com/cls

Internet References

Belfer Center for Science and International Affairs (BCSIA)
http://ksgwww.harvard.edu/csia

U.S. Agency for International Development
www.usaid.gov

The World Bank Group
www.worldbank.org

A defining characteristic of the twentieth century was the intense struggle between proponents of two economic ideologies. At the heart of the conflict was the question of what role government should play in the management of a country's economy. For some, the dominant capitalist economic system appeared to be organized primarily for the benefit of a few wealthy people. From their perspective, the masses were trapped in poverty, supplying cheap labor to further enrich the privileged elite. These critics argued that the capitalist system could be changed only by gaining control of the political system and having the state own the means of production. In striking contrast to this perspective, others argued that the best way to create wealth and eliminate poverty was through the profit motive, which encouraged entrepreneurs to create new products and businesses. An open and competitive marketplace, from this point of view, minimized government interference and was the best system for making decisions about production, wages, and the distribution of goods and services.

Violent conflict at times characterized the contest between capitalism and socialism/communism. The Russian and Chinese revolutions overthrew the old social order and created radical changes in the political and economic systems in these two important countries. The political structures that were created to support new systems of agricultural and industrial production (along with the centralized planning of virtually all aspects of economic activity) eliminated most private ownership of property. These two revolutions were, in short, unparalleled experiments in social engineering.

The economic collapse of the Soviet Union and the dramatic market reforms in China have recast the debate about how to best structure contemporary economic systems. Some believe that with the end of communism and the resulting participation of hundreds of millions of new consumers in the global market, an unprecedented era has been entered. Many have noted that this process of "globalization" is being accelerated by a revolution in communication and computer technologies. Proponents of this view argue that a new global economy is emerging that will ultimately eliminate national economic systems.

Others are less optimistic about the prospects of globalization. They argue that the creation of a single economic system where there are no boundaries to impede the flow of both capital and goods and services does not mean a closing of the gap between the world's rich and poor. Rather, they argue that multinational corporations, government financed enterprises, and global financial institutions will have fewer legal constraints on their behavior, and this will lead to not only increased risks of periodic financial crises but also greater exploitation of workers and the accelerated destruction of the environment. Further, these critics point out that drug trafficking and other criminal enterprises are adapting more rapidly than appropriate remedies can be developed.

© Frederic Charpentier/Alamy

The use of the term "political economy" for the title of this unit recognizes that economic and political systems are not separate. All economic systems have some type of marketplace where goods and services are bought and sold. Government (either national or international) regulates these transactions to some degree; that is, government sets the rules that regulate the marketplace.

One of the most important concepts in assessing the contemporary political economy is "development." For the purposes of this unit, the term *development* is defined as an improvement in the basic aspects of life: lower infant mortality rates, longer life expectancy, lower disease rates, higher rates of literacy, healthier diets, and improved sanitation. Judged by these standards, some countries are more developed than others. A fundamental question that a thoughtful reader must consider is whether globalization is resulting in increased development not only for a few people but also for all of those participating in the global political economy.

The unit is organized into three sections. The first is a general discussion of the globalized economy and some of the differing perspectives on this economic structure. Included in this discussion is a description of the Millennium Development Goals and a call for their redefinition to goals that are sustainable.

Following the first section are two sets of case studies. The first focuses on specific countries and/or economic sectors. The second examines the global energy sector. All of the case studies have been selected to challenge the reader to develop her or his own conclusions about the positive and negative consequences of the globalization process. Does the contemporary global political economy result in increasing the gap between economic winners and losers, or can everyone positively benefit from its system of wealth creation and distribution?

Go Glocal

Globalization used to be a one-way street that led away from America. Now high energy prices, political risk and technological shifts are bringing opportunity back home. Welcome to the era of localnomics.

RANA FOROOHAR

If there's a single company that illustrates the huge range of opportunities and challenges facing the U.S. economy today, it might be Caterpillar, the heavy-machinery giant based in Peoria, Ill. Like most other firms, Cat took a hit following the financial crisis. But since then, it's bounced back—and how. After a strong second quarter, the firm is on track for a second record-breaking year in a row and will likely sell $70 billion of its famous yellow earthmovers, tractors and mining equipment globally.

As products roll off the line at the recently expanded East Peoria factory, every one is marked with a flag that designates its final destination. There are a lot of Chinese, Indian and Australian flags. But there are plenty of American ones too, and their numbers are growing. "We put those flags on a few years back. I wanted our workers to understand that globalization isn't necessarily about someone taking your job," says Caterpillar CEO Doug Oberhelman. Indeed, Caterpillar thinks less about a single world market than many regional ones. The company is global, but where it can, it sources and produces locally, which is a natural hedge against everything from oil prices to currency risk to changing customer tastes. The bottom line: jobs and growth are split more or less equally between the U.S. and the rest of the world.

This isn't how globalization was supposed to work. Until quite recently, it was seen as a one-way street. American companies, which led the charge four decades or so ago into growing global markets, were its ambassadors, and American workers, whose wages and upward mobility were flattened, were the victims. The core idea was that globalization, technological innovation and unfettered free trade would erase historical and geographic boundaries, making the world ever more economically interconnected and alike. (Foreign-affairs writer Tom Friedman famously encapsulated this notion with the title of his book *The World Is Flat*.) In this vision, all nations would be on an even playing field, and the U.S. would come under more and more competitive pressure from eager upstart nations. It worked something like that from the mid-1980s to 2008, a period of unprecedented market calm that economists call the Great Moderation. Not so much anymore.

The truth is that the world was never as flat as we thought, and it's getting bumpier. The flaws in the premise are coming into focus. Consider the following: when energy prices and political risk go up, far-flung global supply chains make less economic sense. Low-wage workers in China look attractive—until robots operated by highly skilled laborers at home are able to do their jobs even more cheaply. Unfettered free trade seems

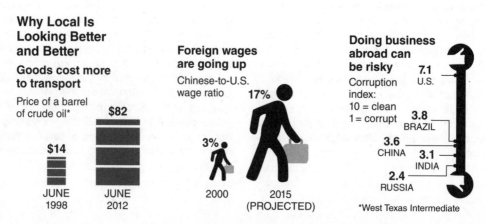

Sources: Energy Information Administration; Boston Consulting Group; Transparency International

great until the world's fastest-growing economies won't play by the rules of the game.

Since the financial crisis, fragmentation rather than unity has become the norm. You can see it everywhere, from the eurozone crisis to Communist Party infighting in China. In just the past few months, Argentines renationalized their biggest oil company, and several nations put capital controls on their currencies. Rich and poor regions from the E.U. to Japan and from China to Turkey are ramping up tariff increases, export restrictions and self-serving regulatory changes. World Trade Organization director general Pascal Lamy calls the rise in protectionism "alarming" and frets that we are headed back to the 1930s.

Given all the risks out there in the world, the 2% economy—in place of our historical 3%-to-4% yearly growth—has become the new normal for the foreseeable future. So is it possible to survive or even thrive in the new normal?

The answer is yes, but only if you know where to look and how to pivot. A key truism in this new age of volatility is that "everything local will take clear priority," says Peter Atwater, a financial researcher who studies social mood and the markets. That means much more focus on regional economic ecosystems and how to foster job creation at home instead of relying on global markets to raise all boats. In short, we need to be aware of the myths of globalization and how we can unleash untapped economic power closer to home. Here are some of the new rules of localnomics.

Rule No. 1
Hometown Bankers Know Best

During the Great Moderation, finance was the industry that ruled the world. It greased the wheels of globalization, spreading capital like pixie dust, and came to represent some 30% of total corporate profitability in the U.S., up from about 11% in 1975. Even after the financial crisis, banks represent a greater percentage of the economy than ever before. Slowly but surely, that's changing. The Dodd-Frank banking legislation, which is still under construction, may well be toughened in the wake of several new banking scandals. Regulators on both sides of the Atlantic are making a new push to rein in banks, and even the Fed may be considering ways to goose the mortgage market by forcing banks to lend.

As public cries for a safer financial system grow louder, it's quite likely that banks will eventually be broken up into smaller, more manageable pieces and forced to hold more capital, moving the industry away from global laissez-faire business as usual and toward a more traditional banking model.

Already, in Europe, banking is balkanizing along national lines. There, the rollback of the decade-long, cross-border integration of banking may turn out to be a bad thing, because it underscores a lack of faith in the euro and will expose deeper rifts in the continental economy as a whole.

But in the U.S., the shifts in banking may be a happy event. Too-big-to-manage institutions may be reined in or even split up, allowing smaller entities to focus on what they do best,

be it high-flying trading or local lending. (Being closer to the ground, such commercial banks will know their consumers better, which could mitigate risk and increase capital flows to small businesses.) As profit margins shrink, the fees banks charge may get higher. But banking may also become more the way it is in *It's a Wonderful Life,* "which has certain advantages in terms of reconnecting people back to their local communities," says Atwater.

30%: Percentage of U.S. corporate profitability accounted for by banks, a number likely to fall

Rule No. 2
Manufacturing Matters

As finance fades into the backdrop, manufacturing takes center stage, and each hometown accomplishment brings crucial carryover effects for the surrounding economy.

It's not being overly dramatic to say that the world is on the verge of a new industrial revolution as manufacturing regains its traditional role as a global growth driver. Manufacturing's share of global output is 17.4%, the highest it's been in over a decade. The growth has been driven not only by China but also by the U.S. (the second-biggest factory nation by output), which got a boost from the government's Detroit bailouts. Indeed, if the U.S. manufacturing economy were a nation, it would be the ninth largest in the world.

Government support is certainly one of the reasons for the boom. Manufacturing is politically very important because it's one of the few areas of the economy that is creating solid middle-income jobs. (See Rule No. 3. Export-oriented jobs pay 9% more on average.) The reason the latest U.S. jobs numbers aren't worse than they are is that Detroit has been holding its own. A weaker dollar and more-competitive global wage rates have also helped U.S. manufacturing, as have two other key trends: the rise of emerging markets, which buy a growing chunk of American exports, and a homegrown energy boom in shale gas and oil, which is goosing other parts of the economy like commercial construction and agriculture. This underscores manufacturing's important spillover effect for the rest of the economy. The Bureau of Economic Analysis calculates that every $1 of manufacturing GDP drives an incremental $1.42 of activity in the nonmanufacturing economy.

That fact was recently heralded by, of all people, Airbus CEO Fabrice Brégier in a July 2 announcement in Mobile, Ala., where the European aircraft giant is opening a new plant, citing a more competitive labor and growth climate in the U.S. as compared with Europe. It was a bitter day for the French and the Germans. Manufacturing is a key source of innovation, accounting for 70% of private-sector R&D and 90% of patents issued in the U.S. When a high-end manufacturing operation like Airbus sets up shop in a community, the benefits stay disproportionately within the local ecosystem. Spillover benefits decline by half when you go 700 miles beyond a manufacturing site, according to economist Wolfgang Keller.

So how to create more of these local hubs? Ensure access to a highly skilled labor force, connect educators to job creators, and help smaller businesses become suppliers to big firms. (See Rules 3 and 4.)

Rule No. 3
Blue Collar Jobs Go High-Tech

At the Caterpillar factory line in East Peoria, yet another important trend of the new normal is on display: labor bifurcation. Extremely cheap workers—robots—now do much of the tedious, physically demanding welding at the plant. Other work is done by high-end technicians, many of whom need computer skills to manipulate the robots. The number of human employees hasn't actually decreased over the past few years as the firm has added robots, but their skill level has increased. Welding is no longer a job for someone with only a high school degree. It's something that requires advanced in-house training or a community-college certification.

This situation is a microcosm of the global labor market. Even as Apple recently announced it would work with its supplier Foxconn to cut hours and boost pay for laborers in its Chinese factories, Foxconn itself has plans to deploy about 1 million new industrial robots in factories across the Middle Kingdom over the next three years. Chinese workers are getting more expensive, with pay rising about 17% a year, but their productivity isn't increasing quite so fast.

That's one reason the Boston Consulting Group estimates that within five years, as many as 3 million manufacturing jobs could come back to the U.S. But they won't be old-style, cheap-labor jobs. They'll be high-skill, high-demand positions.

Indeed, 63% of U.S. jobs will require postsecondary training by 2018. The U.S. economy will create more than 14 million new jobs over the next 10 years, but only for workers with at least a community-college degree. These jobs—for people like dental hygienists, electricians and entry-level software engineers—would allow millions of people to move from living on the edge to being middle class. The problem is that a low percentage of college students in the U.S.—30% at four-year colleges and 1 in 4 at two-year colleges—finish their degrees.

Some of that is about money, but it also reflects a relative lack of effort in the U.S. to connect educators with companies, particularly compared with what's being done in growth machines like Germany. The result is a mismatch between degrees and jobs that some economists, like Harvard's Rosabeth Moss Kanter, believe is responsible for as much as a third of the increase in unemployment since the Great Recession.

Tech-oriented community colleges with links to industry are an obvious solution, and the Obama Administration's latest budget proposes $8 billion to fund such institutions. But political gridlock has stalled the proposal. So businesses like Caterpillar and Siemens are taking matters into their own hands, setting up programs with local community colleges. (Cities, take note: these programs can be job magnets. Caterpillar set up an engineering design center in South Dakota because of a strong community-college system there.) High-tech service companies like Microsoft, Cisco and IBM are starting six-year combined high school and community-college programs designed to churn out qualified midlevel employees. One such program, P-Tech, a public-private partnership led by IBM, has been adopted by Mayor Michael Bloomberg of New York City and Mayor Rahm Emanuel of Chicago as part of an effort to boost employment and growth. Expect private companies to take on an even greater role in education while local leaders become major economic actors.

Help Wanted

By 2020, the world will have a surplus of **93 million** low-skilled workers

In advanced economies, 35 million

and a shortage of **85 million** high- and medium-skilled workers

In advanced economies, 18 million

Source: McKinsey & Co.

Rule No. 4
Closer Is Faster, and Faster Is Good

One of the most amazing things about globalization is that for all the press it gets, it's not nearly as broad-based as you would think. European business-school professor Pankaj Ghemawat's recent book *World 3.0* lays out in detail how the world was never really all that flat to begin with. His numbers, which tweak some official tallies to account for what he believes are various errors in calculation, are compelling: by his estimates, exports account for only about 20% of the world economy, cross-border foreign direct investment is only 9% of all investment, only 15% of venture-capital money is deployed outside home borders, less than 2% of all phone calls are international, less than a quarter of Internet traffic is routed across a national border and about 90% of the world's people will never leave the country in which they were born. "The challenge isn't too much globalization," says Ghemawat. "It's too little."

But that's a hard sell politically at a time when the dark side of globalization—namely, growing inequality within nations—has resulted in a strong sense that an elite group of people and companies are flying safely above all the troubles in the global economy while the majority of those on the ground suffer. This was brought front and center earlier this year when an Apple executive being interviewed by *The New York Times* about why the iPhone is mostly made outside the U.S. was quoted as saying, "We [Apple] don't have an obligation to solve America's problems."

The statement implied that not only should Apple put jobs wherever it was cheapest to do so globally (which is still mainly in Asia) but that this was a relatively seamless process. But the company's recent labor problems with its supplier Foxconn in China prove that doing business globally is hardly simple. And companies with complex global supply chains have not only labor issues to contend with but also natural disasters (remember how last year's tsunami and earthquakes in Japan disrupted auto-supply chains and sank industry growth for several quarters), high energy costs that make shipping more expensive and risks of corruption (as in the case of Walmart's scandal in Mexico). The laissez-faire attitude toward globalization that prevailed during the Great Moderation seems decidedly naive today. "For much of the last 15 years, it seemed like the attitude was that anytime you could find a lower cost anywhere in the global supply chain, you did it, with no thought of the difficulties or risks that things could go wrong," says Gene Sperling, head of the National Economic Council. "More U.S. companies are rethinking that calculation, and that holds open the promise of more location and insourcing here."

UPS, which moves 2% to 3% of global GDP annually, says it views supply-chain disruption as the No. 1 risk facing multinational businesses today. Mitch Free, who runs MFG.com, one of the world's largest online marketplaces for the manufacturing industry, says he's seeing a big trend toward regional and local insourcing not only because of risk mitigation but because consumer demand for all things to be newer, faster, better is shortening the life cycle for products (as little as six weeks from production to market in many cases). The trend toward hyperlocal product customization to suit individual customer needs in everything from jeans to ditch diggers also favors just-in-time, local supply chains. "The dynamic is not so much that American firms are bringing jobs back to the U.S. from abroad as it is that companies everywhere are bringing jobs and operations closer to where their customers are," says Free. "It's all about regionalization and localization rather than globalization."

Indeed, Caterpillar nurtures a network of about 2,000 local suppliers in the Illinois area alone, many of whom make a good living designing and producing customized goods for the firm—items destined for particular U.S. markets or specialized needs. Where things can be sourced locally, they are, in every Caterpillar territory internationally. "It allows us to better understand the needs of the local market and adjust the product

quickly," says Oberhelman, "but it's also a natural currency and energy-cost hedge."

Companies are also starting to realize that localnomics can help support their revenue growth. Suppliers can also buy things from their customers, and customers can be suppliers too. IBM, which sells a lot of its products and services to small and midsize firms, recently founded an online network to source more of its business needs from such companies in the U.S. Sixteen other companies, including Caterpillar, Dell and AMD, are taking part. Since the project, called Supplier Connection, went live in March, the companies have booked tens of millions of dollars in new business from small firms. This has an exponential growth effect. A recent study by the Center for an Urban Future found that most small businesses that became suppliers to multinationals saw their employment go up, on average, 164% within two years. For the large firms, it's just smart business; many of the small and medium-size enterprises they fuel will undoubtedly become customers at some point.

Rule No. 5
Local Leaders Must Step Up

Localnomics has great potential. But how much can governments do to nurture local economies? And how much should they do?

Economists on both sides of the political spectrum have begun to argue that we need to rethink laissez-faire trade policies when we are up against state-run capitalist systems in places like China, which openly gives preference to homegrown firms and limits foreign capital even as it exports massive amounts of cheap goods. Groups like the Council on Foreign Relations and the Information Technology and Innovation Foundation agree that the U.S. needs to get more aggressive about pursuing trade violations and punishing violators. Some economists call for sanctions or temporary tariffs.

There's even a push in some quarters for the U.S. to shed its Alan Greenspan–era taboo on economic planning. "Manufacturing is thriving in China, Germany, Sweden and Singapore only because their governments set up specific vocational institutes to prepare workers for new industries," wrote Kishore Mahbubani, head of the Lee Kuan Yew School of Public Policy in Singapore, in a *Financial Times* op-ed. "China has rapidly overtaken the U.S. in green technology because of a coordinated national response, not because Chinese businesses alone invested in green technology."

In the U.S., industrial policy remains a third-rail notion. (See what happens if you mention Solyndra.) And developing policies to support localnomics is tricky, as many factors that support it—currency, oil prices and even labor rates—can change quickly. In just the past couple of months, manufacturing in the U.S. has begun to soften a bit as Europe and emerging markets slow down.

There's a risk of pitting state against state and city against city in a battle for short-term gains that can easily become a

164%: Average employment growth for smaller businesses within two years of becoming a big-company supplier

race to the bottom. Caterpillar decided to put a new factory in Texas because of, according to a spokesman, "port access, proximity to supply base and a more positive business climate." A good chunk of that last factor has to do with superlow tax rates and nonunion labor. But states that try to outdo one another on tax cuts may eventually undermine infrastructure and services needed to fuel longer-term growth. And localnomics doesn't mean the pressure on labor ends. Caterpillar creates lots of jobs, but even as profits and revenue rise, the company is seeking worker concessions and is embroiled in union skirmishes.

Yet many economists continue to believe that localnomics is America's best hope for a real recovery. The McKinsey Global Institute recently published research noting that a large portion of the difference in economic growth between the U.S. and Europe is due to America's more vibrant cities and regional centers of growth, rather than just a few large capitals that generate most of the nation's wealth.

So count on cities to become more aggressive about protecting their economic future. Witness how Californian communities like San Bernardino and Stockton, driven to bankruptcy by mass foreclosures and frustrated by banks' reluctance to renegotiate mortgages, have announced plans to seize loans on underwater homes and forcibly restructure them. Or how Ohio and Tennessee are making sizable commitments to attract high-tech research institutions. Or how Seattle and Philadelphia are cementing niches in the global clean-tech arena. All these initiatives represent a bracing response to gridlocked politics as usual in Washington. And they also add up to local-centric approaches that may someday take us beyond the slow growth of a 2% economy.

Critical Thinking

1. How does this article describe the challenges facing the U.S. economy?
2. What reasons are offered to support this point of view?
3. What are the new rules of localnomics?
4. How does this article relate to Articles 1, 3 and 5?

issue of planning — economic planning not thought/well of

Innovation's Long March

State capitalism IS NOT — socialism

— growth in states with no seperation of political affairs + economics

After years in the dark, state-run economies such as China's are now cutting-edge. Is free-market capitalism obsolete?

Issues — starts talking about state capitalism

State has financial stake in private enterprise — requires results

— does indeed foster innovation

JOSHUA KURLANTZICK

Over the past five years, as much of the developed world has staggered through crisis, a new type of capitalism has emerged as a challenger to laissez-faire economics. Across much of the developing world, state capitalism—in which the state either owns companies or plays a major role in supporting or directing them—is replacing the free market. By 2015 state-owned wealth funds will control some $12 trillion in assets, far outpacing private investors. From 2004 through 2009, 120 state-owned companies made their debut on the *Forbes* list of the world's largest corporations, while 250 private companies fell off it. State companies now control about 90 percent of the world's oil and large percentages of other resources—a far cry from the past, when BP and ExxonMobil could dictate terms to the world.

Even as state capitalism has risen, some writers, business leaders, and politicians contend that such systems fail to encourage innovation, the key to long-term growth and economic wealth. Ian Bremmer, the president of Eurasia Group and author of *The End of the Free Market: Who Wins the War Between Corporations and States,* argues that state capitalists "fear creative destruction—for the same reason they fear all other forms of destruction that they cannot control." In *China 2030,* a recent analysis of China's economy, the World Bank concurred, noting that the country needs "a better innovation policy, [which] will begin with a redefinition of government's role in the national innovation system . . . [and] a competitive market system."

It is a mistake, however, to underestimate the innovative potential of state capitalism. Rising powers such as Brazil and India have used the levers of state power to promote innovation in critical, targeted sectors of their economies, producing world-class companies in the process. Despite its overspending on some state sectors, the Chinese government has nevertheless intervened effectively to promote skilled research and development in advanced industries. In so doing, the state capitalists have shattered the idea that they can't foster innovation to match developed economies. State capitalists' combination of government resources and innovation could put U.S. and European multinationals at a serious disadvantage competing around the globe.

State intervention in economic affairs runs against the established wisdom that the market is best for promoting ideas. At the same time, throughout history, the governments of many developed nations have actively fostered groundbreaking companies, from Bell Labs in the U.S. to Airbus in Europe.

Brazil is perhaps the best current example of how a state-capitalist system can build innovative industries. Successive Brazilian governments have intervened—with incentives, loans, and subsidies—to promote industries that otherwise would have needed long—term private investment to make them competitive with U.S. and European rivals. At the same time, Brazil preserved strong, independent management of state-backed firms, ensuring they did not become political boondoggles.

Three decades ago, for example, the Brazilian government gave aircraft manufacturer Embraer lucrative contracts and various subsidies, recognizing that it could potentially find a niche in producing smaller, regional aircraft. Private investors were dubious of Embraer's chances. Had it relied solely on private investment, the company probably would have failed; instead, it flourished, becoming the world's biggest maker of regional jets. Similarly, by investing in deep-sea drilling technology, Petrobras, a state oil company with an independent management board, has made itself competitive with multinational giants such as Chevron, Shell, and BP.

By picking industries it could dominate and supporting them even when private capital was scarce, Brazil has created internationally competitive companies in a range of industries, from aerospace to clean energy. Today the government often backs companies as a minority shareholder or through indirect vehicles, allowing for corporate independence while still helping companies make important investments in research and skills. Many of Brazil's state-backed companies have survived the global slump far better than multinationals because they can rely on government assistance to see them through.

Combining government support with a mandate for profitability and independent management has yielded successful businesses in other state-capitalist economies. Singapore has used government incentives to push companies to move into industries such as solar and other clean energies, which, although not necessarily profitable now, will be the emerging technologies of this century. A comprehensive 2009 paper by Harvard Business School looked at India's more than 40 state-owned science and engineering research laboratories, which have used a similar type of public-private collaboration. It found that the Indian state labs had "more U.S. patents than all domestic [Indian] private firms combined." In China, greater political interference in state-supported companies has been worse for profitability and innovation than in places like Brazil. And yet in recent years, China's score has steadily risen on the Global Competitiveness Index, a World Economic Forum ranking of nations, even as the score of the U.S. has dropped.

$360 BILLION: Total assets of China's 121 largest state-owned enterprises in 2002. $2.9 TRILLION: Total assets of China's 121 largest state-owned enterprises in 2010.

The rise of innovative state capitalists presents a more than formidable challenge to U.S. and European businesses; it could push multinationals out of some markets entirely. In oil and gas, for example, state companies already control most of the world's reserves, and as state companies like Petrobras become as innovative as multinationals, they will not require foreign companies for exploration, deepwater technology, or refining. In their own large domestic markets the innovative state capitalists will be able to match multinationals' technology, giving them dominance over mobile communications, high-end retailing, and other businesses.

Some developed countries may respond by either curbing state-capitalist companies' access to their markets or by intervening heavily in their own economies. Neither of these solutions is really viable. As the state capitalists' biggest companies expand their global operations, their technology, connections, and capital will be almost impossible to keep out. And aging, heavily indebted nations face huge challenges reforming their entitlement programs: They're in no position to pour the amount of resources into companies that Brazil, India, or China can.

Aging, indebted nations are in no position to pour the resources into companies that Brazil and India can.

Instead of trying to prevent—or worse, dismiss altogether—the rise of state-capitalist systems, U.S. and European companies and governments would do better to learn from them. Singapore offers one model of how the state can intervene in the economy without stifling entrepreneurship. The government there identifies industries that are critical to innovation and future technology, helps provide initial angel investments in small companies, tries to woo talented men and women from other countries who work in these industries, and uses state resources to ensure that universities focus on basic science research that will yield dividends in the future.

All these strategies require only modest state investment, and nothing on the scope of China's or Brazil's large-scale lending to state companies. The U.S. itself has effectively employed such policies in the past—before restrictive immigration policies kept skilled foreigners out, state and federal governments robbed funds from universities for other programs, and even the idea of the government helping foster new industries such as clean energy became politically toxic. (See Solyndra.)

Developed nations still possess a huge advantage over their emerging-market competitors: The U.S. and countries in Europe have mature, large venture capital firms, while places like India don't. In emerging markets, when innovative companies become large enough to leave the state's embrace, they may have nowhere to turn. Venture capital giants, on the other hand, can help small groundbreakers grow. This advantage can be enormous for countries like the U.S. And in a world where the emerging-market giants are learning to innovate, any advantage will be critical.

Critical Thinking

1. Article 1 introduces the concept of state capitalism. How does this article elaborate this concept?

2. What reasons does this article offer that question the future of free-market capitalism?

3. Describe the role of state companies in the global energy sector.

4. How does this article support or contradict Articles 1, 4, 5, and 16?

Joshua Kurlantzick is Fellow for Southeast Asia at the Council on Foreign Relations.

Government is going to have to start investing in other areas

cooperation between private + public sector will be good and reap benefits towards innovation

Why the World Isn't Flat

Globalization has bound people, countries, and markets closer than ever, rendering national borders relics of a bygone era—or so we're told. But a close look at the data reveals a world that's just a fraction as integrated as the one we thought we knew. In fact, more than 90 percent of all phone calls, Web traffic, and investment is local. What's more, even this small level of globalization could still slip away.

PANKAJ GHEMAWAT

Ideas will spread faster, leaping borders. Poor countries will have immediate access to information that was once restricted to the industrial world and traveled only slowly, if at all, beyond it. Entire electorates will learn things that once only a few bureaucrats knew. Small companies will offer services that previously only giants could provide. In all these ways, the communications revolution is profoundly democratic and liberating, leveling the imbalance between large and small, rich and poor. The global vision that Frances Cairncross predicted in her *Death of Distance* appears to be upon us. We seem to live in a world that is no longer a collection of isolated, "local" nations, effectively separated by high tariff walls, poor communications networks, and mutual suspicion. It's a world that, if you believe the most prominent proponents of globalization, is increasingly wired, informed, and, well, "flat."

It's an attractive idea. And if publishing trends are any indication, globalization is more than just a powerful economic and political transformation; it's a booming cottage industry. According to the U.S. Library of Congress's catalog, in the 1990s, about 500 books were published on globalization. Between 2000 and 2004, there were more than 4,000. In fact, between the mid-1990s and 2003, the rate of increase in globalization-related titles more than doubled every 18 months.

Amid all this clutter, several books on the subject have managed to attract significant attention. During a recent TV interview, the first question I was asked—quite earnestly—was why I still thought the world was round. The interviewer was referring of course to the thesis of *New York Times* columnist Thomas L. Friedman's bestselling book *The World Is Flat*. Friedman asserts that 10 forces—most of which enable connectivity and collaboration at a distance—are "flattening" the Earth and leveling a playing field of global competitiveness, the likes of which the world has never before seen.

It sounds compelling enough. But Friedman's assertions are simply the latest in a series of exaggerated visions that also include the "end of history" and the "convergence of tastes." Some writers in this vein view globalization as a good thing—an escape from the ancient tribal rifts that have divided humans, or an opportunity to sell the same thing to everyone on Earth.

Others lament its cancerous spread, a process at the end of which everyone will be eating the same fast food. Their arguments are mostly characterized by emotional rather than cerebral appeals, a reliance on prophecy, semiotic arousal (that is, treating everything as a sign), a focus on technology as the driver of change, an emphasis on education that creates "new" people, and perhaps above all, a clamor for attention. But they all have one thing in common: They're wrong.

In truth, the world is not nearly as connected as these writers would have us believe. Despite talk of a new, wired world where information, ideas, money, and people can move around the planet faster than ever before, just a fraction of what we consider globalization actually exists. The portrait that emerges from a hard look at the way companies, people, and states interact is a world that's only beginning to realize the potential of true global integration. And what these trend's backers won't tell you is that globalization's future is more fragile than you know.

The 10 Percent Presumption

The few cities that dominate international financial activity—Frankfurt, Hong Kong, London, New York—are at the height of modern global integration; which is to say, they are all relatively well connected with one another. But when you examine the numbers, the picture is one of extreme connectivity at the local level, not a flat world. What do such statistics reveal? Most types of economic activity that could be conducted either within or across borders turn out to still be quite domestically concentrated.

One favorite mantra from globalization champions is how "investment knows no boundaries." But how much of all the capital being invested around the world is conducted by companies outside of their home countries? The fact is, the total amount of the world's capital formation that is generated from foreign direct investment (FDI) has been less than 10 percent for the last three years for which data are available (2003–05). In other words, more than 90 percent of the fixed investment around the world is still domestic. And though merger waves can push the ratio higher, it has never reached 20 percent. In a thoroughly globalized environment, one would expect this number to be much higher—about 90 percent, by my calculation. And FDI isn't an odd or unrepresentative example.

The levels of internationalization associated with cross-border migration, telephone calls, management research and education, private charitable giving, patenting, stock investment, and trade, as a fraction of gross domestic product (GDP), all stand much closer to 10 percent than 100 percent. The biggest exception in absolute terms—the trade-to-GDP—recedes most of the way back down toward 20 percent if you adjust for certain kinds of double-counting. So if someone asked me to guess the internationalization level of some activity about which I had no particular information, I would guess it to be much closer to 10 percent—than to 100 percent. I call this the "10 Percent Presumption."

More broadly, these and other data on cross-border integration suggest a semiglobalized world, in which neither the bridges nor the barriers between countries can be ignored. From this perspective, the most astonishing aspect of various writings on globalization is the extent of exaggeration involved. In short, the levels of internationalization in the world today are roughly an order of magnitude lower than those implied by globalization proponents.

A Strong National Defense

If you buy into the more extreme views of the globalization triumphalists, you would expect to see a world where national borders are irrelevant, and where citizens increasingly view themselves as members of ever broader political entities. True, communications technologies have improved dramatically during the past 100 years. The cost of a three-minute telephone call from New York to London fell from $350 in 1930 to about 40 cents in 1999, and it is now approaching zero for voice-over-Internet telephony. And the Internet itself is just one of many newer forms of connectivity that have progressed several times faster than plain old telephone service. This pace of improvement has inspired excited proclamations about the pace of global integration. But it's a huge leap to go from predicting such changes to asserting that declining communication costs will obliterate the effects of distance. Although the barriers at borders have declined significantly, they haven't disappeared.

To see why, consider the Indian software industry—a favorite of Friedman and others. Friedman cites Nandan Nilekani, the CEO of the second-largest such firm, Infosys, as his muse for the notion of a flat world. But what Nilekani has pointed out privately is that while Indian software programmers can now serve the United States from India, access is assured, in part, by U.S. capital being invested—quite literally—in that outcome. In other words, the success of the Indian IT industry is not exempt from political and geographic constraints. The country of origin matters—even for capital, which is often considered stateless.

Or consider the largest Indian software firm, Tata Consultancy Services (TCS). Friedman has written at least two columns in *The New York Times* on TCS's Latin American operations: "[I]n today's world, having an Indian company led by a Hungarian-Uruguayan servicing American banks with Montevidean engineers managed by Indian technologists who have learned to eat Uruguayan veggie is just the new normal," Friedman writes. Perhaps. But the real question is why the company established those operations in the first place. Having worked as a strategy advisor to TCS since 2000,

I can testify that reasons related to the tyranny of time zones, languages, and the need for proximity to clients' local operations loomed large in that decision. This is a far cry from globalization proponents' oft-cited world in which geography, language, and distance don't matter.

Trade flows certainly bear that theory out. Consider Canadian-U.S. trade, the largest bilateral relationship of its kind in the world. In 1988, before the North American Free Trade Agreement (NAFTA) took effect, merchandise trade levels between Canadian provinces—that is, within the country—were estimated to be 20 times as large as their trade with similarly sized and similarly distant U.S. states. In other words, there was a built-in "home bias." Although NAFTA helped reduce this ratio of domestic to international trade—the home bias—to 10 to 1 by the mid-1990s, it still exceeds 5 to 1 today. And these ratios are just for merchandise; for services, the ratio is still several times larger. Clearly, the borders in our seemingly "borderless world" still matter to most people.

Geographical boundaries are so pervasive, they even extend to cyberspace. If there were one realm in which borders should be rendered meaningless and the globalization proponents should be correct in their overly optimistic models, it should be the Internet. Yet Web traffic within countries and regions has increased far faster than traffic between them. Just as in the real world, Internet links decay with distance. People across the world may be getting more connected, but they aren't connecting with each other. The average South Korean Web user may be spending several hours a day online—connected to the rest of the world in theory—but he is probably chatting with friends across town and e-mailing family across the country rather than meeting a fellow surfer in Los Angeles. We're more wired, but no more "global."

Just look at Google, which boasts of supporting more than 100 languages and, partly as a result, has recently been rated the most globalized website. But Google's operation in Russia (cofounder Sergey Brin's native country) reaches only 28 percent of the market there, versus 64 percent for the Russian market leader in search services, Yandex, and 53 percent for Rambler.

Indeed, these two local competitors account for 91 percent of the Russian market for online ads linked to Web searches. What has stymied Google's expansion into the Russian market? The biggest reason is the difficulty of designing a search engine to handle the linguistic complexities of the Russian language. In addition, these local competitors are more in tune with the Russian market, for example, developing payment methods through traditional banks to compensate for the dearth of credit cards. And, though Google has doubled its reach since 2003, it's had to set up a Moscow office in Russia and hire Russian software engineers, underlining the continued importance of physical location. Even now, borders between countries define—and constrain—our movements more than globalization breaks them down.

Turning Back the Clock

If globalization is an inadequate term for the current state of integration, there's an obvious rejoinder: Even if the world isn't quite flat today, it will be tomorrow. To respond, we have to look at trends rather than levels of integration at one point in time. The results are telling. Along a few dimensions, integration reached its all-time high many years ago. For example, rough calculations suggest that the number of long-term international migrants amounted to 3 percent of the world's population in 1900—the high-water mark of an earlier era of migration—versus 2.9 percent in 2005.

Along other dimensions, it's true that new records are being set. But this growth has happened only relatively recently, and only after long periods of stagnation and reversal. For example, FDI stocks divided by GDP peaked before World War I and didn't return to that level until the 1990s. Several economists have argued that the most remarkable development over the long term was the declining level of internationalization between the two World Wars. And despite the records being set, the current level of trade intensity falls far short of completeness, as the Canadian-U.S. trade data suggest. In fact, when trade economists look at these figures, they are amazed not at how much trade there is, but how little.

It's also useful to examine the considerable momentum that globalization proponents attribute to the constellation of policy changes that led many countries—particularly China, India, and the former Soviet Union—to engage more extensively with the international economy. One of the better-researched descriptions of these policy changes and their implications is provided by economists Jeffrey Sachs and Andrew Warner:

"The years between 1970 and 1995, and especially the last decade, have witnessed the most remarkable institutional harmonization and economic integration among nations in world history. While economic integration was increasing throughout the 1970s and 1980s, the extent of integration has come sharply into focus only since the collapse of communism in 1989. In 1995, one dominant global economic system is emerging."

Yes, such policy openings are important. But to paint them as a sea change is inaccurate at best. Remember the 10 Percent Presumption, and that integration is only beginning. The policies that we fickle humans enact are surprisingly reversible. Thus, Francis Fukuyama's *The End of History,* in which liberal democracy and technologically driven capitalism were supposed to have triumphed over other ideologies, seems quite quaint today. In the wake of Sept. 11, 2001, Samuel Huntington's *Clash of Civilizations* looks at least a bit more prescient. But even if you stay on the economic plane, as Sachs and Warner mostly do, you quickly see counterevidence to the supposed decisiveness of policy openings. The so-called Washington Consensus around market-friendly policies ran up against the 1997 Asian currency crisis and has since frayed substantially—for example, in the swing toward neopopulism across much of Latin America. In terms of economic outcomes, the number of countries—in Latin America, coastal Africa, and the former Soviet Union—that have dropped out of the "convergence club" (defined in terms of narrowing productivity and structural gaps vis-à-vis the advanced industrialized countries) is at least as impressive as the number of countries that have joined the club. At a multilateral level, the suspension of

the Doha round of trade talks in the summer of 2006—prompting *The Economist* to run a cover titled "The Future of Globalization" and depicting a beached wreck—is no promising omen. In addition, the recent wave of cross-border mergers and acquisitions seems to be encountering more protectionism, in a broader range of countries, than did the previous wave in the late 1990s.

Of course, given that sentiments in these respects have shifted in the past 10 years or so, there is a fair chance that they may shift yet again in the next decade. The point is, it's not only possible to turn back the clock on globalization-friendly policies, it's relatively easy to imagine it happening. Specifically, we have to entertain the possibility that deep international economic integration may be inherently incompatible with national sovereignty—especially given the tendency of voters in many countries, including advanced ones, to support more protectionism, rather than less. As Jeff Immelt, CEO of GE, put it in late 2006, "If you put globalization to a popular vote in the U.S., it would lose." And even if cross-border integration continues on its upward path, the road from here to there is unlikely to be either smooth or straight. There will be shocks and cycles, in all likelihood, and maybe even another period of stagnation or reversal that will endure for decades. It wouldn't be unprecedented.

The champions of globalization are describing a world that doesn't exist. It's a fine strategy to sell books and even describe a potential environment that may someday exist. Because such episodes of mass delusion tend to be relatively short-lived even when they do achieve broad currency, one might simply be tempted to wait this one out as well. But the stakes are far too high for that. Governments that buy into the flat world are likely to pay too much attention to the "golden straitjacket" that Friedman emphasized in his earlier book, *The Lexus and the Olive Tree,* which is supposed to ensure that economics matters more and more and politics less and less. Buying into this version of an integrated world—or worse, using it as a basis for policymaking—is not only unproductive; It is dangerous.

Critical Thinking

1. What is Pankaj Ghemawat's point of view?

2. What is the "10 percent presumption"?

3. How do Ghemawat's arguments against a "flat" world differ from Friedman's?

4. How does the point of view of this article fit into the discussion of alternative futures presented in Article 1?

PANKAJ GHEMAWAT is the Anselmo Rubiralta professor of global strategy at IESE Business School and the Jaime and Josefina Chua Tiampo professor of business administration at Harvard Business School. His new book is *Redefining Global Strategy* (Boston: Harvard Business School Press, September 2007).

Globalization and Its Contents

PETER MARBER

Ask ten different people to define the term "globalization" and you are likely to receive ten different answers. For many, the meaning of globalization has been shaped largely by media coverage of an angry opposition: from right-wing nationalist xenophobes and left-wing labor leaders who fear rampant economic competition from low-wage countries to social activists who see a conspiracy on the part of multinational corporations to seek profits no matter what the cost to local cultures and economic equality to environmentalists who believe the earth is being systematically ravaged by capitalism run amok. "Globalization"—as if it were a machine that could be turned off—has been presented as fundamentally flawed and dangerous. But "globalization" is a term that encompasses all cross-border interactions, whether economic, political, or cultural. And behind the negative headlines lies a story of human progress and promise that should make even the most pessimistic analysts view globalization in an entirely different light.

Two decades ago, globalization was hardly discussed. At the time, less than 15 percent of the world's population participated in true global trade. Pessimism colored discussions of the Third World, of "lesser developed" or "backward" countries. Pawns in the Cold War's global chess game, these countries conjured images of famine, overpopulation, military dictatorship, and general chaos. At the time, the prospect of the Soviet Union or Communist China integrating economically with the West, or of strongman regimes in Latin America or Asia abandoning central planning, seemed farfetched. The possibility of these countries making meaningful socioeconomic progress and attaining Western standards of living appeared utterly unrealistic. Yet the forces of globalization were already at work.

On average, people are living twice as long as they did a century ago. Moreover, the world's aggregate material infrastructure and productive capabilities are hundreds—if not thousands—of times greater than they were a hundred years ago.[1] Much of this acceleration has occurred since 1950, with a powerful upsurge in the last 25 years. No matter how one measures wealth—whether by means of economic, bio-social, or financial indicators—there have been gains in virtually every meaningful aspect of life in the last two generations, and the trend should continue upward at least through the middle of the twenty-first century.

Most people are living longer, healthier, fuller lives. This is most evident in poor parts of the world. For example, since 1950, life expectancy in emerging markets (countries with less than one-third the per capita income of the United States, or nearly 85 percent of the world's population) has increased by more than 50 percent, reaching levels the West enjoyed only two generations ago. These longevity gains are linked to lower infant mortality, better nutrition (including an 85 percent increase in daily caloric intake), improved sanitation, immunizations, and other public health advances.

Literacy rates in developing countries have also risen dramatically in the last 50 years. In 1950, only a third of the people in Eastern Europe and in parts of Latin [America] living in these countries (roughly 800 million) could read or write; today nearly two-thirds—more than 3.2 billion people—are literate. And while it took the United States and Great Britain more than 120 years to increase average formal education from 2 years in the early nineteenth century to 12 years by the mid-twentieth century, some fast-growing developing countries, like South Korea, have accomplished this feat in fewer than 40 years.

The world now has a far more educated population with greater intellectual capacity than at any other time in history. This is particularly clear in much of Asia, where mass public education has allowed billions of people to increase their productivity and integrate in the global economy as workers and consumers. Similar trends can be seen in Eastern Europe and in parts of Latin America. This increase in human capital has led to historic highs in economic output and financial assets per capita.

During the twentieth century, economic output in the United States and other West European countries often doubled in less than 30 years, and Japan's postwar economy doubled in less than 16 years. In recent decades, developing country economies have surged so quickly that some—like South Korea in the 1960s and 1970s, or China in recent years—have often doubled productive output in just 7 to 10 years.

We often forget that poverty was the human living standard for most of recorded history. Until approximately two hundred years ago, virtually everyone lived at a subsistence level. As the economist John Maynard Keynes wrote in 1931 in *Essays in Persuasion*: "From the earliest times of which we have record—back, say, to two thousand years before Christ—down to the beginning of the eighteenth century, there was no very great change in the standard life of the average man living in civilized centers of the earth. Ups and downs certainly. Visitation

	1950	2000	2050
Global Output, Per Capita ($)	586	6,666	15,155
Global Financial Market			
Capitalization, Per Capita ($)	158	13,333	75,000
Percent of Global GDP			
Emerging Markets	5	50	55
Industrial Countries	95	75	45
Life Expectancy (years)			
Emerging Markets	41	64	76
Industrial Countries	65	77	82
Daily Caloric Intake			
Emerging Markets	1200	2600	3000
Industrial Countries	2200	3100	3200
Infant Mortality (per 1000)			
Emerging Markets	140	65	10
Industrial Countries	30	8	4
Literacy Rate (per 100)			
Emerging Markets	33	64	90
Industrial Countries	95	98	99

*Sources: Bloomberg, World Bank, United Nations, and author's estimates.
Output and financial market capitalization figures are inflation-adjusted.*

Figure 1   Measured Global Progress, 1950–2050E.

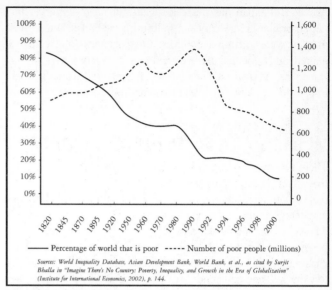

— Percentage of world that is poor   - - - - Number of poor people (millions)

*Sources: World Inequality Database, Asian Development Bank, World Bank, et al., as cited by Surjit
Bhalla in "Imagine There's No Country: Poverty, Inequality, and Growth in the Era of Globalization"
(Institute for International Economics, 2002), p. 144.*

Figure 2   Historic World Poverty Levels, 1820–2000.

of plague, famine, and war. Golden intervals. But no progressive violent change. This slow rate of progress was due to two reasons—to the remarkable absence of technical improvements and the failure of capital to accumulate." Beginning in the early nineteenth century, this picture began to change. The proportion of the world's population living in poverty declined from over 80 percent in 1820 to under 15 percent in 2000; moreover, the actual number of people living in poverty over that period declined, even as the world's population exploded from something over 1 billion to more than 6 billion.

The application of mass production technology, together with excess capital (or "profit") and a free market technologies— is at the root of our modern prosperity. Upon further examination, one can see the virtuous cycle that connects human progress, technology, and globalization. Let's take two countries, one being richer than the other. The richer country has a more educated workforce, with nearly 99 percent literacy, while the poor one has only 50 percent literacy. Due to its less educated workforce and lack of infrastructure, the poor country might only be able to participate in global trade through exporting commodities—let's say fruits and vegetables. The rich country grows fruits and vegetables as well, but it also produces clothing and light manufactured goods such as radios. In the classic Ricardo/Smith models of comparative advantage and free trade, the wealthy country should utilize its skilled workforce to produce more clothing and radios for domestic consumption and export, and it should import more fruits and vegetables from the poorer country. This would, in turn, provide the poorer country with capital to improve education and infrastructure.

As this trade pattern creates profits for both countries, human capital can be mutually developed. Eventually, the poorer country (by boosting literacy and education) should develop its own ability to produce clothes and radios. Over time, the wealthier country—having reinvested profits in higher education, research and development, etc.—will begin to produce higher-tech goods rather than clothes and radios, perhaps televisions and cars. At this stage, the wealthy country would export its cars and televisions, and import clothes and radios. In turn, the poorer country begins to import agricultural products from an even poorer third country while exporting clothing and radios to both countries. As participating countries make progress through crossborder trade and the continuous upgrading of their workforces, it follows naturally that patterns of labor and employment will evolve over time.

It is sometimes argued that free trade harms economic growth and the poor by causing job losses, particularly in wealthier countries. But trade liberalization works by encouraging a shift of labor and capital from import-competitive sectors to more dynamic export industries where comparative advantages lie. Therefore, the unemployment caused by open trade can be expected to be temporary, being offset by job creation in other export sectors (which often requires some transition time). Output losses due to this transitional unemployment should also be small relative to long-term gains in national income (and lower prices) due to production increases elsewhere. In other words, these short-term labor adjustments should be seen as lesser evils when compared to the costs of continued economic stagnation and isolation that occur without open trade.

The shifting U.S. labor pattern from low-wage agricultural labor to manufacturing to higher-paid office and service employment during the nineteenth and twentieth centuries resulted largely from trade. Similar shifts are now seen all over the globe. In the 1950 and 1960s, the United States imported electronics from Japan, and exported cars and other heavy goods. In the 1970s, we began importing small cars from Japan. In the last 30-odd years, Japan has seen its dominance in electronics and economy cars wither amid competition from China and South

Korea. But Japan has made a successful push upmarket into larger, pricier luxury cars and sport utility vehicles. While these markets were shifting over the last three decades, jobs were lost, gained, and relocated in the United States and abroad. But living standards in America, Japan, South Korea, and China have all improved dramatically over that same time.

Working Less, Producing More

There is a growing consensus that international trade has a positive effect on per capita income. A 1999 World Bank study estimates that increasing the ratio of trade to national output by one percentage point raises per capita income by between 0.5 and 2 percent.[2] But the most dramatic illustration of how greater prosperity is spread through globalization is by our increased purchasing power. Ultimately, what determines wealth is the ability to work less and consume more. The time needed for an average American worker to earn the purchase price of various goods and services decreased dramatically during the twentieth century.

In 1919, it took an American worker 30 minutes of labor to earn enough to buy a pound of ground beef. This number dropped to 23 minutes in 1950, 11 minutes in 1975, and 6 minutes in 1997.[3] But this downward trend is even more impressive with respect to manufactured goods and services. For example, in 1895 the list price for an American-made bicycle in the Montgomery Ward catalog was $65. Today an American can buy a Chinese-manufactured 21-speed bike at any mass retailer for the same amount. But an average American needed to work some 260 hours in 1895 to earn the purchase price of the old bicycle, whereas it would take the average worker less than 5 hours to earn enough to buy today's bicycle.[4] In our own lifetimes, the costs of goods and services, everything from televisions to household appliances to telephone calls, computers, and airplane travel have plummeted relative to income—and not just in the United States.

Around the world, both basic commodities and items once considered luxury items now fill store shelves and pantries as increasing output and income have lifted most people above the subsistence level. The 50 most populous countries average more than 95 televisions per 100 households. In the 25 wealthiest countries, there are approximately 450 automobiles per 1,000 people, and China is now among the fastest-growing markets for cars, clothes, computers, cellular phones, and hundreds of household items.

This deflationary effect has also led to a radically improved quality of life. In 1870, the average American worker labored 3,069 hours per year—or six 10-hour days a week. By 1950, the average hours worked had fallen to 2,075.[5] Today, that number is closer to 1,730.[6] This pattern has been repeated around the world. In 1960, the average Japanese worker toiled 2,432 hours a year over a six-day work week; by 1988, this figure had dropped to 2,111 hours a year, and by 2000 it was down to 1,878 hours. There were even more dramatic reductions in European countries like France, Germany, and Sweden.[7] The Nobel Prize–winning economist Robert William Fogel estimates that the average American's lifetime working hours will have declined from 182,100 in 1880 to a projected 75,900 by 2040, with similar trends in other wealthy industrial countries. Fogel notes that while work took up 60 percent of an American's life in 1870, by 1990 it only took up about 30 percent. Between 1880 and 1990, the average American's cumulative lifetime leisure time swelled from 48,300 hours to a remarkable 246,000 hours, or 22 years.[8] This is a pattern of improvement in the human condition that we first saw in the industrialized West and then in Japan, and which is now spreading to dozens of developing countries that are integrating into the global economy.

A Thriving Middle Class

The recent surge in progress is certainly tied to technological advances, but it is also due to the adoption of free-market practices. Cross-border trade has ballooned by a factor of 20 over the past 50 years and now accounts for more than 20 percent of global output, according to the World Bank. Indeed, trade—which grew twice as fast as global output in the 1990s—will continue to drive economic specialization and growth. The global economy is becoming more sophisticated, segmented, and diversified.

The adoption of free-market practices has gone hand-in-hand with greater political freedoms. At the beginning of the twentieth century, less than 10 percent of the world's population had the right to vote, according to Freedom House. By 1950, approximately 35 percent of the global population in less than a quarter of the world's countries enjoyed this right. By 2000, more than two-thirds of the world's countries had implemented universal suffrage.

These symbiotic developments have helped completely recompose the world's "middle class"—those with a per capita income of roughly $10–40 per day, adjusted for inflation and purchasing power parity (PPP). According to the United Nations, in 1960 two-thirds of the world's middle-class citizens lived in the industrialized world—that is, in the United States, Canada, Western Europe, Japan, and Australia. By 1980, over 60 percent of the global middle class lived in developing countries, and by 2000 this number had reached a remarkable 83 percent. It is anticipated that India and China combined could easily produce middle classes of 400–800 million people over the next two generations—roughly the size of the current middle-class populations of the United States, Western Europe, and Japan combined.

A thriving middle class is an important component of economic, political, and social stability that comes with globalization. According to the World Bank, a higher share of income for the middle class is associated with increased national income and growth, improved health, better infrastructure, sounder economic policies, less instability and civil war, and more social modernization and democracy. There are numerous studies that also suggest that increasing wealth promotes gender equality, greater voter participation, income equality, greater concern for the environment, and more transparency in the business and political arenas, all of the quality-of-life issues that concern globalization skeptics.[9]

Measuring Inequality

Even if they concede that the world is wealthier overall, many critics of globalization cite the dangers of growing income inequality. Although the science of analyzing such long-term trends is far from perfect, there are indicators that point toward measurable progress even on this front.[10] The preoccupation with income or gross national product (GNP) as the sole measure of progress is unfortunate. Income is one measure of wealth, but not the only one. And income comparisons do not always reflect informal or unreported economic activity, which tends to be more prevalent in poor countries.

Many social scientists use Gini coefficients (a measure of income dispersion between and within countries) to bolster their arguments about inequality. The lower the Gini figure (between one and zero), the more equal income distribution tends to be. Unfortunately, the Gini index does not take into consideration purchasing power parity, the age dispersion of a population, and other variables that affect the overall picture. When adjusted for PPP, the Gini index for world income distribution decreased from 0.59 to 0.52 between 1965 and 1997, an improvement of nearly 12 percent.[11] Poverty rate trends are also cited by condemners of globalization, but this approach is problematic as well. The impoverished are often defined as those who earn 50 percent less than the median income in a country. But because 50 percent of median American income is very different than 50 percent of median income in Bangladesh, poverty rates may not tell us as much about human progress as we might think.

We can better gauge human progress by examining broader trends in bio-social development than income-centered analyses. A yardstick like the United Nations Development Program's human development index (HDI), for example, which looks at not only income but also life expectancy and education (including literacy and school enrollment), with the higher numbers denoting greater development, provides a clearer picture of global well-being:

	1960	1993	2002
OECD Countries	.80	.91	.91
Developing Countries	.26	.56	.70
Least Developed Countries	.16	.33	.44

What these numbers show is not only that human development has improved overall but that differentials between rich and poor countries are closing. While the HDI figure for wealthy OECD countries in 1960 was five times greater than that for the least developed countries (and three times higher than that for developing countries), those gaps were nearly halved by 1993. And in the most intense period of recent globalization, from 1993 to 2002, these gaps closed even further.

This by no means negates the reality of poverty in many parts of the world. There are still an estimated 1 billion people living in "abject" poverty today, but the World Bank estimates that this number should decline by 50 percent by 2015, if current growth trends hold.

Potholes on the Road to Globalization

The great gains and momentum of the last 25 years should not be seen as sufficient or irreversible. There are still formidable impediments to continued progress, the four most serious being protectionism, armed conflict, environmental stress, and demographic imbalances.

- *Protectionism.* One of the responses to globalization has been the attempt to pull inward, to save traditional industries and cultures, and to expel foreigners and foreign ideas. In India, consumers have protested against McDonald's restaurants for violating Hindu dietary laws. In France, angry farmers have uprooted genetically engineered crops, saying they threatened domestic control over food production.

  Possibly the most harmful protectionism today relates to global agricultural policy. Farming subsidies in wealthy countries now total approximately $350 billion a year, or seven times the $50 billion that such countries provide annually in foreign aid to the developing world.[12] Global trade policies may exclude developing countries from $700 billion in commerce annually, denying them not only needed foreign currency but also the commercial and social interaction necessary to bio-social progress.[13]

  Protectionism in the form of tariffs, rigid labor and immigration laws, capital controls, and regressive tax structures also should be resisted. Wealthy countries should not cling to old industries like apparel or agriculture; it is far more profitable, economically and socially, to look forward and outward, to focus on growing higher-skill industries—like aviation, pharmaceuticals, and entertainment—and to embrace new markets. In turn, poorer countries have generally grown richer through economic interaction with foreign countries, by refocusing nationalistic energies and policies toward future-oriented, internationally engaged commercial activity. The late-twentieth-century march away from closed economies has improved the lives of billions of people. To bow to nationalistic calls for protectionist policies could slow and even reverse this momentum.

- *Armed Conflict.* Countries cannot compete economically, cultivate human capital, or develop financial markets in the midst of armed conflict. According to the Stockholm International Peace Research Institute, there were 57 major armed conflicts in 45 different locations between 1990 and 2001; all but 3 of these were civil wars, which inflict deep economic damage and stunt development. In addition to ongoing civil wars, there are a number of potential cross-border powder kegs (beyond the recent U.S. invasions of Afghanistan and Iraq): Kashmir, over which nuclearized India and Pakistan have been at odds for decades; Taiwan, over which China claims sovereignty; Israel and its Arab neighbors; and the Korean peninsula. The economic, political, and cultural uncertainty surrounding these areas of potential conflict restricts the flow of capital, and paralyzes businesses, investors, and consumers.

To the extent that defense budgets continue to grow in tandem with global tensions and economic resources are used for military purposes, there will be fewer resources devoted to the development of human capital and economic competitiveness.

- *Environmental Stress.* There is no getting around the fact that the success of globalization is underscored by dramatic increases in consumption. With increased consumption comes environmental degradation. Damage to the environment, current or projected, can impede economic progress in many ways. Climatic changes attributed to greenhouse gas emissions and pressure on natural resources are serious problems. Resource scarcity is only one issue we will have to confront as 2–3 billion more people consume like middle-class Americans over the next 50 years. In the face of these environmental dangers, a host of new regulations may be enacted locally or globally. Increased environmental awareness among wealthier populations may lead to domestic policies that will raise costs to businesses and consumers, which in turn could curb economic expansion.

One step in the right direction would be increased public spending on alternative and renewable energy sources in the wealthier countries. The world is clearly underpowered, and the need for diversified energy grows as we speak. The benefits of a burgeoning alternative energy sector could be multiplicative. First, it might spur new economic growth areas for employment in rich countries, supplying them with potential technologies for export while reducing their reliance on foreign oil. Second, it might encourage developing countries that are over-reliant on oil exports to develop and modernize their economies and societies. Third, it would allow developing countries to build their infrastructures with a more diversified, sustainable energy approach than the first wave of industrializing countries.

- *Demographic Imbalances.* There are sharply contrasting population trends around the globe: developing nations are experiencing a youth bulge while industrialized countries are aging rapidly. This divergence may present a variety of challenges to globalization. In poorer developing countries, the youth bulge equals economic opportunity but is also potentially disruptive. In more than 50 of these countries, 50 percent of the population is under the age of 25. In some cases, half the population is under 20, and in extreme cases, even younger. These developing nations are also among the poorest, the fastest urbanizing, and the least politically or institutionally developed, making them susceptible to violence and instability. The large number of unemployed, disenfranchised young men in these countries may explain the growth of Islamic fundamentalism and the existence of pillaging bands of armed warriors in sub-Saharan Africa. Large young populations may also lead to unregulated, unlawful migration that can create long-lasting instability.[14]

While the youth bulge can cause problems that derail global progress, the richest countries may fall victim to their past success. Prosperity, while providing more lifestyle choices and wellness, also results in lower birth rates and increasing longevity which could dampen long-term economic demand. The aging of wealthier populations also stresses public pension schemes that were conceived under different demographic circumstances—eras of robust population and consumption growth. In economies where populations are stagnant or shrinking, the specter of lengthy "aging recessions"—characterized by vicious cycles of falling demand for consumer goods (and deflation), collapsing asset values (including real estate), shrinking corporate profits, deteriorating household and financial institution balance sheets, weakening currencies, and soaring budget pressures—looms large.

Preparing for the Best, Not the Worst

Globalization and its major engines—burgeoning human capital, freer markets, increasing cross-border interaction—have created a new world order that has incited passionate debate, pro and con. However, both sides have more in common than one might imagine.

First, if human capital is a key component of improved living standards, it is arguable that increased spending on education should become a priority in rich and poor countries alike. Wealthier nations continually need to boost productivity and comparative advantage, while poorer countries need to develop skills to compete in the global economy. By adding to the numbers of the educated, there will be a wider base of workers and consumers to contribute to the virtuous cycle of prosperity we have witnessed in the last 50 years.

Second, boosting human capital in poor countries through increased financial and technical aid should also help broaden the marketplace in terms of workers and consumers. Appropriating an extra $100 billion in aid each year—a drop in the bucket for the 20 richest countries—could help some 2 billion people overcome their daily struggles with malnutrition, HIV/AIDS, malaria, and dirty drinking water, thereby increasing the number of healthy, productive workers and consumers.

Third, reorienting wealthy country subsidies away from low-tech areas like agriculture and mining toward higher-tech industries (including alternative energy development) would accelerate comparative advantage and stimulate greater trade. With wealthy countries focusing on higher-value-added industries for domestic consumption and export, poorer countries could pick up the slack in lower-skilled sectors where they can begin to engage the global economy. Over time, the poorer countries would become larger markets for goods and services. This, along with the two attitudinal and policy shifts mentioned above, could have a positive effect on the well-being of the world's population.

Even with its positive trends, globalization is not a perfect process. It is not a panacea for every problem for every person at every moment in time. It is a messy, complicated web of inter-dependent relationships, some long-term, some fleeting. But globalization is too often cited as creating a variety of human miseries such as sweatshop labor, civil war, and corruption—as if such ills never existed before 1980. Poverty is more at the root of such miseries. That is why the wholesale rejection of globalization—without acknowledging its tremendously posi-tive record in alleviating poverty—is shortsighted. Indeed, one could see how simply embracing globalization as inevitable—rather than debating its definition and purported shortcom-ings—could potentially foster more cross-border coordination on a variety of issues such as drug trafficking, ethnic cleansing, illegal immigration, famine, epidemic disease, environmental stress, and terrorism.

Emotion and confusion have unfortunately tainted the glo-balization debate both in the United States and abroad, and the focus is often on anecdotal successes or failures. Anxieties and economies may ebb and flow in the short run, but the responsi-bility to manage these progressive evolutions and revolutions—with worldwide human prosperity as the goal—should be our consistent aim in both government and the marketplace.

Notes

Many of the issues and arguments presented here in abbrevi-ated form are examined at greater length in my book, *Money Changes Everything: How Global Prosperity Is Reshaping Our Needs, Values, and Lifestyles* (Upper Saddle River, NJ: FT Pren-tice Hall, 2003).

1. See Angus Maddison, *Monitoring the World Economy: 1820–1992* (Paris: OECD, 1995).

2. Jeffrey A. Frankel and David Romer, "Does Trade Growth Cause Growth?" *American Economic Review,* vol. 89 (June 1999), pp. 379–99.

3. W. Michael Cox and Richard Alm, *Time Well Spent: The Declining Real Cost of Living in America*, annual report (Dallas: Federal Reserve Bank, 1997), p. 4.

4. Based on average U.S. industrial wages of approximately $15 per hour in 2000.

5. W. Michael Cox and Richard Alm, *These Are the Good Old Days: A Report on US Living Standards*, annual report (Dallas: Federal Reserve Bank, 1994), p. 7.

6. Robert William Fogel, *The Fourth Great Awakening and the Future of Egalitarianism* (Chicago: University of Chicago Press, 2000), p. 185.

7. Ibid., p. 186.

8. Ibid., pp. 184–90.

9. See Marber, *Money Changes Everything*. For more on specific shifts in attitudes and values relative to economic development, the University of Michigan's Ron Inglehart's seminal Human Values Surveys are an invaluable resource.

10. For a balanced study of this subject, see Arne Mechoir, Kjetil Telle, and Henrik Wiig, *Globalisation and Inequality: World Income and Living Standards, 1960–1998*, Norwegian Ministry of Foreign Affairs, Report 6B:2000, October 2000, available at http://odin.dep.no/archive/udvedlegg/01/01/rev_016.pdf.

11. Ibid., p. 14.

12. James Wolfensohn, "How Rich Countries Keep the Rest of the World in Poverty," *Irish Independent*, September 30, 2002.

13. Ibid.

14. See Michael Teitelbaum, "Are North/South Population Growth Differentials a Prelude to Conflict?" at http://csis.org/gai/Graying/speeches/teitelbaum.html.

Critical Thinking

1. What is Peter Marber's point of view?

2. What reasons does he offer to support his point of view?

3. Identify some of the "potholes" to the continuation of globalization.

4. How is this article related to articles 1 and 4?

PETER MARBER is an author, professional money manager, and faculty member at the School of International and Public Affairs at Columbia University.

The Future of History: Can Liberal Democracy Survive the Decline of the Middle Class?

Francis Fukuyama

Something strange is going on in the world today. The global financial crisis that began in 2008 and the ongoing crisis of the euro are both products of the model of lightly regulated financial capitalism that emerged over the past three decades. Yet despite widespread anger at Wall Street bailouts, there has been no great upsurge of left-wing American populism in response. It is conceivable that the Occupy Wall Street movement will gain traction, but the most dynamic recent populist movement to date has been the right-wing Tea Party, whose main target is the regulatory state that seeks to protect ordinary people from financial speculators. Something similar is true in Europe as well, where the left is anemic and right-wing populist parties are on the move.

There are several reasons for this lack of left-wing mobilization, but chief among them is a failure in the realm of ideas. For the past generation, the ideological high ground on economic issues has been held by a libertarian right. The left has not been able to make a plausible case for an agenda other than a return to an unaffordable form of old-fashioned social democracy. This absence of a plausible progressive counter-narrative is unhealthy, because competition is good for intellectual—debate just as it is for economic activity. And serious intellectual debate is urgently needed, since the current form of globalized capitalism is eroding the middle-class social base on which liberal democracy rests.

The Democratic Wave

Social forces and conditions do not simply "determine" ideologies, as Karl Marx once maintained, but ideas do not become powerful unless they speak to the concerns of large numbers of ordinary people. Liberal democracy is the default ideology around much of the world today in part because it responds to and is facilitated by certain socioeconomic structures. Changes in those structures may have ideological consequences, just as ideological changes may have socio-economic consequences.

Almost all the powerful ideas that shaped human societies up until the past 300 years were religious in nature, with the important exception of Confucianism in China. The first major secular ideology to have a lasting worldwide effect was liberalism, a doctrine associated with the rise of first a commercial and then an industrial middle class in certain parts of Europe in the seventeenth century. (By "middle class," I mean people who are neither at the top nor at the bottom of their societies in terms of income, who have received at least a secondary education, and who own either real property, durable goods, or their own businesses.)

As enunciated by classic thinkers such as Locke, Montesquieu, and Mill, liberalism holds that the legitimacy of state authority derives from the state's ability to protect the individual rights of its citizens and that state power needs to be limited by the adherence to law. One of the fundamental rights to be protected is that of private property; England's Glorious Revolution of 1688–89 was critical to the development of modern liberalism because it first established the constitutional principle that the state could not legitimately tax its citizens without their consent.

At first, liberalism did not necessarily imply democracy. The Whigs who supported the constitutional settlement of 1689 tended to be the wealthiest property owners in England; the parliament of that period represented less than ten percent of the whole population. Many classic liberals, including Mill, were highly skeptical of the virtues of democracy: they believed that responsible political participation required education and a stake in society—that is, property ownership. Up through the end of the nineteenth century, the franchise was limited by property and educational requirements in virtually all parts of Europe. Andrew

Jackson's election as U.S. president in 1828 and his subsequent abolition of property requirements for voting, at least for white males, thus marked an important early victory for a more robust democratic principle. In Europe, the exclusion of the vast majority of the population from political power and the rise of an industrial working class paved the way for Marxism. The Communist Manifesto was published in 1848, the same year that revolutions spread to all the major European countries save the United Kingdom. And so began a century of competition for the leadership of the democratic movement between communists, who were willing to jettison procedural democracy (multiparty elections) in favor of what they believed was substantive democracy (economic redistribution), and liberal democrats, who believed in expanding political participation while maintaining a rule of law protecting individual rights, including property rights.

At stake was the allegiance of the new industrial working class. Early Marxists believed they would win by sheer force of numbers: as the franchise was expanded in the late nineteenth century, parties such as the United Kingdom's Labour and Germany's Social Democrats grew by leaps and bounds and threatened the hegemony of both conservatives and traditional liberals. The rise of the working class was fiercely resisted, often by nondemocratic means; the communists and many socialists, in turn, abandoned formal democracy in favor of a direct seizure of power.

Throughout the first half of the twentieth century, there was a strong consensus on the progressive left that some form of socialism—government control of the commanding heights of the economy in order to ensure an egalitarian distribution of wealth—was unavoidable for all advanced countries. Even a conservative economist such as Joseph Schumpeter could write in his 1942 book, *Capitalism, Socialism, and Democracy*, that socialism would emerge victorious because capitalist society was culturally self-undermining. Socialism was believed to represent the will and interests of the vast majority of people in modern societies. Yet even as the great ideological conflicts of the twentieth century played themselves out on a political and military level, critical changes were happening on a social level that undermined the Marxist scenario. First, the real living standards of the industrial working class kept rising, to the point where many workers or their children were able to join the middle class. Second, the relative size of the working class stopped growing and actually began to decline, particularly in the second half of the twentieth century, when services began to displace manufacturing in what were labeled "postindustrial" economies. Finally, a new group of poor or disadvantaged people emerged below the industrial working class—a heterogeneous mixture of racial and ethnic minorities, recent immigrants, and socially excluded groups, such as women, gays, and the disabled. As a result of these changes, in most industrialized societies, the old working class has become just another domestic interest group, one using the political power of trade unions to protect the hard-won gains of an earlier era. Economic class, moreover, turned out not to be a great banner under which to mobilize populations in advanced industrial countries for political action. The Second International got a rude wake-up call in 1914, when the working classes of Europe abandoned calls for class warfare and lined up behind conservative leaders preaching nationalist slogans, a pattern that persists to the present day. Many Marxists tried to explain this, according to the scholar Ernest Gellner, by what he dubbed the "wrong address theory":

> Just as extreme Shi'ite Muslims hold that Archangel Gabriel made a mistake, delivering the Message to Mohamed when it was intended for Ali, so Marxists basically like to think that the spirit of history or human consciousness made a terrible boob. The awakening message was intended for classes, but by some terrible postal error was delivered to nations.

Gellner went on to argue that religion serves a function similar to nationalism in the contemporary Middle East: it mobilizes people effectively because it has a spiritual and emotional content that class consciousness does not. Just as European nationalism was driven by the shift of Europeans from the countryside to cities in the late nineteenth century, so, too, Islamism is a reaction to the urbanization and displacement taking place in contemporary Middle Eastern societies. Marx's letter will never be delivered to the address marked "class." Marx believed that the middle class, or at least the capital-owning slice of it that he called the bourgeoisie, would always remain a small and privileged minority in modern societies. What happened instead was that the bourgeoisie and the middle class more generally ended up constituting the vast majority of the populations of most advanced countries, posing problems for socialism. From the days of Aristotle, thinkers have believed that stable democracy rests on a broad middle class and that societies with extremes of wealth and poverty are susceptible either to oligarchic domination or populist revolution. When much of the developed world succeeded in creating middle-class societies, the appeal of Marxism vanished. The only places where leftist radicalism persists as a powerful force are in highly unequal areas of the world, such as parts of Latin America, Nepal, and the impoverished regions of eastern India.

What the political scientist Samuel Huntington labeled the "third wave" of global democratization, which began in southern Europe in the 1970s and culminated in the fall of communism in Eastern Europe in 1989, increased the number of electoral democracies around the world from around 45 in 1970 to more than 120 by the late 1990s. Economic growth has led to the emergence of new middle classes in countries such as Brazil, India, Indonesia, South Africa, and Turkey. As the economist Moises Naim has pointed out, these middle classes are relatively well educated, own property, and are technologically connected to the outside world.

They are demanding of their governments and mobilize easily as a result of their access to technology. It should not be surprising that the chief instigators of the Arab Spring uprisings were well-educated Tunisians and Egyptians whose expectations for jobs and political participation were stymied by the dictatorships under which they lived.

Middle-class people do not necessarily support democracy in principle: like everyone else, they are self-interested actors who want to protect their property and position. In countries such as China and Thailand, many middle-class people feel threatened by the redistributive demands of the poor and hence have lined up in support of authoritarian governments that protect their class interests. Nor is it the case that democracies necessarily meet the expectations of their own middle classes, and when they do not, the middle classes can become restive.

The Least Bad Alternative?

There is today a broad global consensus about the legitimacy, at least in principle, of liberal democracy. In the words of the economist Amartya Sen, "While democracy is not yet universally practiced, nor indeed uniformly accepted, in the general climate of world opinion, democratic governance has now achieved the status of being taken to be generally right." It is most broadly accepted in countries that have reached a level of material prosperity sufficient to allow a majority of their citizens to think of themselves as middle class, which is why there tends to be a correlation between high levels of—development and stable democracy.

Some societies, such as Iran and Saudi Arabia, reject liberal democracy in favor of a form of Islamic theocracy. Yet these regimes are developmental dead ends, kept alive only because they sit atop vast pools of oil. There was at one time a large Arab exception to the third wave, but the Arab Spring has shown that Arab publics can be mobilized against dictatorship just as readily as those in Eastern Europe and Latin America were. This does not of course mean that the path to a well-functioning democracy will be easy or straightforward in Tunisia, Egypt, or Libya, but it does suggest that the desire for—political freedom and participation is not a cultural peculiarity of Europeans and Americans.

The single most serious challenge to liberal democracy in the world today comes from China, which has combined authoritarian government with a partially marketized economy. China is heir to a long and proud tradition of high-quality bureaucratic government, one that stretches back over two millennia. Its leaders have managed a hugely complex transition from a centralized, Soviet-style planned economy to a dynamic open one and have done so with remarkable competence—more competence, frankly, than U.S. leaders have shown in the management of their own macroeconomic policy recently. Many people currently admire the Chinese system not just for its economic record but also because it can make large, complex decisions quickly, compared with the agonizing policy paralysis that has struck both the United States and Europe in the past few years. Especially since the recent financial crisis, the Chinese themselves have begun touting the "China model" as an alternative to liberal democracy.

This model is unlikely to ever become a serious alternative to liberal democracy in regions outside East Asia, however. In the first place, the model is culturally specific: the Chinese government is built around a long tradition of meritocratic recruitment, civil service examinations, a high emphasis on education, and deference to technocratic authority. Few developing countries can hope to emulate this model; those that have, such as Singapore and South Korea (at least in an earlier period), were already within the Chinese cultural zone. The Chinese themselves are skeptical about whether their model can be exported; the so-called Beijing consensus is a Western invention, not a Chinese one. It is also unclear whether the model can be sustained. Neither export-driven growth nor the top-down approach to decision-making will continue to yield good results forever. The fact that the Chinese government would not permit open discussion of the disastrous high-speed rail accident last summer and could not bring the Railway Ministry responsible for it to heel suggests that there are other time bombs hidden behind the facade of efficient decision-making.

Finally, China faces a great moral vulnerability down the road. The Chinese government does not force its officials to respect the basic dignity of its citizens. Every week, there are new protests about land seizures, environmental violations, or gross corruption on the part of some official. While the country is growing rapidly, these abuses can be swept under the carpet. But rapid growth will not continue forever, and the government will have to pay a price in pent-up anger. The regime no longer has any guiding ideal around which it is organized; it is run by a Communist Party supposedly committed to equality that presides over a society marked by dramatic and growing inequality.

So the stability of the Chinese system can in no way be taken for granted. The Chinese government argues that its citizens are culturally different and will always prefer benevolent, growth-promoting dictatorship to a messy democracy that threatens social stability. But it is unlikely that a spreading middle class will behave all that differently in China from the way it has behaved in other parts of the world. Other authoritarian regimes may be trying to emulate China's success, but there is little chance that much of the world will look like today's China 50 years down the road.

Democracy's Future

There is a broad correlation among economic growth, social change, and the hegemony of liberal democratic ideology in the world today. And at the moment, no plausible rival ideology looms. But some very troubling economic and social trends, if they continue, will both threaten the stability of ontemporary liberal democracies and dethrone democratic ideology as it is now understood. The sociologist Barrington Moore once flatly asserted, "No bourgeois, no democracy." The Marxists didn't get their communist Utopia because mature capitalism generated middle-class societies, not working-class ones. But what if the further development of technology and globalization undermines the middle class and makes it impossible for more than a minority of citizens in an advanced society to achieve middle-class status?

There are already abundant signs that such a phase of development has begun. Median incomes in the United States have been stagnating in real terms since the 1970s. The economic impact of this stagnation has been softened to some extent by the fact that most U.S. households have shifted to two income earners in the past generation. Moreover, as the economist Raghuram Rajan has persuasively argued, since Americans are reluctant to engage in straightforward redistribution, the United States has instead attempted a highly dangerous and inefficient form of redistribution over the past generation by subsidizing mortgages for low-income households. This trend, facilitated by a flood of liquidity pouring in from China and other countries, gave many ordinary Americans the illusion that their standards of living were rising steadily during the past decade. In this respect, the bursting of the housing bubble in 2008–9 was nothing more than a cruel reversion to the mean. Americans may today benefit from cheap cell phones, inexpensive clothing, and Facebook, but they increasingly cannot afford their own homes, or health insurance, or comfortable pensions when they retire.

A more troubling phenomenon, identified by the venture capitalist Peter Thiel and the economist Tyler Cowen, is that the benefits of the most recent waves of technological innovation have accrued disproportionately to the most talented and well-educated members of society. This phenomenon helped cause the massive growth of inequality in the United States over the past generation. In 1974, the top one percent of families took home nine percent of GDP; by 2007, that share had increased to 23.5 percent.

Trade and tax policies may have accelerated this trend, but the real villain here is technology. In earlier phases of industrialization—the ages of textiles, coal, steel, and the internal combustion engine—the benefits of technological changes almost always flowed down in significant ways to the rest of society in terms of employment. But this is not a law of nature. We are today living in what the scholar Shoshana Zuboff has labeled "the age of the smart machine," in which technology is increasingly able to substitute for more and higher human functions. Every great advance for Silicon Valley likely means a loss of low-skill jobs elsewhere in the economy, a trend that is unlikely to end anytime soon. Inequality has always existed, as a result of natural differences in talent and character. But today's technological world vastly magnifies those differences. In a nineteenth-century agrarian society, people with strong math skills did not have that many opportunities to capitalize on their talent. Today,

they can become financial wizards or software engineers and take home ever-larger proportions of the national wealth.

The other factor undermining middle-class incomes in developed countries is globalization. With the lowering of transportation and communications costs and the entry into the global work force of hundreds of millions of new workers in developing countries, the kind of work done by the old middle class in the developed world can now be performed much more cheaply elsewhere. Under an economic model that prioritizes the maximization of aggregate income, it is inevitable that jobs will be outsourced.

Smarter ideas and policies could have contained the damage. Germany has succeeded in protecting a significant part of its manufacturing base and industrial labor force even as its companies have remained globally competitive. The United States and the United Kingdom, on the other hand, happily embraced the transition to the postindustrial service economy. Free trade became less a theory than an ideology: when members of the U.S. Congress tried to retaliate with trade sanctions against China for keeping its currency undervalued, they were indignantly charged with protectionism, as if the playing field were already level. There was a lot of happy talk about the wonders of the knowledge economy, and how dirty, dangerous manufacturing jobs would inevitably be replaced by highly educated workers doing creative and interesting things. This was a gauzy veil placed over the hard facts of deindustrialization. It overlooked the fact that the benefits of the new order accrued disproportionately to a very small number of people in finance and high technology, interests that dominated the media and the general political conversation.

The Absent Left

One of the most puzzling features of the world in the aftermath of the financial crisis is that so far, populism has taken primarily a right-wing form, not a left-wing one.

In the United States, for example, although the Tea Party is anti-elitist in its rhetoric, its members vote for conservative politicians who serve the interests of precisely those financiers and corporate elites they claim to despise. There are many explanations for this phenomenon. They include a deeply embedded belief in equality of opportunity rather than equality of outcome and the fact that cultural issues, such as abortion and gun rights, crosscut economic ones.

But the deeper reason a broad-based populist left has failed to materialize is an intellectual one. It has been several decades since anyone on the left has been able to articulate, first, a coherent analysis of what happens to the structure of advanced societies as they undergo economic change and, second, a realistic agenda that has any hope of protecting a middle-class society.

The main trends in left-wing thought in the last two generations have been, frankly, disastrous as either conceptual frameworks or tools for mobilization. Marxism died many years ago, and the few old believers still around are ready for nursing homes. The academic left replaced it with post-modernism, multiculturalism, feminism, critical theory, and a host of other fragmented intellectual trends that are more cultural than economic in focus. Postmodernism begins with a denial of the possibility of any master narrative of history or society, undercutting its own authority as a voice for the majority of citizens who feel betrayed by their elites. Multiculturalism validates the victimhood of virtually every out-group. It is impossible to generate a mass progressive movement on the basis of such a motley coalition: most of the working- and lower-middle-class citizens victimized by the system are culturally conservative and would be embarrassed to be seen in the presence of allies like this.

Whatever the theoretical justifications underlying the left's agenda, its biggest problem is a lack of credibility. Over the past two generations, the mainstream left has followed a social democratic program that centers on the state provision of a variety of services, such as pensions, health care, and education. That model is now exhausted: welfare states have become big, bureaucratic, and inflexible; they are often captured by the very organizations that administer them, through public-sector unions; and, most important, they are fiscally unsustainable given the aging of populations virtually everywhere in the developed world. Thus, when existing social democratic parties come to power, they no longer aspire to be more than custodians of a welfare state that was created decades ago; none has a new, exciting agenda around which to rally the masses.

An Ideology of the Future

Imagine, for a moment, an obscure scribbler today in a garret somewhere trying to outline an ideology of the future that could provide a realistic path toward a world with healthy middle-class societies and robust democracies. What would that ideology look like?

It would have to have at least two components, political and economic. Politically, the new ideology would need to reassert the supremacy of democratic politics over economics and legitimate a new government as an expression of the public interest. But the agenda it put forward to protect middle-class life could not simply rely on the existing mechanisms of the welfare state. The ideology would need to somehow redesign the public sector, freeing it from its dependence on existing stakeholders and using new, technology-empowered approaches to delivering services. It would have to argue forth-rightly for more redistribution and present a realistic route to ending interest groups' domination of politics.

Economically, the ideology could not begin with a denunciation of capitalism as such, as if old-fashioned socialism were still a viable alternative. It is more the variety of capitalism that is at stake and the degree to which governments should help societies adjust to change. Globalization need

be seen not as an inexorable fact of life but rather as a challenge and an opportunity that must be carefully controlled politically. The new ideology would not see markets as an end in themselves; instead, it would value global trade and investment to the extent that they contributed to a flourishing middle class, not just to greater aggregate national wealth.

It is not possible to get to that point, however, without providing a serious and sustained critique of much of the edifice of modern neoclassical economics, beginning with fundamental assumptions such as the sovereignty of individual preferences and that aggregate income is an accurate measure of national well-being. This critique would have to note that people's incomes do not necessarily represent their true contributions to society. It would have to go further, however, and recognize that even if labor markets were efficient, the natural distribution of talents is not necessarily fair and that individuals are not sovereign entities but beings heavily shaped by their surrounding societies.

Most of these ideas have been around in bits and pieces for some time; the scribbler would have to put them into a coherent package. He or she would also have to avoid the "wrong address" problem. The critique of globalization, that is, would have to be tied to nationalism as a strategy for mobilization in a way that defined national interest in a more sophisticated way than, for example, the "Buy American" campaigns of unions in the United States. The product would be a synthesis of ideas from both the left and the right, detached from the agenda of the marginalized groups that constitute the existing progressive movement. The ideology would be populist; the message would begin with a critique of the elites that allowed the benefit of the many to be sacrificed to that of the few and a critique of the money politics, especially in Washington, that overwhelmingly benefits the wealthy.

The dangers inherent in such a movement are obvious: a pullback by the United States, in particular, from its advocacy of a more open global system could set off protectionist responses elsewhere. In many respects, the Reagan-Thatcher revolution succeeded just as its proponents hoped, bringing about an increasingly competitive, globalized, friction-free world. Along the way, it generated tremendous wealth and created rising middle classes all over the developing world and the spread of democracy in their wake. It is possible that the developed world is on the cusp of a series of technological breakthroughs that will not only increase productivity but also provide meaningful employment to large numbers of middle-class people.

But that is more a matter of faith than a reflection of the empirical reality of the last 30 years, which points in the opposite direction. Indeed, there are a lot of reasons to think that inequality will continue to worsen. The current concentration of wealth in the United States has already become self-reinforcing: as the economist Simon Johnson has argued, the financial sector has used its lobbying clout to avoid more onerous forms of regulation. Schools for the

ell-off are better than ever; those for everyone else con-
nue to deteriorate. Elites in all societies use their superior
ccess to the political system to protect their interests, absent
countervailing democratic mobilization to rectify the situ-
tion. American elites are no exception to the rule.

That mobilization will not happen, however, as long as
ne middle classes of the developed world remain enthralled
y the narrative of the past generation: that their interests
ill be best served by ever-freer markets and smaller states.
he alternative narrative is out there, waiting to be born.

ource

ukuyama, Francis. "The future of history: can liberal democracy
survive the decline of the middle class?" *Foreign Affairs* 91.1
(2012). *General Reference Center GOLD.* Web. 25 Jan. 2012.

Critical Thinking

1. What is Fukuyama's point of view?
2. What are some of the reasons he offers to support this point of view?
3. What contemporary challenges does liberal democracy face?
4. How does globalization undermine the middle class?
5. How does this article relate to Articles 1, 4, 5, 16 and 20?

FRANCIS FUKUYAMA is a Senior Fellow at the Center on Democracy, Development, and the Rule of Law at Stanford University and the author, most recently, of *The Origins of Political Order: From Prehuman Times to the French Revolution.*

kuyuma, Francis. From *Foreign Affairs,* January-February 2012, pp. 1–7. Copyright © 2012 by Council on Foreign Relations, Inc. Reprinted by permission of Foreign Affairs.
ww.ForeignAffairs.com.

Who Will Rule the World?

China may continue to grow in the near term, but this is growth under extractive institutions—mostly relying on politically connected businesses, and technological transfer and catch-up.

DARON ACEMOGLU AND JAMES A. ROBINSON

Voices of both those convinced that China will eclipse the United States as a global economic and military power and those who are confident of continued US leadership are getting louder. Much of this debate focuses on the size of the Chinese economy relative to the US economy or issues of military might.

But what matters for global leadership is innovation, which is not only the key driver of per capita income growth but also ultimately the main determinant of military and diplomatic leadership—it was the US that proved after Pearl Harbor how a prosperous economy can rapidly increase its military power and preparedness when push comes to shove.

So the right question to ask is not who will be the military leader of the next century, but who will be the technological leader.

The answer must be: most probably the US—but only if it can clean up its act.

The odds favor the US not only because it is technologically more advanced and innovative than China at the moment, with an income per capita more than six times that of China. They do so also because innovation ultimately depends on a country's institutions. Inclusive political institutions distribute political power equally in society and constrain how that power can be exercised. They tend to underpin inclusive economic institutions, which encourage innovation and investment and provide a level playing field so that the talents of a broad cross-section of society can be best deployed. Despite all of the challenges that they are facing, US institutions are broadly inclusive, and thus more conducive to innovation. Despite all of the resources that China is pouring into science and technology at the moment, its political institutions are extractive, and as such, unless overhauled and revolutionized soon, they will be an impediment to innovation.

China may continue to grow in the near term, but this is growth under extractive institutions—mostly relying on politically connected businesses, and technological transfer and catch-up. The next stage of economic growth, generating genuine innovation, will be much more difficult unless its political institutions change to create an environment that rewards the challenging of established interests, technologies, firms and authority.

We have a historical precedent for this type of growth and how it runs out of steam: the Soviet Union. After the Bolsheviks took over the highly inefficient agricultural economy from the Tsarist regime and started to use the power of the state to move people and resources into industry, the Soviet Union grew at then-unparalleled rates, achieving an average annual growth rate of over 6 percent between 1928 and 1960. Though there was much enthusiasm about Soviet growth—as there is now about China's growth machine—it couldn't and didn't last. By the 1970s, the Soviets had produced almost all the growth that could be derived from moving people from agriculture into industry, and despite various incentives and bonuses, and even harsh punishments for failure, they could not generate innovation. The Soviet economy stagnated and then totally collapsed.

China has more potential than the Soviet Union. Its growth has not come simply by government fiat, but also because it has reformed its economic institutions, providing incentives to farmers and some firms (though having government connections still helps enormously, and challenging powerful firms can land you in jail or worse). China also had more technological catching up to do than the Soviet Union. But this potential will come to an end as well unless China radically transforms its institutions. This requires not only obvious steps such as introducing an independent judiciary, independent media, and more secure property rights for businesses, but truly inclusive political institutions which necessitate a fundamental political opening so that political power is more equally distributed and can underpin economic institutions that will create a level playing field and encourage and fully reward all sorts of innovation—and especially the disruptive kind.

US inclusive institutions are in decline, and the danger that the US could follow other societies in history—such as the Venetian Republic in the 13th century—that have seen their inclusive institutions dismantled and their economic success undermined is a real one.

The threat for the US is exactly the flip side of the opportunity for China. US inclusive institutions are in decline, and the danger that the US could follow other societies in history—such as the Venetian Republic in the 13th century—that have seen their inclusive institutions dismantled and their economic success undermined is a real one.

The US society has been undergoing profound changes over the last four decades. The huge rise in economic inequality, brought to the headlines partly by the Occupy Wall Street movement, is both an important aspect of these changes and also a warning sign. The problem is that economic inequality often comes bundled with political inequality. Those with great wealth and easy access to the politicians will inevitably try to increase their political power at the expense of the rest of society. This sort of hijacking of politics is a surefire way of undermining inclusive political institutions, and is already under way in the US.

There is also a vicious circle here: Economic inequality is increasing political inequality, and those increasing their political power will use this to tilt the playing field further and gain a greater economic advantage. This will not only take the form of getting more tax breaks and government subsidies for their businesses, but also by blocking more innovative rivals and, directly or indirectly, undermining the opportunities that the rest of society has for acquiring skills, taking risks and innovating.

Economic inequality is increasing political inequality, and those increasing their political power will use this to tilt the playing field further and gain a greater economic advantage.

Ultimately, however, the reason to believe that it will be the US, not China, leading the world in innovation and technology for many, many more decades is the resilience of US inclusive institutions: We have been here before and we have rebounded. Things were much worse during the Gilded Age both in terms of economic inequality and in terms of how totally and unscrupulously the wealthy elite, the so-called robber barons, had come to dominate politics. Yet the robber barons did not prevail. The US political system was also able to tackle the problem of Southern segregation and black disenfranchisement, which if anything looked even more insurmountable. All of this was made possible because Americans stood up and fought for political equality, and the US political system was open enough to allow them to do so. We are optimistic that this time it will not be different.

Critical Thinking

1. What is the answer the authors offer to their central question?
2. What reasons are offered in support of their conclusion?
3. How does this article relate to Articles 4, 5, 15, 16 and 19?

DARON ACEMOCLU AND JAMES A. ROBINSON are the co-authors of *Why Nations Fail: The Origins of Power, Prosperity, and Poverty.*

Mafia States

Moisés Naím

The global economic crisis has been a boon for transnational criminals. Thanks to the weak economy, cash-rich criminal organizations can acquire financially distressed but potentially valuable companies at bargain prices. Fiscal austerity is forcing governments everywhere to cut the budgets of law enforcement agencies and court systems. Millions of people have been laid off and are thus more easily tempted to break the law. Large numbers of unemployed experts in finance, accounting, information technology, law, and logistics have boosted the supply of world-class talent available to criminal cartels. Meanwhile, philanthropists all over the world have curtailed their giving, creating funding shortfalls in the arts, education, health care, and other areas, which criminals are all too happy to fill in exchange for political access, social legitimacy, and popular support. International criminals could hardly ask for a more favorable business environment. Their activities are typically high margin and cash-based, which means they often enjoy a high degree of liquidity—not a bad position to be in during a global credit crunch.

But emboldened adversaries and dwindling resources are not the only problems confronting police departments, prosecutors, and judges. In recent years, a new threat has emerged: the mafia state. Across the globe, criminals have penetrated governments to an unprecedented degree. The reverse has also happened: rather than stamping out powerful gangs, some governments have instead taken over their illegal operations. In mafia states, government officials enrich themselves and their families and friends while exploiting the money, muscle, political influence, and global connections of criminal syndicates to cement and expand their own power. Indeed, top positions in some of the world's most profitable illicit enterprises are no longer filled only by professional criminals; they now include senior government officials, legislators, spy chiefs, heads of police departments, military officers, and, in some extreme cases, even heads of state or their family members.

This fusing of governments and criminal groups is distinct from the more limited ways in which the two have collaborated in the past. Governments and spy agencies, including those of democratic countries, have often enlisted criminals to smuggle weapons to allied insurgents in other countries or even to assassinate enemies abroad. (The CIA's harebrained attempt to enlist American mafia figures to assassinate Fidel Castro in 1960 is perhaps the best-known example.) But unlike normal states, mafia states do not just occasionally rely on criminal groups to advance particular foreign policy goals. In a mafia state, high government officials actually become integral players in, if not the leaders of, criminal enterprises, and the defense and promotion of those enterprises' businesses become official priorities. In mafia states such as Bulgaria, Guinea-Bissau, Montenegro, Myanmar (also called Burma), Ukraine, and Venezuela, the national interest and the interests of organized crime are now inextricably intertwined.

Because the policies and resource allocations of mafia states are determined as much by the influence of criminals as by the forces that typically shape state behavior, these states pose a serious challenge to policymakers and analysts of international politics. Mafia states defy easy categorization, blurring the conceptual line between states and nonstate actors. As a result, their behavior is difficult to predict, making them particularly dangerous actors in the international environment.

A Revolution in Crime

Conventional wisdom about international criminal networks rests on three faulty assumptions. First, many people believe that when it comes to illicit activities, everything has been done before. It is true that criminals, smugglers, and black markets have always existed. But the nature of international crime has changed a great deal in the past two decades, as criminal networks have expanded beyond their traditional markets and started taking advantage of political and economic transformations and exploiting new technologies. In the early 1990s, for example, criminal groups became early adopters of innovations in communications, such as advanced electronic encryption. Criminal syndicates also pioneered new means of drug transportation, such as "narco-submarines": semi-submersible vessels able to evade radar, sonar, and infrared systems. (Drug cartels in Colombia eventually graduated to fully submersible submarines.) In more recent years, criminal organizations have also taken advantage of the Internet, leading to a dizzying growth in cybercrime, which cost the global economy some $114 billion in 2011, according to the Internet security firm Symantec.

A second common misperception is that international crime is an underground phenomenon that involves only a small community of deviants operating at the margins of societies. The truth is that in many countries, criminals today do not bother staying underground at all, nor are they remotely marginal. In fact, the suspected leaders of many major criminal groups have become celebrities of a sort. Wealthy individuals with suspicious business backgrounds are sought-after philanthropists and have come to control radio and television stations and own influential newspapers. Moreover, criminals' accumulation of wealth and power depends not only on their own illicit activities but also on the actions of average members of society: for example, the millions of citizens involved in China's counterfeit consumer-goods industry and in Afghanistan's drug trade, the millions of Westerners who smoke marijuana regularly, the hundreds of thousands of migrants who every year hire criminals to smuggle them to Europe, and the well-to-do professionals in Manhattan and Milan who employ illegal immigrants as nannies and housekeepers. Ordinary people such as these are an integral part of the criminal ecosystem.

A third mistaken assumption is that international crime is strictly a matter of law enforcement, best managed by police departments, prosecutors, and judges. In reality, international crime is better understood as a political problem with national security implications. The scale and scope of the most powerful criminal organizations now easily match those of the world's largest multinational corporations. And just as legitimate organizations seek political influence, so, too, do criminal ones. Of course, criminals have always sought to corrupt political systems to their own advantage. But illicit groups have never before managed to acquire the degree of political influence now enjoyed by criminals in a wide range of African, eastern European, and Latin American countries, not to mention China and Russia.

In the past decade or so, this phenomenon has crossed a threshold, resulting in the emergence of potent mafia states. José Grinda, a Spanish prosecutor with years of experience fighting eastern European criminal organizations, maintains that in many cases, it has become impossible for him and his colleagues to distinguish the interests of criminal organizations from those of their host governments. According to Grinda, Spanish law enforcement officials constantly confront criminal syndicates that function as appendages of the governments of Belarus, Russia, and Ukraine. In confidential remarks contained in U.S. diplomatic cables released by the whistleblower Web site WikiLeaks, he detailed his concerns about the "tremendous control" exercised by what he termed "the Russian mafia" over a number of strategic sectors of the global economy, such as aluminum and natural gas. This control, Grinda suggested, is made possible by the extent to which the Kremlin collaborates with Russian criminal organizations.

In mafia states, government officials and criminals often work together through legal business conglomerates with close ties to top leaders and their families and friends. According to Grinda, Moscow regularly employs criminal syndicates—as when, for example, Russia's military intelligence agency directed a mafia group to supply arms to Kurdish rebels in Turkey. More indicative of the overlap between Russia's government and its criminal groups, however, is the case of a cargo ship, Arctic Sea, that

the Russian government claimed was hijacked by pirates off the coast of Sweden in 2009. Moscow ostensibly sent the Russian navy to rescue the ship, but many experts believe it was actually smuggling weapons on behalf of Russia's intelligence services and that the hijacking and rescue were ruses intended to cover up the trafficking after rival intelligence services had disrupted it. Grinda says that the smuggling was a joint operation run by organized criminal gangs and what he cryptically termed "Eurasian security services." The Russians were embarrassed, but the outcome was essentially benign, even a bit comical. Still, the affair underscored the unpredictability of a security environment in which it is difficult to distinguish the geopolitical calculations of states from the profit motives of criminal organizations.

"The Mafia Has the Country"

Russia is hardly the only country where the line between government agencies and criminal groups has been irreparably blurred. Last year, the Council of Europe published a report alleging that the prime minister of Kosovo, Hashim Thaçi, and his political allies exert "violent control over the trade in heroin and other narcotics" and occupy important positions in "Kosovo's mafia-like structures of organized crime." The state-crime nexus is perhaps even stronger in Bulgaria. A 2005 U.S. diplomatic cable released by WikiLeaks last year is worth quoting at length, given the disturbing portrait it paints of Bulgaria's descent into mafia statehood. The cable read, in part:

> Organized crime has a corrupting influence on all Bulgarian institutions, including the government, parliament and judiciary. In an attempt to maintain their influence regardless of who is in power, OC [organized crime] figures donate to all the major political parties. As these figures have expanded into legitimate businesses, they have attempted— with some success—to buy their way into the corridors of power. . . . Below the level of the national government and the leadership of the major political parties, OC "owns" a number of municipalities and individual members of parliament. This direct participation in politics—as opposed to bribery— is a relatively new development for Bulgarian OC. Similarly in the regional center of Velingrad, OC figures control the municipal council and the mayor's office. Nearly identical scenarios have played out in half a dozen smaller towns and villages across Bulgaria.

This state of affairs led Atanas Atanasov, a member of the Bulgarian parliament and a former counterintelligence chief, to observe that "other countries have the mafia; in Bulgaria the mafia has the country."

Crime and the state are also becoming intertwined in Afghanistan, where top government officials and provincial governors—including President Hamid Karzai's half brother, Ahmed Wali Karzai, who was assassinated last year—have been accused not just of colluding with drug-trafficking networks but of actually leading them. As the drug trade becomes ever more globalized, African countries have been drawn in, too, becoming important transit points for drugs from the Andean region and Asia on their way to drug-hungry European markets. Inevitably, several African rulers and their families, along with lower-level politicians, military officers, and members of the judiciary, have entered the narcotics-trafficking business themselves. In Guinea, for example, Ousmane Conté, son of the late president Lansana Conté, was officially labeled a "drug kingpin" by the U.S. government in 2010.

Police departments, secret services, courts, local and provincial governments, passport-issuing agencies, and customs offices have all become coveted targets for criminal takeovers. Last year, René Sanabria, a retired general who headed Bolivia's antidrug agency, was arrested by U.S. federal agents in Panama and charged with plotting to ship hundreds of kilograms of cocaine to Miami. Sanabria pled guilty and was sentenced to 14 years in prison. Similarly, a succession of generals who held the chief antidrug post in Mexico are now in prison for taking part in the very kind of crime they were supposed to prevent.

A mafia state has also taken root in Venezuela. In 2010, President Hugo Chávez appointed General Henry Rangel Silva as the top commander of the Venezuelan armed forces; earlier this year, he became minister of defense. But in 2008, the U.S. Treasury Department added Rangel Silva to its list of officially designated drug kingpins, accusing him of "materially assisting narcotic trafficking activities." The Treasury Department also recently slapped that label on a number of other Venezuelan officials, including five high-ranking military officers, a senior intelligence officer, and an influential member of congress allied with Chávez. In 2010, a Venezuelan named Walid Makled, accused by several governments of being the head of one of the world's largest drug-trafficking groups, was captured by Colombian authorities. Prior to his extradition to Venezuela, Makled claimed that he had videos, recorded telephone conversations, canceled checks, and other evidence proving he worked for a criminal network that involved 15 Venezuelan generals (including the head of military intelligence and the director of the antinarcotics office), the brother of the country's interior minister, and five members of congress.

Owing in part to such ties, the cocaine business has flourished in Venezuela in recent years, and the country now supplies more than half of all cocaine shipments to Europe, according to the UN Office on Drugs and Crime. And the drug trade is not the only illicit activity that has flourished in Venezuela's era of state-sanctioned crime: the country has also become a base of operations for human trafficking, money laundering, counterfeiting, weapons smuggling, and the trade in contraband oil.

In the past, foreign policy scholars generally considered international crime to be a relatively minor problem that domestic legal systems should handle. The impact of crime, they believed, was insignificant compared with the threat of terrorism or the proliferation of weapons of mass destruction. Fortunately, the conventional wisdom is starting to change. More and more experts and policymakers are recognizing that crime has become a significant source of global instability, especially with the emergence of mafia states.

Criminal gangs, for example, have become involved in for-profit nuclear proliferation. A. Q. Khan, the notorious Pakistani nuclear peddler, claimed that he was spreading bomb-making know-how to other nations in order to advance Pakistan's interests. But the international network he built to market and deliver his goods was organized as an illicit, for-profit enterprise. Nuclear proliferation experts have long cautioned that nonstate actors might not respond to nuclear deterrence strategies in the same way states do; there is reason to worry, then, that as criminal organizations fuse more thoroughly with governments, deterrence might become more difficult. Perhaps most worrisome in this regard is North Korea. Although North Korea recently announced that in exchange for food aid, it would suspend its nuclear weapons tests, stop enriching uranium, and allow international inspectors to visit its main nuclear complex, the country still remains a nuclear-armed dictatorship whose state-directed criminal enterprises have led U.S. officials to nickname it "the Sopranos state." Sheena Chestnut Greitens, an expert on the crime-state nexus in North Korea, has written that the country has "the means and motivation for exporting nuclear material," warning that "proliferation conducted through illicit networks will not always be well controlled by the supplier state," which adds additional uncertainty to an already dangerous situation.

Even putting aside the alarming prospect of nuclear mafia states, governments heavily involved in illicit trade might be more prone to use force when their access to profitable markets is threatened. Take, for example, the 2008 war between Georgia and Russia over the breakaway territories of Abkhazia and South Ossetia. According to the Carnegie Endowment's Thomas de Waal, an expert on the Caucasus, before the conflict, criminal organizations operated highly profitable operations in South Ossetia, where illicit trade accounted for a significant part of the economy. Although direct evidence is difficult to come by, the scale of these illegal activities suggested the active complicity of senior Russian officials, who acted as the criminals' patrons and partners. Of course, the conflict was fueled by many factors, including ethnic strife, domestic Georgian politics, and Russia's desire to assert its hegemony in its near abroad. But it is also conceivable that among the interest groups pushing the Kremlin toward war were those involved in lucrative trafficking operations in the contested areas.

Profiting in the Shadows

Increasingly, fighting transnational crime must mean more than curbing the traffic of counterfeit goods, drugs, weapons, and people; it must also involve preventing and reversing the criminalization of governments. Illicit trade is intrinsically dangerous, but the threat it poses to society is amplified when criminals become high-level government officials and governments take over criminal syndicates. Yet today's law enforcement agencies are no match for criminal organizations that not only are wealthy, violent, and ruthless but also benefit from the full support of national governments and their diplomats, judges, spies, generals, cabinet ministers, and police chiefs. Mafia states can afford the best lawyers and accountants and have access to the most advanced technology. Underfunded law enforcement agencies, overworked courts, and slow-moving bureaucracies are increasingly unable to keep up with such well-funded, agile foes.

Law enforcement agencies are also hamstrung by the fact that they are inherently national, whereas the largest and most dangerous criminal organizations, along with the agents of mafia states, operate in multiple jurisdictions. Mafia states integrate the speed and flexibility of transnational criminal networks with the legal protections and diplomatic privileges enjoyed only by states, creating a hybrid form of international actor against which domestic law enforcement agencies have few weapons. The existing tools that national governments can use to counter the new threat—treaties, multilateral organizations, and cooperation among national law enforcement agencies—are slow, unwieldy, and unsuited to the task. After all, how can a country coordinate its anticrime efforts with government leaders or top police officials who are themselves criminals?

The emergence of mafia states imperils the very concept of international law enforcement cooperation. In 2006, the heads of police of 152 nations met in Brazil for the 75th General Assembly of Interpol, the multilateral organization whose constitution calls on it "to ensure and promote the widest possible mutual assistance between all criminal police authorities." Interpol's president at the time was Jackie Selebi, the national police commissioner of South Africa. In his opening address, Selebi exhorted his colleagues "to find systems to make sure that our borders and border control are on a firm footing"; a noble cause, to be sure. Unfortunately, its champion turned out to be a crook himself. In 2010, Selebi was convicted of accepting a $156,000 bribe from a drug smuggler and is now serving a 15-year prison sentence.

But more troubling for Interpol than any single high-profile embarrassment is what insiders call a "low-trust problem," which has historically stifled the agency's efforts. "The sad truth is I am not going to share my best, most delicate information with the Russian or Mexican police departments," one senior official in the United Kingdom's organized-crime agency told me when asked about Interpol. Even though the agency goes to great lengths to ensure the confidentiality of the information that its member agencies share with it, the reality is that national law enforcement agencies remain wary of revealing too much.

As the role of mafia states has become clearer, law enforcement officers across the globe have begun to develop new policies and strategies for dealing with such states, including requiring high-level public officials to disclose their finances; scrutinizing the accountants, lawyers, and technology experts who protect crime lords; and improving coordination among different domestic agencies. The rise of mafia states has also added urgency to the search for ways to internationalize the fight against crime. One promising approach would be to create "coalitions of the honest" among law enforcement agencies that are less likely to have been penetrated or captured by criminal groups. Some states are already experimenting with arrangements of this kind, which go beyond normal bilateral anticrime cooperation by including not just law enforcement agencies

but also representatives from intelligence agencies and armed forces. A complementary step would be to develop multinational networks of magistrates, judges, police officials, intelligence analysts, and policymakers to encourage a greater degree of cooperation than Interpol affords by building on the trust that exists among senior law enforcement officers who have fought transnational criminal networks together for decades. As is often the case, long-term collaborations among like-minded individuals who know one another well and share values are far more effective than formal, officially sanctioned cooperation between institutions whose officers barely know one another.

Unfortunately, despite the near-universal recognition that combating international crime requires international action, most anticrime initiatives remain primarily domestic. And although mafia states have transformed international crime into a national security issue, the responsibility for combating it still rests almost exclusively with law enforcement agencies. Indeed, even in developed countries, police departments and other law enforcement bodies rarely coordinate with their national security counterparts, even though transnational crime threatens democratic governance, financial markets, and human rights.

An important obstacle to combating the spread of mafia states is a basic lack of awareness among ordinary citizens and policymakers about the extent of the phenomenon. Ignorance of the scope and scale of the problem will make it difficult to defend or increase the already meager budgets of government agencies charged with confronting international crime, especially in a time of fiscal austerity. But such awareness will be hard to generate while so many aspects of the process of state criminalization remain ill understood—and therein lies an even larger problem. Devoting public money to reducing the power of mafia states will be useless or even counterproductive unless the funds pay for policies grounded in a robust body of knowledge. Regrettably, the mafia state is a phenomenon about which there is little available data. The analytic frameworks that governments are currently applying to the problem are primitive, based on outdated understandings about organized crime. Addressing this dearth of knowledge will require law enforcement authorities, intelligence agencies, military organizations, media outlets, academics, and nongovernmental organizations to develop and share more reliable information. Doing so, however, would be only a first step—and an admittedly insufficient one.

Critical Thinking

1. How does the global economic crisis benefit organized crime?
2. What is meant by the term "transnational criminals"?
3. How important are ordinary consumers to the criminal ecosystem?
4. Offer examples of the fusion of some governments and criminal groups.
5. Do the authors of Article 1 give enough importance to the role of transnational criminals?

Bolivia and Its Lithium

Can the "Gold of the 21st Century" help lift a nation out of poverty?

REBECCA HOLLENDER AND JIM SHULTZ

Executive Summary

The resource curse refers to the paradox that countries and regions with an abundance of natural resources, especially minerals and fuels, tend to have less economic growth and worse development outcomes than countries with fewer natural resources.

Bolivia has a long history with that curse, dating back to the theft of its silver at the hands of the Spanish during the colonial era. Today Bolivia seeks to break that curse with what some call "the gold of the 21st century": lithium. This report examines Bolivia's prospects for doing so.

I. Lithium—The Super Hero of Metals

Every time we pick up a cell phone or iPod, look at our watch, or plug-in a laptop we are relying on batteries that contain lithium. It is also used in ceramics and glass production, bi-polar medication, air conditioners, lubricants, nuclear weaponry, and other products. The lightest metal on Earth, lithium is mined from many sources, but most cheaply from underground brines like those found in abundance under Bolivia's vast Salar de Uyuni.

Today the global focus on lithium is about its potential as a key ingredient in a new generation of electric car batteries. Powerful global players are investing billions of dollars in lithium's future. Some predictions speculate that lithium car battery sales could jump from $100 million per year to $103 billion per year in the next 2 decades. If so, the countries that possess lithium are poised to become much bigger players in the global economy.

Despite the growing enthusiasm about lithium's future, there are also real doubts as well. The process for transforming lithium into its commercially valuable form, lithium carbonate, is complex and expensive. The electric vehicle batteries currently being developed with lithium are still too large and heavy, and too slow to charge. The batteries are so expensive that they put the cost of electric cars beyond the reach of most consumers. Lithium batteries also have a record of catching fire. So while lithium car batteries might become a massive global market, they could also turn out to be the energy equivalent of the 8-track tape.

II. The Race for Bolivia's Lithium

Based even on conservative estimates, Bolivia's lithium reserves are the largest in the world. The Salar de Uyuni, a 10,000 square kilometer (3,860 square miles) expanse of salt-embedded minerals, located in Bolivia's department of Southwest Potosí, is ground zero for Bolivia's lithium dreams.

Foreign corporations and governments alike are lining up to court a Bolivian government intent on getting the best deal possible for its people. Among the major players are two Japanese giants, Mitsubishi and Sumitomo, the latter of which already has a stake in the controversial San Cristobal Mine known for contaminating the same region. The French electric vehicle manufacturer, Bolloré, is also courting the Morales government, as are the governments of South Korea, Brazil, and Iran.

The Bolivian government has sketched out a general plan for the various phases of its lithium ambitions, but many of the details of how all this will be done have yet to be defined. To get its feet wet in the technical and economic waters of lithium, the government of Bolivia has invested $5.7 million in the development of a "pilot plant" at the edge of the Salar de Uyuni. The plant is intended to test drive the steps in getting the lithium-rich brine out from under the Salar's crust and separating it into its distinct (and marketable) parts. Based on the experience of this pilot plant, the government aims to then construct a much larger industrial-scale plant, capable of producing up to 30,000 to 40,000 metric tons of lithium carbonate per year. This will be followed by a third phase to produce marketable lithium compounds, which the government plans to undertake in partnership with foreign investors.

To get help in meeting the formidable challenges it faces, the government has assembled a Scientific Advisory Committee (Scientific Research Committee for the Industrialization of the Evaporitic Resources of Bolivia) comprised of experts from universities, private companies, and governments, to give free, and mutually beneficial, advice.

III. The Challenges Ahead on Bolivia's Lithium Highway

At heart, Bolivia's lithium ambitions are simple: to lift a people out of poverty by squeezing the maximum benefit possible from a natural resource on the cutting edge of global markets. But between where Bolivia sits today and where it aims to go on its lithium highway there are major challenges that it will need to face:

Getting the Economics Right

Bolivia's dreams of lithium wealth involve hitting a complicated moving target. The electric car battery market looks like the most lucrative for lithium development, and is the one the Morales government says it's aiming for (Morales also claims that Bolivia will produce electric vehicles), but how big that market will be, and when it will peak, is still just a guessing game. Bolivia could aim for more traditional lithium markets, such as glass and ceramics, but they aren't nearly so potentially profitable. A middle option would be established types of lithium batteries for products such as watches, cell phones, iPods, laptops and other electronic gadgets.

How much will it cost to build a lithium battery industry in Bolivia? That number is one of the most elusive pieces of information in the picture. If Bolivia kicks into full industrial mode the budget would be $200 million or higher just for the main plant. But that still doesn't include massive additional investments in supporting chemical industries and huge infrastructure development in a region where today even keeping the lights on is a technological challenge. One Bolivian official has placed the potential cost at as high as $1 billion. Because of this, Bolivia is looking for serious partnerships with investors, an approach that some local community groups do not support.

The fact that the government might suddenly have substantial new revenues from lithium is also no guarantee that the Bolivian people will end up any better off. Those revenues could easily become a magnet for corruption, waste and favoritism and there will be a constant tension between the demand to use the funds for public goods and reinvesting them into state-controlled lithium production.

Environmental Impacts

Lost in the great Bolivian lithium race is a set of very deep and real environmental concerns. In the name of providing cleaner cars to the wealthy countries of the north, Bolivia's beautiful and rare Salar could end up an environmental wasteland. The adequacy of Bolivia's environmental strategy for lithium development in Southwest Potosí is doubted by several well-regarded Bolivian environmental organizations.

One major problem that lithium development could cause is a major water crisis. The region already suffers from a serious water shortage, impacting quinoa farmers, llama herders, the region's vital tourism industry, and drinking water sources. While Bolivian officials contend that the lithium project's water requirements will be minimal, their estimates are based on very limited and incomplete information.

Contamination of the air, water and soil is also a major concern. Large quantities of toxic chemicals will be needed to process the predicted 30,000 to 40,000 tons of lithium per year that the project expects to mine. The escape of such chemicals via leaching, spills, or air emissions is a danger that threatens the communities and the ecosystem as a whole. Reports from Chile's Salar de Atacama describe a landscape scarred by mountains of discarded salt and huge canals filled with blue chemically contaminated water.

Bolivian officials have dismissed those risks, and the government system in place to protect the environment is inadequate at best. Public institutions, such as Bolivia's Ministry of the Environment and Water, which are responsible for ensuring compliance with environmental requirements, clearly lack the capacity or authority to intervene in an effective way.

The Threat to Communities

How do the people and communities who live in Southwest Potosí feel about their homeland becoming the site of what could soon become one of the biggest industrial projects their nation has ever built? To be sure, many groups in the region have long supported lithium development, seeing it as a vital opportunity for increased income and development. But there are deep concerns as well.

Quinoa producers and tourism operators have expressed concern about supposed benefits that the Bolivian government has promised from lithium, saying that the benefits are irrelevant to local needs and could easily damage the two industries that are thriving in the region—agriculture and tourism. But Bolivia's laws that guarantee community involvement in planning are as weak as its environmental protections. While some local organizations—especially ones that actively support Evo Morales' political party (MAS)—have been engaged, others say they have not.

The Capacity of the Bolivian Government to Manage the Program

Finally, there are concerns about the chronic problems faced by the Bolivian government to manage such an ambitious program—problems that pre-date President Morales. To pull off its lithium ambitions, Bolivia will need highly trained and qualified experts, in the technical and scientific aspects of lithium, in business management and economics, and in social and environmental impacts. And these experts need to be solely accountable to the Bolivian people, not to foreign governments or corporations.

IV. Conclusion—Can Bolivia Beat the Resource Curse?

Whether these challenges are surmountable for the people of Bolivia and their leaders is an open debate. To be certain, there is real potential here. The demand for lithium is clearly on the rise, and with the possibility in the future of a very big rise. Bolivia is indeed sitting on the world's largest supply of lithium and it is being courted by some serious players. And importantly, all this is happening just as Bolivia has a government that has committed itself to a different way of doing resource business.

In practical terms, the government is also doing some important things right, such as beginning with a pilot effort to test the technological and economic waters. But there are many things that can go badly wrong on the lithium road ahead. In the uphill battle to make Bolivia's lithium dreams a reality, clearly the first step is to acknowledge and understand the economic, environmental, social, and capacity challenges.

What Bolivia is trying to do is hard—very hard. It is trying to break a curse—the paradox of plenty—that few impoverished nations escape. Its effort to escape that curse is extremely important, which is why so much of the world is watching. It is an experiment that is economic, social, political, technological and practical all at the same time. The fate of its success lies in the hands of the Bolivian people and in their ability to hold their leaders accountable, both for their own benefit and the planet's.

Critical Thinking

1. Why has lithium become an important raw material?
2. What do the authors mean by a "development paradox"?
3. Is Bolivia's approach to the development of its lithium reserves similar to Sachs's development approach?

Tech's Tragic Secret

The world's most sophisticated smartphones and tablets start in the tin mines of Bangka Island.

Cam Simpson

On May 29, in the bottom of a tin-mining pit on Bangka Island in Indonesia, a wall about 16 feet high collapsed, sending a wave of earth crashing down on a 40-year-old father of two. His name was Rosnan. The dirt crushed his legs, sent something sharp slicing through his right thigh, and buried him from the waist down. His partner, panicked but unhurt, scrambled out of the pit screaming for help. About 20 other miners rushed in to dig Rosnan out with their bare hands.

"He kept repeating, 'Please, please help me,'" recalls Rosnan's son, Dian Chandra, 20, who rode in the back of a car with his father to a nearby hospital. Rosnan lost too much blood. "I couldn't find a pulse," says Dr. Mario, the emergency room physician on duty. Dr. Mario declared Rosnan dead at about 3 P.M. (Like many Indonesians, including Dr. Mario, Rosnan had one name.) Back at the mine, someone stuck a withered sapling into the soft bottom of the pit near the spot where Rosnan fell—a far too frequent sight in the mines of Bangka, where Rosnan was the first of six to die on the job during a single week this spring. The other victims didn't make it to the hospital. All, including a 15-year-old boy, were buried alive.

Three days after Rosnan's death, and following Friday prayers at the local mosque, his family and friends gathered to mourn him at his brother's cinder-block home. They sat on the bare floor, sharing a meal of rice, noodles, and fish stew. Rosnan's 57-year-old brother, Rani, recalls that Rosnan had few options outside the pit. "We have to live," he says. "We need money."

The head of the village said the area where Rosnan was working was an illegal mine, and that it would be refilled and re-seeded. Yet even as Rosnan's family was mourning, three teenage boys, soaking in the rain, scraped for tin ore at the bottom of the same pit, right near the sapling. Two said they were 15 years old, the third 16. All were barefoot in knee-length shorts as they dug into the steep, sheer face. They were among about a dozen miners working in the immediate area. They knew about Rosnan's death, and kept digging.

Rosnan worked among thousands of Indonesians who wield pickaxes and buckets each day on Bangka Island, extracting the tin that becomes the solder that binds components in the world's tablet computers, smartphones, and other electronics. Police figures show Bangka miners died in accidents similar to Rosnan's at an average of almost one a week last year, more than double the rate from 2010. There is good reason to believe it's getting worse. At the end of July, five Bangka miners were killed beneath another mudslide.

In recent years about one-third of all the tin mined in the world has come from Bangka, its sister island Belitung to the east, and the sea-beds off the islands' shores. Because almost half of all tin is turned into solder for the electronics industry, a dominant force in the global tin market today is tablets and smartphones bought by consumers in the U.S. and elsewhere.

The trail from the dangerous mines to the leading names in electronics, including Foxconn Technology Group, the biggest manufacturer for Apple and others, is clear. Shenmao Technology and Chernan Metal Industrial—two of the top solder makers in Asia, both suppliers to Foxconn—say they buy 100 percent of their tin from Indonesia. Shenmao estimates it's the dominant supplier of solder to China, the cradle of electronics manufacturing, and accounts for 16 percent of the global market. Chernan says other clients have included Sony, Panasonic, Samsung Electronics, and LG Electronics. Several other solder makers declined to discuss their tin sourcing. But their product is so crucial to electronics that tin is the most common metal used by Apple suppliers, according to data Apple made public earlier this year; 179 suppliers for the company, maker of the iPad and iPhone, which are assembled by Foxconn, use tin in components for Apple.

The top of seahorse-shaped Bangka is about one degree south of the equator, just off the eastern coast of Sumatra. It has a population of about 960,000 and has been known for tin for centuries. In 1841, when the Dutch controlled the island, an account described an island rumored to be so saturated with the metal that it was poisoning residents until "the unfortunate wretches invariably perished."

Today, swaying palms shade white beaches along its coasts, but inland, mining has wrecked the landscape. Vast patches of the island are stripped of their rubber trees, palm trees, and tropical grasses. In their place are thousands of craters punched into the tan and red sand, as if meteors had showered down from the heavens.

Miners hunt near Bangka's surface for veins of cassiterite, a dark mineral that is the principal tin ore, and virtually all of the work is done by hand. While estimates from tin industry officials are wide-ranging, there may be anywhere from 15,000 to 50,000 miners on permitted and unpermitted sites, scrounging in the pits of Bangka and Belitung. The craters are roughly round and usually about 15 to 40 feet deep. Inside, miners work in groups of three to five, hunched over hoes and pickaxes, or crawling on their knees to scoop the walls with their hands. If they're lucky, the members of a crew find enough "tin sand" to each earn about $5 a day, sometimes a bit more. The quest for tin touches virtually everything on Bangka. Even in the province's capital, Pangkal Pinang, where mining is officially banned, renegades have dug craters near the airport's sole runway. There are pits about 800 feet behind the parking lot of the governor's office. And there are pits within sight of the island's largest hospital.

Demand is pushing the mining offshore, too. There, an armada of dredges suck ore from the seabed with the government's blessing, plying waters that have supplied fishermen since boats were first carved from tree trunks. The dredges, which look like little metal factories bobbing on the surface of the sea, work side by side with thousands of floating small-scale miners, three- or four-man crews atop homemade dredges, made with poles and blue plastic barrels. Each has a diesel-powered pump to suck up the ore. They have overtaken beachside villages once dominated by fishermen or domestic tourists.

Though ubiquitous, the small-scale mines floating along the shore, and many on the island, are technically illegal. This does not seem to matter. Mined legally or illegally, from land or sea, tin ore from Bangka and its neighbor island flows each day into the global supply chain.

Tin is often associated with soup and questionable meats, but tin cans were replaced long ago by containers made from far cheaper steel, lined with plastic or extremely thin coatings of tin, which does not corrode. Tin's real use is for solder. Electronics manufacturers use solder, which today typically contains more than 95 percent tin, to attach and connect components. The solder points are tiny but omnipresent, numbering about 7,000 in just two of the components in an iPad, according to research company IHS's iSuppli. A large flat-screen television can contain as much as 4.8 grams of solder, according to German solder maker Henkel. The iPad or a competing tablet can hold at least 20 percent of that amount, with its tin content weighing in at anywhere from 1 to 3 grams, according to Henkel and ITRI, a U.K.-based industry trade group. That means the construction of as few as five iPads, which weigh about 1.4 pounds each, consumes as much tin solder as the average car, which weighs about 4,000 pounds.

The solder points in an iPad are tiny but omnipresent. They number about 7,000 in just two of the components.

London-based solder maker Cookson Group told investors in a Feb. 27 presentation that growth for its solder was "still underpinned" by "buoyant" sales of three things: smartphones, tablets, and Internet data servers. Foxconn confirmed it uses solder made of Indonesian tin from, at a minimum, Shenmao and Chernan. But the company declined to say what share of its total might come from other solder makers who buy tin elsewhere. In an e-mailed statement, Foxconn said it follows international standards for supplier responsibility and its own internal code of conduct.

Indonesian tin is becoming more desirable for companies hoping to avoid controversy over sourcing materials in Africa. On Aug. 22, as part of the Dodd-Frank act, the Securities and Exchange Commission required U.S.-listed companies to start disclosing whether any "conflict minerals" from Africa's war-torn Democratic Republic of Congo are in the supply chains for their products. Buying Indonesian tin is the expedient route to a "conflict-free" guarantee, solder makers say.

Prompted by concerns about Africa, Apple said in a report this year that it had traced solder used by its component makers to 58 of the world's tin refiners, but it did not publicly identify them. Contacted for this story and told of some of the conditions on Bangka Island, Apple spokesman Steve Dowling declined to comment on the identities of any of the tin refiners in Apple's supply chain or their locations. He did say Apple provides funding for education programs in Indonesia, but this is intended for locals who may be lured into coercive labor at Asian electronics plants.

ITRI says about 70 percent of all tin in the past decade has come, roughly equally, from two countries: Indonesia and China. About 12 percent of China's production comes from small-scale mining pits, too, according to ITRI data. As with many commodities, China does not often export tin, holding on to it for domestic manufacturers. As the world's largest tin consumer, China also must import the metal or unrefined ore from other countries. In the first half of this year, it imported 13,582 metric tons of refined tin, with more than 49 percent coming directly from Indonesia, Chinese customs data show.

Indonesia, by contrast, exports virtually all of its tin, and more than 90 percent of it comes from the Bangka-Belitung province, according to the government. This means the bulk of worldwide tin exports originates in and around Bangka, and that most phones for sale in the U.S. almost certainly have a little piece of the troubled island inside.

Six days after Rosnan died, in a village about six miles away, Robin Simanjuntak, a local Bangka police commander, sat on a rickety wooden bench on the front porch of a one-room home. Inside, the body of 18-year-old Johidi bin Gunadi was laid out in the middle of the reception room's floor, shrouded in a gold, yellow, and black striped blanket. About a dozen family members and friends were present, most sitting cross-legged on the floor. Their heads were bowed, but their voices carried communal prayers out into the evening air as the police commander described what happened.

Only a few hours earlier, Johidi had been working with two older men in a deep tin pit along a mud road a couple of miles behind the village. The pit began to cave in, the commander says, using the Indonesian word *longsor*—"landslide." The two older miners bolted away from the cascading mud, while Johidi, apparently confused, ran toward it, the commander says. It took three hours, about 50 villagers, and two excavators to uncover Johidi's body from beneath 16 feet of dirt. When their search was finished, rescue party members mounted their motorbikes or climbed into the few vehicles parked on the edge of the mining site. Under a tropical downpour, they formed a long procession and streamed toward the village along the wet road. Up front was a black Suzuki flatbed truck carrying Johidi in the back, cradled in the arms of a villager.

Like Johidi, most of the bodies of miners killed in the pits go straight to families for burial, as is Muslim custom. Dr. Mario, the doctor who declared Rosnan dead at the government hospital, says he has seen only a few unclaimed bodies of miners brought into the hospital's morgue, where he also works. These are most likely migrants from impoverished areas of neighboring islands who come to Bangka to scratch out a living in the tin pits. Last year police in Bangka counted 44 deaths in the pits, more than double the 21 from 2010. A police spokesman says many cases may go unreported.

Some pits are unstable because they are dug straight down. Mining in a terraced pattern, with shorter, staggered walls, is far safer; it also takes more time and effort. In one of the pits adjacent to where Johidi died, the dangers were obvious. The pit was deep, and its walls were nearly vertical. Striations showed the walls were freshly cut with the bucket of an excavator—according to miners at the site, one of the same excavators used to unearth Johidi's body.

As the mining continues, it becomes more dangerous. The world's biggest exporter of refined tin, Timah, a publicly traded company based on Bangka, says ore concentrations have plummeted 63 percent on the island in just the past two decades. Scarcity creates the need for deeper mines, which are more likely to cave in. "I don't know about the deposits in the land," says Johan Murod, a portly businessman who owns three tin smelting plants, and a dredge. "But if the price is high, we can just dig deeper."

Murod is a Bangka native and a folk hero to many. As a young political activist, he helped Bangka and Belitung fight for, and win, self-rule in 2000, following years of provincial control from Sumatra. Self-rule was key to unleashing small-scale mining. After authorities in 2006 and 2007 tried to place controls on it, Murod helped organize demonstrations, which spun into riots. He was jailed and became a political martyr. The authorities relented.

Murod says it was his idea to bring in the dredges. "Like a money printer," he says, speaking past a translator and breaking into English. During an interview at an outdoor café, he wears a short-sleeve dress shirt unbuttoned below the middle of his chest, exposing a long gold chain. At one point, he tries a joke in English, apologizing for his inability to understand a reporter's accent. "I usually hear accent of Uzbekistan girl," he says.

Until late last year, Murod was the secretary of an association representing independent refiners on the island, who supply almost half of Bangka's exports. The rest enters the world market through two related mining companies: Timah, which is majority-owned by the Indonesian government, and a smaller company, Koba, which is a closely held partnership between Timah (25 percent) and Malaysia Smelting (75 percent). The Indonesian government owns 65 percent of Timah, while the public owns the rest through shares traded on the Indonesian Stock Exchange under the ticker symbol TINS. Timah says it has almost 4,000 full-time employees and produced 11 percent of the global tin supply last year, making it the world's largest integrated tin miner. But the people not reflected in those numbers are probably more vital to tin production. In 2010 the company said 98 percent of its onshore production came from independent, small-scale miners.

Timah has increased the number of small-scale sites in operation from 2009 to 2010 by close to 100 percent; reaching almost 4,000. Subcontractors run the pits, each with four or five miners, according to Timah's 2010 annual report. The company says all of its subcontractors receive safety training and are required to cut pits with shallow terraces, in order to avoid collapses.

Yet tin ore flows to Timah from communities and pits where miners were killed, where safety was ignored, and from obviously illegal operations, via tin buyers who work as the company's subcontractors in villages across the island. This does not surprise Murod. When questions are raised about environmental damage, or after a miner is killed, he says, Timah and the independent refiners tend to blame each other, or simply claim that the miners involved were rogues. Swatting his open palm back and forth, he likens it to a game of Ping-Pong.

Tjung Ling Siaw, 40, is a third-generation fisherman with spiky black hair, a wide smile, and a tattoo on his left arm featuring a woman wrapped in a snake. During high season, he spends 16 hours a day on the water, seven days a week. His wife and 5-year-old son live in a small house just off Bangka's Rebo beach, but Siaw sleeps on the water. He snoozes in turn with his crew, either on a massive trap floating 17 miles out, or on the 35-foot blue and red fishing prow he built by hand. Even after a productive night, Siaw is pessimistic about the future. "Being a fisherman is like gambling with your life," he says.

On May 29, the day Rosnan was killed, Siaw led a group of about 40 fishermen in a march to the gates of Timah's headquarters in Pangkal Pinang. They carried a banner declaring it was time "to restore people's rights" and accused the company of destroying their livelihoods. Today, Timah gets more than 54 percent of its tin from the sea, compared with just 29 percent in 2008. That jump comes with the addition of a fleet of dredges, called *Kapal Isap Produksi* in Indonesian, or KIPs for short. These are the boats that Murod likens to presses that print money. They are also the focus of the fishermen's ire.

For decades, traditional dredges sent mechanical arms with conveyor belts down to the sea floor. Buckets attached to the conveyors would scoop up the bottom and trundle it to the surface, one load at a time. The process was slow, clunky, and inefficient. The newer dredges use vacuums. The ships move easily, making it possible to find the most fruitful spots quickly. As Timah has expanded its fleet, its take of tin ore has more than doubled to 14,399 metric tons in 2010, up from 6,904 in 2008. The company's motto, and the title of its most recent annual report, is "Go Offshore, Go Deeper." Timah has about 50 ships on contract and 10 more of its own. There are also a handful of vacuum dredges owned by private refiners, such as Murod's.

On a hot afternoon in June, Reza Muftiadi, a 27-year-old dive master, pulls himself out of a swimming pool in Pangkal Pinang, puts down his air tank, and uses his right hand to squeegee the water off his face before extending it. Muftiadi, who teaches diving techniques to a pool full of young students, is a lecturer in the fisheries department at Bangka-Belitung University. He has studied and photographed reefs around the island and says they are being buried by sediment churned up in the quest for tin. Waters once deep and blue as the sky are now brown and silted over, Muftiadi says. "If there's no coral, it means there are no fish," he says. Fishermen say ship captains repeatedly ignore a prohibition on mining in waters within four miles of Bangka's shore.

Tired of being ignored, the fishermen tried a new approach late last year. They teamed up with the local chapter of WALHI, an Indonesian environmental group, and sent crews chasing after the dredges with handheld GPS units and video cameras. With little effort, they documented illegal mining, says Ratno Budi, WALHI's executive director for Bangka and Belitung. Fishermen say illegal operations continue.

The corporate dredges are joined by countless small operators. In a seaside village called Batu Belubang, which is near the capital, 82 floating mines lined the sand or the shallows along a half-mile stretch of beach. More were strung out along the horizon in all directions, their diesel engines providing a sputtering symphony as they mined the seabed. Each platform held a wooden shack with a thatched roof. Some carried names resembling call signs, such as "643 TIGER," scrawled in black paint.

WALHI has estimated that there are about 2,500 such rafts mining the island's coasts at any given time. Timah says these floating poachers "number in the thousands" and mine in waters where the company has exclusive rights. They are often manned by fishermen who have turned to floating tin mines to survive, according to Budi and others. Siaw, the fisherman who's been leading protests, says he understands the difficulties that could force some fishermen to turn to mining, but insists he'll never be one of them. "My philosophy is that I make my life from the sea. I can't make my life destroying it," he says.

Asked what the floating mines have meant for the village, a retired fisherman named Asis wrinkles his forehead. "We hoped it would build our infrastructure, but that was nonsense," he says. "There's nothing good for the community in this."

The Saturday afternoon following Rosnan's death, I go to see a man who was buying tin from the miners on the site. Awakened from an afternoon nap by his wife, Cikung, wearing a traditional sarong, invites me into the living room of his home, where a flat-screen television is airing soccer highlights. Cikung is bald and has a small pot belly. He sits on a couch next to a man summoned from behind the house, identified as his partner, "Billy." Cikung then says that he is indeed the man who buys tin from mining sites in the area and that he is a subcontractor for Timah. Billy, sitting next to him, says the duo then sells the tin ore to both independent refiners and to Timah. Cikung agrees.

Moments later, Cikung changes his mind. He says he sells tin only to Timah and that Billy sells to independent refiners. Subcontractors for Timah are penalized if they sell ore from company concessions to independent concerns, who might pay higher prices in times of peak demand. The men then lead me through a small maze of rooms in a building connected to Cikung's house, and into a walled and gated compound in the backyard. The taste of metal and wood smoke fills the courtyard air.

Hot coals glow beneath what looks like a giant sandbox made of steel. Two men stand beside it, reaching in with rakes they use to spread wet ore across the bottom to dry it. Tin miners use water to form a slush around a vein of ore, which makes it easier to suck up with hoses. Stacked around the courtyard are propylene sacks holding more than four metric tons of ore. "You can't take any pictures," Cikung's wife shouts. Billy says he's not sure where all of this cassiterite was unearthed. "It's hard to know where the tin comes from, because when miners come to us, we just buy it," he says. He then displays permits for purchasing tin that he has from an independent refiner. "If someone comes to ask where my tin comes from, I just show that I have permits," he says. The documents are meant to entitle the holder to buy tin ore mined on specific, legally permitted areas, but Billy says he buys tin ore regardless.

In a neighboring village between where Rosnan died and where 18-year-old Johidi bin Gunadi died, "illegal" small-scale miners say they sell their tin ore to another Timah subcontractor, named Rusmanti. Dressed in cargo shorts, a red Suzuki polo shirt, and a Guinness baseball cap, the 43-year-old pit boss, Rusmanti, explains that he has a Timah permit to run mines on about 20 acres (8 hectares) of company land. One of his pits is clearly safer than the ones where Johidi and Rosnan died. Its walls are low, and the pit is terraced throughout. Still, chunks of one wall slide into the water at the bottom of the pit three times during the interview. Of the dead miners, Rusmanti says, "They are illegal, they are not working for Timah. . . . If you work with Timah, you know how to do good mining."

Moments later, however, Rusmanti acknowledges what the illegal miners in his village say: He buys their tin. When asked if he mixes tin from illegal mines with the tin his legitimate miners have unearthed, he answers, "Yes, I mix it. Timah will never know about this."

Agung Nugroho, a spokesman for Timah, declined to comment on specific cases, but says the company will start instructing its small-scale mine operators to halt any tin buying from illegal and dangerous pits. A clear prohibition will be added to all future contracts, he says, adding that illegal mining on the island damages the company's own operations.

The public prosecutor acknowledges that, at least in recent memory, the government has never charged the owner of a small-scale mine, a pit boss, a tin purchaser, or anyone else in the supply chain following a deadly pit collapse. "Government, no responsibility. Timah, no responsibility. Smelter, no responsibility," Murod says, adding, "We are all the thieves here."

Murod says change is overdue. Independent smelters and e mining companies should be forced to pay a share of their venues into a fund that would be administered by an indepenent group to improve safety, provide insurance for miners who e killed or injured, and to remediate environmental damage, urod says.

Government, no responsibility. Timah, no esponsibility. Smelter, no responsibility," urod says, adding, "We are all the thieves ere."

The companies that dominate the world solder market—such Cookson; Henkel; Metallic Resources, of Twinsburg, Ohio; d Indium of Clinton, N.Y.—are not completely in the dark. ve years ago they expressed alarm about illegal mining. But ey were concerned that a crackdown by Indonesian authorities as driving tin prices up. On March 12, 2007, following one of e first big price spikes for tin in the last decade, a group called e Solder Products Value Council issued a public statement. complained that tightened Indonesian export regulations d the crackdown on "illegal mining operations mostly in the angka-Belitung province" were behind the spike, declaring: A key to our industry's growth will be how we address these ramatic cost increases without driving the Assembly lectronics supply chain to yet another dangerously low level of rofitability." Members of the group say they control more than 0 percent of the global supply of solder for electronics. In a atement this week, the group said it doesn't endorse illegal ining and supports all efforts to eliminate it.

It is not the first time tin buyers on the island have been different to the local costs of global demand. Bangka has only ne building dedicated to preserving history, the Indonesia Tin luseum. It spans four small ground-floor rooms in what used to be the residence of the Dutch colonial mining boss. Schoolchildren on field trips regularly crowd before its glass cases, peering in at hand tools, spools of solder, or a plastic model of a dredge suspended on a faux sea.

The museum's dominant feature is a mural painted across a concave wall like a diorama. The painting shows more than 70 islanders scattered across a vast pit, most hunched over rakes, or stooped under the weight of ore suspended from the tips of shoulder poles. Standing front and just off-center is the Dutch colonial boss. Shaded under a parasol held high by an islander, the boss's back is turned to three miners, who are only a few feet from him. Two of the men are acting as human crutches, assisting a comrade unable to stand on his own. Shoulder poles are a rare sight at Bangka's tin pits these days, and there are no Dutch masters. Otherwise, not much has changed; if anything, the terracing shown in the 19th century pit is an improvement.

Dian Chandra, Rosnan's son, says he blames no one for what happened to his dad. "I just accept it as a fate," he says. He sometimes accompanied his father to the tin pits, sleeping in the makeshift camps miners erect from tarps and palm branches along the pit rims, so he could help his dad dig for tin at sunrise. As he spoke, his mother was mining tin in the pits nearby, as she had been when Rosnan died. "I told her not to go mining again, and to let me look for a job," he says. "I want to make her happy, and I'm worried that something might happen to her."

Critical Thinking

1. Why is tin important to high-tech industries?
2. Describe the "human face" this article presents.
3. How does this article relate to Articles 3, 14, 21, and 22?

With Tim Culpan, in Taiwan; Dwi Sadmoko and Eko Listiyorini, in Indonesia.

Africa's Hopeful Economies: The Sun Shines Bright

The continent's impressive growth looks likely to continue.

Her $3 billion fortune makes Oprah Winfrey the wealthiest black person in America, a position she has held for years. But she is no longer the richest black person in the world. That honour now goes to Aliko Dangote, the Nigerian cement king. Critics grumble that he is too close to the country's soiled political class. Nonetheless his $10 billion fortune is money earned, not expropriated. The Dangote Group started as a small trading outfit in 1977. It has become a pan-African conglomerate with interests in sugar and logistics, as well as construction, and it is a real business, not a kleptocratic sham.

Legitimately self-made African billionaires are harbingers of hope. Though few in number, they are growing more common. They exemplify how far Africa has come and give reason to believe that its recent high growth rates may continue. The politics of the continent's Mediterranean shore may have dominated headlines this year, but the new boom south of the Sahara will affect more lives.

From Ghana in the west to Mozambique in the south, Africa's economies are consistently growing faster than those of almost any other region of the world. At least a dozen have expanded by more than 6% a year for six or more years. Ethiopia will grow by 7.5% this year, without a drop of oil to export. Once a byword for famine, it is now the world's tenth-largest producer of livestock. Nor is its wealth monopolised by a well-connected clique. Embezzlement is still common but income distribution has improved in the past decade.

Severe income disparities persist through much of the continent; but a genuine middle class is emerging. According to Standard Bank, which operates throughout Africa, 60m African households have annual incomes greater than $3,000 at market exchange rates. By 2015, that number is expected to reach 100m—almost the same as in India now. These households belong to what might be called the consumer class. In total, 300m Africans earn more than $700 a year. That's not much, and many of those people could be pushed back into penury by a small change in circumstance. But it can cover a phone and even some school fees. "They are not all middle class by Western standards, but nonetheless represent a vast market," says Edward George, an economist at Ecobank, another African banking group.

As for Africans below the poverty line—the majority of the continent's billion people—disease and hunger are still a big problem. Out of 1,000 children 118 will die before their fifth birthday. Two decades ago the figure was 165. Such progress towards the Millennium Development Goals, a series of poverty reduction milestones set by the UN, is slow and uneven. But it is not negligible. And the mood among have-nots is better than at any time since the independence era two generations ago. True, Africans have a remarkable capacity for being upbeat. But it seems that this time they really do have something to smile about.

Lions and Tigers (and Bears)

Since *The Economist* regrettably labelled Africa "the hopeless continent" a decade ago, a profound change has taken hold. Labour productivity has been rising. It is now growing by, on average, 2.7% a year. Trade between Africa and the rest of the world has increased by 200% since 2000. Inflation dropped from 22% in the 1990s to 8% in the past decade. Foreign debts declined by a quarter, budget deficits by two-thirds. In eight of the past ten years, according to the World Bank, sub-Saharan growth has been faster than East Asia's (though that does include Japan).

Even after revising downward its 2012 forecast because of a slowdown in the northern hemisphere, the IMF still expects sub-Saharan Africa's economies to expand by 5.75% next year. Several big countries are likely to hit growth rates of 10%. The World Bank—not known for boosterism—said in a report this year that "Africa could be on the brink of an economic take off, much like China was 30 years ago and India 20 years ago," though its officials think major poverty reduction will require higher growth than today's—a long-term average of 7% or more.

There is another point of comparison with Asia: demography. Africa's population is set to double, from 1 billion to 2 billion, over the next 40 years. As Africa's population grows in size, it will also alter in shape. The median age is now 20, compared with 30 in Asia and 40 in Europe. With fertility rates dropping, that median will rise as today's mass of young people moves into its most productive years. The ratio of people of

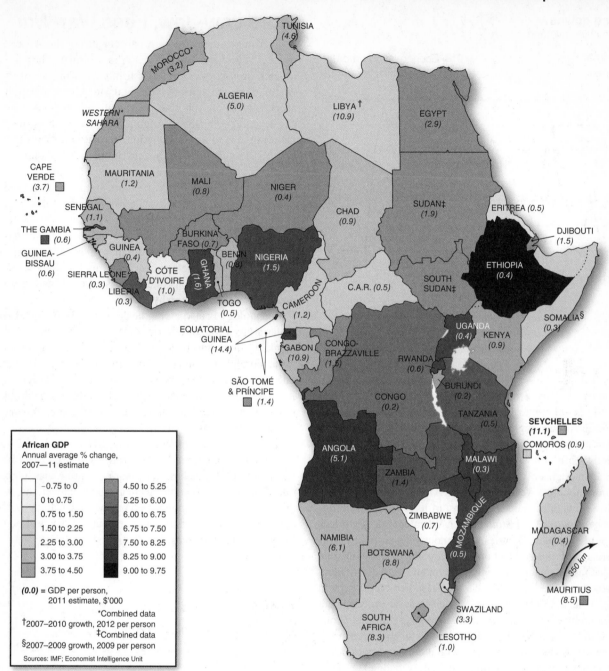

African GDP
Annual average % change,
2007—11 estimate

−0.75 to 0	4.50 to 5.25
0 to 0.75	5.25 to 6.00
0.75 to 1.50	6.00 to 6.75
1.50 to 2.25	6.75 to 7.50
2.25 to 3.00	7.50 to 8.25
3.00 to 3.75	8.25 to 9.00
3.75 to 4.50	9.00 to 9.75

(0.0) = GDP per person,
2011 estimate, $'000

*Combined data
†2007–2010 growth, 2012 per person
‡Combined data
§2007–2009 growth, 2009 per person

Sources: IMF; Economist Intelligence Unit

working age to those younger and older—the dependency ratio—will improve. This "demographic dividend" was crucial to the growth of East Asian economies a generation ago. It offers a huge opportunity to Africa today.

Seen through a bullish eye, this reinforces exuberant talk of "lion economies" analogous to the Asian tigers. But there are caveats. For one thing, in Africa, perhaps even more so than in Asia, wildly different realities can exist side by side. Averaging out failed states and phenomenal success stories is of limited value. The experience of the leaders is an unreliable guide to what will become of the laggards. For another, these are early days, and there have been false dawns before. Those of bearish mind will ask whether the lions can match the tigers for stamina. Will Africa continue to rise? Or is this merely a strong

upswing in a boom-bust cycle that will inevitably come tumbling back down?

More than Diamond Geezers

Previous African growth spurts undoubtedly owed a lot to commodity prices (see chart 1). After all, Africa has about half the world's gold reserves and a third of its diamonds, not to mention copper, coltan and all sorts of other minerals and metals. In the 1960s revenues from mining paid for roads, palaces and skyscrapers. When markets slumped in the 1980s the money dried up. The skylines of Johannesburg, Nairobi and Lagos are still littered with high-rise flotsam from the high-water marks of previous booms.

Ups and downs
2-year moving average

African GDP*,
% increase

The Economist commodity-
price index, % change

[Chart showing African GDP percentage increase (left axis 0-8) and The Economist commodity-price index percentage change (right axis) from 1981 to 2010, with x-axis years 1981, 85, 90, 95, 2000, 05, 10]

*Sub-Saharan excluding
South Africa

Sources: IMF; *The Economist*

Recently revenues from selling oil and metals have helped to fill treasuries, create jobs and feed an appetite for luxury. In gem-rich Angola, high-grade diamonds are reimported after being cut in Europe to adorn the fingers of local minerals magnates and their molls.

Overall, though, only about a third of Africa's recent growth is due to commodities. West and southern Africa are the chief beneficiaries. Equatorial Guinea gets most of its revenues from oil; Zambia gets half its GDP from copper. When commodity prices soften or tumble such countries will undoubtedly suffer. But it is east Africa, with little oil and only a sprinkling of minerals, that boasts the fastest-expanding regional economy on the continent, and there are outposts of similar non-resource-based growth elsewhere, such as Burkina Faso. "Everything is growing, not just commodities," says Mo Ibrahim, a Sudanese mobile-phone mogul who is arguably Africa's most successful entrepreneur.

When the world economy—and with it commodity prices—tanked in 2008, African growth rates barely budged. "Africa has great resilience," says Mthuli Ncube, chief economist of the African Development Bank. "A structural change has taken place."

A long-term decline in commodity prices would undoubtedly hurt. But commodity-led growth on the continent is not as reversible as it used to be. For one thing, African governments have invested more wisely this time round, notably in infrastructure. In much of the continent roads are still dirt. But there are more decent ones than there used to be, and each new length of tarmac will boost the productivity of the people it serves long after the cashflow that paid for it dries up. For another, Africa's commodities now have a wider range of buyers. A generation ago Brazil, Russia, India and China accounted for just 1% of African trade. Today they make up 20%, and by 2030 the rate is expected to be 50%. If China and India continue to grow Africa probably will too.

More Jaw-Jaw, Less War-War

What's more, many foreign participants in the African commodity trade have become less short-termist. They are likely to stick around after they finish mining; Chinese workers, of whom there are tens of thousands in Africa, have shown a propensity to morph into local entrepreneurs. A Cantonese construction company in Angola recently set up its own manufacturing arm to produce equipment that is difficult to import. Few Western competitors would do the same (though many of their colonial forebears did).

Commodity growth may be more assured than it used to be. But two big drivers of Africa's growth would still be there even if the continent held not a barrel of oil nor an ounce of gold. One is the application of technology. Mobile phones have penetrated deep into the bush. More than 600m Africans have one, perhaps 10% of those have access to mobile-internet services. The phones make boons like savings accounts and information on crop prices ever more available.

Technology is also aiding health care. The World Bank says malaria takes $12 billion out of Africa's GDP every year. But thanks to more and better bed nets, death rates have fallen by 20%. Foreign investors in countries with high HIV-infection rates complain about expensively trained workers dying in their 30s and 40s, but the incidence of new infection is dropping in much of the continent, and many more people are receiving effective treatment.

The second big non-commodity driver is political stability. The Africa of a generation ago was a sad place. The blight of apartheid isolated its largest economy, South Africa. Only seven out of more than 50 countries held frequent elections. America and the Soviet Union conducted proxy wars. Capital was scarce and macroeconomic management erratic. Lives were cut short by bullets and machetes.

Open for business

Capital flows into Africa, $bn 2010 prices

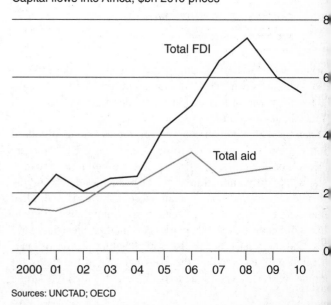

Sources: UNCTAD; OECD

Africa is still not entirely peaceful and democratic. But it has made huge strides. The dead hand of the Soviet Union is gone; countries such as Mozambique and Ethiopia have given up on Marxism. The dictators, such as Congo's leopard-skin-fez-wearing Mobutu Sese Seko, that super-powers once propped up have fallen. Civil wars like the one which crippled Angola have mostly ended. Two out of three African countries now hold elections, though they are not always free and fair. Congo held one on November 28th.

Friends and Neighbours

Even if many of the world's most inept states can still be found between the Sahara and Kalahari deserts, governance has improved markedly in many places. Regulatory reforms have partially unshackled markets. A string of privatisations (more than 100 in Nigeria alone) has reduced the role of the state in many countries. In Nigeria, Africa's biggest resource economy, the much-expanded service sector, if taken together with agriculture, now almost matches oil output.

Trade barriers have been reduced, at least a bit, and despite the dearth of good roads, regional trade—long an African weakness—is picking up. By some measures, intra-African trade has gone from 6% to 13% of the total volume. Some economists think the post-apartheid reintegration of South Africa on its own has provided an extra 1% in annual GDP growth for the continent, and will continue to do so for some time. It is now the biggest source of foreign investment for other countries south of the Sahara.

Somewhat belatedly, Africans are taking an interest in each other. Flight connections are improving, even if an Arab city, Dubai, is still the best hub for African travellers. Blocks of African economies have taken steps towards integration. The East African Community, which launched a common market in 2010, is doing well; the Economic Community of West African States less so. The Southern African Development Community has made the movement of goods and people across borders much easier. That said, barriers remain, and the economy suffers as a result. Africans pay twice as much for washing powder as consumers in Asia, where trade and transport are easier and cheaper.

As in Asia a generation ago, relatively small increases in capital can produce large productivity gains. When, after decades of capital starvation, outside investors started to take that disproportionate return seriously, they helped Asia blossom. Now some of those investors are eyeing Africa. In financial centres such as London barely a week goes by without an Africa investor conference. Private-equity firms that a decade ago barely knew sub-Saharan Africa existed raised $1.5 billion for projects on the continent last year. In 2010 total foreign direct investment was more than $55 billion—five times what it was a decade earlier, and much more than Africa receives in aid (see chart 2 on previous page).

Foreign investors are no longer just interested in oil wells and mines. They are moving on to medium-sized bets on consumer goods. The number of projects—for example by retail chains such as Britain's Marks & Spencer—has doubled in the past three years. Despite the boom in mining, the share of total investment going into extractive activities has shrunk by 13%.

That said, the riches are far from evenly spread: three-quarters of all investments are in just ten big countries.

The increased interest from outsiders that has been triggered by Africa's political and technological changes is not, though, the heart of the story. Economic change has made life more rewarding for Africans themselves. They have more opportunities to start businesses and get ahead than they have enjoyed in living memory, and governments are showing some willingness to get out of their way. According to the World Bank's annual ranking of commercial practices, 36 out of 46 African governments made things easier for business in the past year.

No End to Worries

That said, most African countries are still clustered near the bottom of the table. In all sorts of ways African governments need to run their countries more efficiently, more accountably and less intrusively. They also need to offer much better schooling, an area in which Africa woefully lags behind Asia. African businessmen constantly complain about the shortage of skills. Hiring qualified staff can be prohibitively expensive. The return of skilled exiles has helped in some newly peaceful countries, but often foreigners are needed, usually other Africans. Without better education, Africa cannot hope to emulate the Asian miracle.

Africa's demographic dividend, too, is far from guaranteed. A growing population and a bulge of working-age citizens proved a blessing in Asia. But population growth always has its costs. All those extra people must be fed, educated and given opportunities. If illiberal policies obstruct growth and discourage firms from hiring, Africa's extra millions may soon be jobless and disgruntled. Some may even take up arms—a sure recipe for disaster, both human and economic.

An abundance of young people is like gearing on a balance sheet: it makes good situations better and bad ones worse. It is worrying that some of Africa's fastest-growing populations are in economies not performing well at the moment; and fertility rates are not declining as uniformly, or as swiftly, as they did in Asia.

Africa's extra people are flocking to cities. Some 40% of Africans are city dwellers now, up from 30% a generation ago. By 2025 the number is likely to be 50%. In Asia the rate is currently 52%. This is usually a good thing. Productivity is higher in cities. Transport costs are lower and markets are busier when people live close to each other. In bad times, the tight ethnic jumble of the city can be a powder keg. That said, Africa's worst wars, such as those in Congo, Rwanda, Sudan and Somalia, have been fought in countries where most people are peasants or livestock herders.

Extra mouths will need to be fed. There is scope for this. Though Africa is now a net food importer, it has 60% of the world's uncultivated arable land. It produces less per person now than in 1960. Africa's land is often hard to farm, with large year on year variations in climate (a problem likely to get worse as the Earth heats up). Farmers lack access to capital for fertiliser and irrigation. More roads and storage depots are also needed; much of the harvest rots before it gets to market.

And land ownership often raises thorny issues about who belongs to a place and who does not.

Agriculture is a long-term worry. A shorter term concern is how to deal with a coming slowdown and recession in the north. Investors fleeing risky assets in Europe are unlikely to put their cash into Africa. More likely they will pull back some of the money they have already invested there. The signs are that this is already happening. Bankers say the deal flow is slowing. But many remain generally bullish on Africa, convinced that its growth potential will reward patient investors and eventually lure back fickle ones.

Africa's growth is now underpinned by a permanent shift in expectations. In many African countries people have at last started to see themselves as citizens, with the rights that citizenship brings. Greater political awareness makes it harder for incompetent despots to hold on to power, as north Africa has discovered. Bastions of the continent's past—destitute, violent and isolated—are becoming exceptions.

Africa is not the next China. It provides only a tiny fraction of world output—2.5% at purchasing-power parity. It is as yet not even a good bet for retail investors, given the dearth of stockmarkets. Mr Dangote's $10 billion undeniably make him a big fish, but the Dangote Group accounts for a quarter of Nigeria's stockmarket by value: it is a small and rather illiquid pond. Nonetheless, Africa's boom will continue to benefit Africans, serving the billion as well as the billionaires. That is no small feat.

Critical Thinking

1. How are economic conditions changing in sub-Saharan Africa?

2. What are the reasons for these changes?

3. How does this article relate to Articles 15, 17, and 18?

Women and Work

Here's to the Next Half-Century

It's taking a long time, but things are getting better.

"**W**omen are not at the top anywhere," says Herminia Ibarra, a professor at the INSEAD business school near Paris. "Many get on the high-potential list and then languish there for ever." That is

Speak up

Women in single or lower house of parliament
%, end August 2011

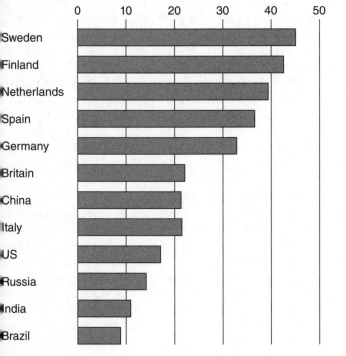

Source: Inter-Parliamentary Union

broadly true not only in business but also in politics, academia, law, medicine, the arts and almost any other field you care to mention.

In parliaments across the world women on average hold just 20% of the seats (see chart), though again the Nordics do much better. In Finland—one of the first countries to give them the vote, in 1906—women have at various times held more than half the ministerial jobs. The prime minister one back was a woman and so is the current president, Tarja Halonen, the first female to hold the post. A lawyer, doughty fighter for women's rights and single mother, she is nearing the end of her second and final term of office but would like to see another woman president soon: "Once is not enough." Elsewhere too female political leaders are becoming less unusual—think of Germany's Angela Merkel, Brazil's Dilma Rousseff, Australia's Julia Gillard or Liberia's Ellen Johnson Sirleaf—but still far from common.

The most egregious gap between men and women is still in the world of work. The World Economic Forum, a Geneva-based think-tank, earlier this month published its latest annual "Global Gender Gap Report", comparing progress in 135 countries towards sex equality in four broad areas. In health and education, says Saadia Zahidi, head of the WEF's Women Leaders and Gender Parity Programme, most countries have largely closed the gap in recent years. In the third, politics, the gap is still wide but progress has been relatively rapid. The fourth, economic opportunity, is proving dishearteningly slow to shift, not just in developing countries but in many rich ones too. Ms Zahidi argues that "smaller gaps in economic opportunity are directly correlated with greater competitiveness, so increased equality helps to promote economic growth."

On the face of it women have done all they possibly could to prepare themselves. Noting that their menfolk got better jobs if they were more highly educated, they piled into the colleges. They went out to look for work in such numbers that in many countries now almost as many women as men hold down jobs. They poured into business and the professions, and a lot more of them these days make it to middle-ranking jobs. But there the vast majority of them stop.

The reasons are complex, but a few stick out. First, work in most organisations is structured in ways that were established many decades ago, when married men were the breadwinners and most married women stayed at home. Yet even though the great majority of families no longer fit that pattern, most workplaces have failed to take the change on board. They think they are being egalitarian by treating women exactly the same as men, but women's circumstances are often different. "We shouldn't be fixing the women but the system," says Alison Maitland, a senior fellow with The Conference Board, a think-tank, and joint author with Avivah Wittenberg-Cox of "Why Women Mean Business", a book about women in leadership roles. A lot of men, as it happens, would also like to see work organised more flexibly to fit their lives better.

Second, though biology need not be destiny, it would be silly to pretend that having babies has no effect on women's careers. Although women now have children later and in smaller numbers, they often start thinking about having a family just at the time when career-oriented people are scrambling madly to get to the top of their particular tree. Most workplaces set critical goals for aspiring leaders (such as making partner or joining the board) at specific ages. Some women join the scramble and forget about having children, but if they take time out to start a family they find it very hard to catch up afterwards.

Third, women can be their own worst enemies. They tend to be less self-confident than men and do not put their hands up, so they do not get the plum assignments or promotions or pay rises. Iris Bohnet, a professor at Harvard's Kennedy School, says that women are less likely than men to negotiate for themselves (although they do very well when negotiating for others), and less willing to volunteer an opinion when they are not sure. They can also be too honest. When a team led by Robin Ely, a professor at the Harvard Business School, was asked to advise a consultancy on the reasons for high turnover among its women, it found that the firm's projects were often badly managed, making for long hours. The men, it discovered, were not happy either, but they quietly rearranged things to make life easier for themselves. The women went part-time or quit.

Fourth, discrimination continues in subtle ways. Business schools that follow their alumni's careers find that men are promoted on their potential but women are promoted on their performance, so they advance more slowly. The women adjust to this, which slows their progress even more, and so the discrimination goes on without either side necessarily being aware of it.

Underusing women across the spectrum of human activity is obviously wasteful. Their cognitive endowment is the same as men's, but because they have different interests and styles, they make for more diverse and probably more innovative workplaces. And since most rich countries' working populations are ageing, women's talents will be needed even more in the future. So what is to be done?

Legislation makes a difference. Over the past few decades most rich countries, and many poorer ones too, have passed laws to ensure equal opportunities and equal pay for women. They do not always work as intended, but they make overt and gross discrimination less likely. The pay gap between men and women, for instance, has significantly narrowed in most countries in the past 30–40 years, even though progress has recently become more sporadic.

Governments can also help in a variety of other ways: by ensuring that tax rules do not discriminate against dual-earner families; by legislating for reasonable (but not excessively long) maternity and paternity leave; and, in the longer term, by pushing for school hours that allow both parents to have paid jobs. Given that education for older children is seen as a public good, there is an argument for also subsidising child care for the very young, or at least making it tax-deductible.

Golden Skirts

Should governments legislate to close the gap between men and women at the top of companies? Norway has become famous for imposing a 40% quota for women on the boards of all state-owned and quoted companies. Over a period of about a decade this raised the proportion of women on boards from 6% to the required figure. Aagoth Storvik and Mari Teigen, two Oslo-based academics who made a detailed study of the experiment last year, found that once the policy was implemented the heated debate over it died down completely and the system now seems to be working smoothly. But the researchers also point out that even now only 5% of the board chairmen (and only 2% of the bosses of companies quoted on the Oslo stock exchange) are women, so this is not a quick fix.

Nevertheless other countries have picked up on the Norwegian example. Spain has set a mandatory 40% target for female directors of large companies by 2015 and France by 2017. Germany is debating whether to impose quotas. In Britain a government-commissioned report earlier this year recommended that companies set themselves voluntary targets, but six months later only a handful seemed to have got around to it and progress is being kept under review. The European Union's justice commissioner, Viviane Reding, has told European business leaders to promote many more women to boards voluntarily, or they may find their hands forced.

Nobody likes quotas: they smack of tokenism and unfair competition. But many people who started off opposing them have changed their minds. Lynda Gratton, a professor at the London Business School, is one of them. She accepts the usual objection that quotas will encourage some women who are not very good but points out that boards also contain lots of men who are not very good.

And there are those who think you just have to keep plugging away. Dame Helen Alexander, until recently president of the Confederation of British Industry (and a former chief executive of The Economist Group), is not in favour of quotas, preferring voluntary targets. She has found progress in large British firms "really patchy" but thinks that companies are getting better. She also reckons that men are changing, noting that "we now hear about husbands of high-earning women staying at home to look after the family." That would have been unthinkable 20 years ago.

Certainly young men now at the start of their career see the world differently from their fathers. They are less inclined to work extreme hours to advance their careers and more interested in achieving a reasonable balance between their work and the rest of their lives. That is what most women have been asking for all along. If both men and women pressed for such a balance, employers would find it harder to refuse and perhaps everyone would be happier. Facebook's Ms Sandberg points to studies showing that couples where both partners work ull-time and share responsibilities in the home equally have ower divorce rates and better sex lives.

In much of the developing world such a balance is still a Jtopian vision, and even in rich countries many women still get a raw deal. But not nearly as raw as they did half a century go, when even in Europe some women did not have the vote, discrimination was rife, women's jobs were second-class and the pay gap was huge. It may be taking far too long, but there is no denying that women's lives have got much better. Listen to the Chinese banker quoted earlier in this report: she works her socks off, looks after her family, supports her ageing parents and has no time for herself. But she still says she considers herself lucky: "In another life I would be a woman again."

Critical Thinking

1. What is the central argument of this article?

2. What reasons are offered to support this argument?

3. What are the future work prospects for women?

It's Still the One

Oil's very future is now being seriously questioned, debated, and challenged. The author of an acclaimed history explains why, just as we need more oil than ever, it is changing faster than we can keep up with.

DANIEL YERGIN

On a still afternoon under a hot Oklahoma sun, neither a cloud nor an ounce of "volatility" was in sight. Anything but. All one saw were the somnolent tanks filled with oil, hundreds of them, spread over the rolling hills, some brand-new, some more than 70 years old, and some holding, inside their silver or rust-orange skins, more than half a million barrels of oil each.

This is Cushing, Oklahoma, the gathering point for the light, sweet crude oil known as West Texas Intermediate—or just WTI. It is the oil whose price you hear announced every day, as in "WTI closed today at. . . ." Cushing proclaims itself, as the sign says when you ride into town, the "pipeline crossroads of the world." Through it passes the network of pipes that carry oil from Texas and Oklahoma and New Mexico, from Louisiana and the Gulf Coast, and from Canada too, into Cushing's tanks, where buyers take title before moving the oil onward to refineries where it is turned into gasoline, jet fuel, diesel, home heating oil, and all the other products that people actually use.

But that is not what makes Cushing so significant. After all, there are other places in the world through which much more oil flows. Cushing plays a unique role in the new global oil industry because WTI is the preeminent benchmark against which other oils are priced. Every day, billions of "paper barrels" of light, sweet crude are traded on the floor of the New York Mercantile Exchange in lower Manhattan and, in ever increasing volumes, at electron speed around the world, an astonishing virtual commerce that no matter how massive in scale, still connects back somehow to a barrel of oil in Cushing changing owners.

That frenetic daily trading has helped turn oil into something new—not only a physical commodity critical to the security and economic viability of nations but also a financial asset, part of that great instantaneous exchange of stocks, bonds, currencies, and everything else that makes up the world's financial portfolio. Today, the daily trade in those "paper barrels"—crude oil futures—is more than 10 times the world's daily consumption of physical barrels of oil. Add in the trades that take place on other exchanges or outside them entirely, and the ratio may be as much as 30 times greater. And though the oil may flow steadily in and out of Cushing at a stately 4 miles per hour, the global oil market is anything but stable.

That's why, as I sat down to work on a new edition of *The Prize* and considered what had changed since the early 1990s when I wrote this history of the world's most valuable, and misunderstood, commodity, the word "volatility" kept springing to mind. How could it not? Indeed, when people are talking about volatility, they are often thinking oil. On July 11, 2008, WTI hit $147.27. Exactly a year later, it was $59.87. In between, in December, it fell as low as $32.40. (And don't forget a little more than a decade ago, when it was as low as $10 a barrel and consumers were supposedly going to swim forever in a sea of cheap oil.)

These wild swings don't just affect the "hedgers" (oil producers, airlines, heating oil dealers, etc.) and the "speculators," the financial players. They show up in the changing prices at the gasoline station. They stir political passions and feed consumers' suspicions. Volatility also makes it more difficult to plan future energy investments, whether in oil and gas or in renewable and alternative fuels. And it can have a cataclysmic impact on the world economy. After all, Detroit was knocked flat on its back by what happened at the gasoline pump in 2007 and 2008 even before the credit crisis. The enormous impact of these swings is why British Prime Minister Gordon Brown and French President Nicolas Sarkozy were recently moved to call for a global solution to "destructive volatility." But, they were forced to add, "There are no easy solutions."

This volatility is part of the new age of oil. For though Cushing looks pretty much the same as it did when *The Prize* came out, the world of oil looks very different. Some talk today about "the end of oil." If so, others reply, we are entering its very long goodbye. One characteristic of this new age is that oil has developed a split personality—as a physical commodity but also now as a financial asset. Three other defining characteristics of this new age are the globalization of the demand for oil, a vast shift from even a decade ago; the rise of climate change as a political factor shaping decisions on how we will use oil, and how much of it, in the future; and the drive for new technologies that could dramatically affect oil along with the rest of the energy portfolio.

The cast of characters in the oil business has also grown and changed. Some oil companies have become "supermajors,"

The Capital of Oil

Within three years of its discovery in 1912, the Cushing field in Oklahoma was producing almost 20 percent of U.S. oil. Two years later, it was supplying a substantial part of the fuel used by the U.S. Army in Europe during World War I. The Cushing area was so prolific that it became known as "the Queen of the Oil Fields," and Cushing became one of those classic wild oil boom-towns of the early 20th century. "Any man with red blood gets oil fever" was the diagnosis of one reporter who visited the area during those days. Production grew so fast around Cushing that pipelines had to be hurriedly built and storage tanks quickly thrown up to hold surplus supplies. By the time production began to decline, a great deal of infrastructure was in place, and Cushing turned into a key oil hub, its network of pipelines used to bring in supplies from elsewhere in Oklahoma and West Texas. Those supplies were stored in the tanks at Cushing before being put into other pipelines and shipped to refineries. When the New York Mercantile Exchange—the NYMEX—started to trade oil futures in 1983, it needed a physical delivery point. Cushing, its boom days long gone, but with its network of pipelines and tank farms and its central location, was the obvious answer. As much as 1.1 million barrels per day pass in and out of Cushing—equivalent to about 6 percent of U.S. oil consumption. But prices for much of the world's crude oil are set against the benchmark of the West Texas Intermediate crude oil—also known as "domestic sweet"—sitting in those 300 or so tanks in Cushing, making this sedate Oklahoma town not only an oil hub but one of the hubs of the world economy.

—Daniel Yergin

much as ExxonMobil and Chevron, while others, such as Amoco and ARCO, have just disappeared. "Big oil" no longer means the traditional international oil companies, their logos instantly recognizable from corner gas stations, but rather much larger state-owned companies, which, along with governments, today control more than 80 percent of the world's oil reserves. Fifteen of the world's 20 largest oil companies are now state-owned.

The cast of oil traders has also much expanded. Today's global oil game now includes pension funds, institutional money managers, endowments, and hedge funds, as well as individual investors and day traders. The managers at the pension funds and the university endowments see themselves as engaged in "asset allocation," hedging risks and diversifying to protect retirees' incomes and faculty salaries. But, technically, they too are part of the massive growth in the ranks of the new oil speculators.

With all these changes, the very future of this most vital commodity is now being seriously questioned, debated, and challenged, even as the world will need more of it than ever before. Both the U.S. Department of Energy and the International Energy Agency project that, even accounting for gains in efficiency, global energy use will increase almost 50 percent from 2006 to 2030—and that oil will continue to provide 30 percent or more of the world's energy in 2030.

But will it?

$147.27—Closing price per barrel of oil on July 11, 2008. Exactly one year later, it had fallen to $59.87.

From the beginning, oil has been a global industry, going back to 1861 when the first cargo of kerosene was sent from Pennsylvania—the Saudi Arabia of 19th-century oil—to Britain. (The potential crew was so fearful that the kerosene would catch fire that they had to be gotten drunk to shanghai them on board.) But that is globalization of supply, a familiar story. What is decisively new is the globalization of demand.

For decades, most of the market—and the markets that mattered the most—were in North America, Western Europe, and Japan. That's also where the growth was. At the time of the first Gulf War in 1991, China was still an oil exporter.

But now, the growth is in China, India, other emerging markets, and the Middle East. Between 2000 and 2007, the world's daily oil demand increased by 9.4 million barrels. Almost 85 percent of that growth was in emerging markets. There were many reasons that prices soared all the way to $147.27 last year, ranging from geopolitics to a weak dollar to the impact of financial markets and speculation (in all its manifold meanings). But the starting point was the fundamentals—the surge in oil demand driven by powerful economic growth in emerging markets. This shift may be even more powerful than people recognize: So far this year, more new cars have been sold in China than in the United States. When economic recovery takes hold again, what happens to oil demand in such emerging countries will be crucial.

The math is clear: More consumers mean more demand, which means more supplies are needed. But what about the politics? There the forecasts are murkier, feeding a new scenario for international tension—a competition, even a clash, between China and the United States over "scarce" oil resources. This scenario even comes with a well-known historical model—the rivalry between Britain and "rising" Germany that ended in the disaster of World War I.

This scenario, though compelling reading, does not really accord with the way that the world oil market works. The Chinese are definitely new players, willing and able to pay top dollar to gain access to existing and new oil sources and, lately, also making loans to oil-producing countries to ensure future supplies. With more than $2 trillion in foreign reserves, China certainly has the wherewithal to be in the lending business.

But the global petroleum industry is not a go-it-alone business. Because of the risk and costs of large-scale development, companies tend to work in consortia with other companies.

Oil-exporting countries seek to diversify the countries and companies they work with. Inevitably, any country in China's position—whose demand had grown from 2.5 million barrels per day to 8 million in a decade and a half—would be worrying about supplies. Such an increase, however, is not a forecast of inevitable strife; it is a message about economic growth and rising standards of living. It would be much more worrying if, in the face of rising demand, Chinese companies were not investing in production both inside China (the source of half of its supply) and outside its borders.

There are potential flash points in this new world of oil. But they will not come from standard commercial competition. Rather, they arise when oil (along with natural gas) gets caught up in larger foreign-policy issues—most notably today, the potentially explosive crisis over the nuclear ambitions of oil- and gas-rich Iran.

Yet, despite all the talk of an "oil clash" scenario, there seems to be less overall concern than a few years ago and much more discussion about "energy dialogue." The Chinese themselves appear more confident about their increasingly important place in this globalized oil market. Although the risks are still there, the Chinese—and the Indians right alongside them—have the same stake as other consumers in an adequately supplied world market that is part of the larger global economy. Disruption of that economy, as the last year has so vividly demonstrated, does not serve their purposes. Why would the Chinese want to get into a confrontation over oil with the United States when the U.S. export market is so central to their economic growth and when the two countries are so financially interdependent?

Oil is not even the most important energy issue between China and the United States. It is coal. The two countries have the world's largest coal resources, and they are the world's biggest consumers of it. In a carbon-constrained world, they share a strong common interest in finding technological solutions for the emissions released when coal is burned.

And that leads directly to the second defining feature of the new age of oil: climate change. Global warming was already on the agenda when *The Prize* came out. It was back in 1992 that 154 countries signed the Rio Convention, pledging to dramatically reduce CO_2 concentrations in the atmosphere. But only in recent years has climate change really gained traction as a political issue—in Europe early in this decade, in the United States around 2005. Whatever the outcome of December's U.N. climate change conference in Copenhagen, carbon regulation is now part of the future of oil. And that means a continuing drive to reduce oil demand.

How does that get done? How does the world at once meet both the challenge of climate change and the challenge of economic growth—steady expansion in the industrial countries and more dramatic growth in China, India, and other emerging markets as tens of millions of their citizens rise from poverty and buy appliances and cars?

The answer has to be in another defining change—an emphasis on technology to a degree never before seen. The energy business has always been a technology business. After all, the men who figured out in 1859, exactly 150 years ago, how to drill that first oil well—Colonel Drake and his New Haven, Conn. investors—would, in today's lingo, be described as a group of disruptive technology entrepreneurs and venture capitalists. Again and again, in researching oil's history, I was struck by how seemingly insurmountable barriers and obstacles were overcome by technological progress, often unanticipated.

9.4 million—Number of barrels by which the world's daily oil demand rose from 2000 to 2007, with 85 percent coming from the developing world.

But the focus today on technology—all across the energy spectrum—is of unprecedented intensity. In the mid-1990s I chaired a task force for the U.S. Department of Energy on "strategic energy R&D." Our panel worked very hard for a year and a half and produced what many considered a very worthy report. But there was not all that much follow-through. The Gulf War was over, and the energy problem looked like it had been "solved."

Today, by contrast, the interest in energy technology is enormous. And it will only be further stoked by the substantial increases that are ahead in government support for energy R&D. Much of that spending and effort is aimed at finding alternatives to oil. Yet the challenge is not merely to find alternatives; it is to find alternatives that can be competitive at the massive scale required.

What will those alternatives be? The electric car, which is the hottest energy topic today? Advanced biofuels? Solar systems? New building designs? Massive investment in wind? The evolving smart grid, which can integrate electric cars with the electricity industry? Something else that is hardly on the radar screen yet? Or perhaps a revolution in the internal combustion engine, making it two to three times as efficient as the ones in cars today?

We can make educated guesses. But, in truth, we don't know, and we won't know until we do know. For now, it is clear that the much higher levels of support for innovation—along with considerable government incentives and subsidies—will inevitably drive technological change and thus redraw the curve in the future demand for oil.

Indeed, the biggest surprises might come on the demand side, through conservation and improved energy efficiency. The United States is twice as energy efficient as it was in the 1970s. Perhaps we will see a doubling once again. Certainly, energy efficiency has never before received the intense focus and support that it does today.

Just because we have entered this new age of high-velocity change does not mean this story is about the imminent end of oil. Consider the "peak oil" thesis—shorthand for the presumption that the world has reached the high point of roduction and is headed for a downward slope. Historically, peak-oil thinking gains attention during times when markets are tight and prices are rising, stoking fears of a permanent shortage. In 2007 and 2008, the belief system built around peak oil helped drive prices to $147.27. (It was actually the fifth time that the world had supposedly "run out" of oil. The first such episode was in the 1880s; the last instance before this most recent time was in the 1970s.)

However, careful examination of the world's resource base—including my own firm's analysis of more than 800 of the largest oil fields—indicates that the resource endowment of the planet is sufficient to keep up with demand for decades to come. That, of course, does not mean that the oil will actually make it to consumers. Any number of "aboveground" risks and obstacles can stand in the way, from government policies that restrict access to tax systems to civil conflict to geopolitics to rising costs of exploration and production to uncertainties about demand. As has been the case for decades and decades, the shifting relations between producing and consuming countries, between traditional oil companies and state-owned oil companies, will do much to determine what resources are developed, and when, and thus to define the future of the industry.

There are two further caveats. Many of the new projects will be bigger, more complex, and more expensive. In the 1990s, a "megaproject" might have cost $500 million to $1 billion. Today, the price tag is more like $5 billion to $10 billion. And an increasing part of the new petroleum will come in the form of so-called "unconventional oil"—from ultradeep waters, Canadian oil sands, and the liquids that are produced with natural gas.

But through all these changes, one constant of the oil market is that it is not constant. The changing balance of supply and demand—shaped by economics, politics, technologies, consumer tastes, and accidents of all sorts—will continue to move prices. Economic recovery, expectations thereof, the pent-up demand for "demand," a shift into oil as a "financial asset"—some combination of these could certainly send oil prices up again, even with the current surplus in the market. Yet, the quest

for stability is also a constant for oil, whether in reaction to the boom-and-bust world of northwest Pennsylvania in the late 19th century, the 10-cents-a-barrel world of Texas oil in the 1930s, or the $147.27 barrel of West Texas Intermediate in July 2008.

Certainly, the roller-coaster ride of oil prices over the last couple of years, as oil markets and financial markets have become more integrated, has made volatility a central pre-occupation for policymakers who do not want to see their economies whipsawed by huge price swings. Yet without the flexibility and liquidity of markets, there is no effective way to balance supply and demand, no way for consumers and producers to hedge their risks. Nor is there a way to send signals to these consumers and producers about how much oil to use and how much money to invest—or signals to would-be innovators about tomorrow's opportunities.

One part of the solution is not only enhancement of the already considerable regulation of the financial markets where oil is traded, but also greater transparency and better understanding of who the players are in the rapidly expanding financial oil markets. But regulatory changes cannot eliminate market cycles or repeal the laws of supply and demand in the world's largest organized commodity market. Those cycles may not be much in evidence amid the quiet tanks and rolling hills at Cushing. But they are inescapably part of the global landscape of the new world of oil.

Critical Thinking

1. How is the "age for oil" changing?

2. Specifically, how is the demand of oil changing?

3. How do these general and specific changes affect the U.S.-China relationship?

4. Does Yergin's analysis complement or contradict Klare's point of view in Article 3?

DANIEL YERGIN received a Pulitzer Prize for *The Prize: The Epic Quest for Oil, Money and Power,* published in an updated edition this year. He is chairman of IHS Cambridge Energy Research Associates.

Yergin, Daniel. Reprinted in entirety by McGraw-Hill with permission from *Foreign Policy,* September/October 2009, pp. 90, 92–95. www.foreignpolicy.com.

Seven Myths about Alternative Energy

As the world looks around anxiously for an alternative to oil, energy sources such as biofuels, solar, and nuclear seem like they could be the magic ticket. They're not."

MICHAEL GRUNWALD

What Comes Next?
Imagining the Post-Oil World

Nothing is as fraught with myths, misperceptions, and outright flights of fancy as the conversation about oil's successors. We asked two authors—award-winning environmental journalist Michael Grunwald and energy consultant David J. Rothkopf—to take aim at some of these myths, and look over the horizon to see which technologies might win the day and which ones could cause unexpected new problems. If fossil fuels are indeed saying their very long goodbye, then their would-be replacements still have a lot to prove.

1. "We Need to Do Everything Possible to Promote Alternative Energy"

Not exactly. It's certainly clear that fossil fuels are mangling the climate and that the status quo is unsustainable. There is now a broad scientific consensus that the world needs to reduce greenhouse gas emissions more than 25 percent by 2020—and more than 80 percent by 2050. Even if the planet didn't depend on it, breaking our addictions to oil and coal would also reduce global reliance on petrothugs and vulnerability to energy-price spikes.

But though the world should do everything sensible to promote alternative energy, there's no point trying to do everything possible. There are financial, political, and technical pressures as well as time constraints that will force tough choices; solutions will need to achieve the biggest emissions reductions for the least money in the shortest time. Hydrogen cars, cold fusion, and other speculative technologies might sound cool, but they could divert valuable resources from ideas that are already achievable and cost-effective. It's nice that someone managed to run his car on liposuction leftovers, but that doesn't mean he needs to be subsidized.

Reasonable people can disagree whether governments should try to pick energy winners and losers. But why not at least agree that governments shouldn't pick losers to be winners? Unfortunately,

that's exactly what is happening. The world is rushing to promote alternative fuel sources that will actually accelerate global warming, not to mention an alternative power source that could cripple efforts to stop global warming.

We can still choose a truly alternative path. But we'd better hurry.

2. "Renewable Fuels Are the Cure for Our Addiction to Oil"

Unfortunately not. "Renewable fuels" sound great in theory, and agricultural lobbyists have persuaded European countries and the United States to enact remarkably ambitious biofuels mandates to promote farm-grown alternatives to gasoline. But so far in the real world, the cures—mostly ethanol derived from corn in the United States or biodiesel derived from palm oil, soybeans, and rapeseed in Europe—have been significantly worse than the disease.

Researchers used to agree that farm-grown fuels would cut emissions because they all made a shockingly basic error. They gave fuel crops credit for soaking up carbon while growing, but it never occurred to them that fuel crops might displace vegetation that soaked up even more carbon. It was as if they assumed that biofuels would only be grown in parking lots. Needless to say, that hasn't been the case; Indonesia, for example, destroyed so many of its lush forests and peat lands to grow palm oil for the European biodiesel market that it ranks third rather than 21st among the world's top carbon emitters.

In 2007, researchers finally began accounting for deforestation and other land-use changes created by biofuels. One study found that it would take more than 400 years of biodiesel use to "pay back" the carbon emitted by directly clearing peat for palm oil. Indirect damage can be equally devastating because on a hungry planet, food crops that get diverted to fuel usually end up getting replaced somewhere. For example, ethanol profits are prompting U.S. soybean farmers to switch to corn, so Brazilian soybean farmers are expanding into cattle pastures to pick up the slack and Brazilian ranchers are invading the Amazon rain forest, which is why another study pegged corn thanol's payback period at 167 years. It's simple economics: the mandates increase demand for grain, which boosts prices, which makes it lucrative to ravage the wilderness.

Deforestation accounts for 20 percent of global emissions, so unless the world can eliminate emissions from all other sources—cars, coal, factories, cows—it needs to back off forests. That means limiting agriculture's footprint, a daunting task as the world's population grows—and an impossible task if vast expanses of cropland are converted to grow middling amounts of fuel. Even if the United States switched its entire grain crop to ethanol, it would only replace one fifth of U.S. gasoline consumption.

This is not just a climate disaster. The grain it takes to fill an SUV tank with ethanol could feed a hungry person for a year; biofuel mandates are exerting constant upward pressure on global food prices and have contributed to food riots in dozens of poorer countries. Still, the United States has quintupled its ethanol production in a decade and plans to quintuple its biofuel production again in the next decade. This will mean more money for well-subsidized grain farmers, but also more malnutrition, more deforestation, and more emissions. European leaders have paid a bit more attention to the alarming critiques of biofuels—including one by a British agency that was originally established to promote biofuels—but they have shown no more inclination to throw cold water on this $100 billion global industry.

3. "If Today's Biofuels Aren't the Answer, Tomorrow's Biofuels Will Be"

Doubtful. The latest U.S. rules, while continuing lavish support for corn ethanol, include enormous new mandates to jump-start "second-generation" biofuels such as cellulosic ethanol derived from switchgrass. In theory, they would be less destructive than corn ethanol, which relies on tractors, petroleum-based fertilizers, and distilleries that emit way too much carbon. Even first-generation ethanol derived from sugar cane—which already provides half of Brazil's transportation fuel—is considerably greener than corn ethanol. But recent studies suggest that any biofuels requiring good agricultural land would still be worse than gasoline for global warming. Less of a disaster than corn ethanol is still a disaster.

Back in the theoretical world, biofuels derived from algae, trash, agricultural waste, or other sources could help because they require no land or at least unspecific "degraded lands," but they always seem to be "several" years away from large-scale commercial development. And some scientists remain hopeful that fast-growing perennial grasses such as miscanthus can convert sunlight into energy efficiently enough to overcome the land-use dilemmas—someday. But for today, farmland happens to be very good at producing the food we need to feed us and storing the carbon we need to save us, and not so good at generating fuel. In fact, new studies suggest that if we really want to convert biomass into energy, we're better off turning it into electricity.

Then what should we use in our cars and trucks? In the short term . . . gasoline. We just need to use less of it.

Instead of counterproductive biofuel mandates and ethanol subsidies, governments need fuel-efficiency mandates to help the world's 1 billion drivers guzzle less gas, plus subsidies for mass transit, bike paths, rail lines, telecommuting, carpooling, and other activities to get those drivers out of their cars. Policymakers also need to eliminate subsidies for roads to nowhere, mandates that require excess parking and limit dense development in urban areas, and other sprawl-inducing policies. None of this is as enticing as inventing a magical new fuel, but it's doable, and it would cut emissions.

In the medium term, the world needs plug-in electric cars, the only plausible answer to humanity's oil addiction that isn't decades away. But electricity is already the source of even more emissions than oil. So we'll need an answer to humanity's coal addiction, too.

4. "Nuclear Power Is the Cure for Our Addiction to Coal"

Nope. Atomic energy is emissions free, so a slew of politicians and even some environmentalists have embraced it as a clean alternative to coal and natural gas that can generate power when there's no sun or wind. In the United States, which already gets nearly 20 percent of its electricity from nuclear plants, utilities are thinking about new reactors for the first time since the Three Mile Island meltdown three decades ago—despite global concerns about nuclear proliferation, local concerns about accidents or terrorist attacks, and the lack of a disposal site for the radioactive waste. France gets nearly 80 percent of its electricity from nukes, and Russia, China, and India are now gearing up for nuclear renaissances of their own.

But nuclear power cannot fix the climate crisis. The first reason is timing: The West needs major cuts in emissions within a decade, and the first new U.S. reactor is only scheduled for 2017—unless it gets delayed, like every U.S. reactor before it. Elsewhere in the developed world, most of the talk about a nuclear revival has remained just talk; there is no Western country with more than one nuclear plant under construction, and scores of existing plants will be scheduled for decommissioning in the coming decades, so there's no way nuclear could make even a tiny dent in electricity emissions before 2020.

The bigger problem is cost. Nuke plants are supposed to be expensive to build but cheap to operate. Unfortunately, they're turning out to be really, really expensive to build; their cost estimates have quadrupled in less than a decade. Energy guru Amory Lovins has calculated that new nukes will cost nearly three times as much as wind—and that was before their construction costs exploded for a variety of reasons, including the global credit crunch, the atrophying of the nuclear labor force, and a supplier squeeze symbolized by a Japanese company's worldwide monopoly on steel-forging for reactors. A new reactor in Finland that was supposed to showcase the global renaissance is already way behind schedule and way, way over budget. This is why plans for new plants were recently shelved in Canada and several U.S. states, why Moody's just warned utilities they'll risk ratings downgrades if they seek new reactors, and why renewables attracted $71 billion in worldwide private capital in 2007—while nukes attracted zero.

It's also why U.S. nuclear utilities are turning to politicians to supplement their existing loan guarantees, tax breaks, direct subsidies, and other cradle-to-grave government goodies with new public largesse. Reactors don't make much sense to build unless someone else is paying; that's why the strongest push for nukes is coming from countries where power is publicly funded. For all the talk of sanctions, if the world really wants to cripple the Iranian economy, maybe the mullahs should just be allowed to pursue nuclear energy.

Unlike biofuels, nukes don't worsen warming. But a nuclear expansion—like the recent plan by U.S. Republicans who want 100 new plants by 2030—would cost trillions of dollars for relatively modest gains in the relatively distant future.

Nuclear lobbyists do have one powerful argument: If coal is too dirty and nukes are too costly, how are we going to produce our juice? Wind is terrific, and it's on the rise, adding nearly half of new U.S. power last year and expanding its global capacity by a third in 2007. But after increasing its worldwide wattage tenfold in a decade—China is now the leading producer, and Europe is embracing wind as well—it still produces less than 2 percent of the world's electricity. Solar and geothermal are similarly wonderful and inexhaustible technologies, but they're still global rounding errors. The average U.S. household now has 26 plug-in devices, and the rest of the world is racing to catch up; the U.S. Department of Energy expects global electricity consumption to rise 77 percent by 2030. How can we meet that demand without a massive nuclear revival?

Wind is terrific, but it produces less than 2 percent of the world's electricity.

We can't. So we're going to have to prove the Department of Energy wrong.

5. "There Is No Silver Bullet to the Energy Crisis"

Probably not. But some bullets are a lot better than others; we ought to give them our best shot before we commit to evidently inferior bullets. And one renewable energy resource is the cleanest, cheapest, and most abundant of them all. It doesn't induce deforestation or require elaborate security. It doesn't depend on the weather. And it won't take years to build or bring to market; it's already universally available.

It's called "efficiency." It means wasting less energy—or more precisely, using less energy to get your beer just as cold, your shower just as hot, and your factory just as productive. It's not about some austerity scold harassing you to take cooler showers, turn off lights, turn down thermostats, drive less, fly less, buy less stuff, eat less meat, ditch your McMansion, and otherwise change your behavior to save energy. Doing less with less is called conservation. Efficiency is about doing more or

the same with less; it doesn't require much effort or sacrifice. Yet more efficient appliances, lighting, factories, and buildings, as well as vehicles, could wipe out one fifth to one third of the world's energy consumption without any real deprivation.

Efficiency isn't sexy, and the idea that we could use less energy without much trouble hangs uneasily with today's more-is-better culture. But the best way to ensure new power plants don't bankrupt us, empower petrodictators, or imperil the planet is not to build them in the first place. "Negawatts" saved by efficiency initiatives generally cost 1 to 5 cents per kilowatt-hour, versus projections ranging from 12 to 30 cents per kilowatt-hour from new nukes. That's because Americans in particular, and human beings in general waste amazing amounts of energy. U.S. electricity plants fritter away enough to power Japan, and American water heaters, industrial motors, and buildings are as ridiculously inefficient as American cars. Only 4 percent of the energy used to power a typical incandescent bulb produces light; the rest is wasted. China is expected to build more square feet of real estate in the next 15 years than the United States has built in its entire history, and it has no green building codes or green building experience.

But we already know that efficiency mandates can work wonders because they've already reduced U.S. energy consumption levels from astronomical to merely high. For example, thanks to federal rules, modern American refrigerators use three times less energy than 1970s models, even though they're larger and more high-tech.

The biggest obstacles to efficiency are the perverse incentives that face most utilities; they make more money when they sell more power and have to build new generating plants. But in California and the Pacific Northwest, utility profits have been decoupled from electricity sales, so utilities can help customers save energy without harming shareholders. As a result, in that part of the country, per capita power use has been flat for three decades—while skyrocketing 50 percent in the rest of the United States. If utilities around the world could make money by helping their customers use less power, the U.S. Department of Energy wouldn't be releasing such scary numbers.

6. "We Need a Technological Revolution to Save the World"

Maybe. In the long term, it's hard to imagine how (without major advances) we can reduce emissions 80 percent by 2050 while the global population increases and the developing world develops. So a clean-tech Apollo program modeled oil the Manhattan Project makes sense. And we do need carbon pricing to send a message to market makers and innovators to promote low-carbon activities; Europe's cap-and-trade scheme seems to be working well after a rocky start. The private capital already pouring into renewables might someday produce a cheap solar panel or a synthetic fuel or a superpowerful battery or a truly clean coal plant. At some point, after we've milked efficiency for all the negawatts and negabarrels we can, we might need something new.

But we already have all the technology we need to start reducing emissions by reducing consumption. Even if we only hold electricity demand flat, we can subtract a coal-fired megawatt every time we add a wind-powered megawatt. And with a smarter grid, green building codes, and strict efficiency standards for everything from light bulbs to plasma TVs to server farms, we can do better than flat. Al Gore has a reasonably plausible plan for zero-emissions power by 2020; he envisions an ambitious 28 percent decrease in demand through efficiency, plus some ambitious increases in supply from wind, solar, and geothermal energy. But we don't even have to reduce our fossil fuel use to zero to reach our 2020 targets. We just have to use less.

If somebody comes up with a better idea by 2020, great! For now, we should focus on the solutions that get the best emissions bang for the buck.

7. "Ultimately, We'll Need to Change Our Behaviors to Save the World"

Probably. These days, it's politically incorrect to suggest that going green will require even the slightest adjustment to our way of life, but let's face it: Jimmy Carter was right. It wouldn't kill you to turn down the heat and put on a sweater. Efficiency is a miracle drug, but conservation is even better; a Prius saves gas, but a Prius sitting in the driveway while you ride your bike uses no gas. Even energy-efficient dryers use more power than clotheslines.

More with less will be a great start, but to get to 80 percent less emissions, the developed world might occasionally have to do less with less. We might have to unplug a few digital picture frames, substitute teleconferencing for some business travel, and take it easy on the air conditioner. If that's an inconvenient truth, well, it's less inconvenient than trillions of dollars' worth of new reactors, perpetual dependence on hostile petrostates, or a fricasseed planet.

After all, the developing world is entitled to develop. Its people are understandably eager to eat more meat, drive more cars, and live in nicer houses. It doesn't seem fair for the developed world to say: Do as we say, not as we did. But if the developing world follows the developed world's wasteful path to prosperity, the Earth we all share won't be able to accommodate us. So we're going to have to change our ways. Then we can at least say: Do as we're doing, not as we did.

Critical Thinking

1. What is Grunwald's point of view?
2. How does this article complement or contradict the point of views in Articles 3, 11, 12, 13, 26, 27, 28, and 30?

MICHAEL GRUNWALD, a senior correspondent at *Time* magazine, is an award-winning environmental journalist and author of *The Swamp: The Everglades, Florida, and the Politics of Paradise*.

Grunwald, Michael. Reprinted in entirety by McGraw-Hill with permission from *Foreign Policy,* September/October 2009, pp. 130–133. www.foreignpolicy.com.

King Coal's Comeback

Asia needs coal, and the U.S. has plenty. Will expanding exports make climate change that much worse?

BRYAN WALSH

The Powder River Basin in southeastern Montana and north-eastern Wyoming can be as beautiful as its name suggests, but that's not why mining companies call it home. The region has one of the richest deposits of coal in the world, enough to yield more than 400 million tons last year—nearly half the coal mined in the U.S. There's enough coal in the Powder River Basin to keep American lights burning for decades, except for one thing—the U.S. is using less and less of the stuff. Thanks to bargain-basement natural gas prices and tougher air-pollution regulations, coal-fired power plants are closing down, and the Energy Information Administration expects coal consumption in the electric-utility sector to drop by 14% this year. That's good news for the environment—coal is a major polluter and contributor to climate change—and bad news for companies that mine coal.

But across the Pacific Ocean, the demand for coal has never been hotter, with China burning 4.1 billion tons in 2010 alone, far more than any other country in the world. That insatiable demand forced China in 2009 to become a net coal importer for the first time, in part because congested rail infrastructure raised the cost of transporting coal from the mines of the country's northwest to its booming southern cities. In April, Chinese coal imports nearly doubled from a year earlier. Right now Australia and Indonesia supply much of China's foreign coal. U.S. coal from the Powder River Basin could be a perfect addition to the Chinese market. Montana and Wyoming are just short train trips to ports on the Pacific Northwest coast, and from there it's a container ship away from Asian megacities where coal doesn't have to compete with cheap natural gas and air-pollution regulations are far weaker than in the U.S. To a wounded Big Coal, China is a potential savior. "We feel U.S. coal is an outstanding product to export to the Asian market as they continue to increase their coal demand," says Vic Svec, a senior vice president at St. Louis–based Peabody Energy, the world's biggest private coal company.

(Not) A Burning Issue

There's just one hitch: right now, ports on the West Coast lack the infrastructure needed to transfer coal from railcars into container ships. (Just 7 million of the 107 million tons of U.S.-exported coal left the country via Pacific Ocean ports last year.) That's why coal companies like Peabody and Ambre Energy are ready to spend millions to build coal-export facilities at a handful of ports in Washington and Oregon. If all those plans go forward, as much as 150 million tons of coal could be exported from the Northwest annually—nearly all of it coming from the Powder River Basin and headed to Asia. Even if the U.S. kept burning less and less coal at home, it would have a reason to keep mining it.

To environmentalists, though—and to many residents of port towns—those plans sound like the outline of a nightmare. There are the local costs of shipping millions of tons of coal via uncovered railcars: the traffic congestion and the air pollution from spilling coal dust and diesel tractor trailers. Valuable waterfront land would be set aside for transporting coal to China, even as the Northwest weans itself off coal power altogether. (The last coal-fired power plant in Oregon will shut down early in 2020.) Residents of small towns like Cheney, Wash.—which sits near heavily trafficked railways—would endure most of the disruption caused by the increased rail traffic without reaping much of the economic benefit. "What's happening to us here is that we're bearing really unacceptable costs," says Cheney Mayor Tom Trulove.

The local environmental and livability concerns are serious enough that the governor of Oregon called in April for the federal government to take a closer look at the proposed port projects under the National Environmental Policy Act. That won't do much to hold back Big Coal. The Army Corps of Engineers would need to approve at least four of the projects, but there's no single lever the White House can use to stop the port construction—which means the decisions will mostly fall to local officials over the next few years. For their part, the coal and rail companies pushing the projects are hyping the economic benefits of new construction and shipping while promising to take steps to reduce any local environmental impact from coal transportation. The Morrow Pacific project in Oregon, developed by Ambre, would off-load coal from trains in an enclosed area to minimize dust, then ship it down the Columbia River in enclosed barges to the port of St. Helens. In addition, Ambre would donate hundreds of thousands of dollars a year to public schools in the area. "There's a tremendous economic benefit here for Oregon," says Liz Fuller, a spokeswoman for Morrow Pacific.

A Global Coal Conundrum

Nimby feelings alone will make any of these projects a difficult sell, especially in the ultra-green Pacific Northwest.

But the larger environmental question isn't about the local impacts but rather the global ones. Environmentalists worry that by making it easy for the U.S. to ship cheap coal to Asia, the port projects would keep American mines humming even as coal use dwindles domestically. They might also encourage China and other rapidly growing Asian countries to burn more coal than they otherwise would by lowering the global price of the product. (One recent study found that a 10% reduction in the cost of coal in China would lead to a 12% increase in consumption.) By exporting coal to Asia, the U.S. would be responsible for further increasing global carbon emissions. "Will China and India have unlimited access to some of the cheapest and most plentiful

Coal consumption is lagging in the U.S.

Coal consumption in quadrillion BTUs

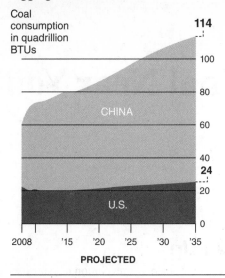

114	
100	
80	
CHINA	60
40	
24	
20	
U.S.	0

2008　'15　'20　'25　'30　'35

PROJECTED

In part because natural gas is so cheap

U.S. natural gas wellhead price per thousand cubic feet

$6.80 — FEBRUARY 2007

$2.46 — FEBRUARY 2012

Down 64% IN FIVE YEARS

Making exports vital for U.S. coal companies

U.S. coal exports in millions of tons

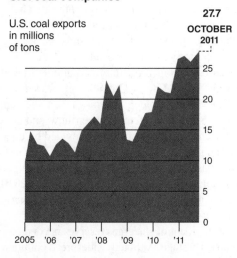

27.7
OCTOBER 2011

25
20
15
10
5
0

2005　'06　'07　'08　'09　'10　'11

Source: U.S. Energy Information Administration

coal on the planet?" says K.C. Golden, policy director for the Seattle-based NGO Climate Solutions. "That's the most important question."

How to act on the answer is another issue. The fact is, no one knows if increased U.S. exports would actually add to the total amount of coal burned globally. Coal companies like Peabody—as well as some economic analysts—say cheap U.S. coal would simply displace more expensive domestic Chinese coal or imports from Australia and Indonesia. If overall coal consumption won't actually increase, why not let U.S. companies—and taxpayers—get the economic benefit of those exports? If the U.S. decides not to build the port facilities, China's hunger for coal will just be met by another dealer.

'Will China and India have unlimited access to the cheapest and most plentiful coal on the planet? That's the important question.'

—K.C. Golden,
Policy Director, Climate Solutions

Some argue that if increasing demand in Asia pushes up global coal prices, it could actually help the environment by forcing more coal-burning countries to start looking for cheaper energy alternatives. In the U.S., higher coal prices could accelerate the switch from coal to natural gas, especially in parts of the Midwest that remain heavily dependent on coal. But that will depend on how Asian markets respond to the potential avalanche of U.S. coal. Chinese demand for coal has been inelastic in recent years, meaning that prices—high or low—haven't had much impact on how much coal China burns. That's partly because the Chinese government exerts control over the energy market, says Richard Morse, director of coal- and carbon-market research at Stanford University, making the effect on emissions of cheaper coal from the U.S. "a complex question. And it's not just about China," he says. "You have to net out the global impacts against the U.S. impacts."

Of course, that kind of modeling is easier said than done, which is why no one's done it. What's clear is that the global rate of consumption of coal—the dirtiest fossil fuel there is—will help decide how fast the planet warms. For their part, environmentalists remain convinced that stopping coal exports to Asia is a must-win battle in the war on climate change. In a fiery speech at a Portland, Ore., protest against the proposed ports last month, environmental activist Robert Kennedy Jr. urged the crowd to fight back. "[Coal companies] are coming to ship their poison, so they can poison the people in China, and that poison is going to come back here," he said. "So don't let them." It's a fight for the people of the Pacific Northwest, but the results will matter to the entire world.

Critical Thinking

1. What is the author's point of view?
2. What reasons are offered to support this point of view?
3. How does this article complement or contradict Articles 3, 11, 13, and 14?
4. Apply this case study to the Allegory of the Balloon.

Coming Soon to a Terminal Near You

Shale gas should make the world a cleaner, safer place.

The Economist

A long the coast of China, six vast liquefied natural gas (LNG) terminals are under construction; by the end of 2015 they should have more than doubled the amount of LNG that the country can import. At the other end of the country, gas is flowing in along a new pipeline from Turkmenistan. In between the two, geologists and engineers are looking at all sorts of new wells that might boost the country's already fast-growing domestic production. China will consume 260 billion cubic metres (260bcm, which is 9.2 trillion cubic feet) of gas a year by 2015, according to the country's 12th five-year plan, more than tripling 2008's 81bcm. The roots of this rapid growth, though, do not lie in China's centralised planning. They are to be found in a piece of deregulation enacted decades ago on the other side of the world: America's Natural Gas Policy Act of 1978.

America's deregulation of its natural-gas market encouraged entrepreneurial energy companies to gamble on new technologies allowing them to extract the gas conventional drilling could not reach. Geologists had long known there was gas trapped in the country's shale beds. Now the incentives for trying new ways of recovering it were greater, not least because, if it could be recovered, it could be got to market through pipelines newly obliged to offer "open access" to all comers.

Decades of development later, the independent companies which embraced horizontal drilling and the use of high-pressure fluids to crack open the otherwise impermeable shales—a process known as "fracking"—have brought about a revolution. Shale now provides 23% of America's natural gas, up from 4% in 2005. That upheaval in American gas markets has gone on to change the way gas is traded globally. A lot of LNG export capacity created with American markets in mind—global supply increased 58% over the past five years—is looking for new outlets.

To the extent that the shale-gas success is repeated elsewhere, a vital source of energy will become available from an ever more diverse and numerous set of suppliers in increasingly free markets. This means that, unlike the boom in oil in the decades following the second world war, this growth in gas may not hand a powerful political weapon to those countries with the biggest reserves. Shale gas could significantly diminish the political clout that Russia, Venezuela and Iran once saw as part and parcel of their gas revenues.

Tanked Up

"The power of the shale-gas revolution has surprised everyone," says Christof Rühl, chief economist at BP. In 2003 America's National Petroleum Council estimated that North America (including Canada and Mexico) might have 1.1 trillion cubic metres (tcm) of recoverable shale gas. This year America's Advanced Resources International reckoned there might be 50 times as much.

The shale-gas bounty is not confined to America. The country's Energy Information Administration released a report in April that looked at 48 shale-gas basins in 32 countries. It put recoverable reserves at 190tcm, and that excludes possible finds in the former Soviet Union and the Middle East, where huge reserves of conventional gas will make investment in shale gas unlikely for years to come. In short order estimates of the Earth's bounty of recoverable gas have expanded by about 40%. Improving extraction technologies and geological inquisitiveness are sure to raise that figure in the years to come.

Nor is shale gas the only new sort of reserve: "tight gas" in sandstones and coal-bed methane (the sort of gas that used to kill canaries down mines) are also promising. Farther in the future and more speculatively, there's the gas frozen into hydrates on the planet's continental shelves, which might offer more than 1,000tcm if a way can be found to exploit it. The cornucopian belief that human ingenuity will always find ways to increase the availability of resources is not a sure bet. With gas, though, the odds look pretty good for decades to come.

A scenario developed for the International Energy Agency's forthcoming "World Energy Outlook" offers a sense of what may unfold. Called the "Golden age of gas", it sees annual world production rising by 1.8tcm between now and 2035, when it reaches 5.1tcm. A fair bit of that is provided by unconventional sources. The growth is about 50% stronger than in the scenario used as a baseline; trade in gas between the world's major regions doubles. Coal use declines from the late 2010s onwards, and by 2030 gas has surpassed it, providing a quarter of all the world's energy.

The development of shale-gas reserves beyond North America is still at an early stage. Although widespread pollution of groundwater by fracking seems unlikely (shales that hold gas typically ie far deeper than groundwater supplies), such risks have raised a great deal of environmental concern about the technology. Coupled with a sensitivity to the rural charms of *la France profonde,* this has led to a moratorium on shale-gas exploration in France. But in Poland, which may have Europe's largest reserves, companies are busily sinking test wells to see what is there.

In South Africa, which may have the largest shale-gas reserves on the continent, the shales in the Karoo basin have attracted the attention of Shell, which is increasingly billing itself as a gas-focused company. Shell is also one of the companies looking at shale-gas reserves in China, which may be the largest on the planet. Chinese interest in shale gas is strong, with state companies buying up American expertise as they take stakes in established shale-gas producers. The country might be producing its first shale gas at scale before the current five-year plan is over.

The Great Decoupling

Gas is currently bought and sold in three distinct global markets—North America, Europe and Asia—and prices differ widely between the three. In deregulated North America, with a competitive market and plenty of shale gas to augment conventional supplies, prices are low. In Asia, where gas is largely traded using a system of long-term contracts tied to the price of oil, prices are high. Europe sits in between: prices at the moment are around $4 per million btu in America, $8 in continental Europe and $11 in Asia (1m btu is about 300 kilowatt-hours).

The origins of long-term contracts and oil-linked pricing go back a long way. When gas first began to be used a lot in the 1960s it was a substitute for home heating oil, and so it made sense to tie its price to that of oil. Because big exploration, extraction and infrastructure investments required pots of capital, long-term contracts became an industry norm.

Today oil is generally no substitute for gas. Gas is used not to fill up cars and lorries—though there are gas-fired transport enthusiasts who would like to do something about that—but to fuel power stations and heat homes. Still, many gas producers are happy enough with the archaic pricing structure, particularly when oil prices are high. Customers with limited choices have had to put up with it. According to a recent study from the Massachusetts Institute of Technology, pipelines carry 80% of all gas traded between regions. The firms at the upstream end of those pipelines, such as Russia's Gazprom, which supplies a quarter of all western Europe's gas, thus have a strong hand in negotiations. Control of the pipelines meant that when Gazprom turned off the gas (as it did in 2009 in a dispute over trans-shipments through Ukraine), buyers had nowhere to turn for alternatives.

In the past couple of years, though, three factors—LNG from Qatar that was no longer needed in shale-gas-rich America, a little energy-market deregulation by the European Union and a drop in overall demand—have helped to loosen the grip of Gazprom. Power-sector reforms allowed smaller European utilities to compete more vigorously, buying LNG on the spot market at a price sometimes as low as half that of long-term contracts from Russia. Bigger utilities that were losing market share

approached Gazprom, not known for sympathetic customer relations, for better terms. The normally intractable Russian company renegotiated contracts with European customers for a three-year "crisis period" to allow up to 15% of gas to be priced on cheaper spot terms. (Norway, also a big supplier to EU countries, had begun to sell gas on contracts that tied an even larger fraction to spot prices.)

Since then the European market has recovered. Prices rose after Libyan gas was cut off as a result of the country's uprising and a lot of Qatari LNG has found a new destination in Japan, deprived of much of its nuclear power since the disaster at its Fukushima plant.

Unsurprisingly, further attempts to pressure Gazprom into revising its terms have faltered. In February it rebuffed appeals by Germany's e.ON, one of its most important customers, to link its gas to spot prices. Gazprom's boss, Alexei Miller, told shareholders at the end of June that oil-indexed long-term gas contracts were here to stay. In private the company is still talking to customers about changing the shape of future contracts, and appears more inclined nowadays to regard European utilities as potential partners rather than spineless adversaries.

Looking reasonable, say cynics, is a ruse to discourage investment in shale reserves and alternative pipelines. If an agreeable-seeming Gazprom, along with increased bullishness about LNG and shale gas, were to dampen European enthusiasm for Nabucco, a long-planned pipeline which might bring 30bcm of gas a year to Europe from the Caspian and the Middle East, that would suit Russia pretty well. But Russia's new attitude could also spring from a realisation that the world really is changing. A study from the James Baker Institute at Rice University, published in July, reckons that, if shale-gas reserves are fully exploited, Gazprom's share of the west European market might fall from 27% in 2009 to 13% by 2040.

And Gazprom is finding that China, with which it has been negotiating pipeline deals since 2005, is not interested in the sort of long-term locked contracts that have previously typified Asian markets; indeed it is not even willing to pay European prices. Its immense shale-gas potential might make it even less willing to pay up, inclining it to depend less on pipeline gas and to take the risk that it can smooth out ebbs and flows through spot markets. If the proportion of imported pipeline gas falls, so does the pricing power of conventional suppliers, even if the overall volume they supply goes up.

Increasingly, it looks as if today's significant regional price differences will be arbitraged away, and that gas could become as fungible and as widely traded as oil. LNG's growth (23% by volume in 2010) shows no sign of slowing. European LNG import capacity has more than doubled since 2000; the costs of building an import terminal have plunged. So far this year twice as many LNG vessels have been ordered from the world's shipyards as in the whole of 2010. Qatar, which along with Iran and Russia holds the world's most impressive conventional gas reserves, is adding new liquefaction plants. Other countries are also busily constructing export terminals; while Australia leads the way, Indonesia, Papua New Guinea and others are all set to bring more LNG to the world markets. There's even work on liquefaction plants in America.

One consequence of a global gas market supplied from widely distributed conventional and unconventional sources is that this diversity will reduce the power of big suppliers to set prices and bully buyers. There has been occasional talk of a "gas OPEC", most audibly when, just before the end of 2008, a dozen or so gas producers met in Moscow under the chairmanship of Russia's prime minister, Vladimir Putin. Despite the rattling of sabres on pipelines, though, something analogous to OPEC looks near impossible under current conditions. For one thing, utilities mostly have spare capacity and can thus adjust their fuel mix in a way that car drivers confronted with an oil shortage cannot. What is more, managing the supply of gas month by month, as the oil cartel seeks to do, would be near impossible when most gas continues to be supplied on long-term contracts that are difficult to break.

The Great Declouting

And the new technologies are widening the production base all the time, weakening the strategic importance of conventional reserves and the power of those who hold them. Before shale gas, it was thought that Venezuela might soon become an important gas source for America, and that Iran's vast gas reserves would motivate potential customers to break the sanctions imposed on it as a result of its nuclear programme. Both things are now less likely; the Baker Institute study suggests that while both countries will grow in importance—it foresees 26% of the world's LNG coming from Venezuela, Iran and Nigeria by 2040—they will do so much more slowly than they would have in a world of constrained supplies.

The growth of the gas market will not be untroubled. Large projects will be delayed sometimes, leading to periods of tight supply; there may also be overcapacity at times, as there have been recently. America's shale-gas success—a matter not just of helpful geology and Yankee ingenuity, but also of various legal and regulatory positions such as those of the 1978 act—may prove hard to replicate in some other countries. Environmental worries could stop shale gas dead in places. But although the pace may slow and the road may have bumps, for the moment the revolution looks set to roll on.

Critical Thinking

1. What are the reasons for a so-called revolution in U.S. natural gas markets?

2. What is fracking?

3. What are the three distinct global markets for natural gas, and how and why do they differ?

4. How is this revolution likely to weaken the strategic importance of some energy producing countries?

Nuclear Energy: The Dream That Failed

Nuclear power will not go away, but its role may never be more than marginal.

OLIVER MORTON

The lights are not going off all over Japan, but the nuclear power plants are. Of the 54 reactors in those plants, with a combined capacity of 47.5 gigawatts (GW, a thousand megawatts), only two are operating today. A good dozen are unlikely ever to reopen: six at Fukushima Dai-ichi, which suffered a calamitous triple meltdown after an earthquake and tsunami on March 11th 2011, and others either too close to those reactors or now considered to be at risk of similar disaster. The rest, bar two, have shut down for maintenance or "stress tests" since the Fukushima accident and not yet been cleared to start up again. It is quite possible that none of them will get that permission before the two still running shut for scheduled maintenance by the end of April.

Japan has been using nuclear power since the 1960s. In 2010 it got 30% of its electricity from nuclear plants. This spring it may well join the ranks of the 150 nations currently muddling through with all their atoms unsplit. If the shutdown happens, it will not be permanent; a good number of the reactors now closed are likely to be reopened. But it could still have symbolic importance. To do without something hitherto seen as a necessity opens the mind to new possibilities. Japan had previously expected its use of nuclear energy to increase somewhat. Now the share of nuclear power in Japan's energy mix is more likely to shrink, and it could just vanish altogether.

In most places any foretaste of that newly plausible future will barely be noticed. Bullet trains will flash on; flat panels will continue to shine; toilet seats will still warm up; factories will hum as they hummed before. Almost everywhere, when people reach for the light switches in their homes, the lights will come on. But not quite everywhere. In Futaba, Namie and Naraha the lights will stay off, and no factories will hum: not for want of power but for want of people. The 100,000 or so people that once lived in those and other towns close to the Fukushima Dai-ichi nuclear power plant have been evacuated. Some 30,000 may never return.

The triple meltdown at Fukushima a year ago was the world's worst nuclear accident since the disaster at Chernobyl in the Ukraine in 1986. The damage extends far beyond a lost power station, a stricken operator (the Tokyo Electric Power Company, or Tepco) and an intense debate about the future of the nation's nuclear power plants. It goes beyond the trillions of yen that will be needed for a decade-long effort to decommission the reactors and remove their wrecked cores, if indeed that proves possible, and the even greater sums that may be required for decontamination (which one expert, Tatsuhiko Kodama of Tokyo University, thinks could cost as much as ¥50 trillion, or $623 billion). It reaches deep into the lives of the displaced, and of those further afield who know they have been exposed to the fallout from the disaster. If it leads to a breakdown of the near-monopolies enjoyed by the country's power companies, it will strike at some of the strongest complicities within the business-and-bureaucracy establishment.

For parallels that do justice to the disaster, the Japanese find themselves reaching back to the second world war, otherwise seldom discussed: to the battle of Iwo Jima to describe the heroism of everyday workers abandoned by the officer class of company and government; to the imperial navy's ill-judged infatuation with battleships, being likened to the establishment's eagerness for ever more reactors; to the war as a whole as a measure of the sheer scale of the event. And, of course, to Hiroshima. Kiyoshi Kurokawa, an academic who is heading a commission investigating the disaster on behalf of the Japanese parliament, thinks that Fukushima has opened the way to a new scepticism about an ageing, dysfunctional status quo which could bring about a "third opening" of Japan comparable to the Meiji restoration and the American occupation after 1945.

To the public at large, the history of nuclear power is mostly a history of accidents: Three Mile Island, the 1979 partial meltdown of a nuclear reactor in Pennsylvania caused by a faulty valve, which led to a small release of radioactivity and the temporary evacuation of the area; Chernobyl, the 1986 disaster in the Ukraine in which a chain reaction got out of control and a reactor blew up, spreading radioactive material far and wide; and now Fukushima. But the field has been shaped more by broad economic and strategic trends than sudden shocks.

The Renaissance That Wasn't

America's nuclear bubble burst not after the accident at Three Mile Island but five years before it. The French nuclear-power programme, the most ambitious by far of the 1980s, continued largely undisturbed after Chernobyl, though other countries did pull back. The West's "nuclear renaissance" much bruited over the past decade, in part as a response to climate change, fizzled out well before the roofs blew off Fukushima's first, third and fourth reactor buildings. Today's most dramatic nuclear expansion, in China, may be tempered by Fukushima, but it will not be halted.

For all that, Fukushima is a heavier blow than the previous two. Three Mile Island, disturbing as it was, released relatively little radioactivity and killed nobody. By causing nuclear safety to be tightened and buttressed with new institutions, it improved the industry's reliability and profitability in America. Chernobyl was far worse, but it was caused by egregious operator error in a totalitarian regime incapable of the sort of transparency and accountability needed to ensure nuclear safety. It put paid to nuclear power in Italy and, for a while, Sweden, but in general it could be treated as an aberration of little direct relevance to the free world's nuclear programmes. Poor regulation, an insufficient safety culture and human error (without which the Japanese tsunami's effects might have been very different) are much more worrying when they strike in a technologically advanced democracy working with long-established reactor designs.

And if the blow is harder than the previous one, the recipient is less robust than it once was. In liberalised energy markets, building nuclear power plants is no longer a commercially feasible option: they are simply too expensive. Existing reactors can be run very profitably; their capacity can be upgraded and their lives extended. But forecast reductions in the capital costs of new reactors in America and Europe have failed to materialise and construction periods have lengthened. Nobody will now build one without some form of subsidy to finance it or a promise of a favourable deal for selling the electricity. And at the same time as the cost of new nuclear plants has become prohibitive in much of the world, worries about the dark side of nuclear power are resurgent, thanks to what is happening in Iran.

Nuclear proliferation has not gone as far or as fast as was feared in the 1960s. But it has proceeded, and it has done so hand in hand with nuclear power. There is only one state with nuclear weapons, Israel, that does not also have nuclear reactors to generate electricity. Only two non-European states with nuclear power stations, Japan and Mexico, have not at some point taken steps towards developing nuclear weapons, though most have pulled back before getting there.

If proliferation is one reason for treating the spread of nuclear power with caution, renewable energy is another. In 2010 the world's installed renewable electricity capacity outstripped its nuclear capacity for the first time. That does not mean that the world got as much energy from renewables as from nuclear; reactors run at up to 93% of their stated capacity whereas wind and solar tend to be closer to 20%. Renewables are intermittent and take up a lot of space: generating a gigawatt of electricity with wind takes hundreds of square kilometres, whereas a nuclear reactor with the same capacity will fit into a large industrial building. That may limit the contribution renewables

can ultimately make to energy supply. Unsubsidised renewables can currently displace fossil fuels only in special circumstances. But nuclear energy, which has received large subsidies in the past, has not displaced much in the way of fossil fuels either. And nuclear is getting more expensive whereas renewables are getting cheaper.

Ulterior Motives

Nuclear power is not going to disappear. Germany, which in 2011 produced 5% of the world's nuclear electricity, is abandoning it, as are some smaller countries. In Japan, and perhaps also in France, it looks likely to lose ground. But there will always be countries that find the technology attractive enough to make them willing to rearrange energy markets in its favour. If they have few indigenous energy resources, they may value, as Japan has done, the security offered by plants running on fuel that is cheap and easily stockpiled. Countries with existing nuclear capacity that do not share Germany's deep nuclear unease or its enthusiasm for renewables may choose to buy new reactors to replace old ones, as Britain is seeking to do, to help with carbon emissions. Countries committed to proliferation, or at least interested in keeping that option open, will invest in nuclear, as may countries that find themselves with cash to spare and a wish to join what still looks like a technological premier league.

Barring major technological developments, nuclear power will continue to be a creature of politics not economics. This will limit the overall size of the industry.

Besides, nuclear plants are long-lived things. Today's reactors were mostly designed for a 40-year life, but many of them are being allowed to increase it to 60. New reactor designs aim for a span of 60 years that might be extended to 80. Given that it takes a decade or so to go from deciding to build a reactor to feeding the resulting electricity into a grid, reactors being planned now may still be working in the early 22nd century.

Barring major technological developments, though, nuclear power will continue to be a creature of politics not economics, with any growth a function of political will or a side-effect of protecting electrical utilities from open competition. This will limit the overall size of the industry. In 2010 nuclear power provided 13% of the world's electricity, down from 18% in 1996. A pre-Fukushima scenario from the International Energy Agency that allowed for a little more action on carbon dioxide than has yet been taken predicted a rise of about 70% in nuclear capacity between 2010 and 2035; since other generating capacity will be growing too, that would keep nuclear's 13% share roughly constant. A more guarded IEA scenario has rich countries building no new reactors other than those already under construction, other countries achieving only half their currently stated targets (which in nuclear matters are hardly ever met) and regulators being less generous in extending the life of existing plants. On that basis the installed capacity goes down a little, and the share of the electricity market drops to 7%.

Developing nuclear plants only at the behest of government will also make it harder for the industry to improve its safety culture. Where a government is convinced of the need for nuclear power, it may well be less likely to regulate it in the stringent, independent way the technology demands. Governments favour nuclear power by limiting the liability of its operators. If they did not, the industry would surely founder. But a different risk arises from the fact that governments can change their minds. Germany's plants are being shut down in response to an accident its industry had nothing to do with. Being hostage to distant events thus adds a hard-to-calculate systemic risk to nuclear development.

The ability to split atoms and extract energy from them was one of the more remarkable scientific achievements of the 20th century, widely seen as world-changing. Intuitively one might expect such a scientific wonder either to sweep all before it or be renounced, rather than end up in a modest niche, at best stable, at worst dwindling. But if nuclear power teaches one lesson, it is to doubt all stories of technological determinism. It is not the essential nature of a technology that matters but its capacity to fit into the social, political and economic conditions of the day. If a technology fits into the human world in a way that gives it ever more scope for growth it can succeed beyond the dreams of its pioneers. The diesel engines that power the world's shipping are an example; so are the artificial fertilisers that have allowed ever more people to be supplied by ever more productive farms, and the computers that make the world ever more hungry for yet more computing power.

There has been no such expansive setting for nuclear technologies. Their history has for the most part been one of concentration not expansion, of options being closed rather than opened. The history of nuclear weapons has been defined by avoiding their use and constraining the number of their possessors. Within countries they have concentrated power. As the American political commentator Gary Wills argues in his book, "Bomb Power", the increased strategic role of the American presidency since 1945 stems in significant part from the way that nuclear weapons have redefined the role and power of the "commander-in-chief" (a term previously applied only in the context of the armed forces, not the nation as a whole) who has his finger on the button. In the energy world, nuclear has found its place nourishing technophile establishments like the "nuclear village" of vendors, bureaucrats, regulators and utilities in Japan whose lack of transparency and accountability did much to pave the way for Fukushima and the distrust that has followed in its wake. These political settings govern and limit what nuclear power can achieve.

Critical Thinking

1. What is the central argument of this article?
2. What factors will likely determine the future of nuclear energy?
3. How does this article complement or contradict the other global energy case studies?

UNIT 5
Conflict

Unit Selections

Learning Outcomes

After reading this unit you should be able to:

• Identify what Kaplan argues are the underlying dynamics of contemporary international conflicts.

• Make some predictions on future hot spots where war might break out.

• Discuss the basic issues surrounding the proliferation of nuclear weapons.

• Speculate about the future of armed conflict.

• Offer insights into additional international relations theories that are summarized in some of the articles.

• Assess your on-going effort at identifying your theory of international relations and how this unit changes/complements it.

Student Website
www.mhhe.com/cls

Internet References

DefenseLINK
　　www.defenselink.mil
Federation of American Scientists (FAS)
　　www.fas.org
ISN International Relations and Security Network
　　www.isn.ethz.ch
The NATO Integrated Data Service (NIDS)
　　www.nato.int/structur/nids/nids.htm

Do you lock your doors at night? Do you secure your personal property to avoid theft? These are basic questions that have to do with your sense of personal security. Most individuals take steps to protect what they have, including their lives. The same is true for groups of people, including countries.

In the international arena, governments frequently pursue their national interest by entering into mutually agreeable "deals" with other governments. Social scientists call these types of arrangements "exchanges" (i.e., each side gives up something it values in order to gain something in return that it values even more). On an economic level, it functions like this: "I have the oil that you need and am willing to sell it. In return I want to buy from you the agricultural products that I lack." Whether on the governmental level or the personal level ("If you help me with my homework, then I will drive you home this weekend."), exchanges are the process used by most individuals and groups to obtain and protect what is of value. The exchange process, however, can break down. When threats and punishments replace mutual exchanges, conflict ensues. In the short run, neither side benefits, for there are costs to both. If efforts at intimidation and coercion fail, the conflict may escalate into violent confrontation.

With the end of the cold war, issues of national security and the nature of international conflict have changed. There are both new and old dynamics at play creating areas of potential and actual armed conflict. Central to the national security debate in the twenty-first century is the issue of nuclear proliferation. Many experts initially predicted that the collapse of the Soviet Union would decrease the arms race and diminish the threat of nuclear war. However, some analysts now believe that the threat of nuclear war has in fact increased as control of nuclear weapons has become less centralized and the command structure less reliable. The proliferation of nuclear weapons into North Korea, South Asia (India and Pakistan), and potentially Iran presents new security challenges. Further, there are concerns about both totalitarian governments and terrorist organizations obtaining weapons of mass destruction. What these changing circumstances mean for U.S. policy is a topic of considerable debate.

The unit begins with a unique perspective on the sources of international conflict. It is followed by a series of case studies and concludes with an article on a new domain of warfare, cyberspace.

© Natalie Roeth

As in the case of the other global issues described in this anthology, international conflict is a multi-dimensional problem. It is important to understand that conflicts are not random events, but follow patterns and trends. Forty-five years of cold war established discernable patterns of international conflict as the superpowers deterred each other with vast expenditures of money and technological know-how.

The changing circumstances of the post–cold war era generate a series of important new policy questions: Will there be more nuclear proliferation? Is there an increased danger of so-called "rogue" states destabilizing the international arena? Is the threat of terror a temporary or permanent feature of world affairs? Will there be a growing emphasis on low-intensity conflicts related to the interdiction of drugs, or will some other unforeseen issue determine the world's hot spots? Will the United States and its European allies lose interest in security issues that do not directly involve their economic interests and simply look the other way, for example, as age-old ethnic conflicts become brutally violent? Can the international community develop viable institutions to mediate and resolve disputes before they lead to war? The answers to these and related questions will determine the patterns of conflict in the twenty-first century.

The Revenge of Geography

People and ideas influence events, but geography largely determines them, now more than ever. To understand the coming struggles, it's time to dust off the Victorian thinkers who knew the physical world best. A journalist who has covered the ends of the Earth offers a guide to the relief map—and a primer on the next phase of conflict.

ROBERT D. KAPLAN

When rapturous Germans tore down the Berlin Wall 20 years ago it symbolized far more than the overcoming of an arbitrary boundary. It began an intellectual cycle that saw all divisions, geographic and otherwise, as surmountable; that referred to "realism" and "pragmatism" only as pejoratives; and that invoked the humanism of Isaiah Berlin or the appeasement of Hitler at Munich to launch one international intervention after the next. In this way, the armed liberalism and the democracy-promoting neoconservatism of the 1990s shared the same universalist aspirations. But alas, when a fear of Munich leads to overreach the result is Vietnam—or in the current case, Iraq.

And thus began the rehabilitation of realism, and with it another intellectual cycle. "Realist" is now a mark of respect, "neocon" a term of derision. The Vietnam analogy has vanquished that of Munich. Thomas Hobbes, who extolled the moral benefits of fear and saw anarchy as the chief threat to society, has elbowed out Isaiah Berlin as the philosopher of the present cycle. The focus now is less on universal ideals than particular distinctions, from ethnicity to culture to religion. Those who pointed this out a decade ago were sneered at for being "fatalists" or "determinists." Now they are applauded as "pragmatists." And this is the key insight of the past two decades—that there are worse things in the world than extreme tyranny, and in Iraq we brought them about ourselves. I say this having supported the war.

So now, chastened, we have all become realists. Or so we believe. But realism is about more than merely opposing a war in Iraq that we know from hindsight turned out badly. Realism means recognizing that international relations are ruled by a sadder, more limited reality than the one governing domestic affairs. It means valuing order above freedom, for the latter becomes important only after the former has been established. It means focusing on what divides humanity rather than on what unites it, as the high priests of globalization would have it. In short, realism is about recognizing and embracing those forces beyond our control that constrain human action—culture, tradition, history, the bleaker tides of passion that lie just beneath the veneer of civilization. This poses what, for realists, is the central question in foreign affairs: Who can do what to whom? And of all the unsavory truths in which realism is rooted, the bluntest, most uncomfortable, and most deterministic of all is geography.

Indeed, what is at work in the recent return of realism is the revenge of geography in the most old-fashioned sense. In the 18th and 19th centuries, before the arrival of political science as an academic specialty, geography was an honored, if not always formalized, discipline in which politics, culture, and economics were often conceived of in reference to the relief map. Thus, in the Victorian and Edwardian eras, mountains and the men who grow out of them were the first order of reality; ideas, however uplifting, were only the second.

And yet, to embrace geography is not to accept it as an implacable force against which humankind is powerless. Rather, it serves to qualify human freedom and choice with a modest acceptance of fate. This is all the more important today, because rather than eliminating the relevance of geography, globalization is reinforcing it. Mass communications and economic integration are weakening many states, exposing a Hobbesian world of small, fractious regions. Within them, local, ethnic, and religious sources of identity are reasserting themselves, and because they are anchored to specific terrains, they are best explained by reference to geography. Like the faults that determine earthquakes, the political future will be defined by conflict and instability with a similar geographic logic. The upheaval spawned by the ongoing economic crisis is increasing the relevance of geography even further, by weakening social orders and other creations of humankind, leaving the natural frontiers of the globe as the only restraint.

So we, too, need to return to the map, and particularly to what I call the "shatter zones" of Eurasia. We need to reclaim those thinkers who knew the landscape best. And we need to update their theories for the revenge of geography in our time.

I f you want to understand the insights of geography, you need to seek out those thinkers who make liberal humanists profoundly uneasy—those authors who thought the map determined nearly everything, leaving little room for human agency.

One such person is the French historian Fernand Braudel, who in 1949 published *The Mediterranean and the Mediterranean World in the Age of Philip II*. By bringing demography and nature itself into history, Braudel helped restore geography to its proper place. In his narrative, permanent environmental forces lead to enduring historical trends that preordain political events and regional wars. To Braudel, for example, the poor, precarious soils along the Mediterranean, combined with an uncertain, drought-afflicted climate, spurred ancient Greek and Roman conquest. In other words, we delude ourselves by thinking that we control our own destinies. To understand the present challenges of climate change, warming Arctic seas, and the scarcity of resources such as oil and water, we must reclaim Braudel's environmental interpretation of events.

So, too, must we reexamine the blue-water strategizing of Alfred Thayer Mahan, a U.S. naval captain and author of *The Influence of Sea Power Upon History, 1660–1783*. Viewing the sea as the great "commons" of civilization, Mahan thought that naval power had always been the decisive factor in global political struggles. It was Mahan who, in 1902, coined the term "Middle East" to denote the area between Arabia and India that held particular importance for naval strategy. Indeed, Mahan saw the Indian and Pacific oceans as the hinges of geopolitical destiny, for they would allow a maritime nation to project power all around the Eurasian rim and thereby affect political developments deep into Central Asia. Mahan's thinking helps to explain why the Indian Ocean will be the heart of geopolitical competition in the 21st century—and why his books are now all the rage among Chinese and Indian strategists.

Similarly, the Dutch-American strategist Nicholas Spykman saw the seaboards of the Indian and Pacific oceans as the keys to dominance in Eurasia and the natural means to check the land power of Russia. Before he died in 1943, while the United States was fighting Japan, Spykman predicted the rise of China and the consequent need for the United States to defend Japan. And even as the United States was fighting to liberate Europe, Spykman warned that the postwar emergence of an integrated European power would eventually become inconvenient for the United States. Such is the foresight of geographical determinism.

But perhaps the most significant guide to the revenge of geography is the father of modern geopolitics himself—Sir Halford J. Mackinder—who is famous not for a book but a single article, "The Geographical Pivot of History," which began as a 1904 lecture to the Royal Geographical Society in London. Mackinder's work is the archetype of the geographical discipline, and he summarizes its theme nicely: "Man and not nature initiates, but nature in large measure controls."

His thesis is that Russia, Eastern Europe, and Central Asia are the "pivot" around which the fate of world empire revolves. He would refer to this area of Eurasia as the "heartland" in a later book. Surrounding it are four "marginal" regions of the Eurasian landmass that correspond, not coincidentally, to the four great religions, because faith, too, is merely a function of geography for Mackinder. There are two "monsoon lands": one in the east generally facing the Pacific Ocean, the home of Buddhism; the other in the south facing the Indian Ocean, the home of Hinduism. The third marginal region is Europe, watered by the Atlantic to the west and the home of Christianity. But the most fragile of the four marginal regions is the Middle East, home of Islam, "deprived of moisture by the proximity of Africa" and for the most part "thinly peopled" (in 1904, that is).

Realism is about recognizing and embracing those forces beyond our control that constrain human action. And of all the unsavory truths in which realism is rooted, the bluntest, most uncomfortable, and most deterministic of all is geography.

This Eurasian relief map, and the events playing out on it at the dawn of the 20th century, are Mackinder's subject, and the opening sentence presages its grand sweep:

> When historians in the remote future come to look back on the group of centuries through which we are now passing, and see them fore-shortened, as we to-day see the Egyptian dynasties, it may well be that they will describe the last 400 years as the Columbian epoch, and will say that it ended soon after the year 1900.

Mackinder explains that, while medieval Christendom was "pent into a narrow region and threatened by external barbarism," the Columbian age—the Age of Discovery—saw Europe expand across the oceans to new lands. Thus at the turn of the 20th century, "we shall again have to deal with a closed political system," and this time one of "world-wide scope."

> Every explosion of social forces, instead of being dissipated in a surrounding circuit of unknown space and barbaric chaos, will [henceforth] be sharply re-echoed from the far side of the globe, and weak elements in the political and economic organism of the world will be shattered in consequence.

By perceiving that European empires had no more room to expand, thereby making their conflicts global, Mackinder foresaw, however vaguely, the scope of both world wars.

Mackinder looked at European history as "subordinate" to that of Asia, for he saw European civilization as merely the outcome of the struggle against Asiatic invasion. Europe, he writes, became the cultural phenomenon it is only because of its geography: an intricate array of mountains, valleys, and peninsulas; bounded by northern ice and a western ocean; blocked by seas and the Sahara to the south; and set against the immense, threatening flatland of Russia to the east. Into this confined landscape poured a succession of nomadic, Asian invaders from the naked steppe. The union of Franks, Goths, and Roman provincials against these invaders produced the basis for modern France. Likewise, other European powers originated, or at least matured, through their encounters with Asian nomads. Indeed, it was the Seljuk Turks' supposed ill treatment of Christian pilgrims in Jerusalem that ostensibly led to the Crusades, which Mackinder considers the beginning of Europe's collective modern history.

Russia, meanwhile, though protected by forest glades against many a rampaging host, nevertheless fell prey in the 13th century to the Golden Horde of the Mongols. These invaders decimated and subsequently changed Russia. But because most of Europe knew no such level of destruction, it was able to emerge as the world's political cockpit, while Russia was largely denied access to the European Renaissance. The ultimate land-based empire, with few natural barriers against invasion, Russia would know forevermore what it was like to be brutally conquered. As a result, it would become perennially obsessed with expanding and holding territory.

Key discoveries of the Columbian epoch, Mackinder writes, only reinforced the cruel facts of geography. In the Middle Ages, the peoples of Europe were largely confined to the land. But when the sea route to India was found around the Cape of Good Hope, Europeans suddenly had access to the entire rimland of southern Asia, to say nothing of strategic discoveries in the New World. While Western Europeans "covered the ocean with their fleets," Mackinder tells us, Russia was expanding equally impressively on land, "emerging from her northern forests" to police the steppe with her Cossacks, sweeping into Siberia, and sending peasants to sow the southwestern steppe with wheat. It was an old story: Europe versus Russia, a liberal sea power (like Athens and Venice) against a reactionary land power (like Sparta and Prussia). For the sea, beyond the cosmopolitan influences it bestows by virtue of access to distant harbors, provides the inviolate border security that democracy needs to take root.

In the 19th century, Mackinder notes, the advent of steam engines and the creation of the Suez Canal increased the mobility of European sea power around the southern rim of Eurasia, just as railways were beginning to do the same for land power in the Eurasian heartland. So the struggle was set for the mastery of Eurasia, bringing Mackinder to his thesis:

> As we consider this rapid review of the broader currents of history, does not a certain persistence of geographical relationship become evident? Is not the pivot region of the world's politics that vast area of Euro-Asia which is inaccessible to ships, but in antiquity lay open to the horse-riding nomads, and is today about to be covered with a network of railways?

Just as the Mongols banged at, and often broke down, the gates to the marginal regions surrounding Eurasia, Russia would now play the same conquering role, for as Mackinder writes, "the geographical quantities in the calculation are more measurable and more nearly constant than the human." Forget the czars and the commissars-yet-to-be in 1904; they are but trivia compared with the deeper tectonic forces of geography.

Mackinder's determinism prepared us for the rise of the Soviet Union and its vast zone of influence in the second half of the 20th century, as well as for the two world wars preceding it. After all, as historian Paul Kennedy notes, these conflicts were struggles over Mackinder's "marginal" regions, running from Eastern Europe to the Himalayas and beyond. Cold War containment strategy, moreover, depended heavily on rimland bases across the greater Middle East and the Indian Ocean. Indeed, the U.S. projection of power into Afghanistan and Iraq, and today's tensions with Russia over the political fate of Central Asia and the Caucasus have only bolstered Mackinder's thesis. In his article's last paragraph, Mackinder even raises the specter of Chinese conquests of the "pivot" area, which would make China the dominant geopolitical power. Look at how Chinese migrants are now demographically claiming parts of Siberia as Russia's political control of its eastern reaches is being strained. One can envision Mackinder's being right yet again.

The wisdom of geographical determinism endures across the chasm of a century because it recognizes that the most profound struggles of humanity are not about ideas but about control over territory, specifically the heartland and rimlands of Eurasia. Of course, ideas matter, and they span geography. And yet there is a certain geographic logic to where certain ideas take hold. Communist Eastern Europe, Mongolia, China, and North Korea were all contiguous to the great land power of the Soviet Union. Classic fascism was a predominantly European affair. And liberalism nurtured its deepest roots in the United States and Great Britain, essentially island nations and sea powers both. Such determinism is easy to hate but hard to dismiss.

To discern where the battle of ideas will lead, we must revise Mackinder for our time. After all, Mackinder could not foresee how a century's worth of change would redefine—and enhance—the importance of geography in today's world. One author who did is Yale University professor Paul Bracken, who in 1999 published *Fire in the East*. Bracken draws a conceptual map of Eurasia defined by the collapse of time and distance and the filling of empty spaces. This idea leads him to declare a "crisis of room." In the past, sparsely populated geography acted as a safety mechanism. Yet this is no longer the case, Bracken argues, for as empty space increasingly disappears, the very "finite size of the earth" becomes a force for instability. And as I learned at the U.S. Army's Command and General Staff College, "attrition of the same adds up to big change."

One force that is shrinking the map of Eurasia is technology, particularly the military applications of it and the rising power it confers on states. In the early Cold War, Asian militaries were mostly lumbering, heavy forces whose primary purpose was national consolidation. They focused inward. But as national wealth accumulated and the computer revolution took hold, Asian militaries from the oil-rich Middle East to the tiger economies of the Pacific developed full-fledged, military-civilian postindustrial complexes, with missiles and fiber optics and satellite phones. These states also became bureaucratically more cohesive, allowing their militaries to focus outward, toward other states. Geography in Eurasia, rather than a cushion, was becoming a prison from which there was no escape.

Now there is an "unbroken belt of countries," in Bracken's words, from Israel to North Korea, which are developing ballistic missiles and destructive arsenals. A map of these countries' missile ranges shows a series of overlapping circles: Not only is no one safe, but a 1914-style chain reaction leading to wider war is easily conceivable. "The spread of missiles and weapons of mass destruction in Asia is like the spread of the six-shooter in the American Old West," Bracken writes—a cheap, deadly equalizer of states.

The other force driving the revenge of geography is population growth, which makes the map of Eurasia more claustrophobic still. In the 1990s, many intellectuals viewed the 18th-century English philosopher Thomas Malthus as an overly deterministic thinker because he treated humankind as a species reacting to its physical environment, not a body of autonomous individuals. But as the years pass, and world food and energy prices fluctuate, Malthus is getting more respect. If you wander through the slums of Karachi or Gaza, which wall off multitudes of angry lumpen faithful—young men mostly—one can easily see the conflicts over scarce resources that Malthus predicted coming to pass. In three decades covering the Middle East, I have watched it evolve from a largely rural society to a realm of teeming megacities. In the next 20 years, the Arab world's population will nearly double while supplies of groundwater will diminish.

A Eurasia of vast urban areas, overlapping missile ranges, and sensational media will be one of constantly enraged crowds, fed by rumors transported at the speed of light from one Third World megalopolis to another. So in addition to Malthus, we will also hear much about Elias Canetti, the 20th-century philosopher of crowd psychology: the phenomenon of a mass of people abandoning their individuality for an intoxicating collective symbol. It is in the cities of Eurasia principally where crowd psychology will have its greatest geopolitical impact. Alas, ideas do matter. And it is the very compression of geography that will provide optimum breeding grounds for dangerous ideologies and channels for them to spread.

All of this requires major revisions to Mackinder's theories of geopolitics. For as the map of Eurasia shrinks and fills up with people, it not only obliterates the artificial regions of area studies; it also erases Mackinder's division of Eurasia into a specific "pivot" and adjacent "marginal" zones. Military assistance from China and North Korea to Iran can cause Israel to take military actions. The U.S. Air Force can attack landlocked Afghanistan from Diego Garcia, an island in the middle of the Indian Ocean. The Chinese and Indian navies can project power from the Gulf of Aden to the South China Sea—out of their own regions and along the whole rimland. In short, contra Mackinder, Eurasia has been reconfigured into an organic whole.

The map's new seamlessness can be seen in the Pakistani outpost of Gwadar. There, on the Indian Ocean, near the Iranian border, the Chinese have constructed a spanking new deep-water port. Land prices are booming, and people talk of this still sleepy fishing village as the next Dubai, which may one day link towns in Central Asia to the burgeoning middle-class fleshpots of India and China through pipelines, supertankers, and the Strait of Malacca. The Chinese also have plans for developing other Indian Ocean ports in order to transport oil by pipelines directly into western and central China, even as a canal and land bridge are possibly built across Thailand's Isthmus of Kra. Afraid of being outflanked by the Chinese, the Indians are expanding their own naval ports and strengthening ties with both Iran and Burma, where the Indian-Chinese rivalry will be fiercest.

Much of Eurasia will eventually be as claustrophobic as the Levant, with geography controlling everything and no room to maneuver. The battle over land between Israelis and Palestinians is a case of utter geographical determinism. This is Eurasia's future as well.

These deepening connections are transforming the Middle East, Central Asia, and the Indian and Pacific oceans into a vast continuum, in which the narrow and vulnerable Strait of Malacca will be the Fulda Gap of the 21st century. The fates of the Islamic Middle East and Islamic Indonesia are therefore becoming inextricable. But it is the geographic connections, not religious ones, that matter most.

This new map of Eurasia—tighter, more integrated, and more crowded—will be even less stable than Mackinder thought. Rather than heartlands and marginal zones that imply separateness, we will have a series of inner and outer cores that are fused together through mass politics and shared paranoia. In fact, much of Eurasia will eventually be as claustrophobic as Israel and the Palestinian territories, with geography controlling everything and no room to maneuver. Although Zionism shows the power of ideas, the battle over land between Israelis and Palestinians is a case of utter geographical determinism. This is Eurasia's future as well.

The ability of states to control events will be diluted, in some cases destroyed. Artificial borders will crumble and become more fissiparous, leaving only rivers, deserts, mountains, and other enduring facts of geography. Indeed, the physical features of the landscape may be the only reliable guides left to understanding the shape of future conflict. Like rifts in the Earth's crust that produce physical instability, there are areas in Eurasia that are more prone to conflict than others. These "shatter zones" threaten to implode, explode, or maintain a fragile equilibrium. And not surprisingly, they fall within that unstable inner core of Eurasia: the greater Middle East, the vast way station between the Mediterranean world and the Indian subcontinent that registers all the primary shifts in global power politics.

This inner core, for Mackinder, was the ultimate unstable region. And yet, writing in an age before oil pipelines and ballistic missiles, he saw this region as inherently volatile, geographically speaking, but also somewhat of a secondary concern. A century's worth of technological advancement and population explosion has rendered the greater Middle East no less volatile but dramatically more relevant, and where Eurasia is most prone to fall apart now is in the greater Middle East's several shatter zones.

I'll never forget what a U.S. military expert told me in Sanaa: "Terrorism is an entrepreneurial activity, and in Yemen you've got over 20 million aggressive, commercial-minded, and well-armed people, all extremely hard-working compared with the Saudis next door. It's the future, and it terrifies the hell out of the government in Riyadh."

The Indian subcontinent is one such shatter zone. It is defined on its landward sides by the hard geographic borders of the Himalayas to the north, the Burmese jungle to the east, and the somewhat softer border of the Indus River to the west. Indeed, the border going westward comes in three stages: the Indus; the unruly crags and canyons that push upward to the shaved wastes of Central Asia, home to the Pashtun tribes; and, finally, the granite, snow-mantled massifs of the Hindu Kush, transecting Afghanistan itself. Because these geographic impediments are not contiguous with legal borders, and because barely any of India's neighbors are functional states, the current political organization of the subcontinent should not be taken for granted. You see this acutely as you walk up to and around any of these land borders, the weakest of which, in my experience, are the official ones—a mere collection of tables where cranky bureaucrats inspect your luggage. Especially in the west, the only border that lives up to the name is the Hindu Kush, making me think that in our own lifetimes the whole semblance of order in Pakistan and southeastern Afghanistan could unravel, and return, in effect, to vague elements of greater India.

In Nepal, the government barely controls the countryside where 85 percent of its people live. Despite the aura bequeathed by the Himalayas, nearly half of Nepal's population lives in the dank and humid lowlands along the barely policed border with India. Driving throughout this region, it appears in many ways indistinguishable from the Ganges plain. If the Maoists now ruling Nepal cannot increase state capacity, the state itself could dissolve.

The same holds true for Bangladesh. Even more so than Nepal, it has no geographic defense to marshal as a state. The view from my window during a recent bus journey was of the same ruler-flat, aquatic landscape of paddy fields and scrub on both sides of the line with India. The border posts are disorganized, ramshackle affairs. This artificial blotch of territory on the Indian subcontinent could metamorphose yet again, amid the gale forces of regional politics, Muslim extremism, and nature itself.

Like Pakistan, no Bangladeshi government, military or civilian, has ever functioned even remotely well. Millions of Bangladeshi refugees have already crossed the border into India illegally. With 150 million people—a population larger than Russia—crammed together at sea level, Bangladesh is vulnerable to the slightest climatic variation, never mind the changes caused by global warming. Simply because of its geography, tens of millions of people in Bangladesh could be inundated with salt water, necessitating the mother of all humanitarian relief efforts. In the process, the state itself could collapse.

Of course, the worst nightmare on the subcontinent is Pakistan, whose dysfunction is directly the result of its utter lack of geographic logic. The Indus should be a border of sorts, but Pakistan sits astride both its banks, just as the fertile and teeming Punjab plain is bisected by the India-Pakistan border. Only the Thar Desert and the swamps to its south act as natural frontiers between Pakistan and India. And though these are formidable barriers, they are insufficient to frame a state composed of disparate, geographically based, ethnic groups—Punjabis, Sindhis, Baluchis, and Pashtuns—for whom Islam has provided insufficient glue to hold them together. All the other groups in Pakistan hate the Punjabis and the army they control, just as the groups in the former Yugoslavia hated the Serbs and the army they controlled. Pakistan's raison d'être is that it supposedly provides a homeland for subcontinental Muslims, but 154 million of them, almost the same number as the entire population of Pakistan, live over the border in India.

To the west, the crags and canyons of Pakistan's North-West Frontier Province, bordering Afghanistan, are utterly porous. Of all the times I crossed the Pakistan-Afghanistan border, I never did so legally. In reality, the two countries are inseparable. On both sides live the Pashtuns. The wide belt of territory between the Hindu Kush mountains and the Indus River is really Pashtunistan, an entity that threatens to emerge were Pakistan to fall apart. That would, in turn, lead to the dissolution of Afghanistan.

The Taliban constitute merely the latest incarnation of Pashtun nationalism. Indeed, much of the fighting in Afghanistan today occurs in Pashtunistan: southern and eastern Afghanistan and the tribal areas of Pakistan. The north of Afghanistan, beyond the Hindu Kush, has seen less fighting and is in the midst of reconstruction and the forging of closer links to the former Soviet republics in Central Asia, inhabited by the same ethnic groups that populate northern Afghanistan. Here is the ultimate world of Mackinder, of mountains and men, where the facts of geography are asserted daily, to the chagrin of U.S.-led forces—and of India, whose own destiny and borders are hostage to what plays out in the vicinity of the 20,000-foot wall of the Hindu Kush.

Another shatter zone is the Arabian Peninsula. The vast tract of land controlled by the Saudi royal family is synonymous with Arabia in the way that India is synonymous with the subcontinent. But while India is heavily populated throughout, Saudi Arabia constitutes a geographically nebulous network of oases separated by massive waterless tracts. Highways and domestic air links are crucial to Saudi Arabia's cohesion. Though India is built on an idea of democracy and religious pluralism, Saudi Arabia is built on loyalty to an extended family. But while India is virtually surrounded by troubling geography and dysfunctional states, Saudi Arabia's borders disappear into harmless desert to the north and are hielded by sturdy, well-governed, self-contained sheikhdoms o the east and southeast.

Where Saudi Arabia is truly vulnerable, and where the shatter zone of Arabia is most acute, is in highly populous Yemen to the south. Although it has only a quarter of Saudi Arabia's land area, Yemen's population is almost as large, so the all-important demographic core of the Arabian Peninsula is crammed into its mountainous southwest corner, where sweeping basalt plateaus, rearing up into sandcastle formations and volcanic plugs, embrace a network of oases densely inhabited since antiquity. Because the Turks and the British never really controlled Yemen, they did not leave behind the strong bureaucratic institutions that other former colonies inherited.

When I traveled the Saudi-Yemen border some years back, it was crowded with pickup trucks filled with armed young men, loyal to this sheikh or that, while the presence of the Yemeni government was negligible. Mudbrick battlements hid the encampments of these rebellious sheikhs, some with their own artillery. Estimates of the number of firearms in Yemen vary, but any Yemeni who wants a weapon can get one easily. Meanwhile, groundwater supplies will last no more than a generation or two.

I'll never forget what a U.S. military expert told me in the capital, Sanaa: "Terrorism is an entrepreneurial activity, and in Yemen you've got over 20 million aggressive, commercial-minded, and well-armed people, all extremely hard-working compared with the Saudis next door. It's the future, and it terrifies the hell out of the government in Riyadh." The future of teeming, tribal Yemen will go a long way to determining the future of Saudi Arabia. And geography, not ideas, has everything to do with it.

The Fertile Crescent, wedged between the Mediterranean Sea and the Iranian plateau, constitutes another shatter zone. The countries of this region—Jordan, Lebanon, Syria, and Iraq—are vague geographic expressions that had little meaning before the 20th century. When the official lines on the map are removed, we find a crude finger-painting of Sunni and Shiite clusters that contradict national borders. Inside these borders, the governing authorities of Lebanon and Iraq barely exist. The one in Syria is tyrannical and fundamentally unstable; the one in Jordan is rational but under quiet siege. (Jordan's main reason for being at all is to act as a buffer for other Arab regimes that fear having a land border with Israel.) Indeed, the Levant is characterized by tired authoritarian regimes and ineffective democracies.

Of all the geographically illogical states in the Fertile Crescent, none is more so than Iraq. Saddam Hussein's tyranny, by far the worst in the Arab world, was itself geographically determined: Every Iraqi dictator going back to the first military coup in 1958 had to be more repressive than the previous one just to hold together a country with no natural borders that seethes with ethnic and sectarian consciousness. The mountains that separate Kurdistan from the rest of Iraq, and the division of the Mesopotamian plain between Sunnis in the center and Shiites in the south, may prove more pivotal to Iraq's stability than the yearning after the ideal of democracy. If democracy doesn't in fairly short order establish sturdy institutional roots, Iraq's geography will likely lead it back to tyranny or anarchy again.

But for all the recent focus on Iraq, geography and history tell us that Syria might be at the real heart of future turbulence in the Arab world. Aleppo in northern Syria is a bazaar city with greater historical links to Mosul, Baghdad, and Anatolia than to Damascus. Whenever Damascus's fortunes declined with the rise of Baghdad to the east, Aleppo recovered its greatness. Wandering through the souks of Aleppo, it is striking how distant and irrelevant Damascus seems: The bazzars are dominated by Kurds, Turks, Circassians, Arab Christians, Armenians, and others, unlike the Damascus souk, which is more a world of Sunni Arabs. As in Pakistan and the former Yugoslavia, each sect and religion in Syria has a specific location. Between Aleppo and Damascus in the increasingly Islamist Sunni heartland. Between Damascus and the Jordanian border are the Druse, and in the mountain stronghold contiguous with Lebanon are the Alawites—both remnants of a wave of Shiism from Persia and Mesopotamia that swept over Syria a thousand years ago.

Elections in Syria in 1947, 1949, and 1954 exacerbated these divisions by polarizing the vote along sectarian lines. The late Hafez al-assad came to power in 1970 after 21 changes of government in 24 years. For three decades, he was the Leonid Brezhnev of the Arab world, staving off the future by failing to build a civil society at home. His son Bashar will have to open the political system eventually, if only to keep pace with a dynamically changing society armed with satellite dishes and the Internet. But no one knows how stable a post-authoritarian Syria would be. Policymakers must fear the worst. Yet a post-Assad Syria may well do better than post-Saddam Iraq, precisely because its tyranny has been much less severe. Indeed, traveling from Saddam's Iraq to Assad's Syria was like coming up for air.

In addition to its inability to solve the problem of political legitimacy, the Arab world is unable to secure its own environment. The plateau peoples of Turkey will dominate the Arabs in the 21st century because the Turks have water and the Arabs don't. Indeed, to develop its own desperately poor southeast and thereby suppress Kurdish separatism, Turkey will need to divert increasingly large amounts of the Euphrates River from Syria and Iraq. As the Middle East becomes a realm of parched urban areas, water will grow in value relative to oil. The countries with it will retain the ability—and thus the power—to blackmail those without it. Water will be like nuclear energy, thereby making desalinization and dual-use power facilities primary targets of missile strikes in future wars. Not just in the West Bank, but everywhere there is less room to maneuver.

A final shatter zone is the Persian core, stretching from the Caspian Sea to Iran's north to the Persian Gulf to its south. Virtually all of the greater Middle East's oil and natural gas lies in this region. Just as shipping lanes radiate from the Persian Gulf, pipelines are increasingly radiating from the Caspian region to the Mediterranean, the Black Sea, China, and the Indian Ocean. The only country that straddles both energy-producing areas is Iran, as Geoffrey Kemp and

Robert E. Harkavy note in *Strategic Geography and the Changing Middle East*. The Persian Gulf possesses 55 percent of the world's crude-oil reserves, and Iran dominates the whole gulf, from the Shatt al-Arab on the Iraqi border to the Strait of Hormuz in the southeast—a coastline of 1,317 nautical miles, thanks to its many bays, inlets, coves, and islands that offer plenty of excellent places for hiding tanker-ramming speedboats.

It is not an accident that Iran was the ancient world's first superpower. There was a certain geographic logic to it. Iran is the greater Middle East's universal joint, tightly fused to all of the outer cores. Its border roughly traces and conforms to the natural contours of the landscape—plateaus to the west, mountains and seas to the north and south, and desert expanse in the east toward Afghanistan. For this reason, Iran has a far more venerable record as a nation-state and urbane civilization than most places in the Arab world and all the places in the Fertile Crescent. Unlike the geographically illogical countries of that adjacent region, there is nothing artificial about Iran. Not surprisingly, Iran is now being wooed by both India and China, whose navies will come to dominate the Eurasian sea lanes in the 21st century.

Of all the shatter zones in the greater Middle East, the Iranian core is unique: The instability Iran will cause will not come from its implosion, but from a strong, internally coherent Iranian nation that explodes outward from a natural geographic platform to shatter the region around it. The security provided to Iran by its own natural boundaries has historically been a potent force for power projection. The present is no different. Through its uncompromising ideology and nimble intelligence services, Iran runs an unconventional, postmodern empire of substate entities in the greater Middle East: Hamas in Palestine, Hezbollah in Lebanon, and the Sadrist movement in southern Iraq. If the geographic logic of Iranian expansion sounds eerily similar to that of Russian expansion in Mackinder's original telling, it is.

The geography of Iran today, like that of Russia before, determines the most realistic strategy to securing this shatter zone: containment. As with Russia, the goal of containing Iran must be to impose pressure on the contradictions of the unpopular, theocratic regime in Tehran, such that it eventually changes from within. The battle for Eurasia has many, increasingly interlocking fronts. But the primary one is for Iranian hearts and minds, just as it was for those of Eastern Europeans during the Cold War. Iran is home to one of the Muslim world's most sophisticated populations, and traveling there, one encounters less anti-Americanism and anti-Semitism than in Egypt. This is where the battle of ideas meets the dictates of geography.

In this century's fight for Eurasia, like that of the last century, Mackinder's axiom holds true: Man will initiate, but nature will control. Liberal universalism and the individualism of Isaiah Berlin aren't going away, but it is becoming clear that the success of these ideas is in large measure bound and determined by geography. This was always the case, and it is harder to deny now, as the ongoing recession will likely cause the global economy to contract for the first time in six decades. Not only wealth, but political and social order, will erode in many places, leaving only nature's frontiers and men's passions as the main arbiters of that age-old question: Who can coerce whom? We thought globalization had gotten rid of this antiquarian world of musty maps, but now it is returning with a vengeance.

We all must learn to think like Victorians. That is what must guide and inform our newly rediscovered realism. Geographical determinists must be seated at the same honored table as liberal humanists, thereby merging the analogies of Vietnam and Munich. Embracing the dictates and limitations of geography will be especially hard for Americans, who like to think that no constraint, natural or otherwise, applies to them. But denying the facts of geography only invites disasters that, in turn, make us victims of geography.

Better, instead, to look hard at the map for ingenious ways to stretch the limits it imposes, which will make any support for liberal principles in the world far more effective. Amid the revenge of geography, that is the essence of realism and the crux of wise policymaking—working near the edge of what is possible, without slipping into the precipice.

Critical Thinking

1. What does Robert Kaplan mean by "realism"?
2. According to Kaplan, what role does geography have in understanding global issues?
3. Identify Mackinder's "heartland" and what its modern implications are.
4. What are the main reasons that the "map of Eurasia is more claustrophobic"?
5. What are some of the most important "shatter zones"?
6. How does this article complement/contradict Articles 1, 4, 5, 32, 33, and 35?

ROBERT D. KAPLAN is national correspondent for *The Atlantic* and senior fellow at the Center for a New American Security.

Kaplan, Robert D. Reprinted in entirety by McGraw-Hill with permission from *Foreign Policy*, May/June 2009, pp. 96, 98–105. www.foreignpolicy.com. © 2009 Washingtonpost Newsweek Interactive, LLC.

Unfinished Mideast Revolts

JONATHAN BRODER

Nowhere in the world have the latest shocks to the Old Order been more powerful than in the Middle East and North Africa, where massive civic turmoil has swept away long-entrenched leaders in Egypt, Tunisia and Yemen, toppled a despot in Libya and now challenges the status quo in Syria. Over the past sixty years, the only other development of comparable game-changing magnitude was the 1989 fall of the Berlin Wall and the subsequent collapse of the Soviet Union.

It isn't clear where the region is headed, but it is clear that its Old Order is dying. That order emerged after World War II, when the Middle East's colonial powers and their proxies were upended by ambitious new leaders stirred by the force and promise of Arab nationalism. Over time, though, their idealism gave way to corruption and dictatorial repression, and much of the region slipped into economic stagnation, unemployment, social frustration and seething anger.

For decades, that status quo held, largely through the iron-fisted resolve of a succession of state leaders throughout the region who monopolized their nations' politics and suppressed dissent with brutal efficiency. During the long winter of U.S.-Soviet confrontation, some of them also positioned themselves domestically by playing the Cold War superpowers against each other.

The United States was only too happy to play the game, even accepting and supporting authoritarian regimes to ensure free-flowing oil, a Soviet Union held at bay and the suppression of radical Islamist forces viewed as a potential threat to regional stability. Although successive U.S. presidents spoke in lofty terms about the need for democratic change in the region, they opted for the short-term stability that such pro-American dictators provided. And they helped keep the strongmen in power with generous amounts of aid and weaponry.

Perhaps the beginning of the end of the Old Order can be traced to the 1990 invasion of the little oil sheikdom of Kuwait by Iraq's Saddam Hussein—emboldened, some experts believe, by diplomatic mixed signals from the United States. It wasn't surprising that President George H. W. Bush ultimately sent an expeditionary force to expel Saddam from the conquered land, but one residue of that brief war was an increased American military presence in the region, particularly in Saudi Arabia, home to some of Islam's most hallowed religious shrines. That proved incendiary to many anti-Western Islamists, notably Osama bin Laden and his al-Qaeda terrorist forces. One result was the September 11, 2001, attacks against Americans on U.S. soil.

The ensuing decade of U.S. military action in Iraq and Afghanistan produced ripples of anti-American resentment in the region. The fall of Saddam Hussein after the 2003 U.S. invasion represented a historic development that many Iraqis never thought possible. But the subsequent occupation of Iraq and increasing American military involvement in Afghanistan deeply tarnished the U.S. image among Muslims, contributing to a growing passion for change in the region. Inevitably, that change entailed a wave of Islamist civic expression that had been suppressed for decades in places such as Egypt and Tunisia.

Meanwhile, the invasion of Iraq also served to upend the old balance of power in the region. It destroyed the longtime Iraqi counterweight to an ambitious Iran. This fostered a significant shift of power to the Islamic Republic and an expansion of its influence in Syria, Lebanon, the Gaza Strip and the newly Iran-friendly Iraqi government in Baghdad. Iran's apparent desire to obtain a nuclear-weapons capacity—or at least to establish an option for doing so—tatters the status quo further. With Israel threatening to attack Iran's nuclear facilities, many see prospects for a regional conflagration, and few doubt that such a conflict inevitably would draw the United States into its fourth Middle Eastern war since 1991.

In short, recent developments have left the Middle East forever changed, and yet there is no reason to believe the region has emerged from the state of flux that it entered last year, with the street demonstrations in Tunisia and Egypt. More change is coming, and while nobody can predict precisely what form it will take, there is little doubt about its significance. Given the region's oil reserves and strategic importance, change there inevitably will affect the rest of the world, certainly at the gas pump and possibly on a much larger scale if another war erupts.

A careful look at the history of the Middle East reveals that, although the West has sought to hold sway over the region since the fall of the Ottoman Empire following World War I, its hold on that part of the world has been tenuous at best. This has been particularly true since the beginning of the current era of Middle Eastern history, marked by the overthrow of colonial powers and their puppets.

Like so many major developments in the region, this one began in Egypt. On July 22, 1952, Colonel Gamal Abdel Nasser led a coup that toppled the British-installed King Farouk, a corrupt Western lackey. The son of a postal clerk, Nasser was a man of powerful emotions. He had grown up with feelings of shame at the presence of foreign overlords in his country, and he sought to fashion a wave of Arab nationalism that would buoy him up as a regional exemplar and leader. By 1956, he had consolidated power in Egypt and emerged as the strongest Arab ruler of his day—"the embodied symbol and acknowledged leader of the new surge of Arab nationalism," as the influential columnist Joseph Alsop wrote at the time.

From President Eisenhower's secretary of state, John Foster Dulles, Nasser secured a promise of arms sales, but Dulles failed to deliver. So Nasser turned to Soviet leader Nikita Khrushchev, who was happy to comply. The young Egyptian leader's anti-Western fervor impressed Khrushchev, and he saw an opportunity: ship arms to Nasser and gain a foothold in the Middle East. The West's relations with Nasser deteriorated further when Dulles withdrew financial support for the Egyptian leader's Aswan Dam project. Nasser, in retaliation, seized the Suez Canal, the hundred-mile desert waterway that nearly sliced in half the trade route from the oil-rich Persian Gulf to Great Britain.

Britain joined with France and Israel in a military move to recapture the canal, but Eisenhower sternly forced them to halt their offensive and withdraw the troops. Thus did Nasser manage to secure the canal for his country for all time. Alsop and his brother Stewart, both Cold War hawks, complained that Britain's options narrowed down to "the grumbling acceptance of another major setback for the weakening West."

By engineering the anti-Farouk coup, then consolidating his power in Egypt and striking a powerful blow against the West at Suez, Nasser set in motion the events that forged the modern, postcolonial era in Middle Eastern history. In 1958, Iraqi officers toppled the pro-British King Faisal II, and cheering mobs dragged his body through the streets of Baghdad. The long and bloody Algerian revolution against French colonial rule finally forced France to give that country its independence in 1962. Morocco gained its autonomy from France two years later. In 1969, Colonel Muammar el-Qaddafi overthrew the oil-rich King Idris and installed himself as the "Brother Leader and Guide of the Revolution" in Libya.

In those days of Cold War confrontation, Moscow moved quickly to exploit the opportunity posed by this revolutionary wave and the anti-Western sentiment that undergirded it. Soviet diplomats in the region didn't preach against Arab attacks on Israel in the long-running hostilities of the region. Regarding Middle Eastern oil, they said, in essence, "Take it; it was stolen from you." The Soviets rubbed their hands in delight at the prospect of cutting off the West's oil lifeline. They stood by their Middle Eastern clients in good times and bad by helping them rearm and providing political support after the Arab countries suffered humiliating defeats in the 1967 and 1973 wars with Israel.

But even before the 1973 hostilities, Nasser's successor, Anwar Sadat, made a decision that helped tip the scales of influence back toward the United States. He expelled thousands of Soviet military advisers that Nasser had invited into the country and curtailed his ties with Moscow. Then, in a dramatic move in 1977, he flew to Israel to announce his desire for peace before the Israeli Knesset. After two years of U.S.-mediated negotiations, the two countries signed a peace treaty that took Egypt out of the Arab conflict with Israel and altered the strategic landscape in the Middle East. It also bolstered the U.S. position in the region as America's good offices became a significant element of influence.

Recent developments have left the Middle East forever changed, and yet there is no reason to believe the region has emerged from the state of flux that it entered last year

Throughout the remainder of the Cold War and well into the post–Cold War period, events in the Middle East unleashed persistent threats to the stability of the postcolonial order set in motion by Nasser in the 1950s. That status quo survived in general form, but it was constantly beset by major upheavals and ominous rumblings just beneath the surface. This was reflected in the long, bloody Lebanese civil war of 1975–1990. It could be seen in the Iranian Revolution of 1979, which installed an Islamist regime in a nation that had been a steadfast U.S. ally and unleashed a bitter wave of anti-Americanism (culminating in the Tehran hostage crisis that lasted from late 1979 to early 1981). It was also reflected in the bloody Iran-Iraq War, which extended over most of the 1980s and consumed nearly 1.2 million lives on both sides. Another upheaval was the ten-year Algerian civil war of the 1990s, which claimed more than 160,000 lives.

These threats to stability also included, of course, the ongoing Israeli-Palestinian tensions, which defied persistent efforts at negotiation and erupted intermittently into violence of varying degrees of magnitude and intensity.

And yet, for all that, the fundamental contours of the region remained relatively intact as those strongman leaders, many allied with the United States to one extent or another, held firm to their autocratic regimes, their agencies of control and their citadels of corruption. Once again, Egypt set an example for the region. If Nasser's brand of politics was fueled by an idealistic Arab nationalism and Sadat's contribution was a search for accommodation with Israel (for which he won a Nobel Peace Prize), the next Egyptian leader, Hosni Mubarak, seemed fixated on the status quo and the politics of self-aggrandizement. He was the embodied symbol and acknowledged leader of Middle Eastern corruption, and his brand of politics was embraced by other leaders in the region.

For nearly sixty years, these leaders generally managed to enforce the Old Order. But now, with the Arab Spring and its aftermath, that Old Order is fading fast, and much of the region is being remade from the bottom up. What's emerging is a strong sense that the Middle East needs to join the rest of the world and that popular sentiment should direct the destinies of the region's nations and peoples.

As the countries of the former Soviet Union and Eastern Europe joined the West in developing modern global economies, the Arab world lagged far behind. And ordinary Middle Easterners were reminded of that fact every day as new Arab satellite-television networks such as Al Jazeera brought the modernizing world into their homes, over the heads of the state-controlled media.

Anyone who visited the non-oil-producing countries of the Middle East over the past thirty years could see how far behind the rest of the world they were in economic development. In Tangier, legions of unemployed young Moroccan men sat around with nothing to do but stare across the Strait of Gibraltar, hoping for a job on the European side. It was a tableau of despair that was repeated throughout the region.

One of the Arab world's most glaring problems was its outdated educational system. According to the UN's "Arab Human Development Report 2002," few Arab schools could keep pace with the changes caused by globalization and technological advances. Clinging to old teaching methods that emphasized rote learning, Arab schools failed to teach critical thinking. Across the region, these schools produced legions of young Arab graduates who were unprepared for a modern, information-age global economy. In some countries, women were denied education altogether.

"With so little human capital available, relatively few entrepreneurs have invested in the Middle East, other than to harvest the region's plentiful oil and gas resources," wrote Kenneth Pollack, a Middle East specialist at the Brookings Institution, in a 2011 study of the Arab Spring. Those investments, he added, "have benefited the regimes and their cronies, but not the vast majority of the people."

The result was massive unemployment, especially among the young. Many emigrated to Europe in search of work. But many others remained, living with their parents and unable to afford marriage.

Other problems included the lack of democratic rule and the endemic corruption that these regimes tolerated and sometimes encouraged. In most countries, so-called elections consisted of referendums in which voters could choose whether they approved or disapproved of the sitting leaders. Not surprisingly, the leaders often claimed 98 percent approval.

The leaders not only enriched themselves and their cronies but also developed pervasive internal-security forces and questionable legal systems to quash any dissent. In Egypt, Syria, Tunisia, Morocco, Jordan and the Persian Gulf states, torture was a regular practice in government jails, according to the State Department's annual human-rights reports.

With the pressure cooker of unemployment, official corruption and government repression building up for more than three decades, it was simply a matter of time and human nature before something snapped. It came on December 17, 2010, when a Tunisian vegetable peddler named Mohamed Bouazizi set himself on fire to protest the humiliating treatment he persistently received at the hands of a government inspector. His self-immolation would ignite the entire Arab world and eventually help bring down the Old Order.

But what will the new order in the Middle East look like? It is still emerging. The discontent in Algeria, Lebanon, Iraq, Sudan and the Palestinian territories, which also share the demographic profile of high unemployment among young people with few economic prospects at home, has not yet reached a critical mass. Perhaps that is because the memories of civil conflict are still fresh in all of those countries. But unless the governments there take steps to address their economic problems, they easily could become targets of a new round of popular protests.

So far, the only rulers who have managed to hold back the popular pressures of the new Middle East are those who lead oil-rich monarchies. Saudi Arabia succeeded in buying off the malcontents in the kingdom by distributing more than $36 billion in additional benefits to a tiny population that already enjoys cradle-to-grave care. For a few months last year, protests by Bahrain's Shia majority appeared to threaten the tiny island nation's ruling al-Khalifa family, which is Sunni. The United States, which maintains a major naval base in Bahrain, pleaded with Bahrain's rulers to make political reforms. But Saudi Arabia, already aghast at the failure of the United States to support Egypt's Mubarak, a faithful U.S. ally for nearly thirty years, intervened on behalf of the regime. Without informing the Americans, Riyadh sent armored units across the causeway that links Bahrain to the Saudi mainland to help crush the Shia rebellion. For now, at least, Saudi Arabia and the other wealthy Gulf states have bought compliance with the status quo.

But Jordan and Morocco, the Arab monarchies that don't have oil, are talking seriously about political changes in an effort to stay ahead of the revolution. In Morocco, King Mohammed VI is considering a new form of government that would transform his country into a constitutional monarchy.

As for the countries where the old autocrats fell, the Arab revolutions are still a work in progress. Public opinion will direct events to a much larger extent, in foreign policy as much as in domestic affairs. This can be seen in Egypt, which seems to be reclaiming its former role as the region's center of gravity. If the recent contretemps over the detention of Americans working for several prodemocracy NGOS is any indication, Washington can expect more anti-American episodes in the future. Israel can also expect greater hostility. It is wildly unpopular in Egypt because of its treatment of the Palestinians. Few, however, expect the Israel-Egypt peace treaty to unravel. The Egyptian military still maintains enough power to keep both the peace treaty and U.S. ties intact.

But the West will have to get used to political Islam as a major force in the Middle East. In Tunisia, Islamists are behaving in accordance with the country's moderate, pro-Western traditions. The Islamist Al Nahda party, long banned under Tunisia's former rulers, won parliamentary elections last year but assembled a coalition with two liberal parties in an effort to form a government of national consensus. In Egypt, the Muslim Brotherhood, also banned under Mubarak's rule, captured one-third of the seats in parliamentary elections, while the more conservative Salafist party won another 20 percent. Democracy in Egypt is pushing the country toward some form of Islamist structure, though its precise nature remains unclear. The test in Egypt is what kind of constitution the Islamists will write. Will it move the country from autocracy to the rule of law? Will the constitution guarantee individual rights for both men and women as well as protect minorities such as Egypt's beleaguered Coptic Christian population? Will sharia law play a role? And how will the country's ruling party behave the next time there is an election? Will it hand over power peacefully if it loses?

Only the future can answer these questions. After decades of political stagnation, the political ferment in the Middle East is only beginning, and any new order there could take years or even decades to develop. Adding to the region's uncertain trajectory are the unresolved Israeli-Palestinian conflict and the growing threat of a war between Israel and Iran over Tehran's nuclear-enrichment program.

Indeed, the only certainty in the new Middle East is the countless opportunities for statesmanship—and miscalculation—that will lie along the way.

Critical Thinking

1. How/why does the author trace the political roots of the contemporary Middle East to Egypt in 1952?

2. Identify three reasons the region's non-oil-producing economies have lagged behind.

3. How do the monarchs of the oil-producing countries differ from the governments of other countries in the region?

4. What predictions about the future does the author make?

JONATHAN BRODER is a senior editor at *Congressional Quarterly*. He spent seventeen years in the Middle East as a foreign correspondent for the *Associated Press*, NBC News and the *Chicago Tribune*.

Living with a Nuclear Iran

Iran can be contained. The path to follow? A course laid out half a century ago by a young Henry Kissinger, who argued that American chances of checking revolutionary powers such as the Soviet Union depended on our credible willingness to engage them in limited war.

ROBERT D. KAPLAN

IN 1957, A 34-year-old Harvard faculty member, Henry Kissinger, published a book, *Nuclear Weapons and Foreign Policy,* putting forth a counterintuitive proposition: that at the height of the Cold War, with the United States and the Soviet Union amassing enough hydrogen bombs for Armageddon, a messy, limited war featuring conventional forces and a tactical nuclear exchange or two was still possible, and the United States had to be prepared for such a conflict. Fresh in Kissinger's mind was the Korean War, which had concluded with a truce only four years earlier—"a war to which," as he wrote, "an all-out strategy seemed particularly unsuited." But President Dwight D. Eisenhower believed that any armed conflict with Moscow would accelerate into a thermonuclear holocaust, and he rejected outright this notion of "limited" nuclear war.

The absence of a nuclear exchange during the Cold War makes Eisenhower and what became the doctrine of mutual assured destruction look wise in hindsight. But more than half a century after *Nuclear Weapons and Foreign Policy* was published, it still offers swift, searing insights into human nature and a deeply troubling contemporary relevance. Eurasia—from the Mediterranean Sea to the Sea of Japan—is today an almost unbroken belt of overlapping ballistic-missile ranges: those of Israel, Syria, Iran, Pakistan, India, China, and North Korea. Many of these nations have or seek to acquire nuclear arsenals; some are stirred by religious zealotry; and only a few have robust bureaucratic control mechanisms to inhibit the use of these weapons. This conjunction of circumstances increases the prospect of limited nuclear war in this century. Kissinger long ago considered this problem in full, and the current nuclear impasse with Iran gives fresh reason to bring his book back into the debate.

Kissinger begins his study by challenging the idea that peace constitutes the "'normal' pattern of relations among states." Indeed, he describes a world that seems anything but peaceful:

On the ideological plane, the contemporary ferment is fed by the rapidity with which ideas can be communicated and by the inherent impossibility of fulfilling the expectations aroused by revolutionary slogans. On the economic and social plane, millions are rebelling against standards of living as well as against social and racial barriers which had remained unchanged for centuries.

Continuing his description of a world that matches our own, he writes, "International relationships have become truly global . . . There are no longer any isolated areas." In 2010, that sounds utterly mundane; but then again, in Eisenhower's day, the idea that North Korea would help Syria to build a nuclear plant and thereby precipitate an Israeli military raid (as happened in 2007) would have seemed wildly improbable. Kissinger foresaw an interconnected world incessantly roiled by unsettling ideologies and unmet expectations.

Out of this turbulence inevitably come revolutionary powers, whose emergence is a critical theme in Kissinger's book:

Time and again states appear which boldly proclaim that their purpose is to destroy the existing structure and to recast it completely. And time and again, the powers that are the declared victims stand by indifferent or inactive, while the balance of power is overturned.

Obviously, Kissinger was concerned here with the Soviet Union. As he told me in an interview last spring in his Manhattan office, he considered Moscow a revolutionary power because of its instigation of the 1948–49 Berlin blockade, and its encouragement of the Korean War in 1950, which were very much recent history when he wrote—Stalin had been dead for only four years. Over nearly five decades, thanks at least in part to a Western strategy of containment that resulted in no limited nuclear exchanges, the behavior of the Soviet regime evolved. The revolutionary power had been tamed, if not by us, then by its own longevity.

To insert a nuclearizing Iran in place of the mid-20th-century Soviet Union is to raise several tantalizing possibilities. In his book, Kissinger writes that, by acquiring nuclear weapons, a nation becomes able, for the first time, to change the regional or global balance of power without an invasion or a declaration of war. Let us assume that Iran develops a nuclear capability—an outcome that seems likely despite the imposition of sanctions and the threat by Israel of some kind of preemptive military strike. Would a nuclear Iran be as dangerous a revolutionary power as the old Soviet Union? More broadly, how should the United States contend with the threat posed by Iran, North Korea, and other would-be revolutionary powers that seek to use their possession of nuclear weapons to overturn the status quo?

Kissinger's 1957 analysis of how the status quo powers respond to revolutionary powers seems sadly applicable to the situation with Iran today: "All their instincts will cause them to seek to integrate the revolutionary power into the legitimate framework with which they are familiar and which to them seems 'natural'." They see negotiations as the preferred way to manage emerging differences. The problem is that for a revolutionary power, a negotiation is not "in itself a symptom of reduced tension," as the status quo powers would have us believe, but merely a tactic to gain time. Whereas for normal nations, a treaty has legal and moral weight, for the revolutionary power, treaty talks are merely a concessionary phase in the continuing struggle. Think of how North Korea has skillfully—and repeatedly—used the promise of giving up its nuclear capability as a negotiating tool to secure other benefits, from fuel oil to relief from sanctions.

"Iran," Kissinger told me, "merely by pursuing nuclear weapons, has given itself a role in the region out of proportion to its actual power, and it gains further by the psychological impact of its being able to successfully defy the United Nations Security Council." Nevertheless, he went on, he does not consider Iran a threat of the "same order of magnitude" as the 1950s' Soviet Union, even as it "ideologically and militarily challenges the Middle East order."

When I asked Kissinger whether a nuclear Iran would be containable, he suggested that he would want to take tough measures to prevent a nuclear Iran in the first place. He did tell me that the United States had "different deterrence equations" to consider: Iran versus Israel, Iran versus the Sunni Arabs, Iran versus its own dissidents, and Islam versus the West. All of these dynamics, he explained, would interact in the event of an Iran that goes nuclear, and lead to "even more-frequent crises" than we currently have in the Middle East.

But in spite of Iran's refusal thus far to avail itself of "the genuine opportunity to transform itself from a cause to a nation," Kissinger told me, the country's true strategic interests should "run parallel with our own." For example, Iran should want to limit Russia's influence in the Caucasus and Central Asia, it should want to limit the Taliban's influence in neighboring Afghanistan, it should accept stability in Iraq, and it should want to serve as a peaceful balancing power in the Sunni Arab world.

Indeed, I would argue that because Sunni Arabs from Saudi Arabia, the United Arab Emirates, Lebanon, and Egypt perpetrated the attacks of September 11, 2001, and because Sunni hostility to American and Israeli interests remains a conspicuous problem, the United States should theoretically welcome a strengthened Shiite role in the Middle East, were Iran to go through an even partial political transformation. And demographic, cultural, and other indicators all point to a positive ideological and philosophical shift in Iran in the medium to long term. Given this prognosis, and the high cost and poor

chances for success of any military effort to eliminate Iran's nuclear program, I believe that containment of a nuclear Iran is the most sensible policy for the United States.

The success of containment will depend on a host of regional factors. But its sine qua non will be the ability of the United States to underline any policy toward a nuclear-armed Iran with the credible threat of military action. As Kissinger told me, "I want America to sustain whatever measures it takes about Iran." As he writes in *Nuclear Weapons and Foreign Policy*, "Deterrence . . . is achieved when one side's readiness to run risks in relation to the other is high; it is least effective when the willingness to run risks is low, however powerful the military capability."

Kissinger well knows from personal experience that domestic politics temper U.S. willingness to run such risks. Limited wars—those conflicts when a nation chooses for political reasons not to bring to bear all the weapons at its disposal—have always been difficult for Americans. "My book" he told me, "was written after one limited war, in Korea, where the U.S. achieved some of its objectives. Since the book was published, we had a limited war in Vietnam, in which a sector of the U.S. population wanted to lose the war in order to purify America's soul. To a lesser extent, that was also the case in Iraq. That is a new experience. You can't fight a war for an exit strategy." His conclusion: "America can no longer engage in a conflict unless it knows it can win it."

The crux of Kissinger's book and, in many ways, his professional life is this ongoing tension between his belief that limited war is something that the United States must be prepared to wage and his recognition of the domestic upheavals that such wars inevitably trigger. To refuse as a matter of principle to fight limited wars is to leave America powerless, with only an inflexible and reactive policy against the subtle maneuvers of adversaries: "Our empiricism," Kissinger writes, "dooms us" to requiring all the facts of a case beforehand, by which point it is too late to act. The search for certainty, he goes on, reduces us to dealing with emergencies, not preventing them. But for a democracy that needs to mobilize an entire population through patient argument in order to deploy troops for war—and, therefore, requires a good-versus-evil cause to ensure public support—limited wars, with their nuanced objectives, are far more challenging than all-out ones.

We must be more willing, not only to accept the prospect of limited war but, as Kissinger does in his book of a half century ago, to accept the prospect of a limited nuclear war between states. For most of the 1950s, observes Lawrence Freedman, a strategic theorist and historian at King's College London, in *The Evolution of Nuclear Strategy,* "the imminence of a strategic stalemate was taken as a basic premise." Although Kissinger was not the first or only thinker to advocate that the West develop strategies for the limited use of nuclear weapons, his "challenging, confident, and assertive style" made him easily the most forceful and articulate.

Kissinger recognizes the inherent dangers of this new strategic approach. Indeed, writing in 1957 about a possible superpower confrontation, he is also describing a possible 21st-century India-Pakistan one:

A limited nuclear war which had to be improvised in the midst of military operations would be undertaken under the worst possible conditions. . . . Because of the need for rapid reaction which is imposed by the speed and power of modern weapons, a misinterpretation of the opponent's intentions . . . may well produce a cataclysm . . . And [the two adversaries'] difficulties would be compounded by the fact that they would have had no previous experience to serve as a guide.

As Kissinger argues in his book, the psychological advantage in limited war will constantly shift in favor of the side that convincingly conveys the intention of escalating, particularly if the escalation entails nuclear weapons. Armed with nuclear weapons, in other words, a cornered Pakistan in a limited war with India would be a fearsome thing to behold.

At the time of his writing *Nuclear Weapons and Foreign Policy,* some analysts took Kissinger to task for what one reviewer called "wishful thinking"—in particular, his insufficient consideration of civilian casualties in a limited nuclear exchange. Moreover, Kissinger himself later moved away from his advocacy of a NATO strategy that relied on short-range, tactical nuclear weapons to counterbalance the might of the Soviet Union's conventional forces. (The doctrinal willingness to suffer millions of West German civilian casualties to repel a Soviet attack seemed a poor way to demonstrate the American commitment to the security and freedom of its allies.) But that does not diminish the utility of Kissinger's thinking the unthinkable. Indeed, now that the nuclear club has grown, and nuclear weaponry has become more versatile and sophisticated, the questions that his book raises are even more relevant. The dreadful prospect of limited nuclear exchanges is inherent in a world no longer protected by the carapace of mutual assured destruction. Yet much as limited war has brought us to grief, our willingness to wage it may one day save us from revolutionary powers that have cleverly obscured their intentions—Iran not least among them.

Critical Thinking

1. What is the central premise of Kissinger's containment policy toward revolutionary powers?

2. How does Robert Kaplan interpret this 1950s-era doctrine in the context of contemporary Iran?

3. Robert Kaplan is the author of Articles 31 and 33. How does this article complement/contradict Article 32?

ROBERT D. KAPLAN is an *Atlantic* national correspondent, a senior fellow at the Center for a New American Security, and a member of the Defense Policy Board. His newest book is *Monsoon: The Indian Ocean and the Future of American Power.*

America's Nuclear Meltdown towards "Global Zero"

"The Obama Administration ought to ensure that, in making moves toward zero, the U.S. will, in fact, receive concrete, reciprocal concessions from China and India regarding their own nuclear disarmament. . . ."

LAVINA LEE

CHINA'S 2008 "White Paper on National Defense"—still the most definitive statement of Beijing's strategic doctrine—asserts that "all nuclear-weapon states should make an unequivocal commitment to the thorough destruction of nuclear weapons." Consistent with this statement, China already has responded favorably to the New START (Strategic Arms Reduction Treaty) agreement between the U.S. and Russia. Although this response should be encouraging to the Obama Administration, New START likely is to be viewed in Beijing as merely a first, tentative step toward global zero, rather than a dramatic signal that alters Chinese strategic calculations and threat perceptions regarding America. In China's view, the U.S. and Russia, as "the two countries possessing the largest nuclear arsenals, bear special and primary responsibility for nuclear disarmament" and should "further drastically reduce their nuclear arsenals in a verifiable and irreversible manner, so as to create the necessary conditions for the participation of other nuclear-weapon states in the process of nuclear disarmament."

Although New START commits the U.S. and Russia to significant reductions in deployed strategic warheads, limiting them to no more than 1,550 each, it places no limits on either state's nondeployed nuclear warheads. Given that the U.S. currently has 5,113 warheads in its nuclear stockpile (not including "several thousand" warheads that are retired and awaiting dismantlement), and China's nuclear capabilities are estimated at around 240 nuclear warheads, it is unlikely that the Chinese will believe that New START has created anywhere near the "necessary conditions" to enable China to begin force reductions of its own. The Chinese have not placed a precise number on the level of force reductions they expect of the U.S. and Russia, but it almost is certain that some semblance of nuclear parity with Beijing will be required.

In any case, given Pres. Barack Obama's own admission that global zero is unlikely to be achieved in his lifetime, the Chinese have cause to question whether the U.S. and Russia voluntarily will relinquish their nuclear superiority any time soon. Under these circumstances, America will be waiting a long time for any Chinese reciprocity on nuclear force reductions. At a minimum, Beijing's posture will stiffen domestic opposition in the U.S. to further cuts in America's own arsenal.

At the April 2010 Nuclear Security Summit in Washington, D.C., Prime Minister Manmohan Singh of India welcomed New START as a "step in the right direction" toward global zero and stated that he was "encouraged" by the "U.S. Nuclear Posture Review" (NPR). That position is consistent with the stance of successive Indian governments of various political persuasions that have advocated global nuclear disarmament since India gained independence. The present Congress Party-led government has called for negotiations on a multilateral, "nondiscriminatory" and "verifiable" Nuclear Weapons Convention that would ban the "development, production, stockpiling, and use of nuclear weapons" in a "time-bound" manner.

India's development of an indigenous nuclear capacity, despite New Delhi's strong stance on nuclear disarmament, would appear at first glance to undermine the credibility of its stance on global zero. However, Indian leaders have maintained that the indefinite extension of the Nuclear Proliferation Treaty (NPT) in 1995, despite the failure of the nuclear weapons states to take concrete steps toward nuclear disarmament in a time-bound manner, left New Delhi no choice but to seek a nuclear deterrent to protect its "autonomy of decisionmaking" (i.e., as a defense against nuclear blackmail). In light of its own experience, India's response to the Obama Administration's global zero agenda has emphasized the connection between comprehensive nuclear disarmament and nonproliferation as "mutually reinforcing processes."

Apart from rhetorical support for nuclear disarmament, India has not made any commitment to join the U.S. and Russia on the path to zero in the near future. Given the historical and existing defense linkages between India and the USSR/Russia, and the developing security partnership between the U.S. and India, New Delhi has little reason to view the continuing strategic nuclear superiority of America and Russia as a security threat. However, in keeping with its moral and political stance against nuclear weapons, India will continue to insist that both states must take the lead by making even further cuts to their nuclear arsenals. For example, Singh, while welcoming the New START agreement, also called on "all states with substantial nuclear arsenals to further accelerate this process by making deeper cuts that will lead to meaningful disarmament."

India vs. China and Pakistan

The greatest influence over when India will begin nuclear force reductions remains its assessment of the security threats emanating from its nuclear armed regional competitors, China and Pakistan. India maintains a minimum credible deterrent nuclear posture aimed primarily toward these states, with which it has a history of unresolved territorial disputes that have erupted into outright conflict, including the 1962 border war with China and recurring clashes with Pakistan over Kashmir. Any commitments India is likely to make on nuclear force reductions will be linked to both of these states doing the same.

From the Chinese perspective, NPR takes some of the essential steps necessary to achieve the eventual eradication of nuclear weapons. These steps include the decisions to abstain from the development of new nuclear warheads, limit the potential targets and the circumstances under which the U.S. might use nuclear weapons, and elevate nuclear proliferation and terrorism as security threats above the possible threat posed by other nuclear weapons states. China will, however, view NPR as not going far enough in a number of areas. First, the U.S. has stopped short of committing to a "no first use" policy or unconditionally exempting non-nuclear weapons states or states within nuclear-weapon-free-zones from the threat or use of nuclear weapons," all policies that China has adopted. Regardless of whether those commitments are themselves believable or reliable, Chinese officials will use them as a reason to be skeptical of U.S. commitments toward global zero, given that the retention of offensive options will require America to maintain a much larger nuclear arsenal at a higher level of alert than China possesses.

Second, although the U.S. has stated in NPR that it only will use nuclear weapons in "extreme circumstances" where its "vital interests" are at stake, as long as those terms remain undefined— particularly where the status of Taiwan is concerned—China will argue that NPR remains strategically ambiguous and does not, therefore, reduce Beijing's threat perceptions of U.S. nuclear forces. Chinese officials will use this ambiguity within NPR to deflect U.S. calls to improve the transparency of China's own nuclear force modernization program, which has the ostensible goal of avoiding destabilization of the strategic balance between the two countries. Thus, this aspect of NPR will not reduce the incentives for China to magnify its deterrent capabilities by maintaining opacity about the nature and scope of its nuclear modernization activities. Yet, prodding China to increase transparency regarding its arsenal and doctrine is an important goal of the U.S. in getting to zero.

Third, the Chinese are likely to be concerned particularly about the greater emphasis within NPR and Washington's "2010 Ballistic Missile Review" on ballistic missile defense and the upgrade of conventional ballistic missile capabilities, both of which most directly threaten the strategic balance between the two countries. Within NPR, the U.S. specifically links the pursuit of ballistic missile defense as a means to reduce reliance on nuclear weapons for deterring an attack (nuclear, biological, or chemical) on America or its allies. However, U.S. theater missile defense cooperation with Japan, or potentially with Taiwan, provides the opposite incentive to China by raising the prospect that its smaller arsenal and delivery capabilities will be unable to penetrate U.S. missile defenses, thereby calling into question the credibility of Beijing's nuclear deterrent.

Although aware of China's concerns, the "U.S. Ballistic Missile Review Report, 2010" explicitly foresees a role for missile defense to counter China's military modernization program, including the development and deployment of advanced and anti-ship ballistic missile capabilities. The report describes Chinese advances in those systems as having created a "growing imbalance of power across the Taiwan Strait in China's favor."

Strategic arms reductions and the possibility of missile defense cooperation between the U.S. and Russia, suggested within NPR, have become possible only because the underlying conflict of strategic interests between the two countries has dissipated significantly since the end of the Cold War. These conditions do not apply in the case of China, because each side remains uncertain about the other's future intentions within the Asian theater. That especially is true in relation to Taiwan, but there is mutual wariness more generally in terms of China's regional aspirations and Washington's reaction to them.

The continued US. emphasis on—and development of— ballistic missile defense, however understandable, has the potential to undermine the Obama Administration's global zero agenda, particularly by eroding Chinese support for the Comprehensive Test Ban Treaty (CTBT) or a fissile material cutoff treaty. If improvements in U.S. ballistic missile defense capabilities undermine the credibility of China's nuclear deterrent, Beijing likely will be compelled to increase the number and quality of its nuclear warheads, which would, in turn, increase requirements for fissile material. In short, from China's perspective, NPR does not go far enough to reduce Beijing's concerns about U.S. nuclear forces and, therefore, does not provide significant additional incentives to join America on the path to global zero.

India, meanwhile, has made a number of proposals to the Conference on Disarmament regarding steps toward the elimination of nuclear weapons, including the "reduction of the salience of nuclear weapons in security doctrines," the negotiation of a treaty among nuclear weapons states on the "no first use" of nuclear weapons and the nonuse of nuclear weapons against non-nuclear weapons states. The specific steps within NPR to limit the potential targets and the circumstances in which the U.S. nuclear arsenal may be used certainly reduces the "salience" of nuclear weapons within Washington's nuclear posture. However, India is likely to argue that it is the U.S. that needs to go much further in establishing its bona fides on disarmament by emulating New Delhi's nuclear doctrine, which explicitly commits to a no-first-use policy and exempts all non-nuclear weapons states from attack.

The specific measures contained in NPR also are unlikely to influence the future development of India's own nuclear doctrine, because India is an emerging strategic partner of the U.S. and, therefore, an unlikely target of America's nuclear forces. Rather, India's nuclear posture and decisions to join arms control treaties, such as the CTBT and a fissile material cutoff treaty, will be influenced most by developments in the nuclear programs of its regional competitors, Pakistan and China.

Apart from the no-first-use posture and negative security assurance given to non-nuclear weapons states, India's nuclear doctrine centers on the maintenance of a "credible minimum deterrent." Precisely what that means in terms of the adequacy of the size and quality of India's nuclear arsenal and delivery systems is calculated primarily with China, rather than Pakistan (much less the U.S.), in mind.

China has loomed large in India's strategic calculations since Chinese forces defeated the Indian army decisively in the October–November 1962 border war. The decision to develop a nuclear capability largely was spurred by China's first nuclear weapons test in 1964. Likewise, India's 1998 nuclear tests were motivated at least as much by increasing fears about being exposed to Chinese nuclear coercion if New Delhi failed to take the next step from fission to thermo-nuclear weapons—as it was by serious and continuing conflicts with Pakistan over control of the disputed territory of Kashmir.

China's positioning of tactical nuclear weapons on the Tibetan plateau, force projection into the Indian Ocean, and willingness to supply missile and nuclear technology to Pakistan all are seen by New Delhi as indicators of a Chinese strategy to hobble Indian influence within South Asia. Further tensions between the two countries continue regarding unresolved border disputes from the 1962 war over geostrategically significant territory in Arunachal Pradesh (claimed as part of Tibet by China but controlled by India) and Aksai Chin (controlled by China but claimed by India). India particularly has been concerned about China's infrastructure-building programs within the disputed border areas, which would enable the efficient movement of land forces during a crisis.

In response, New Delhi has stationed 100,000 troops and two squadrons of advanced Sukhoi-30 MKI aircraft in the northeastern state of Assam as of June 2009. Given these continuing sources of tension between the two countries, Indian support for either the CTBT or a fissile material cutoff treaty most immediately is influenced by how adherence to either treaty will affect the balance of nuclear forces between it and China, rather than any disarmament initiatives of the Obama Administration. Indian negotiators successfully resisted the Bush Administration's pressure to sign the CTBT as a prerequisite to the successful conclusion of the U.S.–India nuclear cooperation agreement in 2008. Instead, New Delhi merely reiterated its commitment to a voluntary moratorium on nuclear testing announced after the 1998 tests.

Questioning Nuclear Testing

The political commitment of India's Congress-led government to this moratorium was tested in August 2009 after a prominent nuclear official involved in the 1998 tests, Kumitithadai Santhanam, publicly expressed doubts about the officially claimed yield of the devices tested in 1998, thereby calling into question the credibility of India's nuclear deterrent. That allegation set off a vigorous internal debate about whether India should resist pressure to sign the CTBT. Nevertheless, members of the Indian government vigorously have disputed Santhanam's claims and maintained that no new testing will be required.

The government is well aware that any resumption of nuclear testing would trigger the termination of the U.S.–India nuclear cooperation agreement, and potentially the reversal of the September 2008 Nuclear Suppliers Group waiver, which allowed its members to trade with India for the first time. Further testing therefore also would put at risk recently signed contracts for nuclear materials and reactors with countries such as Russia and France, which are essential to the success of the government's ambitious plans to expand nuclear energy capacity. In all likelihood, India will maintain a voluntary moratorium on testing to keep its options open unless—and until—the U.S. and China agree to ratify the CTBT.

In terms of a fissile material cutoff treaty, India officially supports the future development of a multilateral and verifiable treaty that will limit future production of fissile material, but has refused to commit to a voluntary moratorium in the meantime. Clearly, India does not believe it has sufficient fissile material to support a nuclear arsenal in keeping with a "credible minimum deterrent" nuclear posture. India's nuclear arsenal is similar in size to Pakistan's at around 60–70 warheads, but only about one-quarter the size of China's. Nongovernmental sources also estimate that China has sufficient enriched uranium and weapons-grade plutonium to produce between 500 and 1,500 additional warheads.

The U.S.–India nuclear deal potentially has increased India's capacity to produce fissile material by allowing domestic sources of uranium to be reserved for military purposes. The completion of a Prototype Fast Breeder Reactor, due this year, will increase that capacity as well. While there is the potential for a nuclear arms race to develop between the two countries, India so far has shown no signs of attempting to reach parity, in terms of numbers of nuclear weapons, with China. New Delhi instead seeks to maintain a credible minimum deterrent by establishing a survivable nuclear triad of bombers, land-based missiles, and missiles deployed aboard submarines.

Whereas Pakistan remains vocally opposed to a fissile material cutoff treaty that prohibits only the future production of fissile material, India has been able to keep a low profile and avoid making any commitment to a treaty either way. Should this obstacle to negotiations be removed, India still is likely to seek to avoid a firm commitment to a treaty on fissile material until it has built up greater stocks. To buy time, India will seek to link support for a fissile material agreement to additional binding disarmament commitments by the U.S. and Russia within a specific time frame. The most fruitful potential point of leverage for the U.S. on this issue is the prospect of cooperation in the field of high technology, particularly the development of ballistic missile defense systems.

Within the NPR and elsewhere, the Obama Administration clearly has elevated disarmament to the center of its nuclear agenda. The Administration hopes that credible moves toward the goal of zero nuclear weapons will lead to reciprocity in terms of disarmament by other states, as well as encourage greater cooperation on measures to limit nuclear proliferation and the threat of nuclear terrorism.

The question remains, though, how far should America move beyond symbolism in "getting to zero"? The Obama Administration ought to ensure that, in making moves toward zero, the U.S. will, in fact, receive concrete, reciprocal concessions from China and India regarding their own nuclear disarmament and their commitments to joining the CTBT. However, the prospects for both results look quite doubtful at this juncture.

Critical Thinking

1. Define "global zero."
2. What steps have Russia and the United States taken to reduce the number of deployed nuclear weapons?
3. Compare and contrast India, China, and Pakistan's nuclear weapons policies.

LAVINA LEE is a lecturer in the Department of Modern History, Politics, and International Relations at Macquarie University, Sydney, Australia, and the author of *U.S. Hegemony and Legitimacy: Norms, Power, and Followership in the War on Iraq.*

Peacekeepers at War

In the eastern Congo, a onetime rebel leader charged with a range of war crimes lived in high style for three years, in full view of a large United Nations peacekeeping force.

How did the U.N. find itself in the middle of one of the world's bloodiest and most unmanageable conflicts? And why are its troops picking sides?

CHRISTOPHER RHOADS

The Congo has long had a knack for bringing out the worst in foreign adventurers, from King Leopold II of Belgium to Joseph Conrad's fictional Kurtz. Now it is forcing a well-intentioned visitor, the United Nations, to reconsider how it keeps the peace in time of war.

The U.N. faced harsh criticism in the mid-1990s when its peacekeepers stood aside as atrocities unfolded in Rwanda and in Srebrenica during the Bosnian war. Determined not to repeat such failures, the U.N. resolved to use force in the name of protecting civilians.

Thirteen years, hundreds of peacekeeper deaths and billions of dollars later, the U.N. mission in the Congo, its largest and most expensive, has shown the problems of what became known as "robust peacekeeping."

A rebellion triggered in early April by a general in the Congolese army—an army that the U.N. supports—has caused hundreds of deaths and tens of thousands of refugees. Last month, Congolese villagers angry at the U.N. for failing to protect them fired on a U.N. base, injuring at least 11 Pakistani peacekeepers. Constrained budgets from a weak global economy have forced the U.N., for the first time in years, to cut its peacekeeping budget and reduce troops on the ground in places like Congo, and the Congolese government has begun putting pressure on the U.N. to pull out entirely.

For more than a century, Congo's natural resources and geopolitical position have drawn the interest of global powers. By the time Belgium granted Congo independence in 1960, the country found itself at the center of Cold War machinations between Washington and Moscow. There's also guilt in the West from a more recent source: France, which supported the ethnic group that perpetrated the genocide in Rwanda,

Thirteen years, hundreds of deaths and billions of dollars later, the U.N. mission in the Congo has shown the problems of 'robust peacekeeping.'

and the U.S., which declined to act to prevent it, are determined to bring stability to the region. When a U.N. mission was proposed in 1999, the U.S. readily gave its support, and other countries quickly got on board. Poorer nations such as Pakistan, Bangladesh and India now provide the bulk of the U.N. troops, both for the prestige and, in some cases, for the financial compensation.

The U.N. mission in Congo has encountered many obstacles, not the least because of Bosco Ntaganda, the former Congolese general at the center of the recent violence there. For three years he lived the high life in Goma, a chaotic city beside an active volcano. He played tennis by the lake at the Hotel Karibu, a favorite spot for Western humanitarian workers in Congo. He took late breakfasts poolside at the Mbiza Hotel and was a fixture at Goma's nightclubs and bars.

U.N. peacekeeping forces in eastern Congo left Mr. Ntaganda alone in Goma, despite accusations against him of human-rights abuses and a 2006 warrant for his arrest issued by the International Criminal Court in The Hague. The peacekeepers said that their hands were tied. As part of a 2009 pact that sought an elusive peace, the onetime rebel leader had become a general in the Congolese army. The U.N.—along with its 19,000 uniformed peacekeepers, special-forces units, armored personnel carriers and attack helicopters—in effect found itself supporting units accused of mass killings and rapes of civilians.

Mr. Ntaganda, 39, ended the charade in April, when he defected from the army with hundreds of followers, blowing up military vehicles and munitions depots. Tens of thousands of refugees fled into neighboring Uganda and Rwanda, the U.N. says. Mr. Ntaganda remains at large.

U.N. peacekeeping today bears little resemblance to what it looked like in its early days. The first mission, in 1948, was a small, unarmed observer force sent to monitor a buffer zone between Arabs and Israelis. During the entire Cold War, the U.N. launched just 18 missions.

The end of the Cold War brought both an increase in conflict within states and, particularly in Africa, a rise in humanitarian crises. Global terrorism highlighted the dangers of failed states.

Suddenly, demands on peacekeepers became larger and more complicated.

Since 1990, the U.N. has launched close to 50 missions. The number of U.N. peacekeepers world-wide has grown sevenfold since 1999, to 100,000, and the global peacekeeping budget has increased by a similar degree to $7.8 billion, of which the U.S. is assessed 27%.

Many missions launched since 1999, when the U.N.'s current mission in Congo began, have carried the mandate to fight to protect civilians—a sharp break from the era when peacekeepers used force only in self-defense.

The Congo mission "has taken peacekeeping to a whole new level in that the U.N. has effectively become a party to the conflict," says Philip Alston, who in 2009, at the request of the U.N. secretary-general, investigated the mission's cooperation with the national army.

There is now debate among member nations about whether the U.N. has taken on too much.

"It's appropriate to start questioning where the hell we're going with all this," says Lt. Gen. Romeo Dallaire, the U.N. force commander in Rwanda during the 1994 genocide and now a Canadian senator, referring to the U.N.'s expanded role. When Hutus began slaughtering Tutsis on his watch in Rwanda, his pleas for U.N. action fell on deaf ears. Now, he says he is concerned that peacekeepers aren't sufficiently trained for what they are expected to do.

"What we can conclude is there is no more peacekeeping, as that term was used historically," he says.

Many recent missions have carried the mandate to fight to protect civilians—a sharp break from the past.

The unrest in Congo has claimed more than five million lives since the late 1990s—most of them civilians, from starvation and disease—according to a study by the International Rescue Committee and Australia's Burnet Institute. The U.N. mission there has suffered 204 peacekeeper deaths, more than in any of its 16 other current missions except the 34-year-old Lebanon deployment.

Congo's current problems are rooted in the Hutu genocide against the Tutsis in Rwanda. Mr. Ntaganda, a Rwandan, was part of a Tutsi rebel group that invaded from Uganda and stopped the genocide.

The defeated Hutu forces fled into eastern Congo. In 1996, the Rwandan national army, with Mr. Ntaganda in its ranks, invaded Congo, toppling the longtime dictator Mobutu Sese Seko. War broke out again in 1998 when relations between Rwanda and the new Congolese government soured.

The U.N. waded into the mess in 1999, deploying 90 political officers and staffers to the Congo to monitor a short-lived cease-fire. After fighting flared anew, the Security Council was initially divided over whether to send armed troops. The Netherlands cautioned against a buildup, citing the 1995 massacre in Srebrenica, in Bosnia, as an example of what can go wrong. The Republic of the Gambia cited the Rwandan genocide to argue for more troops without delay.

In the end, the Security Council passed a resolution in 2000 to send armed troops, and by late the following year 1,868 were on the ground. They arrived just as the U.N. was rethinking its approach to peacekeeping, including allowing the use of force to protect civilians.

Mr. Ntaganda was moving among several armed groups in northeastern Congo during that period. In 2002, he joined a militia whose leader, Thomas Lubanga, was later charged by the ICC with the crime of using child soldiers.

Civilians bore the brunt of the violence. Militias often would signal their power by massacring people in villages where a rival group had just made camp.

In 2002, in a northeastern Congo town called Kisangani, a militia killed at least 103 civilians. More than 1,000 U.N. peacekeepers, including the brigadier general in charge, were present and observed gunfire without taking action, U.N. records show.

Survivors of other massacres in the region in 2002 and 2003 described to Human Rights Watch how soldiers under Mr. Ntaganda's command forced civilians to dig their own graves before they were roped together and killed with sledgehammers and machetes.

Mr. Ntaganda "himself has raped and killed innocent civilians," says Anneke Van Woudenberg, a senior researcher with Human Rights Watch.

Mr. Ntaganda declined to comment for this story, through one of his top officers.

Some at the U.N.'s peacekeeping division in New York saw the Congo mission as ill-equipped to prevent such violence. The mission's own force commander, however, blasted its performance as "totally and utterly unacceptable" after a 2003 episode in which an armed group killed 563 civilians, according to U.N. records.

The U.N. beefed up the Congo peacekeeping force to 10,800 and strengthened its mandate, authorizing the use of "all necessary means" to carry out the mission and placing a higher priority on protecting civilians.

During deliberations on the matter, Italy's ambassador expressed concern about "changing the current practices of peacekeeping operations and plunging the troops into very complicated situations in which they may be required to engage in combat as if they are parties to the conflict."

In 2006, the ICC issued a warrant for Mr. Ntaganda's arrest on charges relating to the use of child soldiers. The U.N. Congo mission began dispatching special forces to capture or kill him.

At one point, U.N. officials learned that Mr. Ntaganda was staying with a girlfriend. U.N. forces surrounded the designated house one night and broke down the door. It was the wrong house. Mr. Ntaganda was staying across the street, according to people familiar with the events. He escaped into the night.

A failed U.N. operation targeting another militia leader killed more than 15 rebels but also eight Guatemalan peacekeepers. On another occasion, U.N. attack helicopters with troops on the ground killed more than 200 members of a militia group moving on Goma.

Some criticized the actions as going too far. Patrick Cammaert, the Dutch U.N. force commander for eastern Congo who oversaw them, disagrees, saying he "never doubted this was the way we should do business."

By 2006, the most significant armed group in Congo was the National Congress for the Defense of the People, or CNDP, a Tutsi-led militia backed by Rwanda. Mr. Ntaganda joined that group and rose to become its chief of military operations.

In November 2008, the CNDP executed more than 150 civilians in Kiwanja, less than a mile from a U.N. base, according to an investigation by Human Rights Watch.

In recent interviews, witnesses to the massacre—identified here by their first names—recalled what CNDP soldiers had done. Kavira, 30, said soldiers stabbed to death eight of her family members and dumped their bodies in a river. Justin, 28, said soldiers shot off his right foot. Anosiate, 62, said soldiers shot her husband and dumped his body with six others in a latrine.

In 2009, Congo and Rwanda attempted to make peace. Congo agreed to take the CNDP militia into the national army. Mr. Ntaganda was made a general and deputy commander of the army's operation in eastern Congo—the same forces receiving U.N. support.

The peace deal caused problems for the U.N. almost immediately. That spring, while participating in a joint operation with U.N. forces, Congolese army troops under Mr. Ntaganda's deputy command were accused of raping and killing civilians. A subsequent fact-finding mission dispatched by U.N. Secretary General Ban Ki-moon concluded that the U.N. Congo mission was "certainly compromised" in lending support to an army that had committed atrocities.

In response, the U.N. began using a database of human-rights abuses to vet army officers before allowing U.N. troops to support their troops. That so-called conditionality policy went into effect world-wide last year.

U.N. officials in Goma say they began to insist on the exclusion of Mr. Ntaganda from all operations involving the U.N. Despite the policy, Congolese officers say, Mr. Ntaganda remained actively involved in army operations.

The tables began to turn on Mr. Ntaganda in March, when the ICC announced a guilty verdict against his former militia boss, Mr. Lubanga, on the same child-soldier charges that Mr. Ntaganda faced. Foreign governments pressured Congolese President Joseph Kabila to arrest Mr. Ntaganda. But before the president could act, the general fled.

U.N. officials say that they are relieved to have Mr. Ntaganda out of the army. The ICC has added rape, murder and pillage to the charges against him. President Kabila has said that the Congolese government seeks his arrest.

U.N. officials in Congo say they have made more changes to how they operate. Their support for the army, they say, is now narrower, on a mission-by-mission basis, and their peacekeepers are trying to limit human-rights violations by getting more involved with local communities.

But Mr. Ntaganda hasn't gone quietly. Late one night in April, in the midst of the rebellion, soldiers loyal to the ex-general appeared in Goma. At a bar called Treichville, Mr. Ntaganda drank with his senior officers, according to people who saw him. Eventually, he hopped into a pickup truck and sped into the night. He is now believed to be hiding with troops loyal to him in Virunga National Park.

Hardeep Singh Puri, India's ambassador to the U.N., says the 13-year Congo mission illustrates the risks inherent in the international body's new, more aggressive notion of peacekeeping.

"There are those that are completely aghast that the Security Council has provided this kind of mandate," he says. "We have to be careful about where this is going. The U.N. charter never talks about going in and being a participant."

Critical Thinking

1. Describe the role of UN peacekeepers in the eastern Congo.

2. What is meant by "robust peacekeeping"?

3. Does this article contradict or complement Article 31?

Rhoads, Christopher. From *The Wall Street Journal*, June 23–24, 2012. Copyright © 2012 by Dow Jones & Company, Inc. Reprinted by permission via Rightslink.

War in the Fifth Domain

Are the mouse and keyboard the new weapons of conflict?

At the height of the cold war, in June 1982, an American early-warning satellite detected a large blast in Siberia. A missile being fired? A nuclear test? It was, it seems, an explosion on a Soviet gas pipeline. The cause was a malfunction in the computer-control system that Soviet spies had stolen from a firm in Canada. They did not know that the CIA had tampered with the software so that it would "go haywire, after a decent interval, to reset pump speeds and valve settings to produce pressures far beyond those acceptable to pipeline joints and welds," according to the memoirs of Thomas Reed, a former air force secretary. The result, he said, "was the most monumental non-nuclear explosion and fire ever seen from space."

This was one of the earliest demonstrations of the power of a "logic bomb". Three decades later, with more and more vital computer systems linked up to the internet, could enemies use logic bombs to, say, turn off the electricity from the other side of the world? Could terrorists or hackers cause financial chaos by tampering with Wall Street's computerised trading systems? And given that computer chips and software are produced globally, could a foreign power infect high-tech military equipment with computer bugs? "It scares me to death," says one senior military source. "The destructive potential is so great."

After land, sea, air and space, warfare has entered the fifth domain: cyberspace. President Barack Obama has declared America's digital infrastructure to be a "strategic national asset" and appointed Howard Schmidt, the former head of security at Microsoft, as his cyber-security tsar. In May the Pentagon set up its new Cyber Command (Cybercom) headed by General Keith Alexander, director of the National Security Agency (NSA). His mandate is to conduct "full-spectrum" operations—to defend American military networks and attack other countries' systems. Precisely how, and by what rules, is secret.

Britain, too, has set up a cyber-security policy outfit, and an "operations centre" based in GCHQ, the British equivalent of the NSA. China talks of "winning informationised wars by the mid-21st century". Many other countries are organising for cyberwar, among them Russia, Israel and North Korea. Iran boasts of having the world's second-largest cyber-army.

What will cyberwar look like? In a new book Richard Clarke, a former White House staffer in charge of counter-terrorism and cyber-security, envisages a catastrophic breakdown within 15 minutes. Computer bugs bring down military e-mail systems; oil refineries and pipelines explode; air-traffic-control systems collapse; freight and metro trains derail; financial data are scrambled; the electrical grid goes down in the eastern United States; orbiting satellites spin out of control. Society soon breaks down as food becomes scarce and money runs out. Worst of all, the identity of the attacker may remain a mystery.

In the view of Mike McConnell, a former spy chief, the effects of full-blown cyberwar are much like nuclear attack. Cyberwar has already started, he says, "and we are losing it." Not so, retorts Mr Schmidt. There is no cyberwar. Bruce Schneier, an IT industry security guru, accuses securocrats like Mr Clarke of scaremongering. Cyberspace will certainly be part of any future war, he says, but an apocalyptic attack on America is both difficult to achieve technically ("movie-script stuff") and implausible except in the context of a real war, in which case the perpetrator is likely to be obvious.

For the top brass, computer technology is both a blessing and a curse. Bombs are guided by GPS satellites; drones are piloted remotely from across the world; fighter planes and warships are now huge data-processing centres; even the ordinary foot-soldier is being wired up. Yet growing connectivity over an insecure internet multiplies the avenues for e-attack; and growing dependence on computers increases the harm they can cause.

By breaking up data and sending it over multiple routes, the internet can survive the loss of large parts of the network. Yet some of the global digital infrastructure is more fragile. More than nine-tenths of internet traffic travels through undersea fibre-optic cables, and these are dangerously bunched up in a few choke-points, for instance around New York, the Red Sea or the Luzon Strait in the Philippines. Internet traffic is directed by just 13 clusters of potentially vulnerable domain-name servers. Other dangers are coming: weakly governed swathes of Africa are being connected up to fibre-optic cables, potentially creating new havens for cyber-criminals. And the spread of mobile internet will bring new means of attack.

The internet was designed for convenience and reliability, not security. Yet in wiring together the globe, it has merged the garden and the wilderness. No passport is required in cyberspace. And although police are constrained by national borders, criminals roam freely. Enemy states are no longer on the other side of the ocean, but just behind the firewall. The ill-intentioned can mask their identity and location, impersonate others and con their way into the buildings that hold the digitised wealth of the electronic age: money, personal data and intellectual property.

Mr Obama has quoted a figure of $1 trillion lost last year to cybercrime—a bigger underworld than the drugs trade, though such figures are disputed. Banks and other companies do not like to admit how much data they lose. In 2008 alone Verizon, a telecoms company, recorded the loss of 285m personal-data records, including credit-card and bank-account details, in investigations conducted for clients.

About nine-tenths of the 140 billion e-mails sent daily are spam; of these about 16% contain moneymaking scams, including "phishing" attacks that seek to dupe recipients into giving out passwords or bank details, according to Symantec, a security-software vendor. The amount of information now available online about individuals makes it ever easier to attack a computer by crafting a personalised e-mail that is more likely to be trusted and opened. This is known as "spear-phishing".

The ostentatious hackers and virus-writers who once wrecked computers for fun are all but gone, replaced by criminal gangs seeking to harvest data. "Hacking used to be about making noise. Now it's about staying silent," says Greg Day of McAfee, a vendor of IT security products. Hackers have become wholesale providers of malware—viruses, worms and Trojans that infect computers—for others to use. Websites are now the favoured means of spreading malware, partly because the unwary are directed to them through spam or links posted on social-networking sites. And poorly designed websites often provide a window into valuable databases.

Malware is typically used to steal passwords and other data, or to open a "back door" to a computer so that it can be taken over by outsiders. Such "zombie" machines can be linked up to thousands, if not millions, of others around the world to create a "botnet". Estimates for the number of infected machines range up to 100m. Botnets are used to send spam, spread malware or launch distributed denial-of-service (DDoS) attacks, which seek to bring down a targeted computer by overloading it with countless bogus requests.

The Spy Who Spammed Me

Criminals usually look for easy prey. But states can combine the criminal hacker's tricks, such as spear-phishing, with the intelligence apparatus to reconnoitre a target, the computing power to break codes and passwords, and the patience to probe a system until it finds a weakness—usually a fallible human being. Steven Chabinsky, a senior FBI official responsible for cybersecurity, recently said that "given enough time, motivation and funding, a determined adversary will always—always—be able to penetrate a targeted system."

Traditional human spies risk arrest or execution by trying to smuggle out copies of documents. But those in the cyberworld face no such risks. "A spy might once have been able to take out a few books' worth of material," says one senior American military source. "Now they take the whole library. And if you restock the shelves, they will steal it again."

China, in particular, is accused of wholesale espionage, attacking the computers of major Western defence contractors and reputedly taking classified details of the F-35 fighter, the mainstay of future American air power. At the end of 2009 it appears to have targeted Google and more than a score of other IT companies. Experts at a cyber-test-range built in Maryland

by Lockheed Martin, a defence contractor (which denies losing the F-35 data), say "advanced persistent threats" are hard to fend off amid the countless minor probing of its networks. Sometimes attackers try to slip information out slowly, hidden in ordinary internet traffic. At other times they have tried to break in by leaving infected memory-sticks in the car park, hoping somebody would plug them into the network. Even unclassified e-mails can contain a wealth of useful information about projects under development.

"Cyber-espionage is the biggest intelligence disaster since the loss of the nuclear secrets [in the late 1940s]," says Jim Lewis of the Centre for Strategic and International Studies, a think-tank in Washington, DC. Spying probably presents the most immediate danger to the West: the loss of high-tech know-how that could erode its economic lead or, if it ever came to a shooting war, blunt its military edge.

Western spooks think China deploys the most assiduous and most shameless cyberspies, but Russian ones are probably more skilled and subtle. Top of the league, say the spooks, are still America's NSA and Britain's GCHQ, which may explain why Western countries have until recently been reluctant to complain too loudly about computer snooping.

The next step after penetrating networks to steal data is to disrupt or manipulate them. If military targeting information could be attacked, for example, ballistic missiles would be useless. Those who play war games speak of being able to "change the red and blue dots": make friendly (blue) forces appear to be the enemy (red), and vice versa.

General Alexander says the Pentagon and NSA started cooperating on cyberwarfare in late 2008 after "a serious intrusion into our classified networks". Mr Lewis says this refers to the penetration of Central Command, which oversees the wars in Iraq and Afghanistan, through an infected thumb-drive. It took a week to winkle out the intruder. Nobody knows what, if any, damage was caused. But the thought of an enemy lurking in battle-fighting systems alarms the top brass.

That said, an attacker might prefer to go after unclassified military logistics supply systems, or even the civilian infrastructure. A loss of confidence in financial data and electronic transfers could cause economic upheaval. An even bigger worry is an attack on the power grid. Power companies tend not to keep many spares of expensive generator parts, which can take months to replace. Emergency diesel generators cannot make up for the loss of the grid, and cannot operate indefinitely. Without electricity and other critical services, communications systems and cash-dispensers cease to work. A loss of power lasting just a few days, reckon some, starts to cause a cascade of economic damage.

Experts disagree about the vulnerability of systems that run industrial plants, known as supervisory control and data acquisition (SCADA). But more and more of these are being connected to the internet, raising the risk of remote attack. "Smart" grids, which relay information about energy use to the utilities, are promoted as ways of reducing energy waste. But they also increase security worries about both crime (eg, allowing bills to be falsified) and exposing SCADA networks to attack.

General Alexander has spoken of "hints that some penetrations are targeting systems for remote sabotage". But precisely what is happening is unclear: are outsiders probing SCADA systems only for reconnaissance, or to open "back doors" for future use? One senior American military source said that if any country were found to be planting logic bombs on the grid, it would provoke the equivalent of the Cuban missile crisis.

Estonia, Georgia and WWI

Important thinking about the tactical and legal concepts of cyber-warfare is taking place in a former Soviet barracks in Estonia, now home to NATO's "centre of excellence" for cyber-defence. It was established in response to what has become known as "Web War I", a concerted denial-of-service attack on Estonian government, media and bank web servers that was precipitated by the decision to move a Soviet-era war memorial in central Tallinn in 2007. This was more a cyber-riot than a war, but it forced Estonia more or less to cut itself off from the internet.

Similar attacks during Russia's war with Georgia the next year looked more ominous, because they seemed to be coordinated with the advance of Russian military columns. Government and media websites went down and telephone lines were jammed, crippling Georgia's ability to present its case abroad. President Mikheil Saakashvili's website had to be moved to an American server better able to fight off the attack. Estonian experts were dispatched to Georgia to help out.

Many assume that both these attacks were instigated by the Kremlin. But investigations traced them only to Russian "hacktivists" and criminal botnets; many of the attacking computers were in Western countries. There are wider issues: did the cyber-attack on Estonia, a member of NATO, count as an armed attack, and should the alliance have defended it? And did Estonia's assistance to Georgia, which is not in NATO, risk drawing Estonia into the war, and NATO along with it?

Such questions permeate discussions of NATO's new "strategic concept", to be adopted later this year. A panel of experts headed by Madeleine Albright, a former American secretary of state, reported in May that cyber-attacks are among the three most likely threats to the alliance. The next significant attack, it said, "may well come down a fibre-optic cable" and may be serious enough to merit a response under the mutual-defence provisions of Article 5.

During his confirmation hearing, senators sent General Alexander several questions. Would he have "significant" offensive cyber-weapons? Might these encourage others to follow suit? How sure would he need to be about the identity of an attacker to "fire back"? Answers to these were restricted to a classified supplement. In public the general said that the president would be the judge of what constituted cyberwar; if America responded with force in cyberspace it would be in keeping with the rules of war and the "principles of military necessity, discrimination, and proportionality".

General Alexander's seven-month confirmation process is a sign of the qualms senators felt at the merging of military and espionage functions, the militarisation of cyberspace and the fear that it may undermine Americans' right to privacy. Cyber-command will protect only the military ".mil" domain. The government domain, ".gov", and the corporate infrastructure, ".com" will be the responsibility respectively of the Department of Homeland Security and private companies, with support from Cybercom.

One senior military official says General Alexander's priority will be to improve the defences of military networks. Another bigwig casts some doubt on cyber-offence. "It's hard to do it at a specific time," he says. "If a cyber-attack is used as a military weapon, you want a predictable time and effect. If you are using it for espionage it does not matter; you can wait." He implies that cyber-weapons would be used mainly as an adjunct to conventional operations in a narrow theatre.

The Chinese may be thinking the same way. A report on China's cyber-warfare doctrine, written for the congressionally mandated US-China Economic and Security Review Commission, envisages China using cyber-weapons not to defeat America, but to disrupt and slow down its forces long enough for China to seize Taiwan without having to fight a shooting war.

Apocalypse or Asymmetry?

Deterrence in cyber-warfare is more uncertain than, say, in nuclear strategy: there is no mutually assured destruction, the dividing line between criminality and war is blurred and identifying attacking computers, let alone the fingers on the keyboards, is difficult. Retaliation need not be confined to cyberspace; the one system that is certainly not linked to the public internet is America's nuclear firing chain. Still, the more likely use of cyber-weapons is probably not to bring about electronic apocalypse, but as tools of limited warfare.

Cyber-weapons are most effective in the hands of big states. But because they are cheap, they may be most useful to the comparatively weak. They may well suit terrorists. Fortunately, perhaps, the likes of al-Qaeda have mostly used the internet for propaganda and communication. It may be that jihadists lack the ability to, say, induce a refinery to blow itself up. Or it may be that they prefer the gory theatre of suicide-bombings to the anonymity of computer sabotage—for now.

Critical Thinking

1. What is meant by the term "cyberwar"?

2. In addition to hostile governments, what other types of international actors employ this tactic?

3. How serious a problem is cyberwar and what efforts are being made to address it?

UNIT 6

Cooperation

Unit Selections

Learning Outcomes

After reading this unit you should be able to:

- Describe the role of non-governmental organizations in developing international cooperative processes.

- Provide examples of cooperation between NGOs, government, and corporations.

- Describe challenges to existing international agreements such as the Geneva Conventions.

- Summarize case studies where NGOs have contributed to solving serious social and environmental problems.

- Assess your on-going effort at identifying your theory of international relations and how this unit changes/complements it.

Student Website
www.mhhe.com/cls

Internet References

Carnegie Endowment for International Peace
    www.ceip.org
OECD/FDI Statistics
    www.oecd.org/statistics
U.S. Institute of Peace
    www.usip.org

An individual can write a letter and, assuming it is properly addressed, be confident that it will be delivered to just about any location in the world. This is true even though the sender pays for postage in the country of origin and not in the country where it is delivered. Every day thousands of international flights transport people from countries around the world, but when boarding an airplane, a traveler has no need to worry about potential language or technical barriers. Similar patterns of cooperation are true when making an international phone call, sending an email, or using an ATM machine while visiting another country.

Many of the most basic activities of our lives are the direct result of governments cooperating across borders. International organizational structures, for example, have been created to eliminate barriers to trade; monitor and respond to public health threats; set standards for international telecommunications; arrest and judge war criminals; protect prisoners of war; and monitor changing atmospheric conditions. Individual governments, in other words, have recognized that their self-interest directly benefits from cooperation (in most cases by giving up some of their sovereignty through the creation of international governmental organizations, or IGOs).

Transnational activities are not limited to the governmental level. There are now tens of thousands of non-governmental organizations (NGOs). The activities of international NGOs include staging the Olympic Games, organizing scientific meetings, and actively discouraging the hunting of seals. The number of international NGOs, along with their influence, has grown tremendously in the past 60 years.

During the same period in which the growth in importance of IGOs and NGOs has taken place, there also has been a parallel expansion of corporate activity across international borders. U.S. consumers are as familiar with Japanese and German brand-name products as they are with items made in their own country. The multinational corporation (MNC) is an important non-state actor. The value of goods and services produced by the biggest MNCs is far greater than the gross domestic product (GDP) of many countries. The international structures that make it possible to buy a German automobile in Sacramento or a South Korean television in Buenos Aires have been developed

© U.S. Air Force photo by Tech. Sgt. James L. Harper Jr.

over many years. They are the result of governments negotiating treaties that create IGOs to implement the agreements (e.g., the World Trade Organization). As a result, corporations engaged in international trade and manufacturing have created complex transnational networks of sales, distribution, and service that employ millions of people.

To some observers these trends indicate that the era of the nation-state as the dominant player in international politics is passing. Other experts have observed these same trends and have concluded that the state system has a monopoly of power and that the diverse variety of transnational organizations depends on the state system and, in significant ways, perpetuates it.

In many of the articles that appear elsewhere in this book, the authors have concluded their analysis by calling for greater international cooperation to solve the world's most pressing problems. The articles in this section provide examples of successful cooperation. In the midst of a lot of bad news, it is easy to overlook the fact that we are surrounded by international cooperation and that basic day-to-day activities in our lives often directly benefit from it.

The Healing Fields

Land mines once crippled a war-ravaged Cambodia. Today the nation is a model for how to recover from this scourge.

MARK JENKINS

Delicately brushing away the soil with his fingers, Aki Ra uncovers a dark green land mine buried two inches beneath the overgrown dirt road. The size of a large soup can, the mine was planted by the Khmer Rouge about 15 years ago on this ox track in northwestern Cambodia—the most densely mined region of one of the most heavily mined countries in the world.

"This is the type 69 Bouncing Betty made in China," says Aki Ra, his breath fogging the blastproof visor of his helmet. Bouncing Betty is the American nickname for a bounding fragmentation land mine. The pressure of a footstep causes it to leap out of the ground and then explode, spraying shrapnel in every direction. It can shred the legs of an entire squad.

Soft-spoken and cherubic, Aki Ra knows the inner workings of the Bouncing Betty and just about every other variety of mine. In the mid-1970s, when he was five, the Khmer Rouge separated him from his parents and took him into the jungle with other orphans. At that time, Pol Pot, commander of the Khmer Rouge, had plunged the country into chaos, closing schools, hospitals, factories, banks, and monasteries; executing teachers and businessmen; and forcing millions of city dwellers into a gulag of labor camps and farms. The small hands of children like Aki Ra were invaluable tools. He was trained to lay land mines, defuse and deconstruct enemy mines, and reuse the TNT for what are now called improvised explosive devices (IEDs).

Some years later, when Vietnamese forces invaded Cambodia, they dragooned Aki Ra into their army, and he was forced to fight against his former captors. When the United Nations' peacekeeping forces finally arrived in 1992, he'd been living in the jungle for some 15 years. He joined the UN as a deminer. When the peacekeepers left two years later, much of the best agricultural lands—vegetable gardens, pastures, rice fields—were still mined. Farmers trying to reclaim their fields were being blown to pieces. For a decade and a half, using only a knife and a stick, Aki Ra worked as an unpaid sapper, defusing rather than detonating land mines, reclaiming his country one square foot at a time. By his own count, he has defused

some 50,000 devices: blast mines, antitank mines, bounding mines, and other explosives.

"I found a lot of mines that I laid," he says with a conflicted sense of pride and shame.

Now a certified deminer, he has his own squad, the Cambodian Self Help Demining team, partially funded by the U.S. The deminers use special metal detectors to search for explosives; that's how they found the Bouncing Betty.

Sweat is dripping off Aki Ra's face as he carefully places a small charge beside the land mine, attaches wires, and runs a thin cable a hundred yards away. Like all official demining organizations, Aki Ra's team no longer defuses land mines but detonates them in situ instead. Squatting behind a tree, he pushes the red button. The explosion is terrifying. With half a grin, Aki Ra says, "One less land mine, one less child without a leg."

In the warfare that raged in Cambodia from 1970 until 1998, all sides used land mines. There are more than 30 different types. Villagers have prosaic names for them based on their appearance: the frog, the drum, the betel leaf, the corncob. Most were manufactured in China, Russia, or Vietnam, a few in the United States. Pol Pot, whose regime was responsible for the deaths of some 1.7 million Cambodians between 1975 and 1979, purportedly called land mines his "perfect soldiers." They never sleep. They wait with limitless patience. Although weapons of war, land mines are unlike bullets and bombs in two distinct ways. First, they are designed to maim rather than kill, because an injured soldier requires the help of two or three others, reducing the enemy's forces. Second, and most sinister, when a war ends, land mines remain in the ground, primed to explode. Only 25 percent of land mine victims around the world are soldiers. The rest are civilians—boys gathering firewood, mothers sowing rice, girls herding goats.

Despite its horrific history, Cambodia has now become a model for how a nation can recover from the scourge of land mines. There are more than a dozen programs for demining, land mine risk education, and survivor assistance in the country. The number of men, women, and children killed or injured each year by mines (both antipersonnel and antitank), explosive remnants of war, or IEDs has fallen from a high of 4,320 in 1996 to 286 in 2010. Survivors are offered medical and vocational assistance. Every schoolchild is taught about the dangers of explosives. Contests have even been held for the best hip-hop songs about land mine awareness.

"I've been rude since I was young," a male performer boasts in one winning song. "I can only make things from bombs."

"No need to exaggerate and show off to me," the female chorus replies. "I don't care and don't want to hear about this."

Major minefields have been mapped and are being systematically demined. There's even a Cambodia Landmine Museum, created by Aki Ra. Located outside Siem Reap, a provincial capital, it displays the mines and ordnance that he deactivated. With support from Americans Bill and Jill Morse, who founded the Landmine Relief Fund, Aki Ra also cares for and educates 35 children at an orphanage.

Worldwide, millions of land mines are buried in nearly 80 countries and regions—from Angola to Afghanistan, Vietnam to Zimbabwe. That's one of every three nations. Many of them are following Cambodia's example. In 2002 almost 12,000 people worldwide were reported killed or maimed by land mines or other explosives. Since then, annual casualties have fallen to fewer than 4,200. This dramatic improvement is a direct result of the Mine Ban Treaty signed in Ottawa, Canada, in 1997, an international agreement banning the use, production, or transfer of land mines and calling for mandatory destruction of stockpiles. Today 157 countries have become party to the treaty, including Afghanistan, Liberia, Nicaragua, and Rwanda; but 39 countries have refused to join, including China, Russia, North Korea, and the U.S.

The American position is complicated. The United States has not used antipersonnel land mines since 1991, not exported them since 1992, and not produced them since 1997. But the nation has a stockpile of some 10 million land mines, and prior to the '90s, it exported 4.4 million antipersonnel land mines, an unknown number of which are still in the ground. Ian Kelly, a State Department spokesman, described the government's official position in 2009: "We would not be able to meet our national defense needs nor our security commitments to our friends and allies if we signed this convention." Nonetheless, under pressure from the United States Campaign to Ban Landmines, the Obama Administration has been conducting a comprehensive review of its land mine policy.

Despite its refusal to join the treaty, the U.S. has done more to counteract mines than any other country, spending $1.9 billion during the past 18 years through the Humanitarian Mine Action Program—roughly a quarter of the total spent on demining and other remediation activities around the world. There's been a special emphasis on helping Cambodia, which has received more than $80 million since 1993.

As in many countries, the vast majority of demining in Cambodia is done by hand. Demining machines—30-ton, dinosaur-size rototillers that flail the earth to a depth of 12 inches—are exceedingly expensive. Only three are in use,

along with 50 or so dogs trained to sniff out a mine. But in the end, a human must dig it out.

Demining operations have strict protocols. Outfitted in heavy, high-collared, crotch-protecting flak jackets and thick-visored helmets, a team of 10 to 25 deminers line up along the edge of a minefield with garden tools and a metal detector. Moving forward in yard-wide lanes, they first clear the vegetation from each three-foot-square block, then sweep the ground with the detectors. They toil straight through monsoonal rains and scorching heat, moving the detectors across the ground, listening for the telltale beep.

The salary is decent for Cambodia—about $160–$250 a month—but money is not the main motivation. When Hong Cheat was five or six years old, a cow he was tending stepped on a land mine. The explosion killed his mother and father and blew off his right leg. He was surviving on the streets of Phnom Penh as a beggar when Aki Ra adopted him and trained him to be a deminer.

"I like to clear the land mines," says Cheat. "I don't want to see any more people like me in my country."

There's a new sense of hope spreading across Cambodia. The country is becoming a place where you can dream of a better life—and where sometimes, those dreams come true. Just ask Miss Landmine Cambodia.

Dos Sopheap, a young woman from Battambang Province, lost her leg to a mine when she was six years old. Her father, then a soldier, was carrying her in his arms through the forest at night when someone in front of them stumbled on a trip wire. Her leg was amputated high above the knee, and she has always used crutches with her false leg—until now.

To the tearful clapping of her family, Sopheap is taking her new titanium prosthesis for a test run around their dirt front yard, scattering the ducks and chickens. As befits a beauty queen, she is wearing a flouncy, peach-colored dress lit up like a rose by the setting sun. Her twin sisters hang on to each arm as she walks stiffly in circles, and her mother weeps.

Competing against 19 other women who had also lost limbs, Sopheap won the 2009 title of Miss Landmine Cambodia through an Internet vote based on her photo. She was awarded $1,000 in cash and a $15,000 state-of-the-art prosthesis. The beauty pageant was founded by Morten Traavik, an eccentric Norwegian theater director who organized the first contest in Angola in 2008.

"The goal is to bring attention to the global issue of land mine contamination," Traavik had told me earlier at a beauty parlor in Battambang where Sopheap was being coiffed and made up for a photo shoot, "and to make us think about how we, able-bodied people, look at disabled people, and not least how disabled people perceive themselves and present themselves."

"It was so hard to watch other children run and play in the schoolyard," says Sopheap's mother. The other children teased the young girl. But that didn't discourage her. Beautiful and quiet, she became a top student, ranking fifth in her high school class. The other kids now call her Miss Landmine, which pleases her. She hopes to become an accountant someday. Her mother later confides that Sopheap also "just wants to be like the other girls and be able to wear jeans."

People aren't the only victims of land mines. A country's economy is crippled too. More than 60 percent of Cambodians are farmers, who can't work a field if it's mined, can't earn an income, and can't feed their families. This is one reason why so many other mine-poisoned countries have struggled for so long after armed conflict has ended.

"There's a clear link between land mine contamination and poverty," says Jamie Franklin of Mines Advisory Group (MAG), one of the major demining operations in Cambodia. Franklin has a large map of the country on the wall of his office in Phnom Penh. The eastern half is splattered with thousands of tiny red and purple dots, representing U.S. bombing raids during the Vietnam War. The western half is marked with hundreds of yellow squares, representing minefields. Unexploded ordnance and minefields are huge obstacles to increased agricultural production, which the government believes is necessary for economic development and recovery.

MAG has demined thousands of acres of contaminated land during the past two decades, including the village of Prey Pros in central Cambodia, where brilliant green squares of flooded rice fields shimmer as far as the eye can see. In Prey Pros, you can hear hammers and laughter. Crops have been good for the past few years, and residents are building homes.

Thath Khiev, the village chief, bounced a naked baby on his knee while his wife stirred a cauldron of bubbling rice. Seventeen years ago, their world was very different.

"We did not have enough food to eat," Khiev tells me. "We could not grow rice on our own land because the soldiers had laid the mines." Prey Pros was once a garrison for Cambodian government forces. Two companies of soldiers were stationed here to protect a nearby bridge. To deter the Khmer Rouge, the bridge was mined and the village's rice fields were also heavily mined as a no-man's-land perimeter. Even footpaths in the village were mined. "It was very difficult," Khiev says.

MAG demined the area around Prey Pros in 1994 and 1995, removing 379 antipersonnel mines and 32 unexploded ordnance.

"Now we can walk safely to the rice fields and work freely without fear of mines," Khiev says. Tossing his grandson in the air, he adds, "It's safe for little children. If they want to swim in the river, in the lake, they can."

As villages and rice paddies like Prey Pros have been cleared, Cambodia's economy has grown stronger. In 1999, the first full year of peace, Cambodia had a gross national income (GNI) of $10 billion and a per capita annual income of $820; 11 years later, in 2010, the GNI had almost tripled to $29 billion, and personal income had more than doubled to $2,040.

Since 1992 demining has cleared about 270 square miles, but there are still some 250 square miles of contaminated land left. Currently, 23 to 31 square miles are cleared a year, which means it will take another decade to rid Cambodia of mines and other explosives—a goal that has been achieved in less heavily mined countries like El Salvador, Honduras, and Albania.

"We simply cannot clear them fast enough," Franklin says.

Even though deminers are still busy, Cambodia is no longer a devastated nation. Cities and villages throb with industriousness.

"We have a future now," says San Mao.

Short and muscled, Mao is an elite runner. He rises at four o'clock every morning to train, threading five miles through the wet, black streets of Phnom Penh. An hour later, after changing his curved fiberglass prosthesis for a rubber foot, he goes to work, whizzing around town as a motorcycle taxi driver. At five in the afternoon, he picks up his young daughter from school, then goes out for another run. His efforts have paid off.

Nine times in recent years, Mao has won the Angkor Wat International artificial leg ten-kilometer foot race, part of the Angkor Wat International Half Marathon, which was founded in 1996 to help land mine survivors.

He doesn't run just to win races. Running has calmed his mind. He used to get headaches from thinking too much about the past. "Now I focus on making a living for just one day, on eating for one day," he says, almost smiling.

Mao was a 15-year-old farm boy in 1987 when he was kidnapped by the Khmer Rouge. Soldiers dragged him away from his family into the jungle near the Thai border, forcing him to carry ammunition and refusing to feed him. One morning he spotted fruit beneath a tree. The next thing he remembers, he was lying in the mud, blood everywhere. The tree had been booby-trapped. "I cannot find anything to compare to the pain," whispers Mao. "I died there."

Three days later, unconscious but alive, he was found by other soldiers, who carried him to a hospital across the border in Thailand. Doctors amputated his leg below the knee. Upon returning to Cambodia, he began vocational training sponsored by Handicap International. That's where he met Ouch Vun, his future wife.

Today the couple live in central Phnom Penh with their daughter and ten other tenants. Their corrugated metal shack is set on stilts above a swamp with floating garbage. Inside, the walls are papered with pages from a pop culture magazine. Mao's race medals hang from nails behind the TV.

When I visit, Regina, their seven-year-old, offers me a bottle of water, then sits in her father's lap. Ouch Vun hobbles over and places a whirring electric fan before me, then awkwardly seats herself beside her husband, tucking her sarong over her artificial leg.

Vun is so shy she barely speaks. Her eyes drop when I look at her. She tells me that her right leg was blown off in 1990 when she was digging for gold with her impoverished family. "When the doctor cut off my leg, I cried for months," she says.

Regina has been watching first her father, then her mother, tell their stories. Mao is stroking her hair, Vun lightly touching her arm. Unlike her parents when they were her age, she can walk without fear of suffering the same fate.

A week later, on a mild December morning, a crowd of hundreds cheers the start of the Angkor Wat ten-kilometer race. It's a fitting location for the biggest race of its kind in Cambodia, with 50 or more runners. The famous ruins were once indiscriminately planted with land mines. Today Angkor Wat is one of the world's most popular tourist destinations.

When San Mao first comes into view, the clapping and cheering swell. Sweat streaks his cropped black hair; his round face is as calm as Buddha's. Whether he knows it or not, Mao is the embodiment of a country transcending its past. His feet, one muscle and bone, the other bowed fiberglass, are like wings.

When they carry him first across the finish line, Cambodians erupt in jubilation.

Critical Thinking

1. Describe the scope of the land mine problem.
2. Describe the "human face" of the problem.
3. Describe how governments and non-profit organizations are collaborating to solve this problem.

Mark Jenkins is a contributing writer.

Jenkins, Mark. From *National Geographic,* January 2012. Copyright © 2012 by National Geographic Society. Reprinted by permission.

Geneva Conventions

They help protect civilians and soldiers from the atrocities of war. But these hard-won rules of battle are falling by the wayside: Terrorists ignore them, and governments increasingly find them quaint and outdated. With every violation, war only gets deadlier for everyone.

STEVEN R. RATNER

"The Geneva Conventions Are Obsolete"

Only in the minor details. The laws of armed conflict are old; they date back millennia to warrior codes used in ancient Greece. But the modern Geneva Conventions, which govern the treatment of soldiers and civilians in war, can trace their direct origin to 1859, when Swiss businessman Henri Dunant happened upon the bloody aftermath of the Battle of Solferino. His outrage at the suffering of the wounded led him to establish what would become the International Committee of the Red Cross, which later lobbied for rules improving the treatment of injured combatants. Decades later, when the devastation of World War II demonstrated that broader protections were necessary, the modern Geneva Conventions were created, producing a kind of international "bill of rights" that governs the handling of casualties, prisoners of war (POWs), and civilians in war zones. Today, the conventions have been ratified by every nation on the planet.

Of course, the drafters probably never imagined a conflict like the war on terror or combatants like al Qaeda. The conventions were always primarily concerned with wars between states. That can leave some of the protections enshrined in the laws feeling a little old-fashioned today. It seems slightly absurd to worry too much about captured terrorists' tobacco rations or the fate of a prisoner's horse, as the conventions do. So, when then White House Counsel Alberto Gonzales wrote President George W. Bush in 2002 arguing that the "new paradigm" of armed conflict rendered parts of the conventions "obsolete" and "quaint," he had a point. In very specific—and minor—details, the conventions have been superseded by time and technology.

But the core provisions and, more crucially, the spirit of the conventions remain enormously relevant for modern warfare. For one, the world is still home to dozens of wars, for which the conventions have important, unambiguous rules, such as forbidding pillaging and prohibiting the use of child soldiers. These rules apply to both aggressor and defending nations, and, in civil wars, to governments and insurgent groups.

The conventions won't prevent wars—they were never intended to—but they can and do protect innocent bystanders, shield soldiers from unnecessary harm, limit the physical damage caused by war, and even enhance the chances for cease-fires and peace. The fundamental bedrock of the conventions is to prevent suffering in war, and that gives them a legitimacy for anyone touched by conflict, anywhere and at any time. That is hardly quaint or old-fashioned.

"The Conventions Don't Apply to Al Qaeda"

Wrong. The Bush administration's position since Sept. 11, 2001, has been that the global war on terror is a different kind of war, one in which the Geneva Conventions do not apply. It is true that the laws do not specifically mention wars against nonstate actors such as al Qaeda. But there have always been "irregular" forces that participate in warfare, and the conflicts of the 20th century were no exception. The French Resistance during World War II operated without uniforms. Vietcong guerrillas fighting in South Vietnam were not part of any formal army, but the United States nonetheless treated those they captured as POWs.

So what treatment should al Qaeda get? The conventions contain one section—Article 3—that protects all persons regardless of their status, whether spy, mercenary, or terrorist, and regardless of the type of war in which they are fighting. That same article prohibits torture, cruel treatment, and murder of all detainees, requires the wounded to be cared for, and says that any trials must be conducted by regular courts respecting due process. In a landmark 2006 opinion, the U.S. Supreme Court declared that *at a minimum* Article 3 applies to detained al Qaeda suspects. In other words, the rules apply, even if al Qaeda ignores them.

And it may be that even tougher rules should be used in such a fight. Many other governments, particularly in Europe, believe that a "war" against terror—a war without temporal or geographic imits—is complete folly, insisting instead that the fight against errorist groups should be a law enforcement, not a military, matter. For decades, Europe has prevented and punished terrorists by treating them as criminals. Courts in Britain and Spain have tried suspects for major bombings in London and Madrid. The prosecutors and investigators there did so while largely complying with obligations enshrined in human rights treaties, which constrain them far more than do the Geneva Conventions.

"The Geneva Conventions Turn Soldiers into War Criminals"

Only if they commit war crimes. For centuries, states have punished their own soldiers for violations of the laws of war, such as the mistreatment of prisoners or murder of civilians. The Geneva Conventions identify certain violations that states must prosecute, including murder outside of battle, causing civilians great suffering, and denying POWs fair trials, and most countries have laws on the books that punish such crimes. The U.S. military, for example, has investigated hundreds of servicemembers for abuses in Iraq and Afghanistan, leading to dozens of prosecutions. Canada prosecuted a group of its peacekeepers for the murder of a young Somali in 1993.

Yet the idea that ordinary soldiers could be prosecuted in a foreign country for being, in effect, soldiers fighting a war is ridiculous. Yes, many countries, including the United States, have laws allowing foreigners to be tried for various abuses of war committed anywhere. Yet the risk of prosecution abroad, particularly of U.S. forces, is minuscule. Those foreign laws only address bona fide war crimes, and it is rarely in the interest of foreign governments to aggravate relations with the United States over spurious prosecutions.

The idea that the International Criminal Court could one day put U.S. commanders on trial is unlikely in the extreme. That court could theoretically prosecute U.S. personnel for crimes committed in, say, Afghanistan, but only if the United States failed to do so first. What's more, the court is by its charter dedicated to trying large-scale, horrendous atrocities like those in Sudan. It is virtually inconceivable that this new institution will want to pick a fight with the United States over a relatively small number of abuses.

"The Conventions Prevent Interrogations of Terrorists"

False. If you've seen a classic war movie such as *The Great Escape,* you know that prisoners of war are only obligated to provide name, rank, date of birth, and military serial number to their captors. But the Geneva Conventions do not ban interrogators from asking for more. In fact, the laws were written with the expectation that states will grill prisoners, and clear rules were created to manage the process. In interstate war, any form of coercion is forbidden, specifically threats, insults, or punishments if prisoners fail to answer; for all other wars, cruel or degrading treatment and torture are prohibited. But questioning

detainees is perfectly legal; it simply must be done in a manner that respects human dignity. The conventions thus hardly require rolling out the red carpet for suspected terrorists. Many interrogation tactics are clearly allowed, including good cop-bad cop scenarios, repetitive or rapid questioning, silent periods, and playing to a detainee's ego.

The Bush administration has engaged in legal gymnastics to avoid the conventions' restrictions, arguing that preventing the next attack is sufficient rationale for harsh tactics such as waterboarding, sleep deprivation, painful stress positions, deafening music, and traumatic humiliation. These severe methods have been used despite the protests of a growing chorus of intelligence officials who say that such approaches are actually counterproductive to extracting quality information. Seasoned interrogators consistently say that straightforward questioning is far more successful for getting at the truth. So, by mangling the conventions, the United States has joined the company of a host of unsavory regimes that make regular use of torture. It has abandoned a system that protects U.S. military personnel from terrible treatment for one in which the rules are made on the fly.

"The Geneva Conventions Ban Assassinations"

Actually, no. War is all about killing your enemy, and though the Geneva Conventions place limits on the "unnecessary suffering" of soldiers, they certainly don't seek to outlaw war. Assassinating one's enemy when hostilities have been declared is not only permissible; it is expected. But at the core of the conventions is the "principle of distinction," which bans all deliberate targeting of civilians. The boundless scope of the war on terror makes it difficult to decide who is and is not a civilian. The United States claims that it can target and kill terrorists at any time, just like regular soldiers; but the conventions treat these individuals like quasi-civilians who can be targeted and killed only during "such time as they take a *direct* part in hostilities" [emphasis mine]. The Israeli Supreme Court recently interpreted this phrase to give Israel limited latitude to continue targeted killings, but it insisted on a high standard of proof that the target had lost protected status and that capture was impossible. What standards the United States might be using—such as when the CIA targeted and killed several al Qaeda operatives in Yemen in 2002—are highly classified, so there's no way to know how much proof is insisted upon before the trigger is pulled or the button pushed.

For European countries and others who reject the idea of a "war" against terrorists to begin with, targeted killings are especially abhorrent, as international law prohibits states in peacetime from extrajudicial killings. There are very specific exceptions to this rule, such as when a police officer must defend himself or others against imminent harm. To that end, a suicide bomber heading for a crowd could legally be assassinated as a last resort. By contrast, suspected terrorists—whether planning a new attack or on the lam—are to be captured and tried.

"The Conventions Require Closing Guantánamo"

No, but changes must be made. The Geneva Conventions allow countries to detain POWs in camps, and, if someone in enemy hands does not fit the POW category, he or she is automatically accorded civilian status, which has its own protections. But none of the residents of Guantánamo's military prison qualifies as either, according to the Bush administration, thus depriving the roughly 275 detainees who remain there of the rights accorded by the conventions, such as adequate shelter and eventual release.

The possibility that detainees could remain in legal limbo indefinitely at Guantánamo has turned the issue into a foreign-relations disaster for the United States. But let's be clear—the Geneva Conventions don't require the United States to close up shop in Cuba. The rules simply insist that a working legal framework be put in place, instead of the legal vacuum that exists now.

There are several options worth consideration. The prison at Guantánamo could be turned into a pre-trial holding area where detainees are held before they are brought before U.S. courts on formal charges. (The hiccup here is that most of the detainees haven't clearly violated any U.S. law.) Alternatively, the U.S. Congress could pass legislation installing a system of preventive detention for dangerous individuals. The courts could occasionally review detainees' particular circumstances and judge whether continued detention is necessary and lawful. (The problem here is that such a system would run against 200 years of American jurisprudence.) In the end, closing Guantánamo is probably the only option that would realistically restore America's reputation, though it isn't required by any clause in the conventions. It's just the wisest course of action.

"No Nation Flouts the Geneva Conventions More than the United States"

That's absurd. When bullets start flying, rules get broken. The degree to which any army adheres to the Geneva Conventions is typically a product of its professionalism, training, and sense of ethics. On this score, U.S. compliance with the conventions has been admirable, far surpassing many countries and guerrilla armies that routinely ignore even the most basic provisions. The U.S. military takes great pride in teaching its soldiers civilized rules of war: to preserve military honor and discipline,

lessen tensions with civilians, and strive to make a final peace more durable. Contrast that training with Eritrea or Ethiopia, states whose ill-trained forces committed numerous war crimes during their recent border war, or Guatemala, whose army and paramilitaries made a policy of killing civilians on an enormous scale during its long civil conflict.

More importantly, the U.S. military cares passionately that other states and nonstate actors follow the same rules to which it adheres, because U.S. forces, who are deployed abroad in far greater numbers than troops from any other nation, are most likely to be harmed if the conventions are discarded. Career U.S. military commanders and lawyers have consistently opposed the various reinterpretations of the conventions by politically appointed lawyers in the Bush White House and Justice Department for precisely this reason.

It is enormously important that the United States reaffirms its commitment to the conventions, for the sake of the country's reputation and that of the conventions. Those who rely on the flawed logic that because al Qaeda does not treat the conventions seriously, neither should the United States fail to see not only the chaos the world will suffer in exchange for these rules; they also miss the fact that the United States will have traded basic rights and protections harshly learned through thousands of years of war for the nitpicking decisions of a small group of partisan lawyers huddled in secret. Rather than advancing U.S. interests by following an established standard of behavior in this new type of war, the United States—and any country that chooses to abandon these hard-won rules—risks basing its policies on narrow legalisms. In losing sight of the crucial protections of the conventions, the United States invites a world of wars in which laws disappear. And the horrors of such wars would far surpass anything the war on terror could ever deliver.

Critical Thinking

1. What reasons are given to support Steven Ratner's contention that the hard-won rules of battle are falling by the wayside?

2. Do the Geneva Conventions prevent the interrogation of terrorists?

3. Do the Geneva Conventions ban assassinations?

STEVEN R. RATNER is professor of law at the University of Michigan.

Africa: MCC and Coca-Cola's Shared Commitment to Water

More than 800 million people around the world lack access to clean drinking water; women spend 200 million hours a day collecting water; and every 20 seconds, a child dies from a water-related illness. These statistics are staggering and both the Millennium Challenge Corporation (MCC) and The Coca-Cola Company are committed to finding new ways for those millions to access sustainable clean water and sanitation.

Water, sanitation and hygiene (WASH) are fundamental pillars to improving the livelihoods and well-being of the poor. Investments in clean water and adequate sanitation lead to improvements in health, school attendance, productivity and entrepreneurship. MCC has invested $793 million in WASH-related projects in nine of its partner countries. This investment demonstrates the high demand for water security and the sound returns associated with these types of investments.

"There is a link between MCC's mission to reduce poverty through economic growth and our commitment to expand access to water and sanitation for the world's poor," said MCC CEO Daniel Yohannes. "The bottom line is that improved access to clean water and reliable sanitation improves lives. We can't afford not to invest in water and sanitation. True to the MCC principle of country-owned, led-, designed-, and implemented development solutions, more and more of our partners worldwide are seeking investments in water and sanitation."

MCC's WASH investments are contributing to water security around the world. Three countries in particular—Cape Verde, Jordan, and Mozambique—have prioritized water sector development as the primary focus of their MCC compacts. Zambia has also prioritized water and sanitation in its compact development process.

Coca-Cola Leads Private Sector Participation in Improving Water Access for Communities

Building on its long history of water stewardship, The Coca-Cola Company is responding to global water issues by leaving lasting legacies of water sustainability in Africa and across the world. In response to the severe water challenges faced by the nearly 300 million Africans living without access to clean water, The Coca-Cola Africa Foundation introduced the Replenish Africa Initiative (RAIN) in 2009 to provide at least 2 million people in Africa with sustainable access to clean water by 2015. Backed by a $30MM commitment, RAIN, together with its partners, addresses the region's greatest needs through projects that provide clean drinking water, expand access to sanitation, and promote hygiene. In this way, RAIN contributes to achieving the United Nation's Millennium Development Goals on water and sanitation.

"Water is a key ingredient in the manufacture of our beverages and is central to the prosperity of communities where we do business. Community water access as a key focus of our sustainability efforts is both central to our business and to our future. The Replenish Africa Initiative (RAIN) is The Coca-Cola Company's response to Africa's water crisis. We believe that our water sustainability efforts are best accomplished by focusing on empowering the communities we work with to become leaders in their own development," said William Asiko, President of The Coca-Cola Africa Foundation.

Since 2005, The Coca-Cola Africa Foundation has provided safe water access to over 350,000 people and the 42 projects supported to date are expected to reach over 1.3 million beneficiaries across 27 countries. Recognizing the importance of a holistic approach to addressing the continent's most pressing water challenges, RAIN, with its partners, has also provided over 100,000 people with access to sanitation and established over 100 watershed protection groups across Africa.

The Coca-Cola Africa Foundation continues to advance RAIN objectives by forming strategic partnerships with organizations that seek long-lasting solutions to Africa's water challenges. In collaboration with various partners, volunteers, patrons, and organizations, RAIN is not just for the immediate future of Africa, but also for the long-term sustainability of its resources.

Critical Thinking

1. Describe the problem of the lack of safe drinking water.
2. Describe the role of a major corporation in addressing this problem.
3. Describe how governments, non-profits, entrepreneurs, and corporations are collaborating to address the problem.
4. How is this case study related to Articles 8, 18, and 24?

Humanitarian Workers
Comprehensive Response

In February's edition of *The World Today,* Lieutenant General Louis Lillywhite argued that "humanitarian aid has been 'politicised' in the context of the current conflicts by becoming part of the Comprehensive Approach." Here, Médecins Sans Frontières (MSF) presents a different angle.

MARC DUBOIS AND VICKIE HAWKINS

Lieutenant General Louis Lillywhite argues in his article that the delivery of aid has become one component within a broader military and political strategy. Such an approach blurs the distinction between humanitarian (emergency) assistance to save lives and other forms of aid falling under the rubric of development or delivery of state services, which are designed to build the legitimacy of governments, win hearts and minds in a conflict zone, and contribute to stabilisation efforts.

Lillywhite astutely notes that it then becomes "entirely rational" for insurgents to perceive humanitarian operations as a key component of their enemy's approach, with the outcome being increased violence against humanitarian workers. This politicisation of humanitarian aid will thereby lead to a reduced ability to provide relief, hence contrary to the intended outcome of the 'Comprehensive Approach' itself. From our perspective, Lillywhite then exactly reverses the question at hand. He examines the measures that could be taken by humanitarians to protect the Comprehensive Approach. The better question is this: Why continue with the Comprehensive Approach in a place like Afghanistan if it endangers humanitarians and, ultimately, fails to deliver aid to those most in need?

Humanitarian organisations like our own often talk of three key principles: independence, neutrality and impartiality. Perhaps there is a suspicion that we use these terms in order to claim some moral high ground—but in fact they are essential to the way we must work on the ground. These operating principles act as a 'guarantee' to all civilians and warring parties alike that they can trust us, that our work does not seek to advance the political or military interests of one side, and that our aid is based on immediate need, not ideology.

Put simply, humanitarian action has to be several things in order to be humanitarian. First and foremost, it has to provide aid on the basis of immediate human needs—for medical care, food and water for example. Being humanitarian means making our own assessments of these needs, delivering the aid in a way that ensures it reaches the people who need it, and then making our own examinations of the impact.

In the case of Médecins Sans Frontières (MSF), these principles are partly safeguarded through financial independence. This means a reliance on a majority of private funds, so that we do not have to accept funding from a belligerent party in the war. In fact, for Afghanistan, Pakistan, Somalia and Iraq we exclude all government funding and work only with private resources. Armed groups tell MSF that independence of action matters to those whom we negotiate with, and is fundamental to our access. Hence, the reality of acting in this way means that it is necessary to have relations not just with the local communities that humanitarians are trying to assist, but with all parties in a conflict area: national governments, armed opposition groups, international forces, private security forces and criminal gangs.

It is hard. The Comprehensive Approach makes aid a target to opposition groups. We do our best to build the trust of local communities and belligerents in order to work in the heart of conflict, and at times we see some success. In Afghanistan for example, MSF actually sees an opening. We are in the process of looking to expand our work in several locations including Kunduz in the north. At the same time, access to people who desperately need assistance remains severely inadequate in many of today's most difficult conflict areas. Many conflict-affected parts of north-west Pakistan remain 'off-limits' to MSF teams in the minds of government officials. In Somalia, what MSF is able to do is dwarfed by the massive needs of those war-ravaged communities. And in Iraq, we continue to struggle to have medical impact. Yet we remain present, with both international and national staff on the ground—we continue to talk to people on all sides, and to be as transparent as possible about our motives and our actions.

Is there any escape from the Comprehensive Approach; from the politicization of aid? In his article, General Lillywhite asserts that even our own organisation, while openly rejecting efforts to co-opt us into the Comprehensive Approach, is inadvertently benefiting the Comprehensive Approach in Afghanistan by working in areas of the country of lower priority to western forces. We disagree.

MSF's decision to work in these areas, namely the Ahmed Shah Baba district of Kabul—where the primary health-care system has been put under intense pressure by a quadrupling of the population yet international investment was woefully inadequate—was driven by need alone, and with no regard to counter-insurgency or stabilisation priorities. In Helmand, we provide access to quality secondary health-care for people across the province, a decision again driven solely by our assessment of medical need. By making the decision to work in an area of high-priority to western forces, because the opposition exert a significant level of control over the population, are we inadvertently contributing to the war aims of the opposition?

In both cases, MSF can recognise and accept that that is the case. However, it would be ludicrous to criticise genuine humanitarian aid for such inadvertent outcomes. Firstly, because such aid—aid given to civilians in a highly polarised, fluid and violent context that has no inadvertent benefits to warring parties—does not exist. Secondly, because the integrity of aid is best judged by its lack of direct political intentions/objectives, rather than the inescapable fact of its potential political consequences. Thirdly, because in emergency situations, where communities and sometimes whole populations struggle to survive a precarious existence, the medical impact of our activities far outweighs any arguable contribution that MSF is making to the war efforts of either party. Finally, perhaps the best indication that our activities do not significantly provide inadvertent benefit to the Comprehensive Approach comes from the Taliban themselves, with whom we have negotiated our access and who have thereby approved of our projects.

It is part of the responsibility of every humanitarian organisation to constantly monitor and question the extent to which its efforts support and promote the objectives of one party or other to the conflict. Attempts by political and military forces to co-opt humanitarian assistance into their efforts, are not a new phenomenon—we have witnessed them first hand in many contexts over the last forty years. Yet today, co-option has been achieved on a more categorically different scale than ever before. In a large part this is due to the explicit and public placement of aid at the centre of the west's war effort, and the substantial aid funds available. In turn, this co-option is facilitated by the blurring between humanitarian and development within the NGO sector itself, by accepting funding from belligerent parties, and engaging in activity that is gauged to support the ambitions of one side in the conflict.

General Lillywhite's bottom-line was that the instigators of the Comprehensive Approach may have diminished its effectiveness through politicising humanitarian aid in the process. MSF's by contrast is that much of the sector is responsible itself for the extent of this politicisation. In a war zone like Afghanistan, by not ensuring that the principles of impartiality, neutrality and independence guide decisions around project funding and project objectives, and by not ensuring a negotiated access among all parties to the conflict, many NGOs have become much more than 'inadvertent' supporters of the Comprehensive Approach.

Critical Thinking

1. What is the "comprehensive approach" that the authors argue against?

2. What is the general strategy humanitarian organizations pursue to maintain neutrality in conflict situations?

Dubois, Marc and Hawkins, Vickie. From *The World Today Magazine*, March 2011, pp. 20–22. Copyright © 2011 by The World Today, Chatham House. Reprinted by permission. www.chathamhouse.org/publications/twt.

UNIT 7

Values and Visions

Unit Selections

Learning Outcomes

After reading this unit you should be able to:

- Identify specific examples of the "meta" component of the Allegory of the Balloon, i.e., changing values and new ideas.
- Describe how social media is impacting politics and whether this is a fad or a new component to mobilizing political action.
- Throughout the book there have been examples of the changing role and political and economic impact of women. Summarize these changes and trends.
- Discuss whether core values are common or defined by culture.
- Consider how the "meta" factor impacts social structures and natural resources.
- Assess your on-going effort at identifying your theory of international relations and how this unit changes/complements it.
- Compare your theory to the Allegory of the Balloon. How are they similar/different?

Student Website

www.mhhe.com/cls

Internet References

Human Rights Web
www.hrweb.org

InterAction
www.interaction.org

The final unit of this book considers how humanity's view of itself is changing. Values, like all other elements discussed in this anthology, are dynamic. Visionary people with new ideas can have a profound impact on how a society deals with problems and adapts to changing circumstances. Therefore, to understand the forces at work in the world today, values, visions, and new ideas in many ways are every bit as important as new technology or changing demographics.

Novelist Herman Wouk, in his book *War and Remembrance,* observed that many institutions have been so embedded in the social fabric of their time that people assumed that they were part of human nature; for example, human sacrifice and blood sport. However, forward-thinking people opposed these institutions. Many knew that they would never see the abolition of these social systems within their own lifetimes, but they pressed on in the hope that someday these institutions would be eliminated.

Wouk believes the same is true for warfare. He states, "Either we are finished with war or war will finish us." Aspects of society such as warfare, slavery, racism, and the secondary status of women are creations of the human mind; history suggests that they can be changed by the human spirit.

The articles of this unit have been selected with the previous six units in mind. Each explores some aspect of global issues from the perspective of values and alternative visions of the future.

New ideas are critical to meeting these challenges. The examination of well-known issues from new perspectives can yield new insights into old problems. It was feminist Susan B. Anthony who once remarked that "social change is never made by the masses, only by educated minorities." The redefinition of human values (which, by necessity, will accompany the successful confrontation of important global issues) is a task that few people take on willingly. Nevertheless, in order to deal with the dangers of nuclear war, overpopulation, and environmental degradation, educated people must take a broad view of history. This is going to require considerable effort and much personal sacrifice.

When people first begin to consider the magnitude of contemporary global issues, some become disheartened and depressed.

© GoGo Images Corporation / Alamy

They ask: What can I do? What does it matter? Who cares? There are no easy answers to these questions, but people need only look around to see good news as well as bad. How individuals react to the world is not solely a function of so-called objective reality but a reflection of themselves.

As stated at the beginning of the first unit, the study of global issues is the study of people. The study of people, furthermore, is the study of both values and the level of commitment supporting these values and beliefs.

It is one of the goals of this book to stimulate you, the reader, to react intellectually and emotionally to the discussion and description of various global challenges. In the process of studying these issues, hopefully you have had some new insights into your own values and commitments. In the presentation of the Allegory of the Balloon, the fourth color represented the "meta" component, i.e., all of those qualities that make human beings unique. It is these qualities that have brought us to this special moment in time, and it will be these same qualities that will determine the outcome of our historic challenges.

Gene Sharp: A Dictator's Worst Nightmare

MAIRI MACKAY

London (CNN)—It's a dark January evening, and in an anonymous townhouse near Paddington station, a man is talking about how to stage a revolution.

A young Iranian asks a question: "The youth in Iran are very disillusioned by the brutality of the violence used against them. . . . It has stopped all the street protest," she says. "What would you say to them? How can they get themselves organized again?"

The man thinks for a moment. He's an unlikely looking radical—slightly stooped with white hair, his bent frame engulfed by the low chair he's sitting in. When he opens his mouth to speak, all eyes in the room are fastened on him.

"You don't march down the street towards soldiers with machine guns. . . . That's not a wise thing to do. "But there are other things that are much more extreme. . . . You could have everybody stay at home. "Total silence of the city," he says lowering his voice to a whisper, punctuating the words with his bent hands, as if he's wiping out the noise himself.

"Everybody at home." The man's eyes scan the room. "Silence," he whispers again. "You think the regime will notice?"

He looks around the room, nodding almost imperceptibly. On the wall behind his head hangs a huge print of the Hiroshima atomic bomb mushrooming into the sky.

This is political scientist Gene Sharp, and explosive ideas are his specialty. Gene Sharp, who wrote "From Dictatorship to Democracy," says no regime can survive without the support of its people.

Ruaridh Arrow

He's been called the father of nonviolent struggle. He could be also described as a revolutionary's best friend. Or perhaps, more accurately, as a dictatorship's worst nightmare.

Now 84, the American academic has dedicated most of his life to the study of the bold, some might say reckless, idea that nonviolence—rather than violence—is the most effective way of overthrowing corrupt, repressive regimes.

On this winter night, he's talking at The Frontline Club, London's journalism hub, and it's standing room only. Those without seats have crowded in at the back of the room under a huge photograph of a girl offering a flower to a line of riot police. She could have been inspired by Sharp's writings.

His practical manual on how to overthrow dictatorships, "From Dictatorship to Democracy," has spread like a virus since he wrote it 20 years ago and has been translated by activists into more than 30 languages.

He has also listed "198 Methods of Nonviolent Action"—powerful, sometimes surprising, ways to tear power from the hands of regimes. Examples of their use by demonstrators and revolutionaries pop up over and over again.

In Ukraine, during the 2004 Orange Revolution that propelled opposition leader Viktor Yushchenko to electoral triumph, hundreds of thousands of demonstrators turned Kiev's Independence Square into a sea of orange flags—the color of Yuschenko's campaign.

No. 18 on Sharp's list: Displays of flags and symbolic colors.

In Serbia, activists fighting then-President Slobodan Milosevic in the 2000 presidential elections printed "Gotov Je!" "He's Finished!" on stickers, T-shirts and posters to help the population understand he was not invincible.

No. 7 on Sharp's list: Slogans, caricatures and symbols.

In Cairo during last year's Egyptian revolution, protesters lived in a tent city in Tahrir Square, where they produced art, made music and sung anti-Hosni Mubarak songs. Many Egyptians would gather there for Friday prayers followed by mass political rallies.

Nos. 20, 37 and 47 on Sharp's list: Prayer and worship. Singing. Assembling to protest.

His ideas of revolution are based on an elegantly simple premise: No regime, not even the most brutally authoritarian, can survive without the support of its people. So, Sharp proposes, take it away.

Nonviolent action, he says, can eat away at a regime's pillars of power like termites in a tree. Eventually, the whole thing collapses.

For a half century, Sharp has refined the theory of nonviolent conflict and crafted the tools of his trade. His methods have liberated millions from tyranny—and that makes regimes from Myanmar to Iran quake in their boots.

In 2009, he was nominated for the Nobel Peace Prize. During the Arab Spring uprisings, his methods were cited repeatedly.

The applause comes after "decades of hardships," he says. His methods have been dismissed and misinterpreted—he's even been accused of working for the CIA.

But he's kept on with "the work," sometimes near penniless. He runs his organization, the Albert Einstein Institution, out of his home in East Boston because he cannot afford office space.

He'll give almost anyone a half hour of his time, even a high school kid doing a project. And the pilgrims come. They come from all over the world because they want to change their situation. They come to hear the extraordinary ideas that Sharp has stubbornly built over a lifetime: ideas that have started revolutions.

The First Rebellion

When Sharp graduated college in 1951, he moved to New York and worked odd jobs to put food on the table. He spent his spare time holed up in the New York City Library working on a book about the Indian political leader Mahatma Gandhi, who he still loosely describes as his hero.

He was also dodging the draft. The U.S. was fighting the Korean War, and Sharp was refusing to cooperate with the military draft board. He wouldn't report for physical examinations or carry a draft card.

"I had chosen a particular kind of conscientious objection, I guess the most obnoxious kind that existed—civil disobedience."

It amounted to draft evasion, a criminal offense punishable by up to 14 years in prison.

His father, a Protestant minister, and mother were distraught. He was an outstanding student. Why was he throwing away his future?

"They put all kinds of strong, strong pressures on me," he remembers. But he continued, "It was just something I had to do and be done with it."

At first, Sharp applied for conscientious objector status but was refused. Then he changed his mind: "I realized I shouldn't have done it in the first place, I shouldn't have applied for it." And when the board finally did give it to him, he wouldn't accept it.

By 1953, things weren't looking good for Sharp. He had been arrested by the FBI and locked up in a federal detention center, awaiting trial. But during this tough time, he had an unlikely and important ally: Albert Einstein.

Sharp was just 25, but already he displayed the intellectual chutzpah that would come to characterize his later work. He wrote to the physicist, asking him to pen the foreword to his book and telling him about his court case.

A notable pacifist in later life, Einstein shared Sharp's admiration for Gandhi. He agreed to write the foreword.

"I earnestly admire you for your moral strength and can only hope, although I really do not know, that I would have acted as you did, had I found myself in your situation," Einstein wrote in a letter dated April 2, 1953.

Einstein also wrote the foreword to Sharp's book, describing it as "the art of a born historian" and adding: "How is it possible that a young man was able to create such mature piece of work?"

Sharp used Einstein's name in a speech he made at his trial. In the end, he was sentenced to two years in prison.

His mother, Eve, who had traveled from Ohio for his sentencing also wrote to Einstein. And he wrote her back. Her son, he told her, was "irresistible in his noble sincerity." The letter was, Sharp says, "a big help" to his parents.

In the end, Sharp served nine months and 10 days. "You count the days in those places," he says now, adding that if he hadn't followed his conscience, it would have been tragic for him.

"I would not have had the self-respect and internal integrity to go on and do in the future what might lie ahead."

Eureka Moment

After his release from prison, Sharp concentrated on his work once again. After a short spell in London as an editor at the pacifist journal *Peace News,* he moved to Norway where he joined the Institute for Social Research in Oslo.

"It was the first time I had financial support to do my own research and my own thinking and my own writing," says Sharp.

He had been invited by philosopher Arne Næss, who shared Sharp's interest in Gandhi and who, much later, would gain prominence as the father of environmentalism.

For a while, things looked promising. Næss persuaded the institute to fund a major research program into nonviolent conflict. But almost before it got off the ground, it was bypassed in favor of a new and more fashionable area of study: peace research.

To this day, Sharp has refused to allow his work to be absorbed into the grander narrative of Peace Studies, losing out on immeasurable funding.

"I still think a lot of the peace researchers are quite naïve and romantic under the guise of science," he says.

Amazingly, Sharp was kept on at the institute to do his own research for a couple of years. It was there that he laid the foundations of his work, tapping out page after page on his little portable typewriter.

But in Norway, Sharp also began to see the flaw in his work: He didn't understand political power.

Bashar al-Assad: President Defined by Violence

"That's a great advantage—to know what you don't know," he says now. "You have a chance of learning—if you want to and you're not arrogant."

So he returned to England to pursue a degree in political science at The University of Oxford. He studied under Alan Bullock, the first biographer of Adolf Hitler, reading everything from Machiavelli to Auguste Comte and David Hume; analyses of totalitarianism; histories of dictatorships.

And as he put the pieces of the jigsaw puzzle together, Sharp started revising his work and asking critical questions.

What gives a government—even a repressive regime—the power to rule? The answer, he realized, was people's belief in its power. Even dictatorships require the cooperation and obedience of the people they rule to stay in charge.

So, he reasoned, if you can identify the sources of a government's power—people working in civil service, police and judges, even the army—then you know what a dictatorship depends on for its existence.

Once he'd worked that out, Sharp went back to his theories of nonviolent struggle: "What is the nature of this technique?" he asked himself. "What are its methods . . . different kinds of strikes, protests, boycotts, hunger strikes . . . How does it work? It may fail. If it fails, why? If it succeeds, why?"

Suddenly, he got it. If a dictatorship depends on the cooperation of people and institutions, then all you have to do is shrink that support.

That's when the light went on in Sharp's head. That is exactly what nonviolent struggle does. By its very nature, nonviolent struggle destroys governments, even brutal dictatorships, politically.

It is a weapon as potent as a bomb or a gun—maybe more so. "That was the eureka moment," says Sharp. He remembers sitting in his little room in Oxford, shocked and, he says, relieved. "This was not just a theory. This was actually something that had been applied in many different historical cases."

That moment would evolve into Sharp's first big text, "The Politics of Non-Violence," which was published in 1973. It was immediately hailed a classic and is still considered the definitive study of nonviolent struggle.

The Viral Pamphlet

Sharp's best-known work, "From Dictatorship to Democracy," is a how-to manual for overthrowing dictatorships.

It started life in Myanmar as incendiary advice printed on a few sheets of paper and surreptitiously exchanged by activists living under a military dictatorship. Those found in possession of the booklet were sentenced to seven years in prison.

From Myanmar, it was taken to Indonesia, then to Serbia. After that, Sharp says, he lost track of the book. But it took on a life of its own, spreading from activist to activist and eventually, some say, inspiring the uprisings known as the Arab Spring.

Ahmed Maher, a leading organizer of the April 6 Youth Movement that played a key role in last year's Egyptian revolution, told *The New York Times* that the group read about nonviolent conflict.

He said some members of the group traveled to Serbia to exchange ideas with members of The Centre for Applied Non Violent Actions and Strategies. The Belgrade-based institution was formed in 2004 by former members of Otpor!, the youth group that helped overthrow Slobodan Milosevic in 2000 using Sharp's methods.

Ruaridh Arrow

Journalist and filmmaker Ruaridh Arrow, who made a documentary about Sharp's work called "How to Start a Revolution," was in Egypt during last year's revolution. He says a young activist

told him Sharp's work had been widely distributed in Arabic, but he refused to talk about it on camera for fear that knowledge of the U.S. influence would destabilize the movement.

Sharp has written about 30 books and has a 900-page guide to self-liberation available for free download on his website. He says military people often have taken his work more seriously than pacifists.

"They could understand the clashing of forces and the use of strategy and tactics."

One such convert was Robert Helvey, a retired U.S. Army colonel who met Sharp at Harvard University in 1987. Sharp was director of the Program for Nonviolent Sanctions at the Center for International Affairs at Harvard, and Helvey, a decorated Vietnam veteran, was a senior fellow there.

Helvey's experiences in the Vietnam War had convinced him that there had to be an alternative to killing people. After hearing Sharp speak, he was hooked. Myanmar, Helvey decided, was the perfect place to bring Sharp's theories.

Helvey had been a U.S. military attaché in Rangoon (the former capital of Myanmar, now called Yangon) and had become sympathetic to groups opposing the regime. After leaving the army, he started doing consultancy work for the Karen National Union, conducting a series of courses on nonviolent struggle for the leadership of the democratic opposition.

The Burmese were amazed by Sharp's theories. They couldn't believe they had been fighting and killing for 20 years when there was an alternative.

The late U Tin Maung Win, a prominent exiled Burmese democrat, asked Sharp to write something for them.

"I couldn't write about Burma honestly because I didn't know Burma well," Sharp says, "and you should at least have the humility not to write about something you don't know anything about.

"So I had to write generically—if there was a movement that wanted to bring a dictatorship to an end, how could they do it.'

And so, "From Dictatorship to Democracy: A Conceptual Framework for Liberation" was born.

Today, the book has been translated into Amharic, Farsi, French, German, Serbian, Tibetan, Ukrainian, Uzbek, Arabic and dozens of other languages.

"Clearly the news is getting around that nonviolent struggle exists," says Sharp. "And clearly it comes almost as a revelation to people that they are not helpless."

Despite the Arab Spring pushing his work into the spotlight in 2011 like never before, Sharp remains skeptical about his actual, measurable influence.

"Even today, I'm credited with some major influence in Egypt, for example," he says. "I haven't seen hard data that would prove that."

Einstein's Legacy

Today, Sharp spends much of his time running the Albert Einstein Institution—the organization he founded in 1983 to spread his ideas and secure some much-needed funding, something he's struggled with his whole career.

"(Nonviolent struggle) was not credited with being realistic or with being powerful," he says. It's a shoestring operation with outside influence that he runs alongside Executive

Director Jamila Raqib. She's his right hand; a subtle organizing influence, watchdog and second brain when Sharp's memory occasionally fails him.

She also supervises the people who come from all over the world to visit Sharp, allowing her to see his influence on those struggling against tyranny or living under a dictatorship.

They come from India, Syria, Russia, Sri Lanka—from all over. They leave, says Raqib, "with stars in their eyes."

"There's something happening," she adds. "Oftentimes people would say, you know, 'This can't work for us, my situation is unique, my situation is worse, the repression is particularly harsh.'

"And what he does during those conversations . . . they leave with the understanding that, you know . . . a seed has been planted; a new possibility is there."

Sharp sees himself as a kind of mentor. "I always refuse to tell them what to do. I'm trying to get them to realize that they understand maybe more than they thought they did. "There's one phrase that's been quoted—'Dictatorships are never as strong as they think they are, and people are never as weak as they think they are.'"

Earlier this year, he released "Sharp's Dictionary of Power and Struggle: Language of Civil Resistance in Conflicts." He says the major unsolved problems of our time—genocide, dictatorship, war—require us to rethink the very language we use to define them.

His dictionary contains some 900 terms. It reconceives many words we take for granted—such as power or defense. "The defense force—sometimes they attack," Sharp says.

The institute also supervises translations of Sharp's work into other languages—a task made more complicated by the precisely defined concepts. They rely on activists for translating, rather than professional translators, because they understand the nature of the work the words describe.

For Sharp, the language is crucial: "If our language doesn't have clear meanings and accurate meanings, you can't think clearly. "If you can't think clearly, you have no ability to evaluate or influence what happens. So the distortions of our language help make us helpless."

Sharp has no plans to settle into a comfortable retirement, not now, when things are finally taking off. He admits that he gets tired sometimes." But there's so much to do.

"The last few weeks I've been waking up in the middle of the night and finding some ideas . . . or a solution to a problem I've been trying to solve for a week or two or three."

At The Frontline Club, the questions from the audience keep coming. Sharp's answers, more than anything, underscore his modesty and lack of pretention.

What about government defectors who want to join freedom groups, asks another Iranian. When should you allow them in and when should you reject them?

"An outsider like me can't tell you what to do," he says, "and if I did, you shouldn't believe me. Trust yourselves. You've got to be smart. This takes time and energy . . . know your situation in depth."

For those who are serious, Sharp has a condensed version of what he says are the required readings of his work, a guide to self-liberation, available free on the Albert Einstein Institution website.

"It's only 900 pages in English," he deadpans, raising a chuckle.

"And if you're not interested in reading 900 pages, you're not interested in getting rid of the dictator," he retorts, whip smart. "Quite seriously."

At the end, people crowd forward to speak to him, kneeling at his chair as if he were royalty, asking him to sign copies of his books.

Later, as he's helped into his flecked black coat and handed his walking stick, he grins and says how much he enjoyed the evening: "The questions were good and hard."

Critical Thinking

1. What is the modern history of non-violent action?
2. Describe the work of Gene Sharp.
3. How does this article illustrate the role of the individual in addressing global issues?
4. Do the authors of Article 1 give much attention to the role of non-violent conflict?
5. How does this article relate to Articles 32 and 43?
6. How does this article illustrate the "meta" component of the Allegory of the Balloon?

Power of the iMob

Dot-orgs are now global players, mobilising millions and changing the debate through tech-savvy marketing techniques. Andrew Marshall analyses their rise and evaluates their impact.

ANDREW MARSHALL

Protesting used to mean turning up on cold, rainy days with a badly-made placard and hoping others would be there too. It was a serious, if sometimes fruitless, business that often ended up with complaints against the police, fellow protesters and the way of the world. But in the past decade, a new wave of organisations has emerged. They have taken the arguments online, making involvement much easier—and a lot more social, in a digital way.

Dot-orgs such as Avaaz, MoveOn and 38Degrees have sprung up apparently from nowhere, launching campaigns about the Iraq war, the environment, whales, bees, Burma, Syria and everything else you can imagine.

Advocates believe the process will revolutionise social activism for a new age, and change the way we think about protest and political involvement. Critics say it will never be anything more than a waste of time, a chance for the idle—the "slacktivists"—to pose as real activists.

It all began in a Chinese restaurant in Berkeley, California in 1998. Wes Boyd and Joan Blades, the married digital entrepreneurs famous for inventing the flying toaster screen-saver, were complaining about the planned impeachment of Bill Clinton over his sexual misadventures in the White House. They overheard a nearby couple having the same conversation. A few days later, they e-mailed a petition to a hundred or so friends calling on Congress to censure Clinton and 'move on'. Within a week, it had 100,000 signatures. Within a month, more than 300,000, according to *Wired* magazine.

MoveOn failed to stop the impeachment, though Clinton was acquitted and remained in the White House. But Boyd and Blades had the technological know-how and the money to continue after George W. Bush succeeded him. They had sold their software company for $14 million in 1997. MoveOn turned its membership's attention to environmental and civil liberties issues. But it was the Iraq war which proved the fund-raising possibilities of digital activism. Boyd and Blades decided to publish an anti-war advertisement in *The New York Times*. In three days, they had raised nearly half a million dollars.

A key recruit to MoveOn was a young radical named Eli Pariser. Alarmed by the turn of events after September 11, 2001,

Pariser sent an e-mail urging a restrained response. 'Parise woke up one morning to find 300 e-mail messages in his in-box, according to *The New York Times*. Pariser was to become exec tive director of MoveOn and high priest of the movement.

MoveOn brought together traditional activist tools with ele tronic and digital protest and a democratic, grassroots feel tie to high-profile events. In the 'Virtual March on Washington more than a million Americans sent electronic messages their congressional representatives and senators. Opponents war could find each other quickly on the web, and organise e-mail, call, or meet up. It didn't take months to get together.

> 'In the Virtual March on Washington more than one million Americans sent an electronic message to Congress'

It was an exciting and motivating prospect for anyone wh wanted to become involved in social activism. The post September 11, Bush-Blair era was a good time for youn progressives to get together globally. The dot-com crash 2000–2001 may also have had a positive impact, as the dot-org were flooded with job applicants and donations of old compu ers and office equipment.

MoveOn inspired others. In 2005, GetUp! was founded i Australia by Jeremy Heimans and David Madden. It describe itself as 'a new independent political movement to build a pro gressive Australia'. It ran a campaign to bombard Australia senators with e-mails that said: 'I'm sending you this messag because I want you to know that I'm watching.'

Avaaz, ultimately the largest and most global of the do orgs, also came out of MoveOn and its alumni. Individu co-founders included Ricken Patel (Avaaz's Canadian exec tive director); Tom Pravda, a former British diplomat; To Perriello, who had worked as a legal adviser to the UN an related bodies in Sierra Leone, Darfur and Afghanistan an later became a US congressman; Pariser, formerly of MoveO

Three Activists

Molly Solomons, 26, Social Activist

My name is Molly. I have a full-time job working for a homeless charity, I pay my taxes, I have a brother with autism and come from a single-parent family. I have been involved in organising protests for the past year against the unnecessary cuts that are being enforced by the coalition. UK Uncut takes direct action against the cuts. Our protests are based around creativity, civil disobedience and realistic alternatives to the cuts such as clamping down on tax avoidance by big businesses and stopping subsidies to the banking sector that caused this crisis. Our movement is non-hierarchal, as we believe that the current model of western leadership is corrupt, undemocratic, patriarchal and will cause global unrest to continue until it changes. We believe Vodafone has dodged £6 billion in tax. My mum lost her job because of the cuts. This is not fair, plain and simple, and that is why I organise protests to go into Vodafone shops and demand they pay their tax—to have my voice heard, feel a part of the movement opposed to these cuts and feel an enormous sense of empowerment as I stand up for a fairer society, for my family and for our futures.

Yevgenia Chirlkova, 37, Environmental Activist

Five years ago I was walking in the Khimki forest, in Moscow's green belt, when I saw red markings on the trees. The forest was going to be chopped down to make way for a toll highway from Moscow to St Petersburg. I had not been involved in politics—I run a small business with my husband—but I felt I had to stop this. I believe the road does not need to go through the forest, and that the contract is corrupt. We managed to get the bulldozers stopped, but since Putin's 're-election', things have got much worse. The bulldozers have now returned to work. An environmental activist who was arrested for protesting against development of the Black Sea coastline now faces five years in jail. Foreign governments should not be congratulating Putin. They should pass laws like the Bill before the US Senate in honour of Sergei Magnitsky—the lawyer who died in jail after exposing a $230 million tax scam involving senior tax and interior ministry officials—to ban corrupt Russians from entering the country or using US banks. We cannot change anything at the top, but we can start from the bottom, by getting honest people elected to local councils.

Atiaf Alwazir, 32, Political Activist

I knew early on that the fight for freedom came with a heavy price. My grandfather was executed for his participation in the failed revolution of 1948 calling for the rule of law through the creation of a constitution. My father and uncles were imprisoned at a young age and have been in exile for years from Yemen while continuing their political activities.

Given my family history, it was inevitable that I would pursue such a path. Anyone who sees the mass corruption, poverty, gross inequality, and injustice in Yemen would do the same.

Since the beginning of the revolution in January 2011, I have been deeply involved in calls for change through various means. First, by participating in the peaceful movement as a citizen journalist/blogger where I am documenting and analysing the current situation in my blog and contributing to media outlets. Second, I am involved in the local Support Yemen video advocacy campaign to promote social justice. Finally, my colleagues and I are working to start a library in the Old City of Sana'a as a space for young people to expand their knowledge, enjoy cultural activities, and gain vocational skills.

Andrea Woodhouse, formerly of the United Nations and the World Bank; and Australians Madden and Heimans.

38Degrees, the next in the family, was launched in May 2009 as a British parallel to GetUp! Founders included Ben Brandzel, formerly of MoveOn; Gemma Mortensen of Crisis Action; Paul Hilder, also of Avaaz; and Benedict Southworth of the World Development Movement.

Most of these people had worked with government or international organisations abroad. Madden had served as an army officer, and worked for the World Bank in East Timor and the UN in Indonesia. Heimans had worked for McKinsey. Others had been with NGOs. Patel, for example, had been with International Crisis Group in Sierra Leone, Liberia, Sudan and Afghanistan. Several had been at elite academic institutions: Madden and Heimans at the Kennedy School of Government at Harvard; Woodhouse and Pravda at Balliol College, Oxford; Patel had been to both.

Early funding for some of the groups came from George Soros, the currency trader and international investor, lending credibility to a kind of 'Progressive International' conspiracy theory. But this charge doesn't stand up. Avaaz liberated itself from large external funding quickly, and now relies entirely on members.

Meeting those named quickly reveals some commonalities. They are all passionate internationalists. They tend to be pragmatic about means: government, NGO, private sector—they are not doctrinaire. They have faith in technology—but only as a means.

The tools have varied, but there is one that is key: blast e-mail, based on their large address list and techniques polished by the direct-marketing industry. They test campaigns rigorously on sections of their member base, to see which fly and which fail to catch on. They test the wording of e-mails and subject lines using 'A/B testing'—sending out two versions of an appeal, and seeing which version spreads most rapidly. The track opens (was the e-mail opened?) and clicks (did the reader click through to the petition or fundraiser?). Their aim is to get campaigns to go viral, and spread rapidly. The wording of each e-mail is carefully scrutinised: they use inclusive, rousing language ("let's show the rich and powerful that we won't be shut up!") and images with impact.

There are some grand claims for the movements. As *The New York Times* said: 'Dot-org politics represents the latest manifestation of a recurrent American faith that there is something inherently good in the vox populi. Democracy is at its purest and best when the largest number of voices are heard, and every institution that comes between the people and their government—the press, the political pros, the fund raisers—taints the process.'

The organisational model is light, decentralised and cheap. In 2011, Avaaz recorded income of $6.7 million, which included $890,000 on salaries (about 13 per cent) and $184,000 on fundraising. Its offices were two crumbling rooms above Pret A Manger, close to Union Square in New York. Avaaz is a low-overhead organisation with high operational leverage (it does a lot with not much money and not many employees), and high fundraising leverage (it raises a lot of money without spending much).

It has what in the tech business is called scaleability: it grew very rapidly indeed without needing to increase staffing or infrastructure. Other large NGOs are keeping a close eye on Avaaz in particular; partly from fascination, partly from envy.

That doesn't mean the dot-orgs attract uncritical admiration. Much of the criticism of these movements has come from the Left, which sometimes sees them as a way for the idle and unthoughtful to feel radical.

'The trouble is that this model of activism uncritically embraces the ideology of marketing,' wrote Micah White, a US social activist and writer, in the *Guardian*. 'It accepts that the tactics of advertising and market research used to sell toilet paper can also build social movements. This manifests itself in an inordinate faith in the power of metrics to quantify success. Thus, everything digital activists do is meticulously monitored and analysed. The obsession with tracking clicks turns digital activism into clicktivism.'

Malcom Gladwell, author of books on social psychology including *The Tipping Point,* dismissed internet activism as incapable of getting things done.

'Social networks are effective at increasing *participation*—by lessening the level of motivation that participation requires,' he argued in *The New Yorker*.

'Unlike hierarchies, with their rules and procedures, networks aren't controlled by a single central authority . . . Because networks don't have a centralised leadership structure and clear lines of authority, they have real difficulty reaching consensus and setting goals. They can't think strategically; they are chronically prone to conflict and error. How do you make difficult choices about tactics or strategy or philosophical direction when everyone has an equal say?'

Both White and Gladwell see this as a betrayal of protest.

Adherents of the model say the critics fail to see the revolution. 'Anyone who has read a newspaper or watched a news programme over the past year should understand that while these things may start exploding through networks online or on mobile phones, they lead to earth-shaking social change in governments and corporations, as well as hearts and mind,' says Paul Hilder, formerly of Avaaz and 38Degrees, and now with Change.org.

'The discussions that took off in the coffee shops and pamphlets of 18th-century Europe and America weren't just talktivism. That early public sphere was the crucible of revolutions that defined constitutional orders that have spanned centuries. The exciting thing is that today's transformations may in time prove to be on a similar scale.'

For many people, the apotheosis of the digital activism trend—and its excesses—was provided by the *Kony 2012* campaign, a video on YouTube directed against Joseph Kony, the murderous head of the Lord's Resistance Army in Africa, that went viral in March. The video was the fastest growing social video campaign ever, attracting more than 100 million views in six days. It brought global attention to a serious issue, on a scale previously only associated with the likes of singer Susan Boyle.

The NGO Invisible Children, which led the campaign, attracted brickbats along with the praise—people who saw it as facile, misleading and even dangerous. 'Invisible Children has turned the myopic worldview of the adolescent—"if I don't know about it, then it doesn't exist, but if I care about it, then it is the most important thing in the world"—into a foreign policy prescription,' wrote Kate Cronin-Furman and Amanda Taub, two international lawyers, at the website of *The Atlantic*. They spoke for many.

Most had mixed opinions—admiration for the scale but not the content. 'Maybe Jason Russell's web-based film *Kony 2012 . . .* can't be considered great documentary-making. But as a piece of digital polemic and digital activism, it is quite simply brilliant,' according to Peter Bradshaw, film critic of the *Guardian*. But, he added, it was 'partisan, tactless and very bold' and could be seen as just 'a way of making US college kids feel good about themselves.'

This argument will be worked out over the next few years. Some of the early fights went to the critics; the online brigade have had the last few rounds, though. Technology is moving on and apparently buttressing the dot-orgs, not the naysayers. The Arab Spring protests and the 'colour revolutions' all relied on technology—blogs, Twitter, Facebook, YouTube—as instruments of co-ordination, communication, campaigning and action. Governments responded, stepping up efforts to block, intercept, fake and censor. And others are using the same technologies: petitions, surveys and blast e-mails are increasingly part of the armoury for any activist or political organisation. The political battlefield is increasingly digital.

Other organisations are emerging that have similar tactics if different profiles, and are adapting the tools of online activism. Even Downing Street does e-petitions these days

The dot-orgs are also growing up and moving beyond an online-only presence: indeed they would say that online was never the point. In Syria, Avaaz provided cameras and satellite communication gear to help the opposition to get its story out. This isn't coincidence. Patel's movement may for many people symbolise technology and geekdom, but Patel is much more interested in what technology can actually achieve. The organisation has for some years experimented with the use of new technologies to help activists communicate, broadcast, witness and report atrocities and bring in intervention.

It would be surprising if the tools the organisations use now didn't become mainstream. 'In a decade from now, I look forward to a time when networked campaigning will have become much more pervasive and everyday, rather than exotic,' says Hilder. 'We'll all be involved in hacking the world into better shape, from the supply chains of the companies we buy from to our own behaviours. The power balance between citizens

Key Campaigns

Clinton's Impeachment

MoveOn began in 1998 with a campaign to prevent the impeachment of President Bill Clinton. The group had a one-sentence petition—Congress must immediately censure President Clinton and 'move on' to pressing issues facing the country—which half a million people signed. It failed: Congress impeached Clinton in November, though he was acquitted.

2003 Iraq War

MoveOn had its most dramatic period of growth before and during the US-led invasion of Iraq. It circulated an anti-war petition calling for 'No War on Iraq', which was delivered to members of Congress before a crucial vote, co-ordinated letter-writing campaigns, helped form the Win Without War coalition, and launched a controversial TV commercial. In February 2003, it sponsored a 'Virtual March on Washington'. The war went ahead anyway.

Burma Regime

Avaaz was founded in 2007, and one of its earliest campaigns was over anti-regime protests in Burma and the crackdown that followed. Nearly a million Avaaz members signed an electronic petition, and thousands donated more than $325,000 in four days. Much of the money went on technology to help the opposition 'break the blackout' on the media. The group collaborated with the older and bigger Open Society Institute.

Global Climate

Avaaz, 38Degrees, and GetUp! all campaigned to get agreement at the 2009 Copenhagen Climate Conference. They worked together with other organizations, in part through the TckTckTck group for climate action. The conference failed; it generated some scepticism about working with other groups in this way, and about electronic activism as the only lever.

Uganda Gay Rights

Avaaz mounted a campaign against anti-gay legislation in Uganda in 2010 that would have made homosexuality punishable by death. Its petition attracted more than 450,000 signatures and the Bill was dropped. It was revived in modified form last year, with some key provisions—including the death penalty—removed.

Murdoch's Empire

Avaaz and 38Degrees ran a series of campaigns against Rupert Murdoch and his corporations, over the *News of the World* and his ambition to buy out BskyB, the satellite broadcaster. These included internet campaigning, but also leafleting and street actions. Their campaign helped to mobilise and give shape to opposition to Murdoch. The News Corporation takeover proposal for BSkyB was withdrawn and the *News of the World* closed down.

Syria

Avaaz was slow to move into Arab politics, though it had campaigned actively in Israel. But it reacted quickly to the Arab Spring, raising money and providing backing for protest movements, giving them satellite phones and other communication equipment. It focused on Syria with petitions and financial support. Avaaz claims to have delivered more than $2 million of medical equipment to the worst affected areas to keep underground hospitals going as well as setting up a network of more than 400 citizen journalists across the country. It has also helped smuggle in foreign journalists.

---

and institutions will be much more equal, as will the balance between citizens and elites.'

'In a decade from now we'll all be involved in hacking the world into better shape'

And this is the key to understanding the goals and trajectories of the dot-orgs. Perhaps the most significant thing about them is their style and the causes they champion: increasingly global, trans-border, and outside the traditional framework of political parties.

By reducing the barriers to participation, Avaaz, MoveOn, Getup!, 38Degrees, Change.org and the others are bringing in a generation that feels a desire to get involved in world affairs, but which conventional structures couldn't handle. International negotiations, global corporate power-plays, vast environmental challenges, clamp downs by government thugs—these are all things that seem too far removed from our lives for us to affect, but the dot-orgs want to bring you into them. For those who subscribe, it is a heady sense of involvement, and a window into a world of possibility. The solutions can sometimes seem simplistic, but the aspiration—to inform public opinion across borders and to engage in search of a better world—is mobilising millions: at least as far as their keyboards, and that really is something.

Critical Thinking

1. How are social media impacting political processes?
2. Are these new technologies likely to have a long-term impact or are they a fad?
3. How does this article relate to Articles 32 and 42?

ANDREW MARSHALL is a media consultant and former journalist. He worked for Avaaz as a paid consultant in 2009.

UN Women's Head Michelle Bachelet
A New Superhero?

She wants more female peacekeepers and an end to violence against women. Meet Michelle Bachelet, the former Chilean president and now head of the UN's new women's rights body.

JANE MARTINSON

Let it not be said that those wags at the United Nations don't have a sense of humour. Given the task of finding an office for its new women's rights body, the premises managers found some space in the iconic Daily News building—otherwise known as the home of Superman.

But now, instead of Clark Kent, the world has Michelle Bachelet—taking on the superhuman challenge of redressing gender inequality. Unlike the last son of Krypton, relatively little is known about Bachelet outside her native Chile and the corridors of international diplomacy. And more than 100 days after it was set up, there are still significant questions about UN Women: what exactly will it do, what are its powers, and how it will be financed?

The body takes over from four existing, underfunded and relatively powerless institutions devoted to women's rights, which the UN general council voted to replace after Kofi Annan, former UN secretary general, pointed out "study after study has taught us that there is no tool for development more effective than the empowerment of women". Bachelet, who was Chile's first female head of state, will report directly to the secretary general and should command a start-up budget of $500m (£300m) by 2013, double what was available previously—though only about 1.6% of total UN funding. But just three months in, there are already disappointing signs of foot-dragging by major donors, including the UK.

UN watchers believe Bachelet, however, may have a better chance than most to cajole and bully her way through UN diplomacy. The daughter of an army general who died after months of torture by Augusto Pinochet's forces, Bachelet was herself tortured before being exiled. She then trained as a doctor and returned to Chile. An avowed atheist, her achievements in office include a controversial decree allowing the morning-after pill to be distributed to women older than 14 years of age without parental consent, policies to abolish shanty towns, and daycare for poor children.

In person, this former paediatrician is the opposite of a dry UN bureaucrat. In her first interview to a British newspaper since taking office, she rattles off a list of priorities, ranging from political and economic empowerment to the ending of sexual violence. But first she is apologising, in her fast-paced heavily accented English, for the UN's parsimony with teabags.

"In my country, offering tea is a sign of hospitality," she begins. "In the UN, nothing. You cannot use the money from the UN for that. My God! It's not like I'm going to be offering whisky, you know. Just a cup of tea. Water. Something." Once the team is all together and not in temporary accommodation, she promises to "bring my china cups" and her own tea. Later, she laughs: "I don't mean to change the UN attitude but . . . well, a little bit."

Charming and voluble, she is credited with getting her own way while making relatively few enemies in her home country. (Her approval rating was 84% when she stood down after her presidential term in March 2010.) She will need all her skills of persuasion to convince member states to help her department, some of which place a very low national priority on women's rights.

"I am an optimist," she laughs when asked about the snail-like pace of funding. "My main issue is to have enough arguments to convince [member states] to build capacity." Given such underfunding, she will not be focusing on saving money, but increasing her budget. "We have had scarce investment in women . . . One of my tasks is that everyone spends much more on women."

A woman who took herself off to study military strategy before being elected head of state, her arguments are backed by a wealth of relevant data. In the same breath, she manages to reference a gender study by the World Economic Forum that found greater productivity in countries where women achieved senior positions, and the benefits of a $3m (£1.8m) programme in Liberia to improve conditions of women market traders.

"Just 19% of parliamentarians are women and we are more than half of humanity," she says. "There are 19 female head of states in 192 member states. And just 15 of Fortune 500 chief executives are women. You see we have a problem. Gender equality will only be reached if we are able to empower women."

Sixteen years after the Beijing assembly set a target of 30% women in national parliaments, only 28 countries meet this target. Most of these (23) did so after introducing quotas, a controversial practice that Bachelet makes no bones about supporting. "I am in favour of affirmative action when there is exclusion," she states.

Economic empowerment is high on her agenda and she lays out the huge financial benefit of ending violence against women. "In the US, violence against women costs $5.8bn (£3.5bn) a year in terms of medical costs, loss of productivity and childcare. In Australia they estimated that it cost $A13.6bn (£8.8bn) a year, more than the $10bn (£6.5bn) they spent stimulating economy."

Perhaps the easiest way to understand the five priorities of UN Women—expanding women's leadership; enhancing women's economic empowerment; ending violence against women and girls; bringing women to the centre of the peace and security agenda; focusing national plans and budgets on gender equality—is to think of all the things not necessarily covered by far larger organisations, such as health (WHO), and children (Unicef). However, the new body will also help co-ordinate gender policies at those organisations and, perhaps more importantly, improve accountability.

"We have accountability but we're not going to be the gender police," she says, perhaps hoping to squash any possible resentment felt by those better-funded organisations.

Yet there is work to be done closer to home. UN Women research last year suggested that women made up less than 8% of negotiating teams in 24 peace processes over the past two decades, and she believes women's issues are missing from peace agreements as a result. A survey of 300 peace agreements in 45 conflicts since the end of the cold war found only 18 mentioning sexual and gender violence—even though this has become a widespread violation in modern conflicts.

So Bachelet wants more female peacekeepers and policewomen, pointing out not only that female victims of sexual violence are happier speaking to other women but that "when they [the perpetrators] see women, strong, with arms, they know also that women are not weak".

Keen to start up local outposts to help on the ground, the issue comes back to whether and when donor states are going to cough up. Next month, Bachelet is due to visit London for talks with the government. The Department for International Development was expected to announce its funding commitment earlier this year, but has instead delayed any announcement until the UN Women's strategic plan is unveiled in June. The charity VSO was among those to condemn the move, calling for funding to be announced to help UN Women, "a once-in-a-generation opportunity to end the discrimination and violence that prevents many women worldwide from earning an income, holding political office or giving birth safely".

Zohra Moosa, ActionAid UK women's rights adviser, describes the situation as a catch-22—the money won't be committed until the plans are made but UN Women needs to know the plans can be paid for. So far, only Spain and Norway of the major donor countries have pledged a significant amount. "[The UN] may have a great ambition but where is the matching resource?" asks Moosa. "It may have €33m (£29m) a year from Spain but, let's get real, that's not going to cut it."

As a former head of state, Bachelet is not going to criticise any countries just a few months into the job. "The real owners [of the UN] are the member states. For me, it is easier to understand as I was head of government and I wouldn't have liked to see an agency come to my country and do what they liked."

Ever emollient, she adds: "If we succeed it should mean that the rest of the system should be doing more and better."

It has been more than 30 years since the UN first adopted the Convention on the Elimination of All Forms of Discrimination Against Women, and some would argue that inequality has got worse. Yet Bachelet, in arguing for positive discrimination, believes real change could come. "Maybe one day UN Women won't be necessary because women won't be discriminated against and will be in power. Until then, we need special measures to level the playing field."

Critical Thinking

1. Describe Bachelet's career.
2. What are the five UN priorities for women?

Martinson, Jane. From *The Guardian*, April 22, 2011. Amended on April 28, 2011. Copyright © 2011 by Guardian News & Media Ltd. Reprinted by permission.

The End of Men

Hanna Rosin

Earlier this year, women became the majority of the workforce for the first time in U.S. history. Most managers are now women too. And for every two men who get a college degree this year, three women will do the same. For years, women's progress has been cast as a struggle for equality. But what if equality isn't the end point? What if modern, postindustrial society is simply better suited to women? A report on the unprecedented role reversal now under way—along with its vast cultural consequences.

In the 1970s the biologist Ronald Ericsson came up with a way to separate sperm carrying the male-producing Y chromosome from those carrying the X. He sent the two kinds of sperm swimming down a glass tube through ever-thicker albumin barriers. The sperm with the X chromosome had a larger head and a longer tail, and so, he figured, they would get bogged down in the viscous liquid. The sperm with the Y chromosome were leaner and faster and could swim down to the bottom of the tube more efficiently. Ericsson had grown up on a ranch in South Dakota, where he'd developed an Old West, cowboy swagger. The process, he said, was like "cutting out cattle at the gate." The cattle left flailing behind the gate were of course the X's, which seemed to please him. He would sometimes demonstrate the process using cartilage from a bull's penis as a pointer.

In the late 1970s, Ericsson leased the method to clinics around the U.S., calling it the first scientifically proven method for choosing the sex of a child. Instead of a lab coat, he wore cowboy boots and a cowboy hat, and doled out his version of cowboy poetry. (*People* magazine once suggested a TV miniseries based on his life called Cowboy in the Lab.) The right prescription for life, he would say, was "breakfast at five-thirty, on the saddle by six, no room for Mr. Limp Wrist." In 1979, he loaned out his ranch as the backdrop for the iconic "Marlboro Country" ads because he believed in the campaign's central image—"a guy riding on his horse along the river, no bureaucrats, no lawyers," he recalled when I spoke to him this spring. "He's the boss." (The photographers took some 6,500 pictures, a pictorial record of the frontier that Ericsson still takes great pride in.)

Feminists of the era did not take kindly to Ericsson and his Marlboro Man veneer. To them, the lab cowboy and his sperminator portended a dystopia of mass-produced boys. "You have to be concerned about the future of all women," Roberta Steinbacher, a nun-turned-social-psychologist, said in a 1984 *People* profile of Ericsson. "There's no question that there exists a universal preference for sons." Steinbacher went on, to complain about women becoming locked in as "second-class citizens" while men continued to dominate positions of control and influence. "I think women have to ask themselves, 'Where does this stop?'" she said. "A lot of us wouldn't be here right now if these practices had been in effect years ago."

Ericsson, now 74, laughed when I read him these quotes from his old antagonist. Seldom has it been so easy to prove a dire prediction wrong. In the '90s, when Ericsson looked into the numbers for the two dozen or so clinics that use his process, he discovered, to his surprise, that couples were requesting more girls than boys, a gap that has persisted, even though Ericsson advertises the method as more effective for producing boys. In some clinics, Ericsson has said, the ratio is now as high as 2 to 1. Polling data on American sex preference is sparse, and does not show a clear preference for girls. But the picture from the doctor's office unambiguously does. A newer method for sperm selection, called MicroSort, is currently completing Food and Drug Administration clinical trials. The girl requests for that method run at about 75 percent.

Even more unsettling for Ericsson, it has become clear that in choosing the sex of the next generation, he is no longer the boss. "It's the women who are driving all the decisions," he says—a change the MicroSort spokespeople I met with also mentioned. At first, Ericsson says, women who called his clinics would apologize and shyly explain that they already had two boys. "Now they just call and [say] outright, 'I want a girl.'" These mothers look at their lives and think their daughters will have a bright future their mother and grandmother didn't have, brighter than their sons, even, so why wouldn't you choose a girl?"

Why wouldn't you choose a girl? That such a statement should be so casually uttered by an old cowboy like Ericsson—or by anyone, for that matter—is monumental. For nearly as long as civilization has existed, patriarchy—enforced through the rights of the firstborn son—has been the organizing principle, with few exceptions. Men in ancient Greece tied off their left testicle in an effort to produce male heirs; women have killed themselves (or been killed) for failing to bear sons. In her iconic 1949 book, *The Second Sex*, the French feminist Simone de Beauvoir suggested that women so detested their own "feminine condition" that they regarded their newborn daughters with irritation and disgust. Now the centuries-old preference for sons is eroding—or even reversing. "Women of our generation want daughters precisely because we like who we are," breezes one woman in *Cookie* magazine. Even Ericsson, the stubborn old goat, can sigh and mark the passing of an era. "Did male dominance exist? Of course it existed. But it seems to be gone now. And the era of the firstborn son is totally gone."

Ericsson's extended family is as good an illustration of the rapidly shifting landscape as any other. His 26-year-old grand-daughter—"tall, slender, brighter than hell, with a take-no-prisoners personality"—is a biochemist and works on genetic sequencing. His niece studied civil engineering at the University of Southern California. His grandsons, he says, are bright and handsome, but in school "their eyes glaze over. I have to tell 'em: 'Just don't screw up and crash your pickup truck and get some girl pregnant and ruin your life.'" Recently Ericsson joked with the old boys at his elementary-school reunion that he was going to have a sex-change operation. "Women live longer than men. They do better in this economy. More of 'em graduate from college. They go into space and do everything men do, and sometimes they do it a whole lot better. I mean, hell, get out of the way—these females are going to leave us males in the dust."

Man has been the dominant sex since, well, the dawn of mankind. But for the first time in human history, that is changing—and with shocking speed. Cultural and economic changes always reinforce each other. And the global economy is evolving in a way that is eroding the historical preference for male children, worldwide. Over several centuries, South Korea, for instance, constructed one of the most rigid patriarchal societies in the world. Many wives who failed to produce male heirs were abused and treated as domestic servants; some families prayed to spirits to kill off girl children. Then, in the 1970s and '80s, the government embraced an industrial revolution and encouraged women to enter the labor force. Women moved to the city and went to college. They advanced rapidly, from industrial jobs to clerical jobs to professional work. The traditional order began to crumble soon after. In 1990, the country's laws were revised so that women could keep custody of their children after a divorce and inherit property. In 2005, the court ruled that women could register children under their own names. As recently as 1985, about half of all women in a national survey said they "must have a son." That percentage fell slowly until 1991 and then plummeted to just over 15 percent by 2003. Male preference in South Korea "is over," says Monica Das Gupta, a demographer and Asia expert at the World Bank. "It happened so fast. It's hard to believe it, but it is." The same shift is now beginning in other rapidly industrializing countries such as India and China.

Up to a point, the reasons behind this shift are obvious. As thinking and communicating have come to eclipse physical strength and stamina as the keys to economic success, those societies that take advantage of the talents of all their adults, not just half of them, have pulled away from the rest. And because geopolitics and global culture are, ultimately, Darwinian, other societies either follow suit or end up marginalized. In 2006, the Organization for Economic Cooperation and Development devised the Gender, Institutions and Development Database, which measures the economic and political power of women in 162 countries. With few exceptions, the greater the power of women, the greater the country's economic success. Aid agencies have started to recognize this relationship and have pushed to institute political quotas in about 100 countries, essentially forcing women into power in an effort to improve those countries' fortunes. In some war-torn states, women are stepping in as a sort of maternal rescue team. Liberia's president, Ellen Johnson Sirleaf, portrayed her country as a sick child in need of her care during her campaign five years ago. Postgenocide Rwanda elected to heal itself by becoming the first country with a majority of women in parliament.

In feminist circles, these social, political, and economic changes are always cast as a slow, arduous form of catch-up in a continuing struggle for female equality. But in the U.S., the world's most advanced economy, something much more remarkable seems to be happening. American parents are beginning to choose to have girls over boys. As they imagine the pride of watching a child grow and develop and succeed as an adult, it is more often a girl that they see in their mind's eye.

What if the modern, postindustrial economy is simply more congenial to women than to men? For a long time, evolutionary psychologists have claimed that we are all imprinted with adaptive imperatives from a distant past: men are faster and stronger and hardwired to fight for scarce resources, and that shows up now as a drive to win on Wall Street; women are programmed to find good providers and to care for their offspring, and that is manifested in more-nurturing and more-flexible behavior, ordaining them to domesticity. This kind of thinking frames our sense of the natural order. But what if men and women were fulfilling not biological imperatives but social roles, based on what was more efficient throughout a long era of human history? What if that era has now come to an end? More to the point, what if the economics of the new era are better suited to women?

Once you open your eyes to this possibility, the evidence is all around you. It can be found, most immediately, in the wreckage of the Great Recession, in which three-quarters of the 8 million jobs lost were lost by men. The worst-hit industries were overwhelmingly male and deeply identified with macho: construction, manufacturing, high finance. Some of these jobs will come back, but the overall pattern of dislocation is neither temporary nor random. The recession merely revealed—and accelerated—a profound economic shift that has been going on for at least 30 years, and in some respects even longer.

Earlier this year, for the first time in American history, the balance of the workforce tipped toward women, who now hold a majority of the nation's jobs. The working class, which has long defined our notions of masculinity, is slowly turning into a matriarchy, with men increasingly absent from the home and women making all the decisions. Women dominate today's colleges and professional schools—for every two men who will receive a B.A. this year, three women will do the same. Of the 15 job categories projected to grow the most in the next decade in the U.S., all but two are occupied primarily by women. Indeed, the U.S. economy is in some ways becoming a kind of traveling sisterhood: upper-class women leave home and enter the workforce, creating domestic jobs for other women to fill.

The postindustrial economy is indifferent to men's size and strength. The attributes that are most valuable today—social intelligence, open communication, the ability to sit still and focus—are, at a minimum, not predominantly male. In fact, the opposite may be true. Women in poor parts of India are learning English faster than men to meet the demands of new global call centers. Women own more than 40 percent of private businesses in China, where a red Ferrari is the new status symbol for female entrepreneurs. Last year, Iceland elected Prime Minister Johanna Sigurdardottir, the world's first openly lesbian head of state, who campaigned explicitly against the male elite she claimed had destroyed the nation's banking system, and who vowed to end the "age of testosterone."

Yes, the U.S. still has a wage gap, one that can be convincingly explained—at least in part—by discrimination. Yes, women still do most of the child care. And yes, the upper reaches of society are still dominated by men. But given the power of the forces pushing at the economy, this setup feels like the last gasp of a dying age rather than the permanent establishment. Dozens of college women I interviewed for this story assumed that they very well might be the ones working while their husbands stayed at home, either looking for work or minding the children. Guys, one senior remarked to me, "are the new ball and chain." It may be happening slowly and unevenly, but it's unmistakably happening: in the long view, the modern economy is becoming a place where women hold the cards.

Dozens of college women I interviewed assumed that they very well might be the ones working while their husbands stayed at home. Guys, one senior remarked to me, "Are the new ball and chain."

In his final book, *The Bachelors' Ball,* published in 2007, the sociologist Pierre Bourdieu describes the changing gender dynamics of Beam, the region in southwestern France where he grew up. The eldest sons once held the privileges of patrimonial loyalty and filial inheritance in Beam. But over the decades, changing economic forces turned those privileges into curses. Although the land no longer produced the impressive income it once had, the men felt obligated to tend it. Meanwhile, modern women shunned farm life, lured away by jobs and adventure in the city. They occasionally returned for the traditional balls, but the men who awaited them had lost their prestige and become unmarriageable. This is the image that keeps recurring to me, one that Bourdieu describes in his book: at the bachelors' ball, the men, self-conscious about their diminished status, stand stiffly, their hands by their sides, as the women twirl away.

Men dominate just two of the 15 job categories projected to grow the most over the next decade: janitor and computer engineer. Women have everything else—nursing, home health

assistance, child care, food preparation. Many of the new jobs, says Heather Boushey of the Center for American Progress, "replace the things that women used to do in the home for free." None is especially high-paying. But the steady accumulation of these jobs adds up to an economy that, for the working class, has become more amenable to women than to men.

The list of growing jobs is heavy on nurturing professions, in which women, ironically, seem to benefit from old stereotypes and habits. Theoretically, there is no reason men should not be qualified. But they have proved remarkably unable to adapt. Over the course of the past century, feminism has pushed women to do things once considered against their nature—first enter the workforce as singles, then continue to work while married, then work even with small children at home. Many professions that started out as the province of men are now filled mostly with women—secretary and teacher come to mind. Yet I'm not aware of any that have gone the opposite way. Nursing schools have tried hard to recruit men in the past few years, with minimal success. Teaching schools, eager to recruit male role models, are having a similarly hard time. The range of acceptable masculine roles has changed comparatively little, and has perhaps even narrowed as men have shied away from some careers women have entered. As Jessica Grose wrote in *Slate,* men seem "fixed in cultural aspic." And with each passing day, they lag further behind.

As we recover from the Great Recession, some traditionally male jobs will return—men are almost always harder-hit than women in economic downturns because construction and manufacturing are more cyclical than service industries—but that won't change the long-term trend. When we look back on this period, argues Jamie Ladge, a business professor at Northeastern University, we will see it as a "turning point for women in the workforce."

When we look back at this period we will see it as a "Turning point for women in the workforce."

The economic and cultural power shift from men to women would be hugely significant even if it never extended beyond working-class America. But women are also starting to dominate middle management, and a surprising number of professional careers as well. According to the Bureau of Labor Statistics, women now hold 51.4 percent of managerial and professional jobs—up from 26.1 percent in 1980. They make up 54 percent of all accountants and hold about half of all banking and insurance jobs. About a third of America's physicians are now women, as are 45 percent of associates in law firms—and both those percentages are rising fast. A white-collar economy values raw intellectual horsepower, which men and women have in equal amounts. It also requires communication skills and social intelligence, areas in which women, according to many studies, have a slight edge. Perhaps most important—for better or worse—it increasingly requires formal education credentials, which women are more prone to acquire, particularly early in adulthood. Just about the only professions in which women still make up a relatively small minority of newly minted workers are engineering and those calling on a hard-science background, and even in those areas, women have made strong gains since the 1970s.

Near the top of the jobs pyramid, of course, the upward march of women stalls. Prominent female CEOs, past and present, are so rare that they count as minor celebrities, and most of us can tick off their names just from occasionally reading the business pages: Meg Whitman at eBay, Carly Fiorina at Hewlett-Packard, Anne Mulcahy and Ursula Burns at Xerox, Indra Nooyi at PepsiCo; the accomplishment is considered so extraordinary that Whitman and Fiorina are using it as the basis for political campaigns. Only 3 percent of Fortune 500 CEOs are women, and the number has never risen much above that.

But even the way this issue is now framed reveals that men's hold on power in elite circles may be loosening. In business circles, the lack of women at the top is described as a "brain drain" and a crisis of "talent retention." And while female CEOs may be rare in America's largest companies, they are highly prized: last year, they outearned their male counterparts by 43 percent, on average, and received bigger raises.

If you really want to see where the world is headed, of course, looking at the current workforce can get you only so far. To see the future—of the workforce, the economy, and the culture—you need to spend some time at America's colleges and professional schools, where a quiet revolution is under way. More than ever, college is the gateway to economic success, a necessary precondition for moving into the upper-middle class—and increasingly even the middle class. It's this broad, striving middle class that defines our society. And demographically, we can see with absolute clarity that in the coming decades the middle class will be dominated by women.

We've all heard about the collegiate gender gap. But the implications of that gap have not yet been fully digested. Women now earn 60 percent of master's degrees, about half of all law and medical degrees, and 42 percent of all M.B.A.s. Most important, women earn almost 60 percent of all bachelor's degrees—the minimum requirement, in most cases, for an affluent life. In a stark reversal since the 1970s, men are now more likely than women to hold only a high-school diploma. "One would think that if men were acting in a rational way, they would be getting the education they need to get along out there," says Tom Mortenson, a senior scholar at the Pell Institute for the Study of Opportunity in Higher Education. "But they are just failing to adapt."

Since the 1980s, as women have flooded colleges, male enrollment has grown far more slowly. And the disparities start before college. Throughout the '90s, various authors and researchers agonized over why boys seemed to be failing at every level of education, from elementary school on up, and identified various culprits: a misguided feminism that treated normal boys as incipient harassers (Christina Hoff Sommers); different brain chemistry (Michael Gurian); a demanding, verbally focused curriculum that ignored boys' interests (Richard Whitmire). But again, it's not all that clear that boys have become more dysfunctional—or have changed in any way. What's clear is that schools, like the economy, now value the self-control, focus, and verbal aptitude that seem to come more easily to young girls.

Researchers have suggested any number of solutions. A movement is growing for more all-boys schools and classes, and for respecting the individual learning styles of boys. Some people think that boys should be able to walk around in class, or take more time on tests, or have tests and books that cater to their interests. In their desperation to reach out to boys, some colleges have formed football teams and started engineering programs. Most of these special accommodations sound very much like the kind of affirmative action proposed for women over the years—which in itself is an alarming flip.

Whether boys have changed or not, we are well past the time to start trying some experiments. It is fabulous to see girls and young women poised for success in the coming years. But allowing generations of boys to grow up feeling rootless and obsolete is not a recipe for a peaceful future. Men have few natural support groups and little access to social welfare; the men's-rights groups that do exist in the U.S. are taking on an angry, antiwoman edge. Marriages fall apart or never happen at all, and children are raised with no fathers. Far from being celebrated, women's rising power is perceived as a threat.

In fact, the more women dominate, the more they behave, fittingly, like the dominant sex. Rates of violence committed by middle-aged women have skyrocketed since the 1980s, and no one knows why. High-profile female killers have been showing up regularly in the news: Amy Bishop, the homicidal Alabama professor; Jihad Jane and her sidekick, Jihad Jamie; the latest generation of Black Widows, responsible for suicide bombings in Russia. In Roman Polanski's *The Ghost Writer,* the traditional political wife is rewritten as a cold-blooded killer at the heart of an evil conspiracy. In her recent video *Telephone,* Lady Gaga, with her infallible radar for the cultural edge, rewrites Thelma and Louise as a story not about elusive female empowerment but about sheer, ruthless power. Instead of killing themselves, she and her girlfriend (played by Beyoncé) kill a bad boyfriend and random others in a homicidal spree and then escape in their yellow pickup truck, Gaga bragging, "We did it, Honey B."

The Marlboro Man, meanwhile, master of wild beast and wild country, seems too farfetched and preposterous even for advertising. His modern equivalents are the stunted men in the Dodge Charger ad that ran during this year's Super Bowl in February. Of all the days in the year, one might think, Super Bowl Sunday should be the one most dedicated to the cinematic celebration of macho. The men in Super Bowl ads should be throwing balls and racing motorcycles and doing whatever it is men imagine they could do all day if only women were not around to restrain them.

Instead, four men stare into the camera, unsmiling, not moving except for tiny blinks and sways. They look like they've been tranquilized, like they can barely hold themselves up against the breeze. Their lips do not move, but a voice-over explains their predicament—how they've been beaten silent by the demands of tedious employers and enviro-fascists and women. Especially women. "I will put the seat down, I will separate the recycling, I will carry your lip balm." This last one—lip balm— is expressed with the mildest spit of emotion, the only hint of the suppressed rage against the dominatrix. Then the commercial abruptly cuts to the fantasy, a Dodge Charger vrooming toward the camera punctuated by bold all caps: MAN'S LAST STAND. But the motto is unconvincing. After that display of muteness and passivity, you can only imagine a woman—one with shiny lips—steering the beast.

Critical Thinking

1. What is Hanna Rosin's point of view?
2. What is a patriarchal society?
3. Why does Rosin argue that a modern economy advantages women over men?
4. How does this article complement/contradict Article 25?
5. Do the authors of Article 1 give sufficient attention to changing gender roles in their alternative future scenarios?

HANNA ROSIN is an *Atlantic* contributing editor and the co-editor of *DoubleX*.

Humanity's Common Values
Seeking a Positive Future

Overcoming the discontents of globalization and the clashes of civilizations requires us to reexamine and reemphasize those positive values that all humans share.

WENDELL BELL

Some commentators have insisted that the terrorist attacks of September 11, 2001, and their aftermath demonstrate Samuel P. Huntington's thesis of "the clash of civilizations," articulated in a famous article published in 1993. Huntington, a professor at Harvard University and director of security planning for the National Security Council during the Carter administration, argued that "conflict between groups from differing civilizations" has become "the central and most dangerous dimension of the emerging global politics."

Huntington foresaw a future in which nation-states no longer play a decisive role in world affairs. Instead, he envisioned large alliances of states, drawn together by common culture, cooperating with each other. He warned that such collectivities are likely to be in conflict with other alliances formed of countries united around a different culture.

Cultural differences do indeed separate people between various civilizations, but they also separate groups within a single culture or state. Many countries contain militant peoples of different races, religions, languages, and cultures, and such differences do sometimes provoke incidents that lead to violent conflict—as in Bosnia, Cyprus, Northern Ireland, Rwanda, and elsewhere. Moreover, within many societies today (both Western and non-Western) and within many religions (including Islam, Judaism, and Christianity) the culture war is primarily internal, between fundamentalist orthodox believers on the one hand and universalizing moderates on the other. However, for most people most of the time, peaceful accommodation and cooperation are the norms.

Conflicts between groups often arise and continue not because of the differences between them, but because of their similarities. People everywhere, for example, share the capacities to demonize others, to be loyal to their own group (sometimes even willing to die for it), to believe that they themselves and those they identify with are virtuous while all others are wicked, and to remember past wrongs committed against their group and seek revenge. Sadly, human beings everywhere share the capacity to hate and kill each other, including their own family members and neighbors.

Discontents of Globalization

Huntington is skeptical about the implications of the McDonaldization of the world. He insists that the "essence of Western civilization is the Magna Carta not the Magna Mac." And he says further, "The fact that non-Westerners may bite into the latter has no implications for accepting the former."

His conclusion may be wrong, for if biting into a Big Mac and drinking Coca-Cola, French wine, or Jamaican coffee while watching a Hollywood film on a Japanese TV and stretched out on a Turkish rug means economic development, then demands for public liberties and some form of democratic rule may soon follow where Big Mac leads. We know from dozens of studies that economic development contributes to the conditions necessary for political democracy to flourish.

Globalization, of course, is not producing an all-Western universal culture. Although it contains many Western aspects, what is emerging is a *global* culture, with elements from many cultures of the world, Western and non-Western.

Local cultural groups sometimes do view the emerging global culture as a threat, because they fear their traditional ways will disappear or be corrupted. And they may be right. The social world, after all, is constantly in flux. But, like the clean toilets that McDonald's brought to Hong Kong restaurants, people may benefit from certain changes, even when their fears prevent them from seeing this at once.

And local traditions can still be—and are—preserved by groups participating in a global culture. Tolerance and even the celebration of many local variations, as long as they do not harm others, are hallmarks of a sustainable world community. Chinese food, Spanish art, Asian philosophies, African drumming, Egyptian history, or any major religion's version of the Golden Rule can enrich the lives of everyone. What originated locally can become universally adopted (like Arabic numbers). Most important, perhaps, the emerging global culture is a fabric woven from tens of thousands—possibly hundreds of thousands—of individual networks of communication, influence, and exchange that link people and organizations across civilizational boundaries. Aided by electronic communications systems, these networks are growing stronger and more numerous each day.

Positive shared value: Unity.

Searching for Common, *Positive* Values

Global religious resurgence is a reaction to the loss of personal identity and group stability produced by "the processes of social, economic, and cultural modernization that swept across the world in the second half of the twentieth century," according to Huntington. With traditional systems of authority disrupted, people become separated from their roots in a bewildering maze of new rules and expectations. In his view, such people need "new sources of identity, new forms of stable community, and new sets of moral precepts to provide them with a sense of meaning and purpose." Organized religious groups, both mainstream and fundamentalist, are growing today precisely to meet these needs, he believes.

Positive shared value: Love.

Although uprooted people may need new frameworks of identity and purpose, they will certainly not find them in fundamentalist religious groups, for such groups are *not* "new sources of identity." Instead, they recycle the past. Religious revival movements are reactionary, not progressive. Instead of facing the future, developing new approaches to deal with perceived threats of economic, technological, and social change, the movements attempt to retreat into the past.

Religions will likely remain among the major human belief systems for generations to come, despite—or even because of—the fact that they defy conventional logic and reason with their ultimate reliance upon otherworldly beliefs. However, it is possible that some ecumenical accommodations will be made that will allow humanity to build a generally accepted ethical system based on the many similar and overlapping moralities contained in the major religions. A person does not have to believe in supernatural beings to embrace and practice the principles of a global ethic, as exemplified in the interfaith declaration, "Towards a Global Ethic," issued by the Parliament of the World's Religions in 1993.

Positive shared value: Compassion.

Interfaith global cooperation is one way that people of different civilizations can find common cause. Another is global environmental cooperation seeking to maintain and enhance the life-sustaining capacities of the earth. Also, people everywhere have a stake in working for the freedom and welfare of future generations, not least because the future of their own children and grandchildren is at stake.

Positive shared value: Welfare of future generations.

Many more examples of cooperation among civilizations in the pursuit of common goals can be found in every area from medicine and science to moral philosophy, music, and art. A truly global commitment to the exploration, colonization, and industrialization of space offers still another way to harness the existing skills and talents of many nations, with the aim of realizing and extending worthy human capacities to their fullest. So, too, does the search for extraterrestrial intelligence. One day, many believe, contact will be made. What, then, becomes of Huntington's "clash of civilizations"? Visitors to Earth will likely find the variations among human cultures and languages insignificant compared with the many common traits all humans share.

Universal human values do exist, and many researchers, using different methodologies and data sets, have independently identified similar values. Typical of many studies into universal values is the global code of ethics compiled by Rushworth M. Kidder in *Shared Values for a Troubled World* (Wiley, 1994). Kidder's list includes love, truthfulness, fairness, freedom, unity (including cooperation, group allegiance, and oneness with others), tolerance, respect for life, and responsibility (which includes taking care of yourself, of other individuals, and showing concern for community interests). Additional values mentioned are courage, knowing right from wrong, wisdom, hospitality, obedience, and stability.

The Origins of Universal Human Values

Human values are not arbitrary or capricious. Their origins and continued existence are based in the facts of biology and in how human minds and bodies interact with their physical and social environments. These realities shape and constrain human behavior. They also shape human beliefs about the world and their evaluations of various aspects of it.

Human beings cannot exist without air, water, food, sleep, and personal security. There are also other needs that, although not absolutely necessary for the bodily survival of individuals, contribute to comfort and happiness. These include clothing, shelter, companionship, affection, and sex. The last, of course, is also necessary for reproduction and, hence, for the continued survival of the human species.

Thus, there are many constraints placed on human behavior if individuals and groups are to continue to survive and to thrive. These are *not* matters of choice. *How* these needs are met involves some—often considerable—leeway of choice, but, obviously, these needs set limits to the possible.

Much of morality, then, derives from human biological and psychological characteristics and from our higher order capacities of choice and reasoning. If humans were invulnerable and immortal, then injunctions against murder would be unnecessary. If humans did not rely on learning from others, lying would not be a moral issue.

Some needs of human individuals, such as love, approval, and emotional support, are inherently social, because they can only be satisfied adequately by other humans. As infants, individuals are totally dependent on other people. As adults, interaction with others satisfies both emotional and survival needs. The results achieved through cooperation and division of labor within a group are nearly always superior to what can be achieved by individuals each working alone. This holds true for hunting, providing protection from beasts and hostile groups, building shelters, or carrying out large-scale community projects.

Thus, social life itself helps shape human values. As societies have evolved, they have selectively retained only some of the logically possible variations in human values as norms, rights, and obligations. These selected values function to make social life possible, to permit and encourage people to live and work together.

Socially disruptive attitudes and actions, such as greed, dishonesty, cowardice, anger, envy, promiscuity, stubbornness, and disobedience, among others, constantly threaten the survival of society. Sadly, these human traits are as universal as are societal efforts to control them. Perhaps some or all of them once had survival value for individuals. But with the growth of society, they have become obstacles to the cooperation needed to sustain large-scale, complex communities. Other actions and attitudes that individuals and societies ought to avoid are equally well-recognized: abuses of power, intolerance, theft, arrogance, brutality, terrorism, torture, fanaticism, and degradation.

Positive shared value: Honesty.

I believe the path toward a harmonious global society is well marked by widely shared human values, including patience, truthfulness, responsibility, respect for life, granting dignity to all people, empathy for others, kindliness and generosity, compassion, and forgiveness. To be comprehensive, this list must be extended to include equality between men and women, respect for human rights, nonviolence, fair treatment of all groups, encouragement of healthy and nature-friendly lifestyles, and acceptance of freedom as an ideal limited by the need to avoid harming others. These value judgments are not distinctively Islamic, Judeo-Christian, or Hindu, or Asian, Western, or African. They are *human* values that have emerged, often independently, in many different places based on the cumulative life experience of generations.

Human societies and civilizations today differ chiefly in how well they achieve these positive values and suppress negative values. No society, obviously, has fully achieved the positive values, nor fully eliminated the negative ones.

But today's shared human values do not necessarily represent the ultimate expression of human morality. Rather, they provide a current progress report, a basis for critical discourse on a global level. By building understanding and agreement across cultures, such discourse can, eventually, lead to a further evolution of global morality.

In every society, many people, groups, and institutions respect and attempt to live by these positive values, and groups such as the Institute for Global Ethics are exploring how a global ethic can be improved and implemented everywhere.

Principle for global peace: Inclusion.

The Search for Global Peace and Order

Individuals and societies are so complex that it may seem foolhardy even to attempt the ambitious task of increasing human freedom and wellbeing. Yet what alternatives do we have? In the face of

violent aggressions, injustice, threats to the environment, corporate corruption, poverty, and other ills of our present world, we can find no satisfactory answers in despair, resignation, and inaction.

Rather, by viewing human society as an experiment, and monitoring the results of our efforts, we humans can gradually refine our plans and actions to bring closer an ethical future world in which every individual can realistically expect a long, peaceful, and satisfactory life.

Given the similarity in human values, I suggest three principles that might contribute to such a future: *inclusion, skepticism,* and *social control.*

1. The Principle of Inclusion

Although many moral values are common to all cultures, people too often limit their ethical treatment of others to members of their own groups. Some, for example, only show respect or concern for other people who are of their own race, religion, nationality, or social class.

Such exclusion can have disastrous effects. It can justify cheating or lying to people who are not members of one's own ingroup. At worst, it can lead to demonizing them and making them targets of aggression and violence, treating them as less than human. Those victimized by this shortsighted and counterproductive mistreatment tend to pay it back or pass it on to others, creating a nasty world in which we all must live.

Today, our individual lives and those of our descendants are so closely tied to the rest of humanity that our identities ought to include a sense of kinship with the whole human race and our circle of caring ought to embrace the welfare of people everywhere. In practical terms, this means that we should devote more effort and resources to raising the quality of life for the worst-off members of the human community; reducing disease, poverty, and illiteracy; and creating equal opportunity for all men and women. Furthermore, our circle of caring ought to include protecting natural resources, because all human life depends on preserving the planet as a livable environment.

2. The Principle of Skepticism

One of the reasons why deadly conflicts continue to occur is what has been called "the delusion of certainty." Too many people refuse to consider any view but their own. And, being sure that they are right, such people can justify doing horrendous things to others.

As I claimed in "Who Is Really Evil?" (*The Futurist,* March–April 2004), we all need a healthy dose of skepticism, especially about our own beliefs. Admitting that we might be wrong can lead to asking questions, searching for better answers, and considering alternative possibilities.

Critical realism is a theory of knowledge I recommend for everyone, because it teaches us to be skeptical. It rests on the assumption that knowledge is never fixed and final, but changes as we learn and grow. Using evidence and reason, we can evaluate our current beliefs and develop new ones in response to new information and changing conditions. Such an approach is essential to futures studies, and indeed to any planning. If your cognitive maps of reality are wrong, then using them to navigate through life will not take you where you want to go.

Critical realism also invites civility among those who disagree, encouraging peaceful resolution of controversies by investigating and discussing facts. It teaches temperance and tolerance, because it recognizes that the discovery of hitherto unsuspected facts may overturn any of our "certainties," even long-cherished and strongly held beliefs.

3. The Principle of Social Control

Obviously, there is a worldwide need for both informal and formal social controls if we hope to achieve global peace and order. For most people most of the time, informal social controls may be sufficient. By the end of childhood, for example, the norms of behavior taught and reinforced by family, peers, school, and religious and other institutions are generally internalized by individuals.

Principle for global peace: Skepticism.

Yet every society must also recognize that informal norms and even formal codes of law are not enough to guarantee ethical behavior and to protect public safety in every instance. Although the threats we most often think of are from criminals, fanatics, and the mentally ill, even "normal" individuals may occasionally lose control and behave irrationally, or choose to ignore or break the law with potentially tragic results. Thus, ideally, police and other public law enforcement, caretaking, and rehabilitation services protect us not only from "others," but also from ourselves.

Likewise, a global society needs global laws, institutions to administer them, and police/peacekeepers to enforce them. Existing international systems of social control should be strengthened and expanded to prevent killing and destruction, while peaceful negotiation and compromise to resolve disputes are encouraged. A global peacekeeping force with a monopoly on the legitimate use of force, sanctioned by democratic institutions and due process of law, and operated competently and fairly, could help prevent the illegal use of force, maintain global order, and promote a climate of civil discourse. The actions of these global peacekeepers should, of course, be bound not only by law, but also by a code of ethics. Peacekeepers should use force as a last resort and only to the degree needed, while making every effort to restrain aggressors without harming innocent people or damaging the infrastructures of society.

Expanding international law, increasing the number and variety of multinational institutions dedicated to controlling armed conflict, and strengthening efforts by the United Nations and other organizations to encourage the spread of democracy, global cooperation, and peace, will help create a win-win world.

Conclusion: Values for a Positive Global Future

The "clash of civilizations" thesis exaggerates both the degree of cultural diversity in the world and how seriously cultural differences contribute to producing violent conflicts.

In fact, many purposes, patterns, and practices are shared by all—or nearly all—peoples of the world. There is an emerging global ethic, a set of shared values that includes:

- Individual responsibility.
- Treating others as we wish them to treat us.
- Respect for life.
- Economic and social justice.
- Nature-friendly ways of life.
- Honesty.
- Moderation.
- Freedom (expressed in ways that do not harm others).
- Tolerance for diversity.

The fact that deadly human conflicts continue in many places throughout the world is due less to the differences that separate societies than to some of these common human traits and values. All humans, for example, tend to feel loyalty to their group, and may easily overreact in the group's defense, leaving excluded "outsiders" feeling marginalized and victimized. Sadly, too, all humans are capable of rage and violent acts against others.

In past eras, the killing and destruction of enemies may have helped individuals and groups to survive. But in today's interconnected world that is no longer clearly the case. Today, violence and aggression too often are blunt and imprecise instruments that fail to achieve their intended purposes, and frequently blow back on the doers of violence.

The long-term trends of history are toward an ever-widening definition of individual identity (with some people already adopting self-identities on the widest scale as "human beings"), and toward the enlargement of individual circles of caring to embrace once distant or despised "outsiders." These trends are likely to continue, because they embody values—learned from millennia of human experience—that have come to be nearly universal: from the love of life itself to the joys of belonging to a community, from the satisfaction of self-fulfillment to the excitement of pursuing knowledge and from individual happiness to social harmony.

How long will it take for the world to become a community where every human everywhere has a good chance to live a long and satisfying life? I do not know. But people of [goodwill] can do much today to help the process along. For example, we can begin by accepting responsibility for our own life choices: the goals and actions that do much to shape our future. And we can be more generous and understanding of what we perceive as mistakes and failures in the choices and behavior of others. We can include all people in our circle of concern, behave ethically toward everyone we deal with, recognize that every human being deserves to be treated with respect, and work to raise minimum standards of living for the least well-off people in the world.

We can also dare to question our personal views and those of the groups to which we belong, to test them and consider alternatives. Remember that knowledge is not constant, but subject to change in the light of new information and conditions. Be prepared to admit that anyone—even we ourselves—can be misinformed or reach a wrong conclusion from the limited evidence available. Because we can never have all the facts before us, let us admit to ourselves whenever we take action, that mistakes and failure are possible. And let us be aware that certainty can become the enemy of decency.

In addition, we can control ourselves by exercising self-restraint to minimize mean or violent acts against others. Let us respond to offered friendship with honest gratitude and cooperation; but, when treated badly by another person, let us try, while defending ourselves from harm, to respond not with anger or violence but with verbal disapproval and the withdrawal of our cooperation with that person. So as not to begin a cycle of retaliation, let us not overreact. And let us always be willing to listen and to talk, to negotiate, to compromise.

Toward Planetary Citizenship

A global economy that values competition over cooperation is an economy that will inevitably hurt people and destroy the environment. If the world's peoples are to get along better in the future, they need a better economic system, write peace activists Hazel Henderson and Daisaku Ikeda in *Planetary Citizenship*.

Henderson, an independent futurist, is one of the leading voices for a sustainable economic system; she is the author of many books and articles on her economic theories, including most recently *Beyond Globalization*. Ikeda is president of Soka Gakkai International, a peace and humanitarian organization based on Buddhist principles.

"Peace and nonviolence are now widely identified as fundamental to human survival," Henderson writes. "Competition must be balanced by cooperation and sharing. Even economists agree that peace, nonviolence, and human security are global public goods along with clean air and water, health and education—bedrock conditions for human well-being and development."

Along with materialistic values and competitive economics, the growing power of technology threatens a peaceful future, she warns. Humanity needs to find ways to harness these growing, "godlike" powers to lead us to genuine human development and away from destruction.

Henderson eloquently praises Ikeda's work at the United Nations to foster global cooperation on arms control, health, environmental protection, and other crucial issues. At the heart of these initiatives is the work of globally minded grass-root movements, or "planetary citizens," which have the potential to become the next global superpower, Henderson suggests.

One example of how nonmaterial values are starting to change how societies perceive their progress is the new Gross National Happiness indicators developed in Bhutan, which "[reflect] the goals of this Buddhist nation, [and] exemplify the importance of clarifying the goals and values of a society and creating indicators to measure what we treasure: health, happiness, education, human rights, family, country, harmony, peace, and environmental quality and restoration," Henderson writes.

The authors are optimistic that the grassroots movement will grow as more people look beyond their differences and seek common values and responsibilities for the future.

Source: *Planetary Citizenship: Your Values, Beliefs and Actions Can Shape a Sustainable World* by Hazel Henderson and Daisaku Ikeda. Middleway Press, 606 Wilshire Boulevard, Santa Monica, California 90401. 2004. 200 pages. $23.95. Order from the Futurist Bookshelf, www.wfs.org/bkshelf.htm.

Finally, we can support international law enforcement, global institutions of civil and criminal justice, international courts and global peacekeeping agencies, to build and strengthen nonviolent means for resolving disputes. Above all, we can work to ensure that global institutions are honest and fair and that they hold all countries—rich and poor, strong and weak—to the same high standards.

If the human community can learn to apply to all people the universal values that I have identified, then future terrorist acts like the events of September 11 may be minimized, because all people are more likely to be treated fairly and with dignity and because all voices will have peaceful ways to be heard, so some of the roots of discontent will be eliminated. When future terrorist acts do occur—and surely some will—they can be treated as the unethical and criminal acts that they are.

There is no clash of civilizations. Most people of the world, whatever society, culture, civilization, or religion they revere or feel a part of, simply want to live—and let others live—in peace and harmony. To achieve this, all of us must realize that the human community is inescapably bound together. More and more, as Martin Luther King Jr. reminded us, whatever affects one, sooner or later affects all.

Critical Thinking

1. How does Wendell Bell contrast his argument with Samuel Huntington's "clash of civilizations" thesis?

2. What are some of the shared values that Bell identifies?

3. What is "critical realism"? How does this concept relate to the study of global issues?

4. Describe what Bell calls an "emerging global ethic."

WENDELL BELL is professor emeritus of sociology and senior research scientist at Yale University's Center for Comparative Research. He is the author of more than 200 articles and nine books, including the two-volume *Foundations of Futures Studies* (Transaction Publishers, now available in paperback 2003, 2004). His address is Department of Sociology, Yale University, P.O. Box 208265, New Haven, Connecticut 06520. E-mail wendell.bell@yale.edu.

This article draws from an essay originally published in the *Journal of Futures Studies 6*.

Test-Your-Knowledge Form

We encourage you to photocopy and use this page as a tool to assess how the articles in *Annual Editions* expand on the information in your textbook. By reflecting on the articles you will gain enhanced text information. You can also access this useful form on a product's book support website at www.mhhe.com/cls.

NAME: _____   DATE: _____

TITLE AND NUMBER OF ARTICLE:
_____

BRIEFLY STATE THE MAIN IDEA OF THIS ARTICLE:
_____

_____

LIST THREE IMPORTANT FACTS THAT THE AUTHOR USES TO SUPPORT THE MAIN IDEA:

_____

WHAT INFORMATION OR IDEAS DISCUSSED IN THIS ARTICLE ARE ALSO DISCUSSED IN YOUR TEXTBOOK OR OTHER READINGS THAT YOU HAVE DONE? LIST THE TEXTBOOK CHAPTERS AND PAGE NUMBERS:

_____

LIST ANY EXAMPLES OF BIAS OR FAULTY REASONING THAT YOU FOUND IN THE ARTICLE:

_____

LIST ANY NEW TERMS/CONCEPTS THAT WERE DISCUSSED IN THE ARTICLE, AND WRITE A SHORT DEFINITION: